MULTICULTURAL EDUCATION SERIES

James A. Banks, Series Editor

Education Programs for Improving Intergroup Relations

Theory, Research, and Practice

WALTER G. STEPHAN
W. PAUL VOGT

EDITORS

Teachers College, Columbia University
New York and London

Published by Teachers College Press, 1234 Amsterdam Avenue,
New York, NY 10027

The editors and contributors to this volume wish to note with considerable
gratitude the generosity and support of The American Jewish Committee,
Chicago Chapter; Drs. Stephen Patt and Sharon Greenburg, the co-chairs of the
AJC project that led to this book; and Jonathan Levine, then Executive Director
of the Chicago Chapter, for helping to address the critical issue of prejudice
reduction and its examination in this publication.

Library of Congress Cataloging-in-Publication Data

Education programs for improving intergroup relations : theory, research, and
   practice / edited by Walter G. Stephan, W. Paul Vogt.
     p. cm. — (Multicultural education series)
   Includes bibliographical references (p.).
   ISBN 0-8077-4459-X
   1. Multicultural education—United States. 2. Intergroup relations—United
States. 3. School improvement programs—United States. I. Stephan,
Walter G. II. Vogt, W. Paul. III. Multicultural education series (New York,
N.Y.)

   LC1099.3.E39 2004
   370.117—dc22   2003068701

ISBN 0-8077-4459-X (paper)

Printed on acid-free paper

Manufactured in the United States of America

11 10 09 08 07 06 05 04   8 7 6 5 4 3 2 1

Contents

Series Foreword

The nation's deepening ethnic texture, interracial tension and conflict, and the increasing percentage of students who speak a first language other than English make multicultural education imperative in the 21st century. The U.S. Census Bureau (2000) estimated that people of color made up 28% of the nation's population in 2000 and predicted that they would make up 38% in 2025 and 47% in 2050.

American classrooms are experiencing the largest influx of immigrant students since the beginning of the 20th century. About a million immigrants are making the United States their home each year (Martin & Midgley, 1999). More than seven and one-half million legal immigrants settled in the United States between 1991 and 1998, most of whom came from nations in Latin America and Asia (Riche, 2000). A large but undetermined number of undocumented immigrants also enter the United States each year. The influence of an increasingly ethnically diverse population on the nation's schools, colleges, and universities is and will continue to be enormous.

Forty percent of the students enrolled in the nation's schools in 2001 were students of color. This percentage is increasing each year, primarily because of the growth in the percentage of Latino students (Martinez & Curry, 1999). In some of the nation's largest cities and metropolitan areas, such as Chicago, Los Angeles, Washington, D. C., New York, Seattle, and San Francisco, half or more of the public school students are students of color. During the 1998–1999 school year, students of color made up 63.1% of the student population in the public schools of California, the nation's largest state (California State Department of Education, 2000).

Language and religious diversity is also increasing among the nation's student population. In 2000, about 20% of the school-age population spoke a language at home other than English (U. S. Census Bureau, 2000). Harvard professor Diana L. Eck (2001) calls the United States the "most religiously diverse nation on earth" (p. 4). Most teachers now in the classroom and in teacher education programs are likely to have students from diverse ethnic, racial, language, and religious groups in their classrooms during their careers. This is true for both inner-city and suburban teachers.

An important goal of multicultural education is to improve race relations and to help all students acquire the knowledge, attitudes, and skills needed to participate in cross-cultural interactions and in personal, social, and civic action that will help make our nation more democratic and just. Multicultural education is consequently as important for middle-class White suburban students as it is for students of color who live in the inner city. Multicultural education fosters the public good and the overarching goals of the commonwealth.

The major purpose of the *Multicultural Education Series* is to provide preservice educators, practicing educators, graduate students, scholars, and policy makers with an interrelated and comprehensive set of books that summarizes and analyzes important research, theory, and practice related to the education of ethnic, racial, cultural, and language groups in the United States and the education of mainstream students about diversity. The books in the *Series* provide research, theoretical, and practical knowledge about the behaviors and learning characteristics of students of color, language minority students, and low-income students. They also provide knowledge about ways to improve academic achievement and race relations in educational settings.

The definition of multicultural education in the *Handbook of Research on Multicultural Education* (Banks & Banks, 2004) is used in the *Series:* Multicultural education is "a field of study designed to increase educational equity for all students that incorporates, for this purpose, content, concepts, principles, theories, and paradigms from history, the social and behavioral sciences, and particularly from ethnic studies and women's studies" (p. xii). In the *Series,* as in the *Handbook,* multicultural education is considered a "metadiscipline."

The dimensions of multicultural education, developed by Banks (2004) and described in the *Handbook of Research on Multicultural Education,* provide the conceptual framework for the development of the books in the *Series.* They are: *content integration, the knowledge construction process, prejudice reduction, an equity pedagogy,* and *an empowering school culture and social structure.* To implement multicultural education effectively, teachers and administrators must attend to each of the five dimensions of multicultural education. They should use content from diverse groups when teaching concepts and skills, help students to understand how knowledge in the various disciplines is constructed, help students to develop positive intergroup attitudes and behaviors, and modify their teaching strategies so that students from different racial, cultural, language, and social-class groups will experience equal educational opportunities. The total environment and culture of the school must also be transformed so that students from diverse groups will experience equal status in the culture and life of the school.

Although the five dimensions of multicultural education are highly interrelated, each requires deliberate attention and focus. Each book in the *Series* focuses on one or more of the dimensions, although each book deals with all of them to some extent because of the highly interrelated characteristics of the dimensions.

This book is timely and significant for several reasons. It is being published at a time when the U.S. Department of Education (2002) is requiring programs that it funds to provide research evidence of their effectiveness. The call for empirical evidence to prove the effectiveness of educational programs by the federal government is being echoed by state departments of education and by local school districts. The resounding call in the education community for research evidence is linked to the movement for accountability, standards, and high-stakes testing. "Where can I find research to support multicultural education programs?" is a question I am frequently asked by professional staff in school districts who are committed to multicultural education. They are finding research evidence narrowly defined and the current political and economic environment ominous.

School practitioners working in multicultural education programs, professors who teach multicultural education courses, and graduate students interested in diversity issues will welcome this well conceptualized, engaging, and informative book. It includes a rich collection of chapters that describes research evidence that intergroup relations programs can help students to develop more positive beliefs, attitudes, values, and behaviors. In addition to research evidence, the chapters in this book explicate the theoretical underpinnings of intergroup relations programs as well as provide thick descriptions of them. "Programs" in this book is broadly defined and includes programs such as A WORLD OF DIFFERENCE® and Facing History and Ourselves, as well as instructional approaches such as complex instruction and cooperative learning.

This book has several distinctive and appealing characteristics. These include the diverse disciplinary backgrounds of the contributing authors, the wide scope of grade levels represented by the programs (preschool through the university level), and the extensive range of programs described. It also contains chapters by scholars and researchers who have stayed the course over several decades in intergroup relations work, such as Louise Derman-Sparks, Elizabeth G. Cohen, Robert Slavin, Biren (Ratnesh) A. Nagda, Cookie White Stephan, John F. Dovidio, and Samuel L. Gaertner.

The editors, Walter G. Stephan and W. Paul Vogt, have enriched this indispensable collection with wisdom, knowledge, and editorial skills they have acquired from two lifetimes of visionary and influential research in social psychology (Stephan) and sociology and the history of education (Vogt). I have been personally and professionally edified by their significant work as well as their humanity and commitment to social justice for two decades.

I am pleased to welcome this book to the *Multicultural Education Series* with both enthusiasm and with the hope that the research evidence it provides on the effectiveness of intergroup relations programs will embolden the field of multicultural education and its supporters in challenging times.

James A. Banks
Series Editor

REFERENCES

Banks, J. A. (2004). Multicultural education: Historical development, dimensions, and practice. In J. A. Banks & C. A. M. Banks (Eds.), *Handbook of research on multicultural education* (2nd ed., pp. 3–29). San Francisco: Jossey-Bass.

Banks, J. A., & Banks, C. A. M. (Eds.) (2004). *Handbook of research on multicultural education* (2nd ed.). San Francisco: Jossey-Bass.

California State Department of Education (2000). On-line: [http://data1.cde.ca.gov/dataquest]

Eck, D. L. (2001). *A new religious America: How a "Christian country" has become the world's most religiously diverse nation.* New York: HarperSanFrancisco.

Martin, P., & Midgley, E. (1999). Immigration to the United States. *Population Bulletin, 54* (2), pp. 1–44. Washington, D.C.: Population Reference Bureau.

Martinez, G. M., & Curry, A. E. (1999, September). *Current population reports: School enrollment-social and economic characteristics of students* (update). Washington, D.C.: U.S. Census Bureau.

Riche, M. F. (2000). America's diversity and growth: Signposts for the 21st century. *Population Bulletin, 55* (2), pp. 1–43. Washington, D. C.: Population Reference Bureau.

U.S. Census Bureau (2000). *Statistical abstract of the United States* (120th edition). Washington, D.C.: U.S. Government Printing Office.

U.S. Department of Education (2002). *Meeting the highly qualified teachers challenge: Secretary's annual report on teacher quality.* Washington, D.C.: U.S. Department of Education, Office of Postsecondary Education.

Preface

We are proud to be associated with the publication of this significant volume. It is the most comprehensive book ever written on specific intergroup relations programs and the only one that critically analyzes these programs. It is both practical in describing the actual techniques utilized in these programs, and theoretical in discussing the underlying concepts and theories of intergroup relations. It takes an objective approach to why these programs work and to whether or not the evidence shows that they work. Finally, its contributors are some of the finest practitioners and researchers in the country.

The work that led to this volume began several years ago when we observed confusion and uncertainty within the field of intergroup relations. These programs had become ubiquitous in American schools. Yet despite a vast investment of time and personnel, no one seemed to know what these programs actually accomplished. Further, there was little research into this question, and much that passed for research was not systematic. A related problem was the inadequate communication among professionals working in intergroup relations programs; in fact, many were unaware of the work of like-minded colleagues. In 1999, in an effort to address these problems, and mindful of the untapped promise of intergroup relations programs, we invited a group of prominent professionals to form a Working Group on Anti-Bias Education. In the ensuing years, their mutually stimulating work together has been a model for the end of fragmentation within the field.

This project has been sponsored by the American Jewish Committee. Throughout its history AJC has engaged in a range of strategies designed to limit, prevent, and oppose prejudice and ethnic hatred. It seems to us that intergroup relations programs take this struggle against prejudice to its very roots. It is sobering to reflect that prejudice is universal within intergroup relations. Children are the constant recipients of an informal education in which prejudice is typically "taught" via social customs, ethnic jokes, the example of elders, and so on. If this be true, then it follows that the development of fair-minded, tolerant adults cannot be entrusted to the spontaneous unfolding of human nature, but that it must be taught and routinely reinforced throughout the course of development.

In this regard, it is shocking and tragic to observe that in some countries, the formal educational process functions as a vehicle to inculcate prejudice and ethnic hatred—a veritable "pro-bias education" for young minds. One helpful response to this appalling problem would be the organization of intergroup relations professionals in other countries. This has already occurred in Germany, where a working group modeled on our own group has been formed through the initiative of the Berlin office of the American Jewish Committee.

We are grateful to the many professionals who have participated in our Working Group and to those who contributed to this book. We particularly recognize our colleague, Eva Lichtenberg, who generously provided much of the support for this project. This book is also a tribute to the wisdom and energy of its co-editors, Walter Stephan and Paul Vogt.

Sharon Greenburg
Jonathan Levine
Stephen L. Patt
The American Jewish Committee

Chapter 1

Introduction:
Education's Influence on Beliefs, Attitudes, Values, and Behaviors

W. Paul Vogt

Educational programs can have strong positive effects on students' beliefs, attitudes, values, and behaviors. They can improve intergroup relations among students, and these improvements can last long after the programs are completed and the students have graduated. This general conclusion is well established in the educational research literature (e.g., Hyman & Wright, 1979). It is also well established that beliefs, attitudes, values, and behaviors are related. This means that influencing one of them will tend indirectly to influence the others. Whether and how such indirect influences may occur are classic questions in social psychology and related disciplines (e.g., Fishbein & Ajzen, 1975). But such questions are *not* mostly classical and academic. Nothing could be more contemporary and practical than education programs focusing on intergroup relations. Education gives us our most important tools to deal with destructive and dangerous conflict among people.

Education Programs for Improving Intergroup Relations advances our understanding of how education can improve intergroup relations. By describing and analyzing exemplary intergroup relations programs, it brings us closer to the resolution of some of the most knotty problems in interpreting the links among educational interventions and students' beliefs, attitudes, values, and behaviors. Again, these problems are more practical than theoretical. Today, increased social and cultural diversity, combined with better communications, brings different people together to an extent never before seen in human history. Intergroup relations is the key to deriving the benefits of diversity and avoiding its perils.

PURPOSE AND AUDIENCE

Making knowledge about intergroup relations programs available to educators is the main goal of the book. To do this, we describe a wide variety of these programs at the elementary level (Part I), the secondary level (Part II), and in colleges and universities (Part III). Following these descriptive chapters comes a group of analytic chapters (Part IV) in which the authors pull together common themes and conclusions that have been drawn from their study of these and other programs. By presenting an intentionally diverse sample of programs that vary in their goals, methods, and clients, we hope to give readers a sense of the enormous range of the kinds of programs designed to improve intergroup relations. But we are also able to show that within that diversity resides a common core of issues, concepts, problems, and solutions.

Readers from many areas of educational practice and research are likely to find the book relevant to their interests. Educators looking for insights into how to deliver education that enlightens students about intergroup relations will find much of interest here. We think that the discussions in the following chapters are broad and deep enough that they will be of interest to experienced educators as well as those about to begin their careers. Educational researchers should be interested in both the program descriptions as possible data and in the more analytic chapters in Part IV, which suggest methods of investigation. Practitioners and researchers alike will be especially interested in the two concluding chapters (Chapters 14 and 15), which systematically review what we know about what works.

ORIGINS OF THIS COLLECTION

Diversity among groups and differences in the problems they face when interacting with one another are mirrored in the diversity of the programs described in this book. If one size does not fit all in social life, it surely does not do so in programs dealing with social life. The programs described below can be seen as "experiments" that take varying approaches to common problems. Readers of this book can use the results of these program "experiments" to clarify their own understanding of what they wish to do. The chapters that follow chart the progress of programs at various stages of development, from the design and implementation of new programs at one location to the evolution of long-established programs that have reached hundreds of thousands of students and teachers. All levels of education, from preschool to university, are discussed. The program descriptions are thorough, and most chapters provide web sites where the reader can learn more. Of particular import for teacher education, the chapters address not only the education of students but also, perhaps more importantly, the preparation of teachers and staff who conduct the programs. Staff development and curricula in effective programs function much as inhaling and exhaling do in respiration. It isn't really possible to do one without the other. A similar balance exists between descriptions of how to design and implement programs and analyses of what works in those programs; we have tried to reflect that balance in the chapters that follow.

In brief, diversity of programs—diversity in goals, methods, and clients—has been a main criterion used to choose what would be included in this book. Given our current state of knowledge, it would not have been responsible to recommend only one type of program. Rather, our strategy was to present readers with a broadly representative sampler. Other programs could have been chosen, of course, and they might have represented the field as well as those discussed in the following chapters, but we are sure that no other collection could better represent the range of high-quality programs available in the United States today.

Each of the program descriptions is written by an "insider," someone responsible for its implementation who knows it well. We intentionally selected authors for their unsurpassed knowledge of the programs they describe. "Outsider" perspectives are included in the systematic overview chapters in Part IV.

Among the many ways to organize our thinking about intergroup relations programs, perhaps the most obvious is the ages or developmental stages of the program participants. We have used that criterion to order the nine programs discussed in Chapters 2 through 10. All age groups could benefit from improvements in intergroup relations. There is ample evidence that very young children can easily be tainted by racist beliefs and attitudes (see Derman-Sparks, Chapter 2, this volume; Van Ausdale & Feagin, 2001). And the persistence of terrorism, genocide, and religio-ethnic wars (Kressel, 2002) makes it clear that the incidence of bias and hate, and the willingness to act upon them, are pervasive among adults, too. Our book focuses on school-age participants in intergroup relations programs from early childhood to young adulthood. Elementary pupils are discussed extensively in Chapters 2, 3, and 4, though the programs discussed there are not exclusively targeted toward the youngest children. Adolescents are the center of attention in Chapters 5, 6, and 7, while college students come to the fore in Chapters 8, 9, and 10. And faculty and staff are discussed to one degree or another in all these chapters.

We provide an overview of each chapter in the introductions to Parts I through IV. In this general introduction, it is more valuable to look at cross-cutting themes and overarching questions that are central to the field of education for improving intergroup relations. Doing so allows us to discuss questions from various perspectives and in several conceptually interesting ways. Discussing each of these themes and questions crucial to progress in the field involves clustering the chapters into different groups. What we will be suggesting here, by raising these themes and questions, is ways in which readers could convert this volume into a "hypertext" book and rearrange the chapters in different orders to pursue topics that interest them.

CRITERIA FOR SELECTING PROGRAMS

In addition to choosing programs broadly representative of the state of the art in our field, we were also fundamentally concerned to include programs that were adept at merging the perspectives of practitioners and researchers. In varying degrees, all our authors approach their work from these two perspectives. Some authors are practitioners, people who design and implement educational programs. Others are researchers, people who investigate intergroup relations. But this is by no means a strict division. Several authors are both practitioners and researchers, and all contributors have an abiding concern for tying the two together.

The authors met in a series of seminars initiated and generously sponsored by the American Jewish Committee (Midwest Region) in Chicago. The original idea behind our seminar meetings was that practitioners and researchers each had something to learn from the other about the impact of educational programs. Our experiences together strongly confirmed this expectation. Participants in the seminars learned from one another not only across the practitioner–researcher divide but also within each group. This could happen because one of the striking features of our field is its fragmentation. Practitioners interested in improving intergroup relations often work in comparative isolation from one another. So do academics, especially when they come from different disciplines, such as psychology, sociology, and political science. Our early meetings were an attempt to combat this fragmentation through discussions that reached across intellectual and practical fissures. As we began pulling together what we were discovering in our discussions, we became convinced that other educators and educational researchers would be interested in what we had learned. This book is our first attempt to communicate our findings. (The work continues, most recently at the time of this writing at an international Conference on Anti-Bias Education in June 2003 co-sponsored by the Society for the Study of Social Issues and the American Jewish Committee.)

Diversity in types of program goals was a key criterion we used to select programs to include in this collection. When people design educational programs in order to improve intergroup relations, they usually stress a specific type of outcome. Some concentrate on knowledge, beliefs, and cognitive processes. Others emphasize feelings, attitudes, and values. Still others try to alter behaviors. Program methods differ according to whether one stresses cognitive, emotional, or behavioral outcomes. These differences account for much of the heterogeneity among the approaches depicted in this book. While all the programs have a broad common goal—using education to improve intergroup relations—the means they employ to attain that goal vary widely.

The often-used phrase "improving intergroup relations" can be interpreted in many ways. Strength comes from this diversity of approaches and goals, but so does some confusion and controversy. That is why, to introduce the book, we have focused on several characteristics of programs that the reader can use as a framework to compare them. Toward the end of the book, Dovidio and his colleagues (in Chapter 14) provide a taxonomy of answers to similar questions about how programs work; their chapter focuses on the links between program interventions and program outcomes. And Stephan weaves the threads of the book's several parallel lines of inquiry into his conclusion (Chapter 15). The book culminates, in Stephan's conclusion, not only with an account of what we have learned but also with an inventory of what we need to do to improve both practice and research on practice. Thus, this introduction, Chapter 14, and the conclusion all focus on a similar set of questions about how education programs influence intergroup beliefs, attitudes, values, and behaviors. Each takes a somewhat different approach, but the degree of common understanding is impressive. It is possible to speak, as Stephan does in the conclusion, of the "underlying vision that animates these programs" and also of a consensus about how to learn more by studying them.

Programs were selected to give readers both general conclusions and a large sample of the evidence upon which those conclusions were based. It does not make much sense to try to answer *general* "how" questions until we have seen "whether" *particular* programs have improved intergroup relations. That is why, in the following pages, we have rooted the general discussions about outcomes and processes in empirical descriptions of programs and the details of how they function. Our ultimate aim was to draw some overall conclusions about how intergroup relations programs contribute to pro-social outcomes, but we knew that to reach that goal we needed to ground these conclusions in intensive study of the work of educational practitioners. The programs depicted in this book were thus primary evidence upon which our conclusions were based, but the authors and program implementers have also reviewed two kinds of additional evidence. First, many of the programs described in the following pages were originally designed with reference to, and continue to be adjusted based upon, state-of-the-art syntheses of the research literature. Second, our book contains two systematic overviews of research literature on the effectiveness of several dozen programs. These two meta-analyses—by Cooper and Slavin on cooperative learning (Chapter 4) and by Stephan, Renfro, and Stephan (Chapter 13)—leave no doubt of education's capacity to improve intergroup relations. These two chapters review different kinds of educational impact. Cooper and Slavin analyze the influence of cooperative learning techniques that can be applied in any classroom. Stephan, Renfro, and Stephan, on the other hand, focus more on free-standing intergroup relations programs. But in each case, the evidence of effectiveness is strong.

We also included chapters that enable us to look at these educational programs in the light of the general social contexts of schooling in the United States. The idea was to discover which aspects of U.S. education can be built upon by intergroup relations programs—and which features of U.S. education they might have to overcome. It can be argued that the need for special intergroup relations programs arises from the shortcomings in the schools' regular offerings (Banks, 1997; Niemi & Junn, 1998). If courses in history, civics, literature, and social studies were taught in the best possible way, there might be little call for special programs such as those described in this book. In any case, it is clear that intergroup relations programs do not occur in social and political vacuums. Avery and Hahn in Chapter 11 and Cushner in Chapter 12 undertake the task of situating programs in their broader contexts, again from two distinct perspectives. Cushner reviews the sociological and social psychological literature to analyze social structures and organizational environments that can either foster or frustrate intergroup relations programs. Avery and Hahn use a representative national sample that describes current practices in schools in the United States and that permits comparisons with other nations.

The range of programs discussed in this collection is also broad in the scope of processes they use to deliver curricula. One can categorize the methods of educational programs in two cross-cutting ways that, when combined, yield four basic types of intergroup relations programs (summarized in Table 1.1). First, programs differ according to whether, as their engine of change, they focus on formal instruction of a curriculum or whether they stress socialization and psychological interaction processes. Are a program's main methods and materials instructional—texts, classes, and so on? Or does the program emphasize processes of social interaction among participants? Most of the programs discussed in this book include both a formal curriculum and the interaction of students as they study it, but each tends to stress

Table 1.1. How Education Can Influence Beliefs, Attitudes, Values, and Behaviors

	Directly	Indirectly
Instruction	Multicultural education	Cognitive development
Socialization	Intergroup contact	Personality development

Note: The italicized cells are examples of the processes.

one considerably more than the other. Among the perennial questions intergroup relations programs face is how to strike the right balance between formal instruction and social interaction of the participants. This will vary depending both on the goals of the program and on the characteristics of the participants, such as their ages. What might be an excellent mix for college students could be quite inappropriate for young children. Ultimately the goal, as Dovidio and colleagues put it, is to enable the practitioner to "choose, from a large repertoire of tools, the most effective and appropriate intervention for a given context and audience" (Chapter 14).

The other dimension on which programs differ is whether they attempt to work their effects directly or indirectly. Combining the two dimensions on which programs tend to differ yields the four possibilities illustrated in Table 1.1: direct and indirect instruction and direct and indirect socialization. (For further elaboration, see Vogt, 1997; Chapters 14 and 15, this volume.) For example, direct instruction is commonly associated with civic education and some versions of multicultural education. Indirect instruction is associated with programs that attempt to foster the cognitive development of participants. Prominent among these are programs based on Kohlberg's theories of moral/cognitive development, such as Facing History and Ourselves (Chapter 6) and the Moral Education of Citizens (Chapter 9).

Direct socialization is the method of most programs based on "contact theory," developed by Gordon Allport (1954) and others. Indeed, every program described in this book builds to one degree or another on contact theory's main proposition: Intergroup contact can improve intergroup relations. Historically the best known and most extensive use of contact theory was school desegregation. And, on balance, the research has shown that the effects of intergroup contact have been beneficial (Vogt, 1997). Some programs described in this book focus on methods of direct socialization as the main process of change. They conclude that, *under the right conditions*, contact can be a powerful promoter of increased intergroup harmony. But those conditions are not easy to attain; it requires effort to reap the benefits and avoid unintended negative consequences (Feld & Carter, 1998; Chapters 3 and 8, this volume).

Effects of indirect socialization usually become visible only in the long term. They are hardest to pin down in part because they are often not fully intentional. Most programs discussed in this volume focus more on immediate targeted effects that can be achieved in the comparatively short term. But they also hope to achieve long-term effects that continue after the program is over. Understanding long-term, indirect socialization effects usually involves focusing more on school structures than on programs (Brint, Contreras, & Matthews, 2001). For example, schooling tends greatly to expand children's social horizons; it entails learning how to interact with strangers who might have interests and values different from one's own. By leaving the narrow world of family and neighborhood and entering into a broader, more diverse world, children may develop personal and social skills and values that enable them to cope with diversity and perhaps to enjoy it. The values inculcated can be as minimal and specific as respect for procedural fairness (Jackson, Boostrom, & Hansen, 1993) or they can include broader attitudes, such as appreciation of nonconformity and independence of thought (Miller, Kohn, & Schooler, 1986). By forging new social structures, such as more egalitarian patterns of interaction among educators and students, that persist after the program has concluded, the programs described in this volume also probably contribute indirectly to pro-social goals. I say "probably," because, despite their importance, such effects are elusive and hard to evaluate.

Some of the authors of the following chapters might resist these categorizations and distinctions between program processes. They could well claim that they do all these things in their programs, that they combine direct and indirect approaches to instruction *and* to socialization. Elizabeth Cohen's "complex instruction" (Chapter 3), for example, appears to do just this. But most programs have an emphasis. They ask themselves, at least implicitly, "Which are our most important goals and methods, and which are the fortunate by-products?" Their answers shape their programs. And paying attention to how they answer those questions will help the reader understand the programs better.

SIX CENTRAL QUESTIONS

The chapters that follow are shaped by attempts to answers several questions; these are persistent in our field. Workers in education to improve intergroup relations routinely encounter them. In our seminars six persistent questions emerged, and they are reprised in our chapters. Each chapter in the book endeavors to address them in one way or another, and they are likely to be important in our field for a long time to come.

Question 1. What's in a Name?

Our field is plagued by nominalism. The authors of this book found it fairly easy to agree on the components of what we were interested in, but we found it harder to agree on *what to call* our collection of those components. What is the general rubric under which we should organize our work? The leading contenders were (1) anti-bias education, (2) education to improve intergroup relations, and (3) multicultural education. When broadly defined, each of these may contain all or nearly all the elements of the others. Much debate, not only in our seminars, has occurred about which term is general and which are the subordinate categories. Is "anti-bias education" too narrow and too negative? Is "improving intergroup relations" too broad and too vague? Is "multicultural education" too exclusively focused on racial/ethnic questions? This proliferation of terms can lead to confusion in our field of practice and research on practice. Nonetheless, we decided not to try to stipulate the one best term or to specify logical relations among various labels such as multicultural and anti-bias education. Some chapters use one, others another. But we believe readers will find that this diversity of labels is fairly superficial; it conceals a broader agreement. Thus, one of our goals in presenting an unusually wide range of programs to study was to show their underlying unity.

Question 2. Do We Accentuate the Positive?

Our seminar discussions several times highlighted the differences of emphasis among participants and in our field on whether we should focus on combating "bad" things or promoting "good" things. Is it our priority to work to *oppose* bias, prejudice, and discrimination or to *promote* intergroup understanding, tolerance, and appreciation for diversity and difference? Of course, promoting the positive and opposing the negative are *roughly* equivalent. But it's not algebra, so they are only roughly equivalent—in intergroup relations, negating a negative is not quite the same as establishing a positive. One interesting difference is that the "anti" programs tend to be more instructional and cognitive in orientation, while many "pro" programs focus more on social interaction and affective mechanisms. Be that as it may, the negative targets of our program actions include bias, prejudice, discrimination, hate crimes, ethnocentrism, racism, narrowmindedness, intolerance, and stereotyping. Positive goals have included tolerance, coexistence, broadmindedness, fairness, justice, difference, multiculturalism, and diversity. The negative terms tend to predominate in our field, and there is usually more agreement on how to define them. But that does not necessarily mean that most programs discussed here see themselves as "anti" in orientation. Programs discussed in this book are about evenly divided between efforts to reduce the negative and attempts to increase the positive aspects of intergroup relations. The differences illustrated by the programs in this book have less to do with ultimate goals and more to do with deciding which is the best place to start.

Question 3. Should We Emphasize Programs or Processes?

Our first thought, as we designed the book, was to focus on programs. And examining the success of discrete programs remains our main theme. But as the project evolved, we realized that many key elements of improving intergroup relations and reducing bias in schools and colleges were not, strictly speaking, distinct programs. Rather they were—like cooperative education, or moral development, or intergroup contact—processes that could be a component of or a technique applicable in many different programs. In the chapters that follow, programs are more central to Chapters 2 through 10 (Parts I through III), while processes are stressed more in Chapters 11 through 14 (Part IV).

Question 4. How Are Regular and Special Curricula Related?

Most of the programs described in this book are designed to supplement the "regular" curriculum. Yet several aspects of the regular curriculum can be central to reducing bias and enhancing intergroup relations. Civic education occurs in many high schools, and moral education is undertaken in some as part of the established curriculum. Indeed, sociologists of education have long held that schools engage in moral education regardless of whether they mean to do so. Furthermore, some of schooling's strongest effects are indirect. One persistent finding is that kids who can read and think well are less likely to exhibit intolerance, prejudice, and stereotyping and are more likely to appreciate diversity—quite apart from whether they have had any special courses in intergroup relations, multicultural education, and so on. Ignorance and rigidity of thought may be our greatest foes. If so, any part of the curriculum that increases intellectual flexibility and encourages clear thinking about social relations could help us indirectly with our cause. The regular curriculum is an aspect of our field less well covered in the present volume (see Banks, 1997; Nie, Junn, & Stehlik-Barry, 1996; Vogt, 1997), but the reader will find many suggestions for bridging the gap between regular and special curricula in this book (e.g., in Chapters 3, 9, and 11).

Question 5. Should Programs Maintain Group Distinctiveness or Stress Commonalities?

Are we more likely to improve intergroup relations by maintaining the cultural distinctiveness of the groups we wish to bring together, or is success more probable when people are encouraged to see and to reflect on what they have in common? Or, perhaps, one should first learn about one's own group's distinctiveness as a bridge to cross on the way to appreciating diversity in other groups. The division between those who emphasize the distinctiveness of, versus the similarities among, groups seems to parallel that between those who stress the positive and those who emphasize the negative approaches to our subject. That is, those who want to accentuate the positive (broadmindedness, openness to new experiences, appreciation for diversity, etc.) have a tendency to want to maintain distinctiveness, while those who want to stress commonalities have a tendency to prefer to combat the negative (bias, prejudice, stereotyping). This difference is one of the most fundamental divisions in discussions of pedagogical strategy. Research cannot currently resolve the debate (see Banks, 1997). Both sides can cite high-quality research in support of their positions. It is likely, I think, that each approach—stressing distinctiveness or emphasizing commonalities— is more effective for *some* goals and for *some* program participants than for others. But we will not know *which* goals and participants until we have higher-quality research on the topic.

Question 6. How Can We Improve Research on Programs?

The pages that follow contain strong evidence that educational programs can be effective at reducing bias, prejudice, and discrimination and promoting fairness, tolerance, and respect for diversity. Several of the strongest programs in the United States are described and evaluated in this book's chapters.

But educational programs can also fail to deliver the goods. Students can be unaffected. Even among programs that "work," surely some work better than others do or, more importantly, some aspects of programs are more effective than others are, and some students are affected more than others. What makes programs productive at enhancing students' pro-social and discouraging students' anti-social beliefs, attitudes, values, and behaviors? Which programs have strong positive effects, which do not, and how do we tell? Effects on what? Effects for whom? The next most important

step in our field is to improve our knowledge of which *particular* program elements or processes are most effective for bringing about *specific*
outcomes with *distinct* categories of students (such as age groups). The
route to that more detailed level of knowledge about better practice is
program evaluation.

One criterion the editors used to select programs for inclusion in this
book was whether they had been evaluated. Some programs may not have
been evaluated as thoroughly as they ideally could have been, but nearly
all were evaluated with much more rigor than is the norm. Not all the details of the evaluations have been presented here. In some cases these details are published elsewhere or are available from the authors. We wanted
first to describe how exemplary programs were designed and implemented;
full evaluations, even when available, would have gotten in the way of achieving the goal of full description. But evaluation is a key to further progress in
our field.

Good program evaluation is not easy. It may be more difficult than most
other kinds of research. Because programs tend to be distinct and the evaluations of them even more so, cumulative knowledge is rare. This makes it
hard to know whether we are using our limited resources most effectively.
Many stumbling blocks are strewn in the paths leading to high-quality evaluations. First, because programs exist in the messy real world, not in the
comparatively neat world of the laboratory, researchers tend to have little
control over the variables being studied. Second, a good program frequently
employs a mixture of techniques to accomplish its goals. While this can be
good for delivering services, it is a headache for evaluators, who often cannot separate the effects of the various techniques. Third, we encounter problems with objectivity particular to evaluation research. It is hard enough to
be objective when doing any kind of research, but ordinary difficulties can
be exacerbated in program evaluation. Outside evaluators are often in the
uncomfortable position of being employed by their "subjects," such as program directors. Inside evaluators frequently find it hard to distinguish program evaluation from program advocacy or public relations.

These barriers increase the difficulty of doing evaluations reliable enough
to use to design better programs. What should be done to make evaluations
more reliable so that we can use them to improve education in intergroup
relations? Ideally, at some point, we could come to agreement among program managers to design evaluations together, across programs, in order to
seek answers to common questions. We are not there yet, and very few
evaluators have the luxury of working in that kind of cooperative and comparative environment. But such difficult comparative and cooperative work
has been done in some fields (research on education and social stratifica-
tion is one impressive example [Shavit & Blossfeld, 1993]).

If the results of several evaluations are available, then they can sometimes be united and synthesized via techniques such as meta-analysis (see Chapters 4 and 13). But meta-analyses, which are by definition retrospective, are usually a second-best choice compared to *starting* with a common design. It is also possible to see the range of programs as a sort of "natural experiment" that we can conduct if we pool our knowledge and our evaluation resources. In such "experiments," researchers use naturally occurring variations in programs (in goals, methods, clientele, and so on) and interpret these differences as virtual independent variables. Our book provides some first steps in this direction. We are not yet at the stage of formulating common evaluation projects that cut across separate programs, but we have, at least, made it easier to juxtapose components of programs. Moving forward toward more systematic evaluations might require a degree of coordination rare in social research, though more common in the natural sciences.

Imagine, for example, what it would be like if antibiotics had been developed and dispensed as intergroup relations programs have been. Hundreds of different groups of researchers and practitioners would have created, often in ignorance of one another, many ostensibly different treatments for infections. Some of the medicines would be very similar, but they would have different brand names. Advocates of particular medicines might have a vested interest in stressing differences that weren't very important. Others might try to ignore differences among diseases that were important. This chaos in the production and use of medicine would have negative consequences for treatment of illness. Medical practitioners would have limited knowledge about how *specific* antibiotics worked against *particular* types of infection or which worked best with different kinds of patients. Like educational programs, many antibiotics work to some extent on many different infections; and often any of several antibiotics can reduce the dangers of an infection. But for particular diseases, some antibiotics work much better than others, and no medicine works equally well on everything. If antibiotics had been developed as intergroup relations programs have been, patients might not have much confidence in the medical profession, because the average treatment effects would tend to be small. Because effective and ineffective treatments would be administered almost hit or miss, successes and failures could come close to canceling one another out on average.

Many have called for better coordination of program evaluations as a way to improve practice. So why don't we have better evaluations? There are at least three reasons. First, program professionals have limited incentive to conduct evaluations when "customers," such as schools districts, do not ask for them; and, for the most part, they do not. An important exception is federally sponsored research, where evaluations are routinely mandated. Unfortunately, this has not had as big an effect in the study of intergroup relations programs as in other areas of educational evaluation, in large part because few federal grant dollars are directed toward improving intergroup relations. Second, the risk of immediate harm from educational programs is quite small. It is very rare to see evidence of an intergroup relations program that actually makes things worse. Therefore, most people do not feel the need for an educational equivalent of something like the Food and Drug Administration that would compel evaluations to protect against possibly dangerous programs. Finally, people who work on programs such as those described in this book are often "true believers." They are committed. That is why so many of them work long hours at low pay. Without their commitment, we would have many fewer programs to combat bias and promote understanding. But dedicated people sometimes resist evaluation. If one is already convinced that one's program is effective, then setting aside 5 or 10 percent of the budget for evaluation is wasting resources that could be used for good works.

Another barrier to high-quality, objective program evaluations is the fact that the people most knowledgeable about programs are sometimes reluctant to make their findings publicly available. Some programs are proprietary, which means it would be unrealistic to expect program directors to highlight weaknesses in their programs, because this might discourage people from adopting them. The authors who wrote our program chapters tend to be advocates. They think (and we agree) that their programs are important contributions to solving fundamental problems. While they are advocates and have a distinct point of view, they also have better access to information about their programs than any outsider could hope to attain. As long as this kind of insider evaluation is "advocacy constrained by rules of evidence" (ACRE), and as long as readers are aware that authors are making the *best case* for their programs, these assessments can have great value (Vogt, 2002). Indeed, they are standard practice in educational evaluation.

Barriers to good program assessment can be overcome. They have been in other fields; for example, mandatory clinical trials to approve medicines date only to the 1960s. If there is one thing that all our seminar discussions returned to repeatedly and that all our authors stress to one degree or another, it is that today the most promising route to improvement is through refining methods of program evaluation. At the most basic level, the reason for the significance of evaluation is simple: It is hard to know how to do better if you don't really know how well you're doing.

It is important to be clear about the kind of evaluation needed. If one is to learn from evaluations, they should contain a large number of studies of the type usually called "formative." Formative evaluations are designed to help a program adjust and improve as it is implemented, and they usually involve substantial evidence gathered from insider advocates. More important, formative evaluations put as much emphasis on identifying processes as on measuring outcomes. Formative evaluations are usually contrasted with "summative" evaluations, which focus on outcomes and are more like external audits used to decide whether a program's funding should be continued. Audits can be important, but it is often hard to learn from them about how to improve practice. If we know only *that* a program accomplished its objectives, but we do not know *how* it did so, we do not know much that we can use. Generalizability to other programs, populations, and settings will be limited. Useful evaluations must attend to inputs and processes, for these are the causal links in the chain of events that lead to program outcomes. Of course, useful evaluations must be equally concerned with outcomes. Processes without outcomes are as uninformative as outputs without evidence about how they were achieved. Even summative evaluations that focus on reporting effect sizes (Chapters 4 and 13) can be highly informative when we have at least a general knowledge of the processes employed by the programs, such as complex instruction (Chapter 3) or dialogue groups (Chapter 8).

The processes-versus-outcomes distinction tends to have parallels with the equally unfortunate battle of the "quants" versus the "quals" in educational program evaluation. Advocates of qualitative approaches tend to like verbal descriptions of processes, while proponents of quantitative approaches favor coefficients that measure outcomes. Good evaluation research will forget about the so-called culture wars in order to combine the strengths and avoid the weaknesses of each approach.

CONCLUSIONS

Combating prejudice, intolerance, and discrimination requires all our tools, quantitative and qualitative. That is why readers of this book will find not only a great diversity of programs but also a variety of methodological approaches to describing and evaluating them. The work of improving intergroup relations and fostering multiculturalism goes forward on many fronts in the programs discussed in the following pages. We know less than we would like to know about what leads to successful intergroup relations programs, but nearly all of what we do know is discussed in this book. Several solid generalizations emerge from the diversity of perspectives in the coming chapters. I mention them briefly here to alert the reader.

First, intergroup relations in schools and universities can be improved without sacrificing academic achievement. Indeed, strong evidence indicates that academic achievement is usually enhanced by the same methods that foster better relations among people. Second, discussion or dialogue is a key process in all the programs described in this book, even programs that are otherwise quite dissimilar. Third, the discussions are often long and painfully difficult; they involve engaging people's thoughts and feelings about real issues about which they disagree and which it would be more comfortable for them to ignore. Fourth, the intensity of the discussions is why all the programs require much more than doing something for (or to) students; at minimum, the teachers and the contexts in which students and teachers interact have to be part of the program, too. Success seems never to come from merely purchasing and distributing a prepackaged curriculum or hiring some consultants to "teach at" the students.

Beyond these four generalizations, there is much room for pluralism in the aims and methods of effective intergroup relations programs. For example, some of the programs are built on concepts drawn from the arts and humanities; others are grounded in the social and behavioral sciences. The authors of this book hope that as readers reflect on such program variations on the common theme of improving intergroup relations, they can draw lessons, and even perhaps inspiration, to use in their own efforts.

ACKNOWLEDGMENT

The editors and contributors to this volume wish to note with considerable gratitude the generosity and support of The American Jewish Committee, Chicago Chapter; Drs. Stephen Patt and Sharon Greenburg, the co-chairs of the AJC project that led to this book; and Jonathan Levine, then Executive Director of the Chicago Chapter, for helping to address the critical issue of prejudice reduction and its examination in this publication.

Part I

Programs for Young Children and Their Teachers

Young children provide intergroup relations practitioners with their first opportunity to shape the thinking and behavior of students. These students do not come unbiased into the classroom. Nearly all have nascent group identities, are capable of categorizing people into groups, evaluate these groups positively and negatively, and display the beginnings of discrimination. But these cognitions, emotions, and behaviors are highly malleable at this early stage. Consequently the prejudices, stereotypes, and biases that would develop in the absence of intervention can be forestalled or prevented. The approaches adopted in these interventions must be especially sensitive to the cognitive and emotional developmental stages of these students. It is all too easy to provide materials that are beyond of the grasp of young children or that are not commensurate with their abilities or level of maturity. Nonetheless, it is clear that interventions, even with very young children, can produce significant improvements in intergroup relations.

In this section we present three approaches to intergroup relations with young children. In Chapter 2, Louise Derman-Sparks discusses "anti-bias education," which is an approach to improving intergroup relations, rather than a specific program. Anti-bias education is based on the premise that even when teaching young children, attention must be paid to "systemic power dynamics" and the cultural milieu in which intergroup relations programs are conducted. Anti-bias education attends to issues of individual identity, empathy for other groups, critical thinking about social groups, and anti-bias student activism. In anti-bias curricula, group differences are a focus of attention, the materials are relevant to the lives of children, and teaching techniques are responsive to the children themselves. Derman-Sparks argues that to teach in such classrooms teachers need to explore their own backgrounds and come to terms with their biases and fears. They also need formal, highly interactive, training opportunities.

Elizabeth Cohen discusses a very different approach to improving intergroup relations in Chapter 3. Her "complex instruction" approach concentrates on relations among students from different groups and is aimed toward producing equal-status interaction among them. The curricula is not focused on social groups but rather consists of classroom lessons set up in a unique format requiring cooperative interaction among students. It is the conditions of intergroup contact, not the content of the curriculum materials, that affect intergroup relations in this program. When students cooperate to work on cognitively complex curriculum content, patterns of exclusion and withdrawal, especially among minority-group and low-achieving children, can be overcome. By counteracting group-based expectancies, status differences among children are eliminated. This is accomplished by providing students with tasks requiring multiple abilities and multiple roles. Such tasks allow all students to excel. Teachers create the curriculum tasks and intervene to facilitate equal-status interactions among students. This is a technique that can only be employed in heterogeneous classes. It has the advantage of avoiding the conflict and discomfort that can arise in approaches that rely on the explicit examination of group differences.

Robert Cooper and Robert Slavin (Chapter 4) describe a different set of approaches to cooperative learning. Their own techniques employ standard academic topics that have been modified so the material can be learned in small interethnic cooperative teams. The students must rely on one another if they are all to successfully learn the curriculum materials. In one of their versions of cooperative learning, team scores are based on each student's scores with respect to his or her own prior performance. Teachers observe the teams and praise positive and successful interactions. In other versions of this technique, the teams compete against one another in academic game tournaments or the students receive supplementary individualized instruction. Cooper and Slavin also review related approaches to cooperative learning developed by other educators. A concern with equity is a guiding principle of all of these approaches. Cooper and Slavin's review demonstrates that research consistently indicates that these cooperative learning techniques regularly improve intergroup relations. The authors' research syntheses show a substantial overall influence (measured by "effect sizes") for a range of approaches to cooperative learning.

Chapter 2

Culturally Relevant Anti-Bias Education with Young Children

Louise Derman-Sparks

Culturally relevant anti-bias education seeks to cultivate the dispositions, provide the knowledge, and develop the skills children and adults need in order to work together in diverse and inclusive schools and communities. The creation of settings in which all feel a sense of belonging and experience the affirmation of their identities is a desired outcome of culturally relevant anti-bias education. In these settings, the educational process is ongoing and seeks to engage all members of the community or school in joyful learning from one another across cultural groups. Inherent in the educational process and in the development of these settings is a commitment to ongoing growth through open communication, which involves actively addressing biased behavior. Anti-bias education is a means for traveling the road of individual and institutional change—not an end in itself. It is "an active/activist approach to challenging prejudice, stereotyping, bias and systemic 'isms,' grounded in the premise that is necessary for each individual to actively intervene, to challenge and counter the personal and institutional behaviors that perpetuate oppression" (Derman-Sparks & ABC Task Force, 1989, p. 3).

The publication in 1989 of *Anti-Bias Curriculum: Tools for Empowering Young Children* by the National Association for the Education of Young Children (NAEYC) introduced the concept of anti-bias education to the field of early childhood care and education. The membership of NAEYC includes teachers, administrators, and paraprofessionals in diverse programs that serve young children and their families. These programs include home- and center-based day-care programs, preschool programs of varying formats, cooperatives, for-

Education Programs for Improving Intergroup Relations. ISBN 0-8077-4459-X (paper). Prior to photocopying items for classroom use, please contact the Copyright Clearance Center, Customer Service, 222 Rosewood Drive, Danvers, MA, 01923, USA, telephone (978) 750-8400.

profit programs, and employer-supported programs, as well as federal-, state-, and city-funded programs. More than 200,000 copies of *Anti-Bias Curriculum: Tools for Empowering Young Children* have been purchased, and the book has been translated into several languages. Since its publication, other books, grounded in teachers' practice with an anti-bias approach and published in the late 1990s deepen, refine, and extend its initial ideas (Alvarado et al., 1999; Bisson, 1997; Cronin, Derman-Sparks, Henry, Olatunji, & York, 1998; Pelo & Davidson, 2000; Whitney, 1999; Wolpert, 1999; York, 1998). The core concepts of an anti-bias approach have spread nationally and internationally, articulating a new paradigm of diversity and equity work with young children.

WHY ANTI-BIAS EDUCATION?

In 1985 a multiracial, multiethnic group of early childhood educators from Los Angeles and Pasadena engaged in a year-long participatory action research project, the purpose of which was to rethink how to do diversity and equity work with young children. Motivation for the project arose from dissatisfaction with the prevailing "additive" (Banks, 1988) or "tourist" (Derman-Sparks & ABC Task Force, 1989) approach to multicultural education. Members of the Anti-Bias Curriculum Task Force gathered qualitative data about their young students' thinking and behavior, looking at gender, race, disabilities, language, and other aspects of the children's family cultures. In monthly meetings the group analyzed the data, discussing ways to address the issues that were emerging. Each educator also began to introduce new activities based on these discussions and to observe their impact on children. The task force also discussed feelings and issues related to their own identity, culture, and prejudices that arose as they worked with the children. What we named the anti-bias approach was the outcome of this project.

Three core concepts grounded our work. First, we agreed that it is impossible to teach about diversity without paying attention to the systemic power dynamics in the United States, which assign privilege or lack of privilege based on race, gender, class, physical ability, and sexual orientation. Nor is it possible to ignore the prevailing social attitudes toward various aspects of human diversity in our society, which come from and support systemic inequities. These dynamics influence children's developing ideas and feelings about themselves and others. They also affect every educator's sense of identity, attitudes, and interactions with children, as well as shaping the institutions in which educators and other human service providers work.

Second, we believed that research about young children's identity and attitudes should inform the curriculum. However, in 1985, when the Anti-Bias Task Force began its work, this belief did not inform the fields of child development and early childhood education and so was absent from curriculum, texts, and courses. At this time, the pioneering work of Kenneth Clark (1955), Mary Ellen Goodman (1952), and Helen Trager and Marian Radke-Yarrow (1952) as well as the continuing research sparked by their efforts (see, for example, Aboud, 1997; Cross, 1987; Dennis, 1981; Derman-Sparks, Higa, & Sparks, 1980; Fox & Jordan, 1973; Katz, 1976, 1982; Leahy, 1983) were unknown to almost all educators.

Young children do not come to early childhood programs as blank slates. They bring ideas about themselves and others that affect how they perceive and how they organize new information. For example, 3- and 4-year-old preschoolers are already aware of mainstream gender norms—what girls and boys can and can't do—even when their own families do not subscribe to these norms. In early childhood programs throughout the country, teachers hear children monitoring each other's gender behavior: "Boys can't play with dolls, girls can't climb playground structures, men can't be nurses, girls can't be doctors." Teachers hear these comments even from children whose mothers are doctors and fathers are nurses, even in programs where boys do play with dolls and girls do climb. Societal norms are powerful and unless teachers know what their children are thinking, they will not be able to create effective activities to counter misinformation.

Third, diversity/equity education should utilize principles of constructivist and critical pedagogy. A constructivist approach is grounded in cognitive developmental theory, which treats learners as active participants in their own learning and requires the teacher to scaffold learning experiences in relation to children's ideas (Bredekamp & Rosegrant, 1992). Critical pedagogy is grounded in the notion that teaching and learning occur in historical, cultural, and social contexts and power dynamics; it places both the learner and the teacher in their cultural and historical contexts (Darder, 1991; Freire, 1970). A pedagogy that is both critical and constructivist engages children in interactive activities that support active exploration and cooperative learning about their daily life experiences. Children and adults are encouraged to develop their capacity to think about and give meaning to their experiences, rather than to memorize disembodied information provided by the teacher. Memorizing cannot lead to the dispositions and abilities required for living comfortably with diversity. Curriculum must be grounded in children's daily life experiences, using interactive methods that allow children to explore and act on their world, to learn from one another as well as from their teachers.

Lack of attention to these three core concept results in what the Anti-Bias Task Force called "tourist multicultural education." In a tourist multicultural approach, children visit cultural groups other than the dominant, mainstream, white, middle-class culture from time to time, just as people do when they visit other countries as tourists. Classroom activities focus on special times, such as a holiday celebration, or an occasional "multicultural" event. This might involve inviting parents to share their cultural foods with the children as a unique experience or feature occasional segregated learning units about Africa or China or Mexico. However, the content and teaching styles of the daily or "regular" curriculum continue to reflect only mainstream culture. In addition, materials used during these special multicultural time-outs from the regular curriculum are frequently inaccurate, are set in the past rather than present, focus on countries of origin rather than the U.S. experience of various ethnic groups, and are presented from the perspective of the dominant culture. Consequently, even with good intentions, a tourist multicultural approach results in exposing children to inaccurate information and a biased perspective and has little relationship to children's lives; in addition, the segregation of the multicultural from the regular curriculum implies that the dominant culture is the normative way to be. A tourist multicultural approach with young children was prevalent at the time the Anti-Bias Task Force began its work and, unfortunately, can still be found in many programs.

GOALS OF CULTURALLY RELEVANT ANTI-BIAS EDUCATION

Anti-bias teaching builds on four interacting goals. These goals are for all children, though the ways of working toward these goals will depend on each child's background, age, and life experiences.

Goal One: Nurture Every Child's Construction of Knowledge, Confident Self-identity, and Group Identity. This goal requires the creation of educational settings in which all children are able to like themselves without needing to feel superior to anyone else. It also means enabling children to develop biculturally. For children of color, this means being able to effectively interact within their home culture and within the dominant culture. For children of the dominant culture, who are likely to experience congruence between home culture and school culture, it means developing the capacity for comfortable and equitable cross-cultural interaction.

The works of Cross (1987, 1991) and Tatum (1997) are especially pertinent to this goal. Reinterpreting existing research on African American children's identity development, Cross makes a distinction between individual or personal identity and group identity or "group reference orientation." This distinction provides a more complex framework for nurturing children's identities in ways that take into account the realities of the societal dynamics of power and privilege. It also becomes a conceptual vehicle for avoiding victim-blaming of groups that experience societal discrimination. Tatum (1997) further develops the implications of Cross's paradigm for parents and teachers. Personal identity development begins at home. Most families do attempt to nurture their children's self-esteem. However, societal racism and other forms of bias affect all young children's group identity through messages of superiority or inferiority. Even nurturing, loving families cannot prevent these societal forces from having a negative impact on their children.

For example, White children need guidance in their development of a positive group identity that does not incorporate societal messages of superiority because of their skin color. Conversely, children whose group identity is undermined through racist or anti-Semitic messages need guidance to develop resistance to these messages. Anti-bias education goes beyond the focus on self-concept that is prevalent in early childhood education to address the impact of societal biases on all children's identity development.

Goal Two: Promote Each Child's Comfortable, Empathetic Interaction with People from Diverse Backgrounds. This goal means guiding children's development of the cognitive awareness, emotional disposition, and behavioral skills needed to respectfully and effectively learn about differences, comfortably negotiate and adapt to differences, and cognitively understand and emotionally accept the common humanity that all people share.

Children begin recognizing and are curious about differences related to gender, skin color, hair texture, apparent physical disabilities, and language very early in life. Research over 50 years as well as observational data from parents and teachers documents that, contrary to a persistent myth, young children do notice skin color and other differences among people. (For a summary of research and further references, see Derman-Sparks & Ramsey, 2000; Ramsey, 1998.)

Awareness of differences among people begins in the first year of life. When children begin talking (in the latter part of their second year), their questions and comments make clear that they are becoming aware of the salient features of identity in our society. As they move into their preschool years (3 to 5 years old), children also have their own ideas about human diversity, reflective of their experiences and cognitive strategies for organizing the world. An anecdote from my own family serves to illustrate the way a young child seeks to organize the experience of ethnic diversity.

When my niece (A) was 4½, she and I (L) had the following conversation during a Passover seder:

A: I'm half-Jewish, aren't I?

L: Yes, Dad is Jewish and Mom isn't.

A: The people who were Jewish got to the other shore and didn't get wet (referring to the passage through the Red Sea).

L: Uh-huh.

A: The people who weren't Jewish drowned.

L: Yes, the story says that many of pharaoh's soldiers did drown.
    (*At this point, A was silent, but I could see the wheels turning in her mind.*)

L: What do you think happened to the people who were half-Jewish?
    (*This was the issue I believed my niece was pondering.*)

A: They got to the other side.

L: That's good, because they were safe.

A: Yes, but they got a little bit wet!

There is no mention of "half-Jewish" people in the narrative of the Exodus. However, my niece was putting different pieces of information together in the way young children think and she was trying to figure out her place in the Passover story—a story that was obviously of great significance to the important people in her life.

Children enter preschool and kindergarten with varying, often unexpected, ideas and feelings about their identity, about other people, and about human diversity. Education will likely miss the mark or even reinforce misconceptions unless teachers have a good idea what their young students may be thinking and feeling. For example, consider an activity designed to help children learn about disabilities—introducing a child-size wheelchair into the classroom. This is a good method for promoting understanding of physical differences, but it may backfire unless the teacher is able to help children uncover and express their ideas and feelings. Many young children think that sitting in a wheel chair will make their legs "not work" and therefore will be afraid to participate in the activity. The teacher needs to be aware that this is how a child may think and provide for discussion that expands the child's understanding while accepting and helping the child to articulate his or her feelings.

Goal Three: Foster Each Child's Critical Thinking about Bias. To achieve this goal, we must guide children's development of the cognitive skills to identify unfair and untrue images (stereotypes). We must help children become aware of comments (teasing, name-calling) and behaviors (exclusion, discrimination) directed at someone because of gender, race, ethnicity, disability, class, age, weight, or other such personal characteristics. Further, we as educators must help children to develop empathy so that they know that all kinds of bias hurt someone.

The natural developmental process of awareness of and curiosity about human diversity, which leads to the creation of theories about diversity, takes place in the social-political and cultural contexts of the family *and* the larger society. Common forms of communication convey a myriad of overt and subtle messages to young children about the significance of the various aspects of human diversity. Many of these messages—coming from television, video games, children's books, movies, greeting cards, and images on clothing and lunch boxes—also teach misinformation. For example, consider the messages embedded in the materials and story surrounding Thanksgiving. The prevailing story is one-sided and inaccurate, presented from the European American perspective only. Thanksgiving decorations give young children stereotypical information about how American Indians look, dress, and live. Moreover, Thanksgiving is not a day of celebration for many of the indigenous people of the Americas, a reality ignored by its designation as a national holiday. As Kenneth Clark pointed out almost 50 years ago in his landmark book *Prejudice and the Young Child* (1955), the messages of bias to children come not from direct contact with people different from themselves (as is commonly believed) but from socially prevailing attitudes and beliefs.

Since young children are just beginning to construct their ideas about self and others, they are especially vulnerable to the inaccurate and biased information that is embedded in too many of these messages. They are also quick to pick up emotional responses of bias from the people who are close to them, even though the adults are not aware of conveying any messages. The insidious "microcontaminants" (Pierce, 1980) of racism, anti-Semitism, sexism, ableism, and homophobia interact with young children's developing cognitive and emotional abilities and can be very destructive.

When children enter early childhood programs, the impact of bias on their understanding of self and others comes with them and affects their responses to diversity education. For example, here is a typical scenario.

A preschool teacher invites a person of American Indian ethnicity to her classroom to share some cultural objects and information. If the guest comes dressed in his ritual clothing, the preschool children are afraid of him, because, influenced by racist societal messages, they think "Indians" spend their time shooting bows and arrows. If the guest comes dressed in his daily clothing, the children do not believe he is "Indian," because he does not look like the inaccurate images they see in the media. Unless the teacher knows what her children may bring to the activity and can intentionally help them talk about their ideas and feelings, guide them to new information that contradicts their misconceptions, the activity won't achieve its intended outcomes.

However, with appropriate teaching and nurturing young children can learn to resist the destructive impact of the microcontaminants of racism and other "isms." Here are some examples of children who have been exposed to anti-bias education and have learned that they can take action to counter bias on their own behalf or on behalf of others. These examples show the development of empathy even in quite young children.

A 4-year-old tells a classmate, "Don't say 'No way, José'. It might hurt José's feelings." A 6-year-old writes in awkward printing, "This book is irregular. It doesn't have any women in it." A 5-year-old tells her classmate to keep a stereotypic "Indian warrior" figure in her cubby, because it's "not fair" to their teacher, who is of American Indian background. A 6-year-old tells a first-grade classmate, "You do not have to like me, but it isn't OK to not like me because my skin color is brown."

Goal Four: Cultivate Each Child's Ability to Stand Up for Herself or Himself and for Others in the Face of Bias. This activist goal includes helping every child learn and practice a variety of ways to act when another child acts in a biased manner toward her or him, when one child acts in a biased manner toward another child, *and* when an adult acts in a biased manner. Goal four builds on goal three. Critical thinking and empathy are necessary components of acting for oneself or others in the face of bias. "Anti-bias activism is a natural outgrowth of children's awareness of what's fair and not fair, a natural response to their readiness to act for fairness" (Pelo & Davidson, 2000, p. 9).

Activism projects with young children "nurture self-esteem and empowerment, develop empathy and appreciation for differences, facilitate critical thinking and problem solving, provide a mental model of survival for children at risk from bias, provide a model of equity and justice for privileged, dominant culture children, and contribute to community building" (Pelo & Davidson, 2000, p. 8). Here is an example, from a preschool in Seattle, illustrating the capacity of 4- and 5-year-olds to develop activism skills.

"Hey, there's no brown crayons," Jennifer called out.

"Yes, there is . . . no, there isn't! Where are the brown crayons? I need to draw a picture of my mommy!" Eula complained.

"Brown is just a poopy color anyhow," said Molly, while a few others giggled.

"No, it's not. Fran, these guys don't even know about brown. You have a meeting and tell them."

They did have a meeting. But Fran did little of the "telling." Eula was clearly in charge of the discussion, with some help from Larry and Jennifer. She talked about how all the people in her family had brown skin and that they liked the color of their skin. She also told them about all the things that she liked that were brown, like the earth, her dog, chocolate milk, and raisins. Other children added to the list.

Larry added to the discussion with some information about his family: "I have a pink grandma and a brown grandma, and they are both nice."

Jennifer described the different shades of color in her family, describing her dad as "almost black." She also directed me to fetch the book *All the Colors We Are* (Kissinger, 1997), which describes "mellow stuff" (skin color and melanin production). Sean piped up, "My mom reads me *Black Is Brown Is Tan* [Adoff, 1973]. You can read that, too, Fran."

Fran added to the discussion, "I feel really upset when I hear someone making fun of another person because of the color of their skin. There are many beautiful and different skin colors among the people in our classroom, and none of them are 'poopy.' Eula, is there anything more that you would like to say to Molly right now?" Eula, who had moved closer to her friend Molly and whose anger had dissipated while she talked, turned to look at Molly and said, "How would you like it, Molly, if I called your skin a bad name?" Molly didn't answer right away. The room was quiet until she said, "Hey, guys, let's look for crayons. Maybe we didn't look good enough. Anyway, Fran will have to buy some, if we need more" (Pelo & Davidson, 2000, p. 63).

Including activities that support young children's learning to take action against injustice is essential to anti-bias education and distinguishes it from other multicultural approaches.

IMPLEMENTATION GUIDELINES AND STRATEGIES

While the implementation of culturally relevant anti-bias education should be contextualized to specific groups of children and adults, several underlying guidelines inform practice.

1. Culturally Relevant Anti-Bias Education Is for All Children, in All Classroom Settings. This means homogeneous as well as diverse classrooms. For example, an often-asked question is how to do anti-bias education with a group of all "White," or European American, children. We suggest first working on the diversity that already exists in the group. For example, children will have different kinds of family configurations; their family members will carry out gender roles differently or have different kinds of jobs and incomes. The first step in implementing an anti-bias approach is establishing the valuing of differences as well as commonalties and fostering respectful, fair treatment of the children in the class. Once children are comfortable with the idea of being the same as and different from each other and are experiencing supportive interactions, the teacher can then introduce diversity that exists beyond the classroom in the children's larger community, neighborhood, or city. Thus, the teacher may choose to introduce learning opportunities about people who are Native American because the children live in a state with an indigenous population or about people who are Mexican Americans because there is a Mexican American population in their city. These differences then become part of and enlarge the tapestry of diversity already explored, shared human needs are connected to the children's own needs, and experiences of unfair treatment are related to the children's own such experiences.

2. Culturally Relevant Anti-Bias Education Is a Perspective or Lens through which to Plan and View All Interactions, Teaching Materials, and Activities. It must permeate all of the classroom life every day. For example, materials in the art area should include a range of skin colors in the crayons, felt pens, paper, and paint available to the children every day, not just for a special activity about skin color. If, for example, a theme such as community helpers is developed, then pictures, books, field trips, and visitors should reflect racial, cultural, language, gender, and class diversity as well as diversity of physical abilities among those who do community service work. In addition, the teacher will intentionally choose images, stories, and people that contradict common stereotypes; for example, a scientist is always a White man, a nurse is always a woman, a firefighter is always a man, a teacher is always able-bodied.

3. Culturally Relevant Anti-Bias Education Addresses Multiple Arenas of Identity, Bias, and Institutional Power Dynamics. Although racial/cultural diversity is at the core of anti-bias work, gender, disability, sexual orientation, class, and age are also woven into the overall fabric. For example, when studying families, a common curriculum topic in early childhood education, a teacher can create a planning web that shows how the multiple diversity topics interweave in the scheme of families. This enables the teacher to intentionally bring in materials and activities that support an anti-bias perspective, such as a family in which a parent or child has a disability, an adoptive family, a family with two mommies or two daddies, a lower-income as well as a middle-income family.

4. Culturally Relevant Anti-Bias Education Works in Partnership with Families. Day-to-Day Activities Must Reflect the Real, Concrete, Daily Lives of the Children and Families Being Served in a Particular Center or Classroom. This means that the curriculum will not look the same from program to program, although all practice will reflect the overall mission, goals, and implementation guidelines. For example, those working to support children's development of a strong identity in a program serving low-income children, whether of color or White, will find it a challenge to find materials that reflect the children's lives. They will need to use their creativity, doing such things as taking photos to make puzzles, posters, and books about the children's communities, with help from families and community members. They might ask family and community members to make audio- or videotapes of family stories so the children hear their home language in the classroom. They will want to include people in the children's communities who are working to make a better life for the community in the curriculum, invite them to talk with the children; and make books about these community activists' lives. They might want to institute family literacy programs that create opportunities for parents to strengthen their own sense of identity and history while learning to read.

In contrast, in programs serving higher-income children it will not be difficult to find learning materials reflecting their lives. What will be more of a challenge is developing activities that support their learning to have empathy for people who have less than their families do and to resist stereotyping people who are poor. Children from affluent, financially secure families are often confused and troubled upon learning of homeless people. Teachers and schools serving children of privilege can develop activities that would enable children to act in ways that will expand upon their concern and provide them with information about homelessness. First, the teacher could initiate a discussion with the children about what homeless people might need—blankets or tents might be items the children would think of. Then the class could plan fund-raising activities, go to buy blankets with funds raised, and write letters to accompany the blankets. The director of a homeless shelter might come to the school to answer questions and accept the blankets. At many points during these activities, teachers would provide information and respond to children's questions, such as "Why are people homeless?" "How do you lose your home?" "Where do you go to the bathroom if you are homeless?" They would also raise questions with the children, such as "How do you think it feels to be homeless?" "What do you think people can do to stop anyone from being homeless?"

5. Culturally Relevant Anti-Bias Education Is Developmental and Emergent, Informed by an Understanding of Children's Ages and Stages of Development, and Responsive to Children's Ideas and Behaviors in Relation to Various Aspects of Diversity. "Teachable moments," which arise throughout the day in the course of children's interactions with one another, with materials, and with the teacher, are a rich mother lode for immediate and follow-up discussion and activities. Teachable moments often arise when the children are engaged in dramatic play. For example, the children are arguing about what the "mother" and "father" do: One child wants the mother to go to work and the father to take care of the baby, whereas another child insists daddies cannot take care of the baby and that mommies stay home. Later, two girls decide they will play house and another child says, "You can't have two mommies." The teacher, overhearing these two interactions, decides to develop a series of activities on the theme of the range of gender roles and another series of activities exploring all the ways in which people can make up a family. Comments by children that reflect the impact of prejudice are another kind of teachable moment. Examples include a child telling another child, "You can't play with us because brown skin people aren't allowed" or a child asking a child who speaks a language other than English, "Why do you talk funny?" When teachers overhear these kinds of interactions, they need to intervene immediately to support the recipient of the remark and to uncover the thinking underneath the speaker's comments. The teacher uses this information to plan a series of activities that help children explore their ideas, correct misconceptions, overcome fears, and develop more awareness of and comfort with diversity.

PEDAGOGICAL METHODS FOR IMPLEMENTING GOALS

The four anti-bias education goals also suggest directions for activities and materials.

Goal One: Nurture Every Child's Construction of Knowledge, Confident Self-identity, and Group Identity. Work on this goal lays a foundation for the other three goals. Activities strengthen children's personal and group identities. Children's daily life at home and in their communities becomes a core part of curriculum content as they learn about themselves, their nuclear and extended family, and their ethnic community. Children's continued development in their home languages is fostered, while they are also beginning to learn English. The classroom environment includes objects, art, music, and images of the children, their homes, their family, and the people who work in their communities. Teachers make books about the child and about each child's family. They take photos of the children, their homes, and their families and make matching games and puzzles. People in the children's communities who are working to improve community life are invited to speak with the children. In addition, activities also explore differences *within* the children's ethnic, gender, and class identities. Recognition and appreciation of the vast range of individual differences promote an appreciation of diversity and counteract stereotyping.

Goal Two: Promote Each Child's Comfortable, Empathetic Interaction with People from Diverse Backgrounds. In working toward this goal, the focus is on learning about others. Often teachers make the mistake of moving right into this goal without developing goal one. Learning about diversity should flow out of the nurturing of self-esteem and a strong and positive sense of group identity.

Working to promote comfortable interaction and develop empathy is relatively easy in programs that are racially, ethnically, and culturally diverse. As children explore who *they* are, rich opportunities to develop their awareness of, comfort with, and respect for the differences among the members of the group will also emerge. Many opportunities for exploring commonalities will also arise.

In programs where children and their families are racially and culturally similar, promoting comfort with and respect for differences begins with the existing diversity within the group. Families within the same culture do not live exactly the same way. Family structure, gender roles, physical abilities/disabilities, types of work, and religion all may differ. In racially/ethnically homogeneous early childhood centers and preschools, diversity among the participating children, families, and staff can be explored, while commonalities such as shared group beliefs and traditions can be discussed. This process lays a foundation for awareness of, comfort with, and respect for differences, in part simply by giving permission to notice and talk about difference.

The next step is to find ways to introduce racial, ethnic, and cultural diversity. Activities should focus on the lives of individual people in the children's larger community and city. Teachers should explore the ways in which the children's lives touch on a larger, more diverse community. The discussion of similarities and differences expands to involve people who are different from the children and their families by race, culture, class, religion, language, physical abilities, and family composition. Care should be taken to see and explore individual differences within all groups in order to avoid fostering stereotypes of the groups that are beyond the children's everyday experience.

Teachers using an anti-bias curriculum avoid the use of stereotypic materials or activities and are selective about ideas in published multicultural guides. Holidays are part of a larger set of activities and used in moderation; they are not the sole focus of teaching about others. Diversity is part of the daily environment of the program; it is not an add-on token for special days. The curriculum incorporates the understanding that humans share core similarities (e.g., the need to be fed, sheltered, loved) and that they meet these core needs in different ways. Deconstructing children's misconceptions and providing them with more accurate information and comfortable exposure to differences help them to resist the influence of prejudice.

Goal Three: Foster Each Child's Critical Thinking about Bias. Activities for critical thinking focus on teaching children to make distinctions between inaccurate and untruthful images and messages and accurate and truthful ones. If children insist on rigid gender-role categories, the teacher plans multiple activities that provide counterinformation and guides the children to see the contradictions between narrow gender-role ideas and reality. If young children think, as many do, that darker skin color means dirty skin, the teacher plans activities that enable the children to actually see for themselves that all skin gets dirty and that dark skin color remains dark even when it is clean.

Children's misinformation about American Indians is another arena for critical thinking activities that provide extensive experiences that contrast real people and pictures of real people with stereotypical, inaccurate ones. Teachers working with primary-age children can use a chart activity, with the children first naming "What I think I know about Native Americans" (or whatever topic under discussion) and "What I would like to know." Then the children and teacher spend several weeks gathering information before returning to their chart. They make a list of "What I have learned" and then compare and contrast this third list with the first one to see where they had misconceptions.

Early childhood teachers find storytelling with "persona dolls" to be an effective strategy for developing empathy with differences and critical thinking about prejudice and discrimination. First mentioned in the Anti-Bias Curriculum book, persona doll activities have become very popular. A full discussion of how to use this strategy appears in *Kids Like Us,* the culmination of many years' work by Trisha Whitney (1999), an Oregon early childhood educator. The persona doll technique utilizes a tried-and-true early childhood practice that is itself part of an age-old, cross-cultural tradition: storytelling. The teacher creates individual personalities and imagined lives for dolls chosen to add diversity to the program. Then the teacher regularly relates stories with the dolls based on real issues of diversity and creates anti-bias theater involving issues and events in the classroom and in the children's community. These stories invite children to explore and invent solutions to challenges a particular doll faces. Young children quickly identify with and feel empathy for the dolls. The teacher then helps the children transfer the issues in a particular doll's story to their own lives.

Here is one example. In the following story, a child looks at a persona doll's [Lucia's] drawing of her family and tells her it can't be her family with only a grandma in it. The teacher's goals are to have the children learn to recognize insistence on conformity as a bias, to empathize with Lucia, and to validate many kinds of families. Lucia's feelings are identified as *upset, mad, and confused.* Then the discussion begins.

'Why is Lucia so upset, mad, and confused?'
'Cause of what that kid said.'

'He said her gramma's not her family.'
'Did Lucia cry?'
'She might have been upset enough to cry. Is her grandma her family?'
'Yes. That's right. She told us before.'
'That's why she drew her grandma.'
'It seems like that other kid wanted everybody's family to be the same. But it's not true that all families are the same, is it?'
'No. I live with just my mom and my brother.'
'Yes. That's your family, Han Eul. A family is the people who love and take care of each other. There are many different ways to be a family. How would it feel if someone told you your family isn't right?'
'I'd be mad. I'd say that's not true!'
'That would hurt my feelings.'
'I'll bet it would! That's just how Lucia felt. Now we know that it's not right to try to tell someone they have to be the same as someone else. And we know how much that hurts, don't we?' (Whitney, 1999, p. 140, italics in original)

Goal Four: Cultivate Each Child's Ability to Stand Up for Herself or Himself and for Others in the Face of Bias.

Activities related to this goal work in tandem with critical thinking activities. Educators who use activism projects with young children are keen observers of their interests, ideas, interactions, joys, and hurts. They create activities that engage children in taking actions that are relevant and appropriate in a variety of ways. By first listening to children and observing what is happening in the classroom and learning about what is happening in the children's larger community, the teacher gains important information on which to draw in structuring activism projects that are relevant and important to the children. As a part of the listening, the teacher will seek to understand and acknowledge children's feelings and provide children with a vocabulary for expressing feelings. The teacher can then move to engaging the children in dialogue about feelings and events that will support and foster critical thinking, asking questions and providing information as appropriate. As teachers seek to develop activism projects with children, it is most important that they remain mindful that the purpose of these activities is the empowerment of the children, not the resolution of any adult issues.

Anti-bias early childhood educators have invented a range of activism activities based on issues in their classrooms that the children thought were important. These have included children writing a letter and circulating a petition (when there was no response to their letter) to a calendar company because the pictures were of white children only. Another involved sending a letter to a Band-Aid company protesting the use of the term "flesh-colored" on the box. (The company sent coupons for transparent Band-Aids.) Other children painted over racist slurs found on a wall in the children's playground. Another class made "tickets" to put on cars of teachers who parked inappropriately in the school's handicapped parking space. (The teachers stopped doing so.)

This goal has usually proved the most difficult for teachers. Now, teachers have a new outstanding book, *That's Not Fair! A Teacher's Guide to Activism with Young Children* (Pelo & Davidson, 2000), which is based on several years' work in early childhood programs in Seattle. Step-by-step guidelines and numerous examples of activism projects based on real issues in the children's lives show clearly what this vital aspect of anti-bias education includes. "When teachers follow these steps, they help children move from asking questions to solving problems, from indignation to understanding and action . . . they teach children to act responsibly, consider people's feelings and perspectives and ideas, and notice how their actions might affect other people" (p. 53).

WHERE WE ARE GOING

Two key lessons emerge from over a decade of anti-bias work. The first is that the most successful anti-bias educators are reflective practitioners who build their daily curriculum based on the questions, concerns, behaviors, and real lives of the children and adults they serve, within the overall framework of culturally relevant anti-bias education. Moreover, teachers must also work on the four anti-bias goals for themselves even as they work with children. They must understand how their own cultural backgrounds influence their teaching beliefs, styles, and interactions with children. They must also look honestly and carefully at the societal structures of power and privilege and see the impact of these structures on themselves and the organizations in which they work. In short, becoming an anti-bias educator requires its own developmental journey, which must inform effective training. Traditional training approaches are not sufficient; rather, adults need time and experiential learning to engage in a *process* of change (Alvarado et al., 1999; Chang, Muckrlory, & Pulido-Tobiassen, 1996).

The second lesson is that effective anti-bias education requires more than work within centers and classrooms. It also requires community building and organizing for institutional as well as individual and interpersonal change, along with building a vision of a new society that includes all of us equitably. We have had to extend our concept of an educator to an educator/organizer, a person who can work for change both in and out of the classroom. This means adding new skills to our training. It also means creating ways to connect people committed to anti-bias work to each other locally and nationally. To this end, we are in the process of building an organization, the Early Childhood Equity Alliance. The ECEA will provide the following functions: linking and network building, assistance in local education and community development, dissemination of resources, and participatory action research. (For further information about the ECEA, contact us at info@ecequityalliance.net or 1403 34th Ave., Seattle, WA 98122.)

The anti-bias approach is also developing internationally, influencing work in early care and education in countries such as Australia, Belgium, Canada, Denmark, Greece, Ireland, Japan, the Netherlands, South Africa, and the United Kingdom. Educators in these countries are figuring out what anti-bias education work looks like in the context of their particular histories, demographics, and cultures (Brown, 2001; Creaser & Dau, 1996; Van Heulen, 2000). Their work contributes to our identification of the variables that affect anti-bias work as well as deepening our understanding of shared principles.

Research on the impact of an anti-bias approach on young children is in its infancy. One source of data is teachers' anecdotal documentation of children's ability to utilize anti-bias concepts (Pelo & Davidson, 2000; Whitney, 1999). One published study used a participatory action research design to document children's reactions to experiencing anti-bias curriculum in a kindergarten classroom over a schoolyear (Marsh, 1992). There are many challenges specific to carrying out this research that must be addressed. What exactly do we look for in assessing impacts on young children? How we gather information from young children is a part of the challenge. Another part of the challenge involves finding ways to carry out long-term research when the development of children's cognitive abilities will naturally alter their understandings. And yet another dilemma has to do with how to retain contact with a population that moves away at the end of an early childhood program, coming into contact with other communities and influences. And finally, we must find ways to sort out the various factors that influence a child. We must figure out how to differentiate among the impacts of family, peers, school programs and teachers, the larger community, and the media before we can accurately assess the impact of a culturally relevant anti-bias early childhood program (Ramsey & Williams, in press).

SUMMARY

After a brief historical perspective, this chapter presented four goals for anti-bias education in early childhood programs: (1) to nurture every child's construction of knowledge, self-identity, and group identity; (2) to promote each child's empathic interaction with people from diverse backgrounds; (3) to foster each child's critical thinking about bias; and (4) to cultivate each child's ability to take action against bias. The philosophical, developmental, and practical bases of these goals were explored, with many examples provided to illuminate the approach. There was a detailed discussion of implementation guidelines and pedagogical methods recommended in working toward these goals, again with many vivid examples drawn from practice. Consideration was also devoted to the educators who undertake this work, with a discussion of the developmental path of the anti-bias educator and of training issues for anti-bias educators. The chapter concluded with a brief consideration of the future of anti-bias early childhood education, raising provocative questions for future research.

Chapter 3

Producing Equal-Status Interaction Amidst Classroom Diversity

Elizabeth G. Cohen

Miguel was a shy and withdrawn child who spoke no English and who stuttered when he spoke Spanish. His Spanish reading and writing skills were very low, and although math was his strength, nobody seemed to notice. Recently arrived from a small community in Mexico, Miguel lived with relatives—more than 10 adults and three children in a two-bedroom apartment. He came to school hungry and tired, wearing dirty clothes. Shunned by his classmates, who said he had the "cooties," Miguel was left out of group activities. Even when he had a specific role, other members of the group would take over and tell him what to do. Miguel was obviously a low-status student. When I observed Miguel's group I saw that the other members simply wouldn't give him a chance. Cooperative learning was not helping him at all.

—Shulman, Lotan, & Whitcomb, 1998, p. 69

The story of Miguel is not uncommon. Most teachers who use cooperative learning have observed the problem of one member being left out of the group. Such students talk less than others; when they do speak up, no one takes their ideas seriously or even listens to what they have to say. They may have trouble getting their hands on materials for the group task; others may exclude them physically.

Patterns of exclusion and withdrawal are particularly troubling in classrooms with diverse student populations. In these classrooms, low-achieving

Education Programs for Improving Intergroup Relations. ISBN 0-8077-4459-X (paper). Prior to photocopying items for classroom use, please contact the Copyright Clearance Center, Customer Service, 222 Rosewood Drive, Danvers, MA, 01923, USA, telephone (978) 750-8400.

students from groups perceived as less powerful in society (e.g., members of ethnic minorities, those of low socioeconomic class, English-language learners) are likely to be treated as outcasts within their own cooperative learning group. Teachers choose cooperative learning precisely because they want to see all students actively talking and working together. They want to produce the equal-status conditions that will lessen prejudice and increase intergroup friendliness. Thus it is particularly painful when the group experience reinforces the majority's stereotype about the incompetence of minority groups.

Less often observed by teachers is the dominance of certain students (often European Americans) who take over the group, telling other people what to do and trying to do all the work themselves. They talk much more than other people. Their suggestions often become the group's decision. They are much better at talking than at listening. These patterns of inequality within the group are the product of status differences among the members. Strangely enough, social isolation and social dominance are two sides of the same coin. They are two ways in which status problems reveal themselves in cooperative learning.

Fortunately, there are ways to treat the effects of status differences during group work. However, to make them work requires an understanding of how these differences in behavior in the group come about. Once teachers understand the process that produces Miguel's predicament, they can see how the treatment is designed to change that situation in a way that will change the behavior. For example, it is essential to recognize lack of participation by some group members and dominance of others as a problem experienced by the whole group rather than as a problem of the student who is excluded from participation. Very often, teachers confuse status problems with personality characteristics of individual students such as "assertiveness," "shyness," "low self-esteem," or "low self-concept." The failure to participate is not due to the personality of the low-status student. It is situational, and if the teacher changes the social situation, the behavior will also change.

My colleagues and I have made extensive studies of status problems using a sociological theory called status characteristic theory (Berger, Cohen, & Zelditch, 1966, 1972; Berger, Rosenholtz, & Zelditch, 1980). Status characteristics are social rankings where it is generally agreed that it is better to be high than low. Those who are in the low state of the status characteristic (such as being African American, female, or Mexican-American) are generally expected to be less competent at important new tasks than are Whites, males, or European Americans. According to this theory, the problem starts from the different expectations for competence attached to status characteristics such as race and gender. These differential expectations for competence spread to new collective tasks, where they affect expectations that group members have for each other's competence at the new task. The spread of expectations to new tasks is called a process of status generalization.

The source of these general expectations for competence and incompetence lies in the larger social context and its culture. They reflect differences in power and resources held by high- and low-status groups in the society. Expectations that certain racial and ethnic groups will be incompetent are often referred to as racist beliefs about the intelligence of people of color. Similarly, sexist beliefs are expectations for incompetence on the part of women, who are supposedly less intelligent than men.

When expectations based on status spread to a mixed-status group working on a collective assignment, a type of self-fulfilling prophecy takes place. Those group members who are expected to be more competent become more active and influential. Those group members who are expected to be less competent tend to be less active and therefore less influential in group decisions. At the end of the group activity, the high-status members are perceived as having had the best ideas and as having done most to lead the group. Thus the net result of the group interaction is a ranking of members on prestige and power that is identical with the initial rank order on the status characteristics. Even on group tasks that have nothing to do with race or ethnicity, we have repeatedly shown in laboratory settings that European Americans will be more active and influential, on the average, than African Americans or Mexican Americans (Cohen, 1982).

In addition to societal status characteristics such as race, ethnicity, social class, and gender, students vary on *local status characteristics* such as academic and peer status. These are the two most important status characteristics in the classroom. Academic status correlates with social-class status because children from lower social classes often come to the school less well prepared for academic success than middle-class students, who have had school-like experiences at home and in preschools. When racial- and ethnic-minority students come from poor families with little formal education, they may also arrive at school without a head start in literacy and numeracy, thus making it likely that they will be seen as having low academic status. Peer status refers to student popularity. As children mature, they increasingly see popularity as quite independent of academic status (Cohen, 1997; Lloyd & Cohen, 1999). These local status characteristics work in the same way as those based on race and gender. They have the same power to infect new collective tasks with differential expectations for competence according to differences in status.

When teachers employ cooperative learning techniques, they unwittingly set the stage for the process of status generalization. According to the theory, when there are mixed-status groups faced with a collective task, conditions are favorable for the emergence of status problems. Thus a cooperative learning group that is heterogeneous on achievement and ethnicity will activate differential expectations. Everyone will expect the high-status students to be more competent on the new task than the low-status students. As a result of these differential expectations, high-status students will talk more and, as a result of their high rates of participation, will learn more. Low-status students will talk less and, as a result, will learn less (Cohen, 1997).

OVERVIEW OF CHAPTER

Complex instruction was designed to create equal-status interaction in mixed groups within heterogeneous classrooms. This chapter describes the model of complex instruction, its origins, and its instructional strategies. I summarize the extensive evaluation studies of its effectiveness and share some of what has been learned from the dissemination of the model in the United States and elsewhere. Throughout the chapter, I make the case for creating more equitable classrooms, a change that involves fundamental alteration of the social structure of traditional classrooms.

COMPLEX INSTRUCTION

Heterogeneous classrooms have multilingual, multiethnic student bodies, typically with a wide range of academic achievement. *Equal-status* interaction occurs when minority students, social isolates, and those who are seen as low-achieving students are equally as likely to participate in discussions as are majority students, popular students, and those who are seen as high-achieving students.

Structure of the Program

To create equal-status interaction, the teacher uses research-based interventions. These interventions, called status treatments, change the expectations for competence for low-status students. They do so by helping students to see that each student is capable of making important intellectual contributions to the group's product. Status treatments require multiple-ability cooperative group tasks that use a far wider range of intellectual abilities than is typical of school assignments. Ordinary school tasks repeatedly call on the same verbal and computational skills, so it is no surprise that some students appear to be good at everything while others become chronic failures.

While students are working in heterogeneous groups at tasks requiring multiple abilities, the teacher delegates authority to the groups so that they have considerable intellectual autonomy in solving problems and in creating products on challenging tasks. Teachers foster interaction among the students, who learn not only by listening to the teacher but also by talking and working together. In other words, students use one another as resources while teachers avoid telling students what to think or how to do their tasks. They provide general instructions through an activity card for each group and reserve direct instruction only for the orientation and wrap-up periods prior to and following group interaction.

Complex instruction does not separate the issues of academic achievement from the issues of equal-status interaction. When students work on the open-ended tasks of complex instruction, those who talk more will learn more. Therefore, participation within the group becomes vitally important to learning. Furthermore, in order to maximize learning gains, that participation should be equal-status. At the same time that teachers foster interaction, they will intervene in order to change the expectations for competence held by and for the low-status students. Gains in higher-order thinking skills occur both because of participation and because of the challenging nature of the academic tasks assigned to groups. As a result of these strategies, there is no group of students in complex instruction classrooms who are performing far below all the others (Cohen, Lotan, & Leechor, 1989).

Origin of the Program

Complex instruction grew out of laboratory experiments with the creation of equal-status interaction in interracial groups of middle school students (Cohen & Roper, 1972). It became a practical program for classrooms after a field experiment demonstrated that the effects of status treatments were robust and would last more than 6 weeks (Cohen, Lockheed, & Lohman, 1976). To run this experiment, we created a special summer school program for middle school students of Oakland, California, at the Center for Interracial Cooperation.

Although the status treatments demonstrated effectiveness in a controlled classroom experiment, one cannot simply insert multiple-ability interventions into conventional classrooms. A teacher-dominated classroom with emphasis only on reading, writing, and computing will reconstruct academic status orders as fast as the interventions can treat them (Rosenholtz & Rosenholtz, 1981). When the curriculum emphasizes a narrow set of skills and utilizes whole-group tasks, and when the teacher makes evaluations known to everyone through use of recitation, students can and do rank each other on a single dimension of perceived academic ability. Furthermore, there is a high level of agreement among the students on who is "smart" and who is "dumb." Unless the social structure of the classroom changes so as to become more equitable, the interventions will have no long-lasting effect.

To prevent the academic status order from consistently re-creating it-self, it is necessary to do something about narrow curricula and the traditional teacher role. Since 1979, we have been researching and developing an approach to creating equitable classrooms. Complex instruction is a complete model for altering the social structure of the classroom, a model that includes curriculum, instructional strategies, status treatments, and methods of professional staff development (see Cohen & Lotan, 1997a).

Creating a practicable model for equitable classrooms requires close collaboration of researchers and teachers. I use the pronoun *we* in this chapter because, throughout this research program, there has been tight teamwork. Talented graduate students with years of teaching experience carried out much of the required research and evaluation. My colleague, Dr. Rachel Lotan, also had lengthy teaching experience prior to her graduate work in the sociology of education. Classroom teachers created many procedures for making the model a practical one for classrooms. We have conducted extensive evaluations and have documented achievement results in elementary and middle schools. The program is now widely implemented in the United States, Israel, Europe, and Jamaica. Throughout this lengthy program of research and development, we have used sociological theories and research tools to create and evaluate curriculum and instruction and to provide a strong knowledge base for the advice we give to others (see Cohen & Lotan, 1997b).

TECHNIQUES AND STRATEGIES

To produce equal-status interaction that will maintain itself over time and to improve academic achievement, complex instruction has several important components. These include changes in the teacher's role and methods of instruction, the use of status treatments, and changes in the nature of curriculum.

Instruction and the Teacher's Role

In a complex instruction classroom, there are typically five or six groups each working on a different task. Groups rotate among tasks so that each group completes each task. To manage this "six-ring circus," teachers must learn how to delegate authority. They cannot run from group to group telling students how to carry out their tasks. Instead, teachers need to foster interaction by holding individuals and groups accountable. The group is responsible for presenting a group product at the end of the work session, while each individual must turn in an individual report concerning one of the major intellectual questions underlying the activity. Teachers avoid "hovering" over the groups while they are at work and do not intervene unless students are hopelessly lost. They will often pose a question to the group, telling the students that they will be back to hear the answer in a few moments. In this way, the group is forced to use its members as resources and to take responsibility for both the group functioning and the final group product.

Our research has repeatedly shown that the higher the percentage of students who are talking and working together during this group work, the greater are the average learning gains for the classroom (Cohen et al., 1989). Thus the success of the teacher in fostering interaction by delegating authority to the groups is of critical importance in achieving the desired learning gains. If the teacher fails to delegate authority and tries to supervise in detail what each group is doing, there will be fewer students talking and working together and weaker learning gains (Cohen, Lotan, & Holthuis, 1997).

There is a system of cooperative norms and roles that is invaluable in helping group members take responsibility for one another. Because cooperative groups represent a radical change from traditional classroom behaviors, it is necessary to instruct students in the new rules or norms for behavior. For example, students learn the following rules: *You have the right to ask others for help; you have the duty to assist those who ask for help.* The use of skill builders helps students internalize new norms to such an extent that they will enforce them with one another. For example, students learn how to help each other without taking over and doing the task for another person. They practice this new behavior in the context of an exercise called *master designer*, in which they must explain to others how to put together a pattern of colored tiles without letting them see the model and without touching or pointing at the tiles. (For more on these skill builders, see Cohen, 1994a.)

Having every student play a role does much to help the teacher delegate authority. In roles such as facilitator and materials manager, students carry out some of the ordinary duties of teachers. Roles such as reporter and harmonizer help to hold the group accountable for producing a good group product and for the quality of the group process. Every student plays a different role, and the roles rotate over time. Teachers do not select the "natural leader" to play the role of the facilitator time and again. This will only reinforce the peer status order that preexists in the classroom. (For more on the development of these roles, see Cohen, 1994a.)

Use of Status Treatments

To achieve equal-status interaction, teachers must directly treat the problem of unequal expectations for competence among their students. Two interventions developed using status characteristic theory have been shown to be effective in boosting the participation of low-status students: the multiple-ability treatment and assigning competence to low-status students. To be successful in using these treatments, it is important to understand the theoretical reasons concerning what makes them effective as well as the practical steps one must take in carrying them out.

Multiple-Ability Treatment. One way to minimize the problem of unequal access and learning for low-status students is to broaden the conception of what it means to be "smart." The multiple-ability treatment requires the teacher's public recognition of a wealth of intellectual abilities that are relevant to and valued in the classroom and in daily life. Rather than assuming that all students can be ranked along a single dimension of intelligence, the multiple-ability treatment highlights specific skills and abilities students need for particular tasks. Each student will have different strengths and weaknesses among these multiple abilities. For example, the highly verbal student may have difficulty with tasks that require spatial and visual competence. Likewise, the student who scores poorly on a vocabulary test may be an astute scientific observer. This view of ability is compatible with work in psychology that views intelligence as multidimensional (Gardner, 1983; Sternberg, 1985).

A multiple-ability treatment typically occurs during orientation to the day's work in groups. Teachers start by naming the different skills and abilities necessary for successful completion of an activity and then explain the relevance of these abilities to the tasks assigned to the groups. An effective multiple-ability treatment convinces students that the tasks they are about to undertake are fundamentally different from traditional classroom tasks because they rely on many different kinds of intellectual abilities. For example, a teacher introducing a unit on the concept of the afterlife in ancient Egypt might say, "Let me remind you that for these activities you need many different abilities. You will read, write, sing, and draw. You need to be able to analyze the pictures and have the ability to visualize what the ancient gods were like. Finally, you will need to be creative and have the ability to visualize and build a three-dimensional model of a tomb."

The next step in the treatment is to create a mixed set of expectations for each student. It is essential that each student perceive that he or she will be strong on some of the abilities and weaker on others. The teacher creates a mixed set of expectations by saying explicitly: "Remember: No one of us has all these abilities, but each one of us has some of the abilities we will need today." A successful treatment never omits this step. Herein lies a central premise of creating equal-status interaction: *Each individual brings valuable and different abilities to the task.* For the group to be successful, all members must contribute.

Theoretically, this treatment works because the teacher has helped the students to understand that there are a number of *specific status charac-*

teristics that are directly relevant to the task they are about to undertake. Specific status characteristics, such as the ability to observe and compare, work the same way as academic status or race. Those students who are felt to rank high on this ability will be more active and influential on all aspects of the task than those who are not ranked so highly on this ability. Thus on a computer task, those students who are felt to be expert with computers are likely to dominate the collective discussion. This expertise, once established, will also spread to noncomputer tasks. By breaking up the task so that students perceive that there are many different relevant abilities, the teacher breaks up the assumption that only general academic status or a student's relative popularity will predict competence at this task. Further, telling students that no one will have all of these abilities but that everyone will have at least one means that each student will have a mixed set of expectations for competence rather than uniformly high or uniformly low expectations. Because the teacher has pointed to specific status characteristics that are directly relevant to the task at hand, they will be stronger than academic or peer status characteristics. Because people combine all the status information at hand when assigning expectations for competence to the upcoming task, the new mixed set of expectations will soften the effects of a person's standing on academic, peer, racial, or ethnic status. The net effect will be improved participation and performance on the new task by low-status students. Moreover, the effects of this success will transfer to new and different tasks.

Assigning Competence to Low-Status Students. While research has shown that a multiple-ability treatment can help to equalize interaction between high- and low-status students (Cohen, Lotan, & Catanzarite, 1988), a second treatment shows even stronger potential to boost the participation of low-status students. Teachers use both interventions in association with multiple-ability group-work tasks.

Assigning competence is a *public statement* that specifically recognizes the intellectual contribution a student has made to the group. Teachers can assign competence to any student, but it is especially important and effective to focus attention on those who are behaving as low-status students within their group. This requires teachers to make careful observations of what is happening in different groups during group work. They must first identify who is acting as a low-status member. Then they must watch for important intellectual contributions by low-status members to the group.

Assigning competence is a *positive evaluation*. It relies on the fact that most students are likely to believe the teacher's opinion. After all, the teacher is the only person in the classroom who has the formal right to evaluate the work of students. In order not only to change the student's expectations for competence but also to raise the group's expectations for the student, the teacher must assign competence publicly, so that both the student and the classmates hear it. In essence, the teacher has assigned the low-status student a high state on a specific status characteristic. This positive evaluation must also be truthful. Talking about contributions that the student did not in reality make will do more harm than good.

Assigning competence must be *specific* so that the student and the group know exactly what the student can do well. Finally, it must make the intellectual ability demonstrated by the student *relevant* to the work of the group. When the specific status characteristic is relevant to the work of the group, it will have more power in raising the expectations for competence for the low-status student than the other status characteristics, which caused the group to treat the student as a low-status individual. The power of such a treatment is that its effects will transfer to the next task that the group undertakes. The group will now expect that the formerly low-status student will have something to contribute. They will make greater efforts to listen and to find out what the student is thinking. (For a videotape of teachers using the treatments, see Cohen, 1994b.)

Candida Graves, a fourth-grade teacher in a bilingual classroom, describes what happened when she assigned competence to a low-status student:

> One day I had a student named Juan. He was extremely quiet and hardly ever spoke. He was not particularly academically successful and didn't have a good school record. He had just been in the country for two or three years and spoke just enough English to be an LEP (limited English proficient) student. I didn't notice that he had many friends, but not many enemies either. Not that much attention was paid to him.
>
> We were doing an activity that involved decimal points, and I was going around and noticed he was the only one of his group that had all the right answers. I was able to say, "Juan! You have figured out all of this worksheet correctly. You understand how decimals work. You really understand that kind of notation. Can you explain it to your group? I'll be back in a minute to see how you did." And I left. I couldn't believe it; he was actually explaining it to all the others. I didn't have faith it was going to work, but in fact he explained it so well that all of the others understood it and were applying it to their worksheets. They were excited about it. So then I made it public among the whole class, and from then on they began calling him "the smart one." This spread to the area where he lived, and even today kids from there will come tell me about the smart one, Juan. I thought, "All of this started with a little intervention!" (Graves & Graves, 1991, p. 14)

In a study of 13 elementary schools, Cohen and Lotan (1995) found that status interventions boosted the participation of low-status students while not suppressing the contributions of high-status students. The more frequently the teacher used the multiple-ability treatment and assigned competence to low-status students, the more the low-status students spoke up and were active in their groups. The overall status problems in such classrooms were observably weaker than in classrooms where teachers used these treatments less frequently.

Changing the Curriculum

The success of the two status treatments requires some major changes in the nature of the group assignments made for cooperative learning. Convincing students that many different abilities are important requires a broad curriculum that really does involve multiple intellectual abilities. If the tasks the teacher assigns to groups are typical worksheet tasks involving only reading, writing, and computing, then it is not possible to convince students that multiple abilities are required. If, in contrast, the tasks are open-ended and do not have a single right answer, and if they really do require an array of intellectual skills, then it will be possible for different students to make different contributions. It will be possible for the low-status student to display his or her abilities so that both the low-status student and other members of the group can change their expectations for competence for this individual.

Working with complex instruction (CI), developers and teachers have created multiple-ability curriculum units specifically for CI classrooms. (For more on the principles of this curriculum, see Lotan, 1997.) For example, the unit on Egyptian afterlife is centered around the conceptual question, "How did the ancient Egyptians' concept of the afterlife affect their everyday lives?" Students complete five different activities, each comprised of a performance task conceptually tied to the unit's big idea and intended to provide an opportunity to explore one aspect of the central concept. Each activity gives groups one piece of the academic content of the unit, an open-ended performance task, and a conceptual tie to the big idea. Tasks in this unit include creating a skit of the journey to the afterlife and weighing of the heart ceremony; drawing a tomb painting of the group's conception of the afterlife; designing a pharaoh's tomb; creating a god or goddess for the ancient Egyptian afterlife; and creating a song, rap, or dance that explains mummification. This unit was created by teachers of sixth graders and follows their studies of ancient Egypt. In connection with each activity, there are resource cards with materials from primary sources, both textual and pictorial.

Even without these carefully engineered units, the status treatments will be successful with any multiple-ability task. All the groups in the classroom can carry out the same task. A typical multiple-ability task in social studies might involve creating role plays, building models, analyzing texts, composing songs, or creating murals. Students have a chance to display a wide range of abilities and to use more traditional academic skills such as textual analysis, experimentation, reasoning, and creative and expository writing. (For more on the creation of multiple-ability tasks, see Cohen, 1994a.) Starting in the sixth grade, students may work with not only an activity card but also with resource cards that present background material for the task (without containing answers). Some of the newer mathematics curricula are oriented to group investigation and problem solving using multiple-ability tasks. A rich source of multiple-ability tasks for the younger student is the area of science. For example, second and third graders may try to figure out what makes popcorn pop, working with a Bunsen burner, a test tube, and a kernel of corn. Alternatively, they may work with the parts of a flashlight, trying to determine what makes it light up. (These tasks are adapted for a bilingual population in the curriculum in *Finding Out/Descrubimiento* [DeAvila & Duncan, 1982].)

Multiple-ability tasks have no single right answer, so one person cannot do the work of the group. Instead, the tasks are carefully constructed so that students need one another to complete a reasonable group product. While creating a product, the group has considerable autonomy; they are free to determine how they will attain the goal of the activity, such as the content of a role play, the nature of model, or the words and tune of a song.

A very common misconception is that if you use these open-ended, multiple-ability tasks, then you will have treated the problems of status. However, without a deliberate intervention to change expectations for competence, high-status students are likely to dominate even a multiple-ability task. According to status characteristic theory, as soon as you give a group a collective task, differential expectations for competence come into play. Therefore, regardless of the richness of the task, high-status students will be more active and influential than low-status students. Multiple-ability tasks are a *necessary* but not a *sufficient* condition for achieving equality within cooperative groups.

Teaching at a High Level

Complex instruction is designed for academically, linguistically, ethnically, and culturally heterogeneous settings. If students are able to use one another as resources, it is possible to teach at a very high intellectual level. This is why complex instruction units always involve the use of small cooperative groups.

Those students who lack proficiency in the language of instruction or who do not read well can receive assistance within the groups. These same students, once they understand the nature of the assignment, can make other kinds of contributions to the group. Although many teachers appear to think that such students will have difficulty with abstract, conceptual work, this is by no means the case. Under ordinary classroom conditions, they often do not understand the assignment. Thus they don't have a chance to show their deeper understanding of the underlying concepts. Sometimes they are not even exposed to the more abstract concepts because teachers decide that their lack of basic skills requires that they work only on these skills and not join more conceptually advanced activities.

EVALUATION

In evaluating the effectiveness of these interventions, we made good use of the theories underlying their development. We had clear theoretical ideas about what in the nature of the intervention should produce particular results. For example, if status treatments are successful, they should raise students' competence expectations, particularly for low-status students. These improved expectations should be observable in their rate of participation within groups. We used similar designs to test the importance of delegation of authority and of interaction within the student groups. Systematic observation of implementation of the program revealed variations in both delegation of authority and interaction. We found that teachers who more often delegated authority had more interaction in the groups. Using statistical procedures such as correlation and regression, we related measures of authority and interaction to achievement measures.

Here is an alternative to the experimental method, which has long dominated the field of educational evaluation. This alternative method will work only if one has a well-developed theory about which features of the intervention are critical to desired outcomes. There will always be significant variability among teachers and classes as to how well or thoroughly these features of the intervention are implemented. Systematic observation of that implementation will provide data for testing the relationship between the superior implementation of critical features and better outcomes of the innovation.

Evaluation of Status Treatments

This alternative method of evaluation requires detailed, systematic observations of classroom implementation of the intervention. To find out if better implementation of the status treatments was associated with higher rates of participation of low-status students, Rachel Lotan and I counted the number of times that teachers used the two status treatments. We reasoned that if teachers used the status treatments more frequently, low-status students should participate more actively. In the evaluation study, we took a sample of high- and low-status students as measured by a questionnaire in which students selected those of their classmates who were the best in schoolwork and those who were their friends. Those students chosen often on these measures of academic and peer status received a high score, while those chosen rarely or not at all received a low score. Observers counted the frequency of task-related talk of the low- and high-status students while they were engaged in group work. Results showed that the more the teachers used status treatments, the higher were the rates of participation of low-status students. Treatment had no effect on the participation of high-status students, suggesting that they were not inhibited by the experience (Cohen & Lotan, 1995).

Evaluation of Authority, Interaction, and Learning

The more the students talk and work together on multiple-ability tasks, the more they learn. This holds for the classroom level—the higher the percentage of students talking and working together, the stronger the class gains on test scores (Cohen et al., 1989). It also holds for the individual level—the more individuals participate, the higher their test scores (controlling on their pre-test score) (Cohen, Lotan, & Holthuis, 1997).

Because of this linkage between interaction and learning, teachers must learn to foster interaction by delegating authority. If they fail to do so and try to instruct groups directly while they are in operation, they inadvertently reduce interaction and thus weaken learning gains (Cohen, Lotan, & Holthuis, 1997). Unlike the attempts of *teachers* to facilitate completion of the task, the more that *students* play a facilitator role, the higher the rates of student interaction and the higher the learning gains. Therefore teachers must not only change expectations for competence but also know how to delegate authority while holding groups accountable for their products. Teachers may be successful in treating status problems, but unless they learn how to foster interaction, the net result will not be the desired outcomes in learning gains. Even if low-status students contribute their share to the interaction, if the total amount of interaction is small, the learning outcomes will not be favorable.

These evaluation studies were all carried out with systematic observation instruments—those measuring teacher and student behavior as well as instruments measuring activities of students in the classroom as a whole. All these instruments are described in detail in Cohen and Lotan (1997b). To measure learning outcomes, we used standardized achievement tests and tests based on the content of the complex instruction unit.

Achievement Outcomes of Complex Instruction

Classrooms using complex instruction gained significantly more than conventional classrooms on standardized achievement tests and on questions measuring higher-order thinking in content-referenced tests in social studies. (For further details, see Cohen, Biarchini, et al., 1997.)

Moreover, examination of the distribution of learning gains among students in each classroom showed that low-achieving students were now much closer to the classroom average than they had been on the pre-test (Cohen et al., 1989). These favorable results demonstrated that in a classroom where the focus is on equity and higher-order thinking, one can also achieve gains in basic skills for high- and low-status students. These findings refute the belief among teachers that students must master basic skills before they can work on higher-order thinking skills.

LESSONS LEARNED FROM IMPLEMENTATION

Implementing this approach with teachers working in different countries and under very different classroom conditions has taught us some valuable lessons. These lessons are applicable to those innovations that require basic changes in the classroom and in the teacher's behavior.

Theory and Research for Teachers

Teachers who are working with sophisticated innovations must have a grasp of the theory and research underlying innovations. When they face the particular conditions of their school and classroom, recipes and attractive, ready-made materials are not sufficient. They must make some adaptations, and unless they have a theoretical understanding of what the critical features are that make for effectiveness, they will not be able to adapt without considerable risk of destroying the strength of the program. We have found that the better the teacher's grasp of the underlying theory, the better the quality of his or her implementation (Ellis & Lotan, 1997).

Importance of Prepared Multiple-Ability Curricula

As anyone who has worked in staff development knows, teachers are eager for well-prepared and attractive curriculum materials. If you provide such materials, teachers are willing to undertake major changes in their accustomed methods of instruction in order to use the new curricula. When working for equity in the classroom, there is the additional concern that it is not possible to treat status problems without multiple-ability tasks. Teachers cannot easily create multiple-ability curricula for themselves unless they have had the chance to work with well-developed model units. After a year of work with such units, they are able, with some assistance, to create new units for their own classrooms and for those of other teachers.

Sometimes I have worked with teachers in settings lacking the resources in time and staff development to fully implement complex instruction with the multiple-ability curricular units. Under these conditions, I have stressed the creation of single multiple-ability tasks where each group of pupils will carry out the same task. After I have worked with the teachers, using many examples of such tasks, they see how they could each create one task and build up a repertoire over time and in collaboration with other teachers. In the workshop, they practice using a multiple-ability treatment with the task they have developed. On this basis, they try it out in their classrooms and find that they are able to produce equal-status interaction in these lessons.

Central Role of Achievement

Even with the most powerful method of improving intergroup relations, it is very difficult to persuade schools to adopt that method unless there are demonstrated connections to improved academic achievement. Only by creating curricula that meet current state standards and by presenting evidence of improved learning outcomes have we been able to convince U.S. school administrators and teachers to invest in equitable classrooms. In this era of emphasis on accountability, it is difficult to argue for precious time in the instructional schedule without some proven effects on desired educational goals.

We have found no inconsistency between achieving equal-status interaction and improved achievement at the same time. Because multiple-ability curricula are so challenging and represent higher-order thinking skills as well as basic academic skills, high- and low-status students can show progress in both these areas.

Classroom Follow-Up

Effective methods of professional development for teachers with classroom follow-up are absolutely critical to the implementation of the full model. We use both an extensive initial training (up to 2 weeks) plus nine systematic observations of teachers in their classrooms. Ideally, each teacher receives three feedback visits from the staff developer, who uses the observation data to present a bar graph for discussion. For example, the teacher will see what the average percentage is of students talking and working together in his or her classroom. If there are to be maximum learning gains, it should be greater than 35% when group work is in operation.

We have found that the quality of the teacher's implementation of the demanding features of the program, such as status treatments, is directly related to the number of feedback visits he or she has experienced (Ellis & Lotan, 1997). When we have failed to achieve the ideal number of visits with the staff developer, the quality of the implementation suffers.

Teachers must have some organizational support for undertaking sophisticated innovations. Our research has consistently shown the importance of the principal's role in achieving superior implementation (Lotan, Cohen, & Morphew, 1997). The principal coordinates resources and time around the program. Effective principals also make clear that they expect the teacher to follow though and implement the program after initial training. Collegial relations among the teachers are essential for maintaining the program after the first year of training. Because of the importance of the role of the principal and the ability of the teachers to work together, innovations such as these require a modicum of organizational health. A school where the principal has little respect for the teachers or the teachers have little respect for the principal is a poor choice for staff development.

Scaling Up

After developing and evaluating an innovation, how can it be disseminated without losing its effectiveness? Also, how can new centers for training and development be created that operate more or less independently from the original developers? These are the issues of scaling up. In scaling up complex instruction, we have found a powerful linkage with teacher training programs that introduce the underlying principles and some of the simpler practices to pre-service teachers. If the student teachers are placed with master teachers who are skilled in complex instruction, the beginners are able to practice what they have learned at the university. They are then much more likely to implement the strategies in their own teaching.

As the innovation spreads to new and different sites, there is a very real danger that adaptations to new settings will undermine its effectiveness. The only way to prevent this from happening is continual education concerning the theoretical underpinnings of the program. The better the grasp of underlying principles, the more possible it is to make adaptations that will not weaken critical features of the innovation.

Another danger lies in the opposite direction. If practitioners are obsessed with reproducing the innovation with total fidelity to the original form, there is a danger that the technique will become a fossilized antique. People will no longer know why they are carrying out the methods. Under these conditions, not only will the innovation rapidly disappear from classrooms, but unthinking implementation is unlikely to be effective. If the program is to be sustained over time, then it will be necessary for teachers, staff developers, teacher educators, and researchers to continue to develop the underlying ideas, concepts, and propositions of the model. Teachers continue to grow through their strong interest in developing new multiple-ability curricular units as well as through becoming staff developers themselves. Researchers continue to work with the approach, studying the effect of new tools for assessment, developing variants of the model for English-language learners, and examining the discourse of students in groups in great detail. We have developed international communication with our network through the use of a web site: www.complexinstruction.org. The ideas behind complex instruction will survive only if working with the model provides everyone an opportunity for continuing professional growth.

CONCLUSION

We began with laboratory treatments designed to treat status problems. Laboratory treatments evolved over time to a total model for reconstructing the classroom. If changes in the status structure were to persist and allow students to continue to interact on an equal-status basis, each new step seemed to us necessary. Without changing the teacher's role, the curriculum, and strategies for instruction, I do not think it is possible to prevent classrooms from reproducing the inequities of the outer society. Through the connection between minority-group status and depressed academic status, classrooms tend to replicate the inequality of the outer society. In addition to direct strategies for improving intergroup relations, it is necessary to revise the classroom social structure, which sets the stage for academic failure and reinforcement of widely held stereotypes. Our experience leads us to believe that equitable classrooms are both practicable and possible.

Chapter 4

Cooperative Learning: An Instructional Strategy to Improve Intergroup Relations

Robert Cooper
Robert E. Slavin

A resurgence of interest in research on intergroup relations in schools, particularly in interracial group dynamics, has led to the identification of a variety of approaches that are successful in reducing tension among racial/ethnic groups (Brawarsky, 1996). As American society becomes more varied and its public schools reflect this diversity, the need for programs that encourage positive interracial and interethnic communication and interaction will become even more necessary.

In addition to the growing numbers of established minority groups in America, new ethnicities are also being represented in increasing numbers. Where once we spoke of Asians, Hispanics, and Blacks as monolithic groups, the members of these groups are now demanding to be recognized and valued as separate and independent entities. Eugene Garcia, dean of the Graduate School of Education at the University of California at Berkeley, has labeled the phenomenon of increased ethnic specificity as "new diversity." Citing California as an example, Garcia points out that students of color no longer represent the minority. He argues that by 2010 students of color will predominate in many public school systems, particularly those in urban environments. Policy analysts agree that by 2010 there will be as many as 12 school districts in the country that will serve students from more than 100 different racial, ethnic, and national backgrounds (Clinton, 1997).

As the United States becomes more multicultural, it is important that this unique quality be seen as a national asset rather than as a source of tension. Because the public school system provides the opportunity for intergroup interaction, it seems to be the ideal venue for people to learn the merits of a multicultural society while they are at a stage in their lives when harsh, negative stereotypes can still be confronted and refuted. Simply placing students in an ethnically and racially varied environment, however, does not ensure that students will interact across racial lines or that they will view diversity as a constructive quality of their scholastic environment. By implementing academic programs such as cooperative learning that encourage heterogeneous group interaction, students benefit from both the positive results of group work and the experience of cross-ethnic and -racial interactions. As we have argued in earlier work (Cooper & Slavin, 2001), cooperative learning is a critical component of a larger strategy of "equity infusion" (Mariaskin & Sofo, 1992), creating student learning environments in which equity concerns are used as guiding principles for both policy and practice. Embedded in this approach to school reform is the notion that the social organization of schools must be restructured in ways that support high academic standards for all students while instilling a strong sense of respect and tolerance for social, racial, political, economic, and cultural differences.

THE STUDY OF INTERGROUP RELATIONS IN SCHOOLS

The tenets of Gordon Allport's research have dominated social science inquiry on race and intergroup relations. Allport's *The Nature of Prejudice* (1954) has served as the basis for the study of intergroup relations since the mid-1950s. In *The Nature of Prejudice*, Allport evaluated the effects of desegregation in nonschool settings to anticipate the effects of school desegregation on intergroup relations. Although school integration was illegal in one-third of the states in the country at that time, and rare in the rest, Allport's research was deemed crucial to understanding the future of public education in this country. Furthermore, the coincidence of the publication of Allport's report with the *Brown* decision served to augment further its importance in restructuring the American schools.

The *Brown* decision, which established that segregation leads to unequal educational opportunities for African American students, served as the catalyst to school integration efforts. As school integration became more widespread, the need to address intergroup relations within a school setting took on significant importance. Allport cited evidence that asserts that when students of diverse backgrounds have the opportunity to work and get to know one another on equal footing, they become friends and find it more difficult to hold prejudices against one another (Slavin, 1991, 1995b). Allport's contact theory of intergroup relations was helpful in that his research outlined four major variables needed to produce the desired positive academic and social outcomes integration efforts sought: cooperative interaction, equal status among all participants, individual contact, and individualized support for the contact. Research has since added a broader set of variables in this regard that warrant consideration, including the culture, history, and demographic backgrounds of the groups involved (Stephan & Stephan, 1996).

Research findings in the area of intergroup relations have been consistent over time with regard to diverse school environments. Desegregation is not enough to ensure positive academic or social outcomes (Allport, 1954; Cohen, 1972; Orfield, 1975; J. W. Schofield, 1995). Research on intergroup relations indicated that early integration efforts failed to produce the results researchers and policymakers had expected. A study looking at racial attitudes among students in desegregated school settings found that prejudice among African American students toward White students decreased by 50%, but prejudice among White students toward African American students was reduced only by 13% (Stephan, 1978). This pattern of significant difference between racial groups was pervasive. The study concluded that students in desegregated school settings tended to be more negative toward the other group than were students in segregated schools (Green & Gerard, 1974; Stephan, 1978).

The eradication of segregation is not enough to create the schooling experiences that lead to the once hoped-for academic and social outcomes for minority and majority students. J. W. Schofield (1991), drawing on the work of Pettigrew (1986), suggested that the distinction between desegregation, which refers to the existence of a racially mixed environment, and true integration, which refers to the creation of a setting conducive to the development of positive relations among member of different racial and ethnic groups, is vital to understanding intergroup relations in schools.

While Allport's contact theory has been updated and expanded over the years (Cook, 1978; Hewstone & Brown, 1986; Pettigrew, 1986), the factors that were identified as being critical for the improvement of intergroup relations through direct contact with people from different racial and ethnic groups in the 1950s still apply today. For social interactions between students to result in positive cross-cultural experiences those interactions must be on a level of equal status; they must be sanctioned by the institution and by authority figures. Furthermore, students from differing racial and ethnic backgrounds must have the opportunity to interact as individuals (Brawarsky, 1996). Unfortunately, despite all of the research that informs our thinking on this issue, many schools have failed to create the opportunities for students to interact in these ways. Consequently, positive cross-cultural relationships among students are still an anomaly rather than the norm on desegregated school campuses, particularly in middle and high schools. Despite efforts by educators, policymakers, and researchers, youth from different backgrounds still have limited interactions in school settings (Romo & Falbo, 1996; J. W. Schofield, 1995; Slavin, 1995a). Foster, in a study of relationships in multicultural classrooms (discussed in Brawarsky, 1996), found that as children move through the educational pipeline, they are less likely to have cross-ethnic connections. As students grow older, they select a peer group most like themselves and become estranged from their former friends. Foster also concluded that this phenomenon occurs more quickly for females than for males. She cites the lack of participation of females in school-sponsored activities, particularly sports and other extracurricular activities, as an explanation for this (Brawarsky, 1996).

Foster's conclusions resonate with earlier research looking at student participation in sports and intergroup relations. Slavin and Madden (1979) argued that students rarely engage in meaningful conversations that lead to true social integration. The one major exception is school-related sports participation (Slavin, 1995c). Correlational research shows that in desegregated schools, students who participated in school athletics were more likely to have friends of racial backgrounds other than their own and more positive attitudes toward racial diversity than those students who were not active in the sports programs (Slavin & Madden, 1979).

Because participation in after-school athletics programs and extracurricular activities is not universal among the school population, it is important to consider alternative ways for schools to create the conditions needed to support positive cross-cultural experiences for students. More specifically, schools must consider how they might restructure to allow for meaningful, cooperative interaction to take place between students of different ethnicities.

RESEARCH ON COOPERATIVE LEARNING AND INTERGROUP RELATIONS

Cooperative learning is a term that applies to a set of instructional strategies that involve students working collaboratively in groups with little teacher supervision (Deering, 1989). Grounded in several different theoretical perspectives such as social psychology, developmental psychology, and cognitive psychology, cooperative learning is one of the most effective modes of instruction for higher-learning thinking tasks (Lee, 1997), as well as an effective instructional strategy in combating stereotypes (Johnson et al., 1993; Slavin, 1991). Cooperative learning is a collaborative activity organized so that learning is dependent on the socially structured exchange of information between students grouped together, where each student is held accountable for his or her own learning and is motivated to increase the learning of others. This learning method attempts to reduce competition and/or individualism in classrooms by rewarding students based on the performance of every member of their group (Aronson, 1978; Johnson & Johnson, 1987; Slavin, 1983). With some cooperative learning techniques, the group is awarded points or recognition based on the average academic performance of each member of the group. Teachers often delegate authority and responsibility for group management and learning to the students (Cohen, 1994b). The instructional methods used are structured to give each student a chance to make substantial contributions to the team, so that the teammates will be equal—at least in the sense of role equity as specified by Allport (1954).

In many cases, cooperative learning provides students an opportunity to work in a group that is diverse in academic performance, as well as race, gender, and language proficiency. When using cooperative learning methods, students are asked to work in heterogeneous groups to solve problems and complete tasks. The intent of cooperative work groups is to enhance the academic achievement of students by providing them with increased opportunity for discussion, interactive learning, and group support. Cooperative learning methods explicitly use the strength of the desegregated school—the presence of students of different races or ethnicities—to enhance intergroup relations (Slavin, 1995a). When teachers assign students of different races or ethnicities to work together, students are sent a strong positive message regarding cross-cultural interaction. Although increasing positive intergroup relations may not be an explicit goal of cooperative learning, it would be difficult for students to believe that the teacher supports racial separation when he or she has assigned the class to multiethnic teams.

It is important to note that group work for students does not in itself constitute cooperative learning (Johnson et al., 1993). Cooperative learning differs from group work in that assignments are carefully prepared, planned, and monitored in cooperative learning groups (Lee, 1997). Cooperative learning groups place emphasis on the academic learning success of each individual member of the group (Slavin, 1990). Although cooperative learning involves heterogeneously grouping students of varying academic achievement levels, research has consistently found that the use of such methods improves academic achievement for students across the board (Lopez-Reyna, 1997; Slavin, 1991, 1992, 1995b). Given the changing labor-force demands in this country, schools cannot afford to focus solely on equity concerns. Instead, they must always keep at the forefront of any reform or restructuring effort the need to impact and increase student achievement outcomes. One review of research on cooperative learning (Slavin, 1995b) identified 99 studies conducted over periods of at least 4 weeks in regular elementary and secondary schools that measured effects on student achievement. These studies compared the effects of cooperative learning with effects of traditionally taught control groups on measures of the same objectives pursued in all classes. Teachers and classes were either randomly assigned to cooperative or control conditions, or they were matched based on pre-test achievement levels and other factors. Of 64 studies on cooperative learning methods that provided group rewards based on the sum of group member's individual learning, 50 (78%) found significant positive effects on achievement. No negative effects of cooperative learning were observed. The median effect size reported for these studies from which effect sizes could be computed was +.32 (which means that 32% of a standard deviation separated cooperative learning and control treatments). In contrast, studies of methods that used group goals based on a single group product or provided no group rewards found few positive effects; the median effect size was only +.07. Comparisons of alternative treatments within the same studies found similar patterns; group goals based on the sum of individual learning performances were necessary to the instructional effectiveness of the cooperative learning models (Fantuzzo, Polite, & Grayson, 1990; Fantuzzo, Riggio, Connelly, & Dimeff, 1989).

There are eight well-researched cooperative learning methods that embody the principles of contact theory. Four of these methods were developed and evaluated at the Center for Social Organization of Schools at Johns Hopkins University. These are as follows: Student Teams Achievement Divisions (STAD), Teams–Games–Tournament (TGT) (Slavin, 1986), Team-Assisted Individuation (TAI) (Slavin, Leavy, & Madden, 1984), and Cooperative Integrated Reading and Composition (CIRC) (Stevens, Madden, Slavin, & Farnish, 1987). A fifth technique, Jigsaw teaching (Aronson, 1978), has been evaluated in several desegregated schools and is widely used both in its original form and as modified by Slavin (1986) and by Kagan, Zahn, Widaman, Schwarzwald, and Tyrell (1985). Methods developed and assessed at the University of Minnesota (Johnson & Johnson, 1987) have been studied in desegregated schools, and Group Investigation (Sharan & Sharan, 1992) has been studied in Israeli schools that include European and Middle Eastern Jews. In addition, Wiegel, Wiser, and Cook (1975) evaluated a cooperative learning method in triethnic (African-American, Hispanic, and Anglo) classes. (For more details, see Slavin 1986, 1990, 1995b; Cohen, Chapter 3, this volume.)

Many field experiments have evaluated the effects of cooperative learning methods on intergroup relations. This review emphasizes studies in which the methods were compared to control groups in elementary or secondary schools for at least 4 weeks (median duration = 10 weeks) and in which appropriate research methods and analyses were used to rule out obvious bias. Numbers of students in the studies ranged from 51 to 424 (median = 164), in grade levels from 4 to 12, and with the percentage of minority students ranging from 10% to 61%. Most of the studies used sociometric indices (e.g., "Who are your friends in this class?"), peer ratings, or behavioral observation to measure intergroup relations as pairwise positive relations between individuals of different ethnic backgrounds. Some studies defined intergroup relations in terms of attitudes toward various ethnic groups. Several other studies used such sociometric questions as "Who have you helped in this class?" Because only students in the cooperative learning classes were instructed to help their classmates, such measures are biased toward the cooperative learning treatments; thus, the results of these measures are not discussed. Also, observations of cross-racial interaction during the treatment classes were not considered as intergroup relations measures because they measure implementation rather than outcome.

The experimental evidence on cooperative learning has generally supported the main tenets of contact theory (Allport, 1954). With only a few exceptions, this research has demonstrated that when the conditions outlined by Allport are met in the classroom, students are more likely to have friends outside their own racial groups than they would in traditional classrooms, as measured by responses to such sociometric items as "Who are your best friends in this class?"

Student Teams Achievement Divisions (STAD)

In STAD (Slavin, 1986) the teacher presents a lesson to the whole class. Following the initial presentation, students are organized in heterogeneously grouped four-member teams. Each team is given the opportunity to study the information presented. All members of the team have an obligation to ensure that everyone on the team has mastered the lesson's objectives. Following this, students take individual quizzes, and team scores are computed based on the degree to which each student has improved over his or her own past record. The team scores are recognized in newsletters. For example, in a classroom where the teacher is instructing students on the use of possessives, instead of encouraging them to look over a worksheet dealing with this topic alone, students work together in their "Mastermind" teams. The teacher announces to the class that they will be quizzed on the material in 30 minutes. Up until the quiz is handed out, the students complete a worksheet on possessives, using one another as an academic resource. Two of the students from the group of four may choose to start working on the worksheet together. When they are both unsure of an answer, they can approach the other two students in their group for input. As a team, they are able to ensure that each student has grasped the concept of possessives. While the students are working together on the worksheet, the teacher comes by to observe the group work and to praise positive and successful interaction.

At the end of the 30-minute period, the teacher administers a short quiz on possessives. All four of the students' scores on the quiz are totaled to form a group score. The group score will be added to other scores from this same group of students to determine the "Superteam" status for the week (Slavin, 1994).

The evidence linking STAD to gains in cross-racial friendships is strong. In two studies, Slavin (1977, 1979) found that students who had experienced STAD over periods of 10 to 12 weeks gained more in cross-racial friendships than did control students. In a later study, Slavin and Oickle (1981) noted significant gains in White friendly feelings toward African Americans as a consequence of STAD but found no difference in African American friendly feelings toward Whites. Data from a study by Kagan and colleagues (1985) showed that STAD (and TGT) reversed a trend towards the ethnic polarization of friendship choices among Anglo, Latino, and African American students. Similarly, Sharan, Hertz-Lazarowitz, Bejarano, Raviv, & Sharan (1984) identified positive effects of STAD on ethnic attitudes among both Middle Eastern and European Jews in Israeli schools. Like findings were concluded also in studies by Sharan (1980) and Stallings and Stipek (1986).

In a follow-up effort from the Slavin (1979) study, students who had been in the experimental and control classes were asked to list their friends. Students in the control group listed an average of fewer than 1 friend of another race, 9.8% of all of their friendship choices; those in the experimental group named an average of 2.4 friends outside their own race, 37.9% of their friendship choices.

Teams–Games–Tournament (TGT)

TGT is essentially the same as STAD in rationale and method. However, it replaces the quizzes and improvement score system used in STAD with a system of academic game tournaments, in which students from each team compete with students from other teams at the same level of past performance in an effort to contribute to their team scores (see Slavin, 1986). In most classrooms that have implemented TGT, the tournament will happen at the end of the week after the students have been presented the new material and have had a chance to familiarize themselves with it through the completion of worksheets. The tournament begins with the assignment of students to tournament tables from their four- to five-person heterogeneously grouped teams. The top three scorers from the previous week make up table 1. The students who scored the fourth-, fifth-, and sixth-highest are assigned to table 2. Tables are formed in this manner until all students are members of a table. Once students are at the tables, a reader picks a numbered card and locates the corresponding question on the game sheet. He or she answers the question after reading it aloud to the rest of the table. After hearing the reader's response, the first challenger at the table has the opportunity to agree with the first answer, offer a new answer, or pass. If the first challenger passes, the second challenger has the opportunity to answer the question. After everyone has speculated about the answer, the second challenger checks the answer sheet. The individual who answered correctly keeps the card. If a challenger provided an incorrect solution, he or she must put a previously won card back in the deck. As students score points, the high scorer from the table moves up a table, for example, from table 2 to table 1, the middle scorer stays at the table, and the lower scorer moves down. The points scored by the individuals at the tournament tables will be added to the overall team score. At the end of the tournament, the team scores are acknowledged in the classroom newsletter (Slavin, 1983).

DeVries, Edwards, and Slavin (1978) summarized data analyses from four studies of TGT in desegregated schools. In three of these studies, students in classes that used TGT gained significantly more friends outside their own racial groups than did control students. Only one study showed no change in intergroup behavior. The samples involved in these studies varied in grade level from grade 7 to grade 12 and in percentage of minority students from 10% to 51%. In addition, Kagan and colleagues (1985) found positive effects of TGT on friendship choices among African American, Mexican American, and Anglo American students.

Team-Assisted Individuation (TAI)

TAI combines the use of cooperative teams (like those in STAD and TGT) with individualized instruction in elementary mathematics (Slavin et al., 1984). Students work in four- to five-member teams on self-instructional materials at their own levels and rates. Students take responsibility themselves for all checking, management, and routing. Additionally, students help one another with problems, freeing the teacher to spend more time instructing small groups of students working on similar concepts. Teams are rewarded with certificates if they attain preset standards in terms of the number of units mastered by all team members each week. For example, after having been assessed for an appropriate mathematics level through the use of a diagnostic test, students are given a set of programmed units that they will work through at their own pace. The units are carefully organized into more simplified subsets, which include a directions page and sets of problems. The students work in pairs with self-selected members of their team to compare answers and check solutions. At the point at which a student is able to pass a "checkout" with a grade of 80% or higher, he or she will take a final test. This is administered by a fellow team member. Both the score that the student makes on the test and the number of tests that were taken in a week are totaled to contribute to the weekly group score (Slavin, 1983).

Two studies have assessed the effect of TAI on intergroup relations. Oishi, Slavin, and Madden (1983) found positive effects of TAI on cross-racial nominations on two sociometric scales, "Who are your friends in this class?" and "Who would you rather *not* sit at a table with?" No effects were found on cross-racial ratings of classmates as "nice" or "smart," but TAI students made significantly fewer cross-racial ratings as "not nice" and "not smart" than did control students. In a similar study, Oishi (1983) noted significantly positive effects of TAI on cross-racial ratings as "smart" and on reductions in ratings as "not nice." The effect on "smart" ratings was accounted for primarily in the increases of White students' ratings of their African American classmates.

Jigsaw Methods

The original Jigsaw method (Aronson, 1978) assigned students to heterogeneous six-member teams. Each member was given a unique set of information to be discussed in "expert groups" made up of students from different teams who were given the same information. The "experts" returned to their teams to teach the information to their teammates. As a final stage, all students were quizzed and received individual grades.

A classroom that integrates the Jigsaw method is divided into groups of students who are responsible for studying specific areas, such as, in this example, religion in colonial America. To begin the group work, the teacher prepares cards for all six members of the group, which have suggestions written on them offering ways to help focus the discussion on specific issues. The cards offer both reference sources tailored to the achievement level of the student and performance objectives. Once the students have their cards, they set a time limit for themselves to obtain the information on their card based on a variety of photocopied resources. Students who finish quickly are responsible for helping other students who work more slowly or have more complicated activities. The students monitor the time allowed to various activities. After the student in charge of watching the time for information acquisition calls the students back together, each student spends time presenting his or her topic and orchestrating a discussion about it. During the discussion the students are also responsible for monitoring the group's behavior. At the end of the allotted time, the teacher returns to the group and asks them to take notes on how far they have gotten. Additionally, he or she tells them to spend 5 minutes on "group process" cards, where the students evaluate how well they functioned as a group (Aronson, 1978).

Jigsaw II modifies Jigsaw to correspond more closely to the Student Team Learning format (Slavin, 1986). Students work in four- to five-member teams.

While all students read a chapter or story, each team member is given an individual topic on which to become an expert. Students discuss their topics in expert groups and then teach them to their teammates, as in the original Jigsaw program. Quiz scores in Jigsaw II are summed to form team scores, and team accomplishments are recognized in a class newsletter as in STAD.

The effects of the original Jigsaw method on intergroup relations are less clear than those for STAD, TGT, or TAI. Blaney, Stephan, Rosenfield, Aronson, and Silkes (1977) did find that students in desegregated classes using Jigsaw preferred their Jigsaw groupmates to their classmates in general. However, since students' groupmates and their other classmates were similar in ethnic composition, this cannot be seen as a measure of intergroup relations. No differences between the experimental and control groups in interethnic friendship choices were reported.

Gonzales (1979), using a method similar to Jigsaw, found that Anglo and Asian American students had better attitudes toward Mexican American classmates in the Jigsaw groups than did those in control groups, but he found no differences in attitudes toward Anglo or Asian American students. In a subsequent study, Gonzales (1981) found no differences in attitudes toward Mexican American, African American, or Anglo students in Jigsaw and control bilingual classes.

The most positive effects of a Jigsaw-related intervention were found in a study of Jigsaw II by Ziegler (1981) in classes composed of recent European and West Indian immigrants and Anglo Canadians in Toronto. She found substantially more cross-ethnic friendships in the Jigsaw II classes than in control classes, both "casual friendships" ("Who in this class have you called on the telephone in the last 2 weeks?") and "close friendships" ("Who in this class have you spent time with after school in the last 2 weeks?").

The Johnsons' Methods

In cooperative learning methods developed by David Johnson and Roger Johnson (1987), students work in small heterogeneous groups to complete a common worksheet and are praised and rewarded as a group. Of all the cooperative learning methods, these are the closest to a pure "cooperative" model. In a classroom following the Johnsons' method, the students of the class are assigned to four-person heterogeneous groups. The teacher assigns each group the task of learning a vocabulary list. Through the efforts of the group, each member should learn the list of words. Individually, students are given 8 of the 32 words with the intention that they will teach this subset of the list to the group. After the students have instructed the members of their groups, a tournament is held in the class to test them on their knowledge and to see which group was most successful in mastering the vocabulary.

Additionally, the groups are assigned to write a story collectively, in which 95% of the vocabulary is from the word list. At the end of the unit, the students are tested individually on the material (Johnson & Johnson, 1987).

Two of the Johnsons' studies have examined intergroup relation outcomes. Cooper, Johnson, Johnson, and Wilderson (1980) found greater friendship across racial lines in a cooperative treatment than in an individualized method in which students were not permitted to interact. However, there were no differences in cross-racial friendships between the cooperative condition and the competitive condition in which students competed with equals (similar to the TGT tournaments). Johnson and Johnson (1981) observed more cross-racial interaction in cooperative rather than in individualized classes during free time.

Group Investigation

Group Investigation (Sharan & Sharan, 1992), developed by Shlomo and Yael Sharan and their colleagues in Israel, is a general classroom organization plan in which students work in small groups, using cooperative inquiry, group discussion, and cooperative planning and projects. In this method, students form their own two- to six-member groups. The groups choose subtopics from a unit being studied by the entire class, further break their subtopic into individual tasks, and carry out the activities necessary to prepare a group report. The group then makes a representation or display to communicate its findings to the entire class and is evaluated based on the quality of this report.

When applied to the actual classroom setting, Group Investigation offers the students an opportunity to play an integral part in their educational process. For example, during a unit on animals and their diet, the teacher plans a field trip to the zoo with the explicit intent to investigate what animals eat. However, instead of being provided with a list of questions, the students generate the questions they will need to commence with the project. The teacher's role in this stage of the Group Investigation project is to summarize the students' input in order to highlight the overarching themes of the students' ideas. On the day of the field trip, the teacher provides the students with charts based on the questions generated by the class that they can fill out while they take the tour of the zoo. As a follow-up exercise, the teacher asks the students to write about their impressions of the zoo and their tour, allowing students creative freedom as to the form of the written work. Later, the class is asked to comment on the trip to the zoo. The teacher also summarizes these opinions into an overarching theme.

Having established the general feelings toward the zoo experience, the teacher creates five interest groups, such as the five classes of vertebrates.

In heterogeneous groups of seven, the students decide which class of animals they wish to study. Once the students are aware of their category of animal, they are instructed to bring in pertinent resources from home. On the following day, after the students have brought in their research materials, the groups receive cards that instruct them on the responsibilities of the group and of the individuals. Within the group, the students choose the animal they wish to study. During the research stage, although the students are researching their individual topics, they are encouraged to interact with other students to benefit from the class's widespread knowledge and to take part in research efforts that include the entire class, such as looking at slides or visiting laboratories. Once the groups have finished collecting the data, they are instructed to present their information to the class. They can either draw up a storyboard for a documentary focusing on the specific topic or they can prepare a quiz for the class based on the information discussed on the poster they have created during the research process. After the students present the projects and quizzes, the teacher surveys the students on their feelings about how well they used their resources, how well the group worked together, and how much they enjoyed the project on the whole (Sharan & Sharan, 1992).

In a study in Israeli junior high schools, Sharan and colleagues (1984) compared Group Investigation, STAD, and traditional instruction in terms of their effect on relationships between Jews of Middle Eastern and European backgrounds. They found that students who experienced Group Investigation and STAD had significantly more positive ethnic attitudes than did students in traditional classes. There were no differences between Group Investigation and STAD on this variable.

Wiegel and Colleagues' Method

Wiegel and colleagues (1975), working in triethnic (Mexican American, Anglo, and African American) classrooms, conducted one of the largest and longest studies of cooperative learning. They evaluated a method in which students in multiethnic teams engaged in a variety of cooperative activities in several subjects, winning prizes based on team performance. They reported that their cooperative methods had positive effects on White students' attitudes toward Mexican Americans but not on White–Black, Black–White, Black–Hispanic, Hispanic–Black, or Hispanic–White attitudes. They also found that cooperative learning reduced teachers' reports of interethnic conflict.

The effects of cooperative learning methods are not entirely consistent, but 16 of the 19 studies reviewed here demonstrate that, when the conditions of contact theory are fulfilled, some aspect of friendship between students of different ethnicities improves. In a few studies (e.g., Gonzales, 1979;

Slavin & Oickle, 1981; Wiegel et al., 1975), improvements in attitudes were primarily improvements in the attitudes of Whites toward minority classmates, but in most studies, attitudes toward White and minority students were improved to the same degree.

It is important to note that in addition to positive effects on intergroup relations, cooperative learning methods have positive effects on student achievement. This is particularly true of STAD, TGT, and TAI—structured methods that combine cooperative goals and tasks with a high degree of individual accountability (see Slavin, 1995a), as well as Group Investigation (Sharan & Sharan, 1992). It is, therefore, apparent that cooperative learning methods have positive effects on relationships among students of different races or ethnicities, while simultaneously positively influencing academic achievement.

CONFRONTING THE "NEW DIVERSITY" IN INTERGROUP RELATIONS RESEARCH

Is the American public educational system prepared to deal with the "new diversity" of which Eugene Garcia speaks? Do current efforts to improve intergroup relations on school campuses capture the kaleidoscope of racial and ethnic diversity existent in our schools (and in the larger society)? The rich diversity found in American public schools provides unparalleled learning opportunities, but it also creates some unique challenges. Within the school context, diversity can be viewed as a cultural asset to be built upon and shared with students, or it can be seen as a burden that must be dealt with. This is an important dilemma with which educators must grapple, because public education, more than any other social institution in this country, will determine the course of race relations. Given that students spend more time in school and engaged in school-related activities than anywhere else, it stands to reason that schools play a vital role in helping adolescents understand and give meaning to the multiple ways in which race and ethnicity are socially constructed (Giroux, 1992).

Undeniably, the schooling context for America's youth is increasingly multicultural (Heath, 1995). Unfortunately, the vast majority of research about intergroup relations in schools is now 15 to 20 years old, focusing mostly on improving relations between Whites and Blacks. These studies are insufficient in examining intergroup relations within the context of our new diversity (J. W. Schofield, 1995). Given the enormous diversity found today in many public schools, racial and ethnic relations are much more complicated than they were just a decade ago. Intergroup relations are no longer affected just by the competition for resources and attention, but must now consider the relative power and status of the racial and ethnic groups involved. Research in this area must broaden its scope and generate empirical evidence about how positive intergroup relations must be created in school settings where many different racial and ethnic groups coexist and the boundaries between groups are blurred by overlapping categories (McLoyd, 1990; Quintanilla, 1995).

CONCLUSION

The evidence of effectiveness for cooperative learning, obtained through evaluations of programs, indicates a high success rate in encouraging positive intergroup interactions and increasing academic success. The eight programs reviewed in this chapter are particularly effective in challenging and confronting racial stereotypes and other socially constructed notions about different racial groups. Rather than targeting improvements strictly for the minority population, evidence from evaluations of cooperative learning shows that students of all ethnic and racial backgrounds benefit from learning in a well-structured group environment.

Perhaps one of the most promising aspects of cooperative learning is that the programs that embody this ideology are inexpensive to implement. Furthermore, the instructional strategies are widely applicable in terms of subject matter and grade level. They are easily integrated into existing curricula without requiring additional resources. Because evaluations of the programs identify grouping practices, pedagogical strategies, and curriculum as the three common dimensions that are critical to the intergroup climate on a school campus, the programs are most effective when they address these components in tandem. However, each of these scholastic aspects has great potential not only to create the positive interdependence among students of differing backgrounds that challenge racist and stereotypical notions but also to fundamentally alter the intergroup dynamics in schools.

While all three dimensions of the schooling process are important to the discussion of improving the relations between heterogeneous groups of students, this chapter builds on three decades of research on cooperative learning strategies designed to celebrate the increasing diversity in our public schools. Slavin (1995a, 1995b, 1995c) and other researchers have argued over the years that to establish opportunity for positive intergroup relations, schools must create learning environments in which all students are intellectually challenged and encouraged to demonstrate their knowledge without fear of ridicule, embarrassment, or feelings of inadequacy. Furthermore, these learning environments must allow students to develop a positive sense of self as well as a strong sense of interdependence across racial and ethnic boundaries. There is evidence that suggests that cooperative learning can do both.

Over the last 20 years, cooperative learning has emerged as one of the most promising instructional approaches in education. Research suggests that students who participate in cooperative learning activities tend to have higher academic test scores, higher self-esteem, a greater number of positive social skills, and fewer negative stereotypes of individuals based on their race or ethnic group (Johnson et al., 1993; Slavin, 1991; Stahl & VanSickle, 1992). Equally important, advocates of cooperative learning argue that it promotes some of the most important goals in American education—increasing the academic achievement of all students while simultaneously improving intergroup relations among students of different racial and ethnic backgrounds (Deering, 1989). Research on cooperative learning and intergroup relations tells us that we can choose to create schools in which interethnic relations are positive, respectful, and collaborative. This is a choice we must make.

PART II

PROGRAMS FOR ADOLESCENTS AND THEIR TEACHERS

In the next section we present three programs that are aimed primarily at adolescents and the educators who work with them. Addressing intergroup relations issues with adolescents presents special challenges. The basic issues are to counteract the messages they have acquired from their social experiences, to instill values of respect for and acceptance of differences, and to provide knowledge about the diversity of society and the value of diversity. The challenge is the greater because ethnic, racial, religious, and gender identities are crystallizing during adolescence, and in-group peers exercise a powerful influence that is not easily counteracted by messages in school-based programs. This is not an easy group to work with. As one author notes, adolescents tend to be overly sensitive and critical, self-conscious, moody, passionate, and dramatic. As a consequence, different approaches from those used with younger students are needed when educating teenagers. On the other hand, while adolescents may be harder to work with than younger children, their greater maturity provides educators with a wider range of approaches. More sophisticated and direct messages can be delivered about intergroup similarities and differences. More abstract complexities of social life can be addressed, including issues such as justice, fairness, and equality. And more engaging and challenging exercises can be employed.

The three programs we present in this next section are all highly engaging, yet they are also subtle in their approaches, and they display a deep understanding of the student populations they are addressing. The program developers all discuss the complicated tasks of training teachers and trying to sustain the changes they create. All have also been concerned with systematic evaluation as a technique of improving their programs and demonstrating their effectiveness. Finally, all these programs acknowledge the importance of involving parents and the community in changing the attitudes and behaviors of young people.

One of the largest and best-established programs in the country is the WORLD OF DIFFERENCE® program developed by the Anti-Defamation League and described in Chapter 5 by Ellen Hofheimer Bettmann and Lindsay Friedman. The goals of this program are to sensitize students to the existence of prejudice, bigotry, and discrimination and help them develop the knowledge and skills that will enable them to battle their own biases and effectively respond to those of others. The values of justice and equity inform this approach, and it emphasizes the democratic principles upon which this country is based. The WORLD OF DIFFERENCE® program relies on carefully developed curriculum materials. All participating teachers are provided with training in presenting these materials before they can use them in their classrooms. One variation of their anti-bias programs specifically addresses the important role played by peers during adolescence. It is designed to train selected peer leaders who will influence other students through the leadership roles they assume. The pedagogical approach in these programs is highly interactive and personally involving. The programs attempt to address issues of concern to students in their everyday lives. Ground rules are established early on in the anti-bias workshops. Then the workshops focus on issues of identity, the nature of bias, assessing problems of exclusion in the participants' own schools, and ways of fostering positive intergroup relations.

Next, in Chapter 6, Terry Tollefson, Dennis Barr, and Margot Stern Strom describe the Facing History and Ourselves program. This program is based on the study of a specific historical period (Nazi Germany, especially the Holocaust) that is used to explore contemporary issues of racism, prejudice, and anti-Semitism. It is particularly concerned with developing critical thinking skills concerning moral issues such as justice, human rights, and a concern for the welfare of others. The teachers learn the program by going through an adult version of it themselves. The teachers are provided with ongoing support as they develop and implement their own versions of the program. The students in the program are taught to use the methods of humanities research (inquiry, analysis, and interpretation) to examine the rise to power of the Nazis and the events leading to the Holocaust. The students then relate this information to current events in their schools, communities, and society. Explorations of group identity play an important role in this process. Students read history, watch videotapes, write journals, and hold discussions as they learn about hatred, stereotyping, ethnocentrism, scapegoating, power, obedience, and misplaced loyalty. As in the WORLD OF DIFFERENCE® program, students are encouraged to develop a capacity for empathy with those who differ from them.

In the last contribution to this section, Sharon Hicks-Bartlett describes, in Chapter 7, the Hands Across the Campus program. This program has been employed primarily with older adolescents and is aimed at altering the culture of the school as well as changing individual participants. Again, teacher training forms the foundation of this program, but the program also places a heavy emphasis on enlisting the support of school administrators. Among other things, teachers are trained to recognize and deal with problems of intolerance in schools, including exclusion, bullying, teasing, and fighting. The goals of the curriculum are to create an appreciation of cultural diversity, improve communication across group boundaries, and strengthen the democratic process. A variety of techniques are employed to achieve these goals, such as role playing, team learning, reading about historical incidents and cultural heroes, completing personal surveys, and class discussions. Teachers are encouraged to create a safe environment in which sensitive issues can be discussed. A special component of the program involves training student leaders to raise their awareness of diversity issues and assist them in resolving intergroup conflicts. Finally, this program puts extensive effort into community coalition building and involvement.

All three programs, in sum, work with adolescents by contributing to their teachers' professional development, by fostering students' deeper understanding of the issues involved in human interaction in a diverse society, by actively engaging students in their learning, and by realizing that successful programs require incorporating the perspectives of stakeholders from the schools and from the surrounding community.

Chapter 5

The Anti-Defamation League's A WORLD OF DIFFERENCE® Institute

Ellen Hofheimer Bettmann
Lindsay J. Friedman

Almost everyone can recall the positive and, sometimes more vividly, the negative impact that an educator had in his or her life. As Haim Ginott (1975) wrote about his role as an educator:

> I have come to the frightening conclusion that I am the decisive element in the classroom. . . . As a teacher, I possess a tremendous power to make a child's life miserable or joyous. I can be a tool of torture or an instrument of inspiration. I can humiliate or humor, hurt or heal. In all situations, it is my response that decides whether a crisis will be escalated or deescalated and a child humanized or dehumanized. (p. 7)

Harnessing the power of teachers to create classroom and school communities where all children are valued, respected, and able to succeed was, and remains, the founding principle on which the Anti-Defamation League's A WORLD OF DIFFERENCE® Institute is based.

This chapter explores the foundation, goals, and successes of the Institute, an international organization established in 1985 with anti-bias and diversity education programs used by schools, universities, corporations, and community and law enforcement agencies in the United States and abroad. The program has developed, changed, struggled, and met an array of challenges in its relatively short lifetime to become what it is today.

Today, the Institute is in many ways facing greater and more complex challenges than ever before. While there has been an extraordinary growth in understanding (and, at some levels, embracing) the fact that the United States

Education Programs for Improving Intergroup Relations. ISBN 0-8077-4459-X (paper). Prior to photocopying items for classroom use, please contact the Copyright Clearance Center, Customer Service, 222 Rosewood Drive, Danvers, MA, 01923, USA, telephone (978) 750-8400.

is a multicultural society, putting that awareness into action by confronting the bias and prejudice that remain in society is still a difficult, and, at times, frightening prospect. Despite the fact that the principles surrounding the Institute's programs echo the democratic ideals posited by this country's founders, resistance to such programs can be enormous. The proponents of anti-bias education are often left to defend their programs against outcries that such efforts will weaken and divide rather than strengthen and unify this country. However, most educators and anti-bias experts would agree that many of our country's schools are not meeting the needs of all of their students. Students labeled as "different," for any reason, are often victimized and isolated, and increasingly these young people are taking actions that harm themselves or others as a result. Schools can—and should—play an essential role in helping all students develop the critical thinking abilities to reject stereotypical thinking and prejudiced beliefs. Schools can help students acquire the necessary skills to succeed in a society that is far more diverse than the one in which most of their parents and teachers were raised.

Additionally, high-stakes testing, teacher and school accountability for academic performance, and reduced flexibility in individual curriculum choices have led many schools to limit their professional development days (and resources) to those programs that explicitly meet these test-driven standards. Some, therefore, may consider anti-bias educational programs as "extras" or "add-ons." The challenge that the Institute and many of our counterparts in the field face is helping educators and educational leaders recognize that anti-bias education *is* a core component of providing children with a strong educational foundation. Children cannot learn where they do not feel safe, nor can they learn if they do not feel valued and respected.

EARLY HISTORY

The Anti-Defamation League (ADL), as one of the nation's premier civil rights and human relations agencies, was well suited to initiate a broad-based campaign to combat prejudice. When the ADL was established in 1913, its charter stated: "The immediate object of the League is to stop, by appeals to reason and conscience, and if necessary, by appeals to law, the defamation of the Jewish people. Its ultimate purpose is to secure justice and fair treatment to all citizens alike and to put an end forever to unjust and unfair discrimination against and ridicule of any sect or body of citizens." With this charter, the ADL called for a society in which any minority group would be granted the same rights of citizenship and freedom from discrimination traditionally enjoyed by the majority. The ADL's long-term commitment to fighting anti-Semitism and all forms of bigotry is the basis for all of its anti-bias initiatives.

In 1985, the ADL and WCVB-TV in Boston initiated the A WORLD OF DIF-FERENCE® campaign to combat prejudice, promote democratic ideals, and strengthen pluralism. The program's initial school-based goal was to provide training and resources to Massachusetts educators in public, private, and parochial schools on the subject of racial, religious, and ethnic prejudice and discrimination. Today, training programs are offered through four distinct departments, each reaching a particular segment of the population: A CLASSROOM OF DIFFERENCE™ for teachers, administrators, students, and family members in grades preK–12; A CAMPUS OF DIFFERENCE™ for college and university students, faculty, and staff; A COMMUNITY OF DIFFERENCE™ for members of community, youth service, and social service organizations; and A WORKPLACE OF DIFFERENCE™ for employers and employees in a variety of workplaces and law enforcement settings.

Each program offered through the A WORLD OF DIFFERENCE® Institute has its own goals and objectives targeting its specific audience. However, in general terms the goals of the programs are (1) to raise awareness about the issues of prejudice and discrimination and the harm they inflict on individuals and society and (2) to provide effective strategies and resources to address these issues in homes, workplaces, schools, and communities.

A CLASSROOM OF DIFFERENCE™

I learned through the training that individual differences make us unique and cannot be stripped way without damaging our sense of self—sometimes severely. The Institute provided me with good resources, encouragement and support to effectively teach my class. (tenth-grade educator, Houston, Texas)

The primary component of the Institute—and the focus of this chapter—is A CLASSROOM OF DIFFERENCE™, developed to address diversity issues in the preschool through twelfth-grade communities. Programs include workshops for teachers, support staff, classified staff, administrators, students, and family members.

A CLASSROOM OF DIFFERENCE™ programs include anti-bias training and curricular resources that mobilize people to challenge bigotry and to create bias-free schools where differences are appreciated and all people have opportunities to be successful. Workshops provide opportunities for exploring complex issues in an atmosphere that is nonblaming, open, supportive, and action-oriented.

When first launched in 1985, A WORLD OF DIFFERENCE® materials and training were designed for secondary educators only. The belief then was that these educators were the most appropriate group to address complex issues of bias and prejudice in the classroom. As the Institute grew and recognized the need and importance of addressing prejudice in earlier grades, age-appropriate programs were designed for and introduced to elementary and middle school educators. With current research identifying that the seeds of bias can begin to take root as early as ages 3 and 4, the Institute recently introduced an early childhood program for family members and other care-givers of young children (Van Ausdale & Feagin, 2001).

While educators remain the primary audience for the programs and re-sources of the Institute, throughout the 1980s and early 1990s, many schools also requested programs that directly served students. The Institute has de-veloped a number of programs for students that focus on encouraging stu-dents to serve as agents for positive change in their schools and communities.

Providing programs for several audiences has benefited the Institute on many levels. It has allowed ADL staff to meet a variety of needs within a single school community, which encourages schools to think of their anti-bias efforts in a comprehensive manner. Further, ADL staff have found the once the "door is open" through a program for students, which some schools may request instead of administrator or teacher training, it allows for a re-lationship to be developed to encourage educator programming to sup-port the efforts of the students. A relatively new program under the auspices of A Classroom of Difference™, Names Can Really Hurt Us, combines teachers *and* students in planning, training, and presenting a multifaceted assem-bly program for high school communities.

ANTI-BIAS STUDY GUIDES FOR THE CLASSROOM

The Guide has been a tremendous resource for me. I used it in a
Human Relations course that I taught for my eleventh graders. The
students enjoyed the lessons because they were interactive and about
"real issues" that they cared about and, best of all, they got the
message behind each of the activities. (eleventh-grade educator, San
Diego, California)

The centerpieces of A Classroom of Difference™ programs are the *Anti-Bias Study Guides* for secondary and elementary/intermediate teachers. These resources are interdisciplinary and contain teaching materials to help teachers and students examine issues of diversity. ADL staff have sought to be sensi-tive to the many demands on time and content that educators face in meeting their teaching goals for the year. Therefore, from inception, the ADL designed its curriculum materials to be used in a supplementary manner, not as a stand-alone or new curriculum. The *Guides'* instructional units are divided so that at each level—elementary/intermediate and secondary—students have opportunities to explore their own and others' cultures before examining the complex issues of prejudice and discrimination. The materials have been aligned with National Goals 2000 and the national Social Studies State Standards.

The Institute operates on the premise that educators are most likely to be successful in integrating anti-bias content and methodology in their classrooms when they have had the opportunity to examine their own beliefs and assumptions about issues related to diversity and when they have had hands-on experience and training with the materials. Thus, the *Anti-Bias Study Guides* are available to teachers only within the context of a 6-hour (minimum) staff development workshop.

Individualized adaptation of ADL's resources creates challenges for ADL staff in describing to funders or evaluators exactly what a classroom that is "doing A WORLD OF DIFFERENCE®" would look like. This is because it looks different in every classroom. As a result of training, some educators might use the *Guide* to plan a separate human relations unit; others might pick and choose a lesson from different units; and others might not formally use lessons from the *Guide* at all, but might alter or modify the language they use, the concepts they teach, and/or the methods that they use for instruction.

PEER TRAINING PROGRAM

[As a peer trainer] people really listened to what we were discussing. . . . A lot of new areas were introduced and I know some of [my peers] were hesitant but did open up to us. That's a great thing in itself because they acknowledge that there are issues out there. (peer trainer, New York City)

Another program conducted under the auspices of A CLASSROOM OF DIFFERENCE™ is ADL's Peer Training Program, developed in 1991 in response to the riots in Crown Heights in New York City. In the Peer Training Program, ADL trainers conduct anti-bias training in schools for a specially selected group of high school students. These meetings are designed to encourage dialogue about diversity, prejudice, stereotyping, discrimination, and violence. The workshops equip students with the skills and confidence to become activists against bigotry and agents for change and to lead workshops for their peers. By facilitating discussions with their peers in their schools and the larger community, peer trainers disseminate knowledge and incorporate practices that increase awareness about diversity and foster respect.

The Peer Training Program's philosophy is that peer groups have tremendous influence on the attitudes and behaviors of their members. Peer leaders explore their own and their peers' beliefs and values, and programs incorporate strategies for effective leadership. Research indicates that this skill development works best when students are exposed to a body of knowledge and then provided with the opportunity to integrate that knowledge in the classroom and in their everyday lives (Ender, McCaffrey, & Miller, 1979).

A school-based coordinator (usually a teacher) acts as an adviser and organizer for the group of peer trainers. After the students complete the training, the school-based coordinator organizes workshops and projects in schools and in community-based organizations where the peer trainers practice the skills they have acquired.

PROGRAM AND AGENDA DEVELOPMENT

In the beginning of each workshop, participants were very reserved, but as the workshop progressed, responses became more intense. People revealed more about their own life experiences and their perceptions of others. At times, the room would be filled with conversation and at others absolutely silent except for a single person sharing something with the group. (educator, Richardson, Texas)

Workshop agendas are developed following a needs assessment conducted by ADL staff. Typical workshops have up to 30 participants per group and are facilitated by diverse training teams in 6-, 12-, or 18-hour sessions. Five-day summer institutes offer 40 hours of instruction. In order to maximize the possibilities for success, workshops employ discovery learning in which participants discover connections and concepts through their participation and questioning. A variety of media and methods are used in workshops, including videos, small- and large-group discussion, readings, and simulation activities.

Much of the success of Institute training programs depends on information gathering and relationships developed with a school prior to the presentation of the program. The majority of the Institute teacher training sessions are offered to an entire faculty at a single school. This raises obvious challenges in creating agendas that will meet everyone's needs. This initial data collection and communication between ADL staff and the client are crucial not only for building program support and creating relevant agendas but also for developing reasonable outcomes and goals for the session. If a school is only willing or able, for example, to provide a 4-hour training program, ADL staff must work with the school to create realistic expectations of what can be accomplished in such a short time period.

On a related note, frequent requests to develop meaningful teacher training programs in a single 3- to 4-hour time slot present challenges for the

Institute. Research has consistently affirmed that substantial change occurs when professional development programs are longer and also more frequent (Garet, Porter, Desimore, Birman, & Youn, 2001). However, ADL staff balance this with the knowledge that having one's "foot in the door" can be an important step to starting an important process that might otherwise not begin. Of greatest concern, however, is that a relatively short, single workshop may open the proverbial Pandora's box without a plan to address what comes out. Thus, after the workshop, staff will share evaluation data and feedback from the training team to address follow-up needs with the school contact and other decision makers in order to attempt to develop a thoughtful plan to move forward.

As the Institute has become a leader in educational programming in many communities around the country, there have, of course, been necessary changes to the models offered. One of these changes occurred fairly early in the Institute's development. Initially, Institute programs only addressed bias based on race, religion, and ethnicity. These three areas were at that time considered the primary area of expertise for the Anti-Defamation League, and thus A WORLD OF DIFFERENCE programs were the same. Over the years, the Institute has broadened the focus of its programs and services so that now the anti-bias training program for educators examines a wide range of manifestations of bias and prejudice.

METHODS OF PROGRAM DELIVERY

One of the unique features of the A WORLD OF DIFFERENCE® Institute, and one of which ADL is most proud, is its use of trained specialists to deliver its programs. Looking back to the program's origins is instructive. As the initial teacher training program began to take hold and spread across the country, the ADL staff and leadership were ambitious in planning for the numbers of teachers who could be reached. In order to achieve such goals, many staff would have to be trained to deliver this program. Further, ADL staff recognized that it would be essential for the program's credibility as a broad-based diversity program to have people of diverse backgrounds delivering its message. Thus, the ADL incorporated a train-the-trainer model to prepare "independent consultants" (who were not ADL staff) to serve as per-diem trainers. Today, the ADL has more than 400 training specialists who work with ADL staff around the world to deliver Institute programs.

The independent consultants have, in many ways, been at the core of the Institute's success. Without them, it would have been impossible for the ADL to reach the large number of educators it has: 375,000 in direct-service programs since 1985. These consultants, who come primarily from a variety of educational, training, social service, and consulting backgrounds, participate in an intensive 5-day program to learn about the Institute's content, pedagogy, and methods. After this initial training, the consultants are required to observe training programs and then "apprentice" with an experienced trainer. In order for consultants' contracts to be renewed from year to year, they are required to attend professional development programs led by ADL staff to enhance their skills and understanding.

This well-developed method of recruitment, selection, training, observation, and ongoing professional development was created gradually. And while the A WORLD OF DIFFERENCE® Institute is committed to customizing its programs and services in each region, national staff also realized that programs needed to maintain consistency in methods and content. Throughout the early 1990s, a variety of training manuals and operational procedures were put in place throughout the ADL to ensure this consistency and to create a level of quality control for all Institute programs.

The training and development of per-diem facilitators was a central focus of these quality control measures. These skilled specialists have also been instrumental in helping the ADL evolve and grow. They provide insights into the training program, bring new ideas and perspectives, "push the envelope" for the Institute to explore an issue in different ways, and in many cases consult on the development of new curriculum or training models. Many have continued their association with the Institute for more than a decade and often reflect on the profound personal impact it has had on their lives. As one long-time trainer stated,

> The gains for me are best defined as rewards. As a trainer, I have watched people identify their own biases through self-discovery, witnessed many cope with past acts of discrimination, and marveled at those who feel comfortable enough to expose their fears to others. With each training that I do, I come away a little better, a little wiser.

PHILOSOPHICAL FRAMEWORK

Much research exists about both how prejudice is acquired and about the pedagogical strategies that are effective in combating it (Stephan, 1999). This academic research, in conjunction with empirical evidence gathered by ADL staff, has helped to define and refine the philosophical belief system that underlies all of the ADL's education programs. The ADL's anti-bias training programs are based on the following assumptions and beliefs, which are explicitly addressed during workshops.

Passive Learning

Racist, sexist, anti-Semitic, homophobic, and other negative attitudes, beliefs, and patterns of thought and action are "taught" to young people, consciously and unconsciously, in their families, communities, schools, and religious organizations, as well as through the media. This "teaching" is pervasive, starts early, and is frequently reinforced. Because these negative beliefs are commonly learned unconsciously, many people who hold them disavow them, which makes the "unlearning" of such beliefs a great challenge. While research suggests that people do not completely unlearn their prejudices, it is possible for people to develop the ability to challenge "learned" stereotypes that impede positive intergroup relations (Monteith & Voils, 1998). The learning of prejudice is often unconscious (passive), but the process of "unlearning" must be conscious (active), which often creates internal conflict in workshop participants.

Baggage

Most people have been miseducated, and everyone has baggage regarding prejudicial thinking. People who attend anti-bias workshops do not all have the same baggage. Workshops incorporate the concept that prejudice has affected all people. As issues of prejudice and discrimination frequently evoke strong unconscious beliefs, conflict in workshops is to be expected.

Self-Awareness

Research has shown that one effective method of addressing prejudice and increasing intergroup understanding is to focus initially on participants' own cultures and progress to exploring similarities and differences between and among cultures (Cotton, 1992). Pride and heightened understanding of one's own heritage can be a starting point in combating prejudice. Focusing on one's racial or ethnic identity need not lead to feelings of superiority or be taken as a rationale for exclusivity. Self-identity and awareness activities assist people in focusing on themselves and exploring the filters through which their worldview is formed.

Beyond Factual Information

While some facts and information on different cultural groups can be helpful in enhancing understanding among people, research indicates that facts alone will not lead to improved intergroup relations (Byrnes, 1988).

Effective anti-bias methods for addressing prejudice and improving intergroup understanding among people include cooperative learning, critical thinking skills, and activities that promote self-esteem. For this reason, ADL programs engage people in a combination of affective and cognitive learning, learning that engages people's hearts and spirits as well as their brains.

Responsibility and Blame

People should not be blamed for having been taught biased messages in the past; however, all people must assume responsibility for their current attitudes and behaviors. ADL workshops provide a place for participants to recall times when they intervened successfully in the face of prejudice and challenged inequity. Public affirmation of people who have successfully resisted bigotry can provide much-needed role models for resisting and can inspire people to intervene in future situations.

Empathy Development

Developing empathy is essential to effectively addressing prejudice and improving intergroup understanding (Garcia, Powell, & Sanchez, 1990). ADL's programs are designed to provide opportunities for people to explore the commonality of the "outsider" experience. Most people have had at least one experience of feeling like an outsider. By recalling their own outsider experiences, workshop participants can begin to identify with other people who also have been targeted by hate. However, victimization experiences are not equal. ADL programs and resources do not equate all discriminatory experiences, a practice that would trivialize different "isms," ignoring the uniqueness of each form of bigotry. Further, one person's pain is not seen as more legitimate than another's. By sharing their experiences with prejudice and discrimination and listening to one another's experiences, participants learn to develop empathy and to form coalitions against bigotry.

Self-Esteem

People who feel good about themselves less often feel the need to denigrate others than do people who do not (Byrnes, 1988). The single best thing a parent or teacher can do to raise children who are open and respectful of all people is to help them feel good about themselves. These children grow up able to maintain their sense of self without having to vilify others. When teachers present lessons in which all students can see themselves reflected in the curriculum in a variety of ways, such lessons help to create classroom environments that foster respectful attitudes and behaviors. Additionally, teachers who have high expectations for all impart a positive sense of worth to their students.

GENERAL WORKSHOP FRAMEWORK FOR TEACHER TRAINING

The above learning principles and research guide the development of every A World of Difference® Institute training program. Teacher workshop trainers employ a variety of facilitation techniques that stress the importance of participation, interaction, and constructivist learning. Although workshops vary greatly, the following conceptual framework underlies most agendas.

Establishing the Environment

Creating an environment in which participants feel comfortable express- ing differing opinions, beliefs, and viewpoints is critical to the success of anti-bias programs. A frequently used exercise to establish this environment is ROPES. In this activity, a facilitator writes the words *Ground Rules* on the top of a piece of chart paper and writes the letters *R-O-P-E-S* down the left- hand side of the page. Participants offer words beginning with each of the five letters, and the facilitator records everyone's words on the chart paper. This simple collaborative project sets the tone for the rest of the day and gives workshop participants some measure of control over their learning environment.

Identity

These activities provide participants with opportunities to examine their own identities and belief systems and to explore how their attitudes and behaviors are shaped by their backgrounds, including their ethnicity, reli- gion, sexual orientation, culture, and race. Within the workshop setting, train- ers discuss with participants the fact that "race" is a social, rather than biological, construct. They also make the important distinction that despite the fact that race is socially constructed, "racism" is a real entity in society. In one identity exercise, Four Questions, participants are asked to think about and discuss the following:

1. If I had to describe myself in terms of my culture and heritage in four words, I would say I am a:
   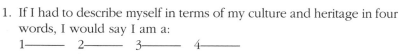
   1———— 2———— 3———— 4————
2. One time that I was very aware that I was at least one of those words was: ————

3. One thing that makes me feel proud about being at least one of these four words is: ———
4. One thing that is difficult or embarrassing about being one of these four words is: ———

In small groups, participants discuss the four questions while a facilitator creates a composite list of all responses to the first question. When the composite list of descriptors is written on chart paper, the facilitator selects several of the words and reads them aloud, one by one, inviting participants to stand as each word is called if the word applies to them. The composite list accomplishes a number of objectives. For one thing, it reveals that there is diversity represented in the room, even in groups that, at first glance, appear to be homogeneous. In that way the exercise helps to define the word *diversity* broadly. For another, it provides an opportunity for participants to discuss feelings associated with being a member of a group that is part of the dominant culture in society and to examine feelings associated with identifying oneself as a member of a subordinated or minority group in society.

Language

Language activities provide opportunities for participants to define key concepts and terms related to diversity and bias. In this segment of the workshop, participants identify manifestations of various forms of bigotry in their personal and professional lives. Many people define *prejudice* in terms of individual actions without including the societal and institutional components of such behavior. In ADL programs, *prejudice* is defined as both personal and institutional. Defining key words is a core component of workshops. The ADL's definition of an institutional "ism" is prejudice against a group or individual that is supported, sanctioned, legitimized, or reinforced by society. Such "isms" include, but are not limited to, racism, sexism, anti-Semitism, ageism, heterosexism, ableism, and classism. During the Language segment of the workshop, participants working in small groups identify both personal and institutional manifestations of various "isms."

Examining Bias

Cultural diversity and anti-bias activities explore current demographics and cultural norms operating in the United States. Research has long indicated that a first critical step in addressing prejudice is for people to come to terms with their own unconscious stereotyping and the damage it can do (Allport, 1954). One method facilitators use to address this concept in workshops is posing a question to participants regarding a negative message they remember hearing or "learning" when they were growing up about a cultural group different from their own. Following dyad discussions, the facilitator elicits from all participants the *sources* of the messages, such as parents, teachers, media, neighborhood, or religious institutions. This process allows participants to see that everyone has been affected by negative messages. Establishing this concept removes some of the onus from participants for having learned these "bad" things, and it decreases the need for defensiveness on the part of workshop participants. Additionally, this exercise allows participants to see that biased messages and thinking are pervasive in U.S. society.

School Assessment

Personal and institutional assessment and action-planning exercises encourage participants to determine necessary steps to make their classrooms inclusive and their schools bias-free. Several workshop exercises provide educators with methods to explore their school's environment. The following are sample questions from an assessment in which participants are asked to rate the extent to which their school has examined procedures and practices related to understanding diversity and promoting positive intergroup relations. They are asked to indicate, in response to each of the following statements, whether "we do this well" or whether "we need to give this more attention."

1. We have examined our school's resources for multicultural and antibias content.
2. We incorporate human relations issues into an orientation program for all new students and staff.
3. Staff development opportunities are available in anti-bias training.
4. We have established a code of conduct for what constitutes racial, religious, ethnic, gender, and sexual orientation harassment, including appropriate sanctions for violating the code.
5. Programs, assemblies, speakers, bulletin boards, holiday celebrations, and so on reflect our multicultural society.
6. We have a plan to evaluate human relations programs and progress at designated intervals.

PROGRAM EVALUATION

Since its inception, the Institute's programs have been continuously evaluated through both informal and formal mechanisms. Given the individualized nature of Institute programming, creating standard instruments to be used in all regions and for all programs has been a challenge. The ADL has been cautious not to ascribe certain broad outcomes to its intervention or treatment without sufficient evidence. Institute staff recognize that many variables can be at play in the work that we do: Findings may be positive due to factors over which the organization may have no control; findings may also be negative for the same reason. If an incident of bias occurs at a school in the midst of a program evaluation, does this mean the program has not been successful? ADL staff would know that this is not the case; however, to the staff or students at that school—or to the funder—it may feel as if the program has failed.

Despite some of these challenges, the Institute has engaged in several studies, particularly since 1998, on both a regional and national level. Collaborative studies have been undertaken with institutions including Teachers College of Columbia University, the Claremont Graduate School, and the University of Pennsylvania. Further, independent, non-university-affiliated evaluators have been hired in several regions and also nationally to assess programs. The evaluation project completed under the auspices of the Cantor-Fitzgerald Center for Research on Diversity in Education at the University of Pennsylvania has been one of the most comprehensive evaluation studies to date of ADL's anti-bias programs and resources. This study, funded through the Bildner Family Foundation, was launched to assess the effectiveness of ADL's A World of Difference® Institute comprehensive training initiative in three public school districts in New York, St. Louis, and New Jersey. The study tracked the activities in each site for 18 months, from August 1998 to December 1999. Selected findings from this study are included in the following pages.

Impact on Educators

One of the first national evaluation studies of A World of Difference® Institute was conducted in 1993 and was designed to measure attitudinal changes of participants in the ADL's teacher training programs. Since many ADL staff development program formats existed at that time, in order to limit the considerable variables, the decision was made to include only programs that were 6 hours long in this evaluation. In consultation with a social science researcher, ADL staff created a Teacher Training Evaluation Survey for educators. This was administered immediately prior to and following the teachers' participation in a 6-hour A Classroom of Difference™ workshop.

The survey was created to ascertain respondents' attitudes and self-reported actions related to issues of bias and prejudice. In order to examine patterns of change in respondents, the survey questions were grouped in six clusters, each cluster associated with one of the workshop objectives. The six clustered areas of inquiry are cultural awareness, personal responsibility, anxiety, denial, "modern" racism, and "old-fashioned" racism. The evaluation relied on self-reporting about how participants viewed themselves in a number of situations before and after taking part in the 6-hour workshop.

A participant profile used in conjunction with the Teacher Training Evaluation Survey included questions regarding the participating teacher's gender, race, ethnicity and cultural heritage, number of years in teaching, and subject and grade level taught. In addition, the profile asked participants to assess their life experiences from "monocultural" to "very multicultural" on a 5-point scale. They rated, for example, things like family of origin, neighborhood as a child, current family, friendships, and work situation. In addition, respondents were asked to identify whether their attendance at the workshop was voluntary or mandatory. Survey questions, with a 5-point scale from "strongly agree" to "strongly disagree," included the following:

- When I hear someone make a racial or ethnic slur, I believe it is always my responsibility to respond. (The same question was used for gender, religion, disability, and sexual orientation.)
- My family never owned slaves, and I do everything I can to try to be sensitive. I am not responsible for racism.
- My biases do not influence my evaluation of my students.
- Inclusion of multicultural materials should not come at the expense of core curriculum.
- Institutional discrimination is no longer a problem in the United States.
- I feel uncomfortable when I am interacting with someone with a different sexual orientation from my own. (The same question was used for religion, race, and physical disability.)

To evaluate whether there was a change in participants' attitudes, dependent-sample *t*-tests were performed on each item. This test, like other inferential statistical procedures, produces a *p*-value, which represents the probability that the change that was observed would have occurred by chance. In general, results that are unlikely to occur by chance are considered statistically significant. Analysis of this study found that approximately one-third of the items on the survey showed significant differences in the expected direction, that is, more positive attitudes regarding diversity.

A number of interesting additional observations came from this evaluation. While some ADL staff initially expressed concern that a 6-hour workshop could not accomplish statistically significant change on two-thirds of the items, a more optimistic interpretation was possible: The pre–post surveys showed that in less than one day many people's attitudes had indeed changed.

Another assumption held by many ADL staff was that mandatory workshops produced such resistance that it would be better to offer Institute workshops for teachers *only* on a voluntarily basis. While the evaluation results showed very little difference in response by gender or number of years in teaching, there were statistically significant differences between people whose attendance was mandatory and voluntary and between people who identified as "White" or a "person of color." Changes in attitude in the mandated attendees and in the participants who identified as "White" were far greater than in the voluntary and "people of color" groups (Hofheimer Bettmann, Green, & Dovidio, 1993; for similar conclusions about college students, see Pascarella, Edison, Hagedorn, Nora, & Terenzini, 1996; Chapter 9, this volume).

Anti-Bias Study Guide: Review and Impact

The ADL's *Anti-Bias Study Guide,* secondary level, was a key component in the successful implementation of the pilot program in the University of Pennsylvania study. Initially, all sites experienced reluctance on the part of staff to incorporate this resource into their curriculum. The key to overcoming this resistance was the successful alignment of the materials to the existing curriculum within the school and the respective state standards in social studies. Once teachers were able to see how the *Guide* could be used within their existing courses, they became increasingly willing and excited about the material and its use with students.

As part of the evaluation study, an independent external panel was formulated to offer a critique of the Institute's *Anti-Bias Study Guide,* secondary level. This panel was comprised of secondary-level teachers and college professors from California State University at Long Beach; the University of California at Berkeley; New York University; Teachers College, Columbia University; and school districts in Manassa, Virginia, and Philadelphia. The findings of the panel were very favorable. General conclusions about the *Guide* were that it offers a comprehensive approach to anti-bias education, is "user-friendly" for teachers, is easily infused into a standards-based curriculum, and is appropriate for all students within a variety of courses and disciplines. The following are selected comments from the panelists:

- "The *Guide* links so directly to the kinds of thinking current standards emphasize—namely, analysis and critical thinking, performance and experiential learning, and integration of multiple disciplines."
- "Students [using the *Guide*] learn about bias conceptually, they think about it personally, they learn how to recognize it in their environ-

ments and lives, they study its history, they examine examples of social action, and they engage in planning for initiating social action themselves."

- "The *Guide* deals with personal values, different perspectives, and looking below the surface. These emphases help students understand bias and anti-bias actions as complex and evolving."

Data compiled from students who participated in lessons from the *Anti-Bias Study Guide* in their classes further supported the positive findings of the independent panel:

- 81% of students reported the lessons helped increase their understanding of other viewpoints different from their own.
- 76% reported the lessons helped them communicate with students different from themselves.
- 66% reported the lessons helped them develop a broader view of issues and problems in society.
- 78% reported the lessons helped to increase their respect for students in their school who are different from themselves.
- 70% reported the lessons helped them better get along with all types of people in their lives.

Of course, when some 60% to 80% say they are helped by a program, this also means that about 20% to 40% say they were *not* helped. Efforts at improvement focus importantly on understanding how to revise the program to reach those for whom it was less effective.

Peer Training Program

Of all the programs of the Institute, the Peer Training Program has been most frequently evaluated and has shown the most positive findings. One reason for this is that this program lends itself more readily to evaluation because it has a fairly prescribed set of materials and training components. Further, the "treatment" is longer and more consistent than that in staff development programs, in that students selected to become peer trainers have a standard training and then a series of meetings and follow-up trainings to prepare them to deliver training to their peers.

Quantitative data collected by Teachers College, Columbia University with peer trainers in New York City in 1998 support the University of Pennsylvania's findings that the Peer Training Program has a strong positive influence on students' academic, personal and social development:

- 84% of the peer trainers reported increased confidence in their ability to prepare and organize a presentation for peers.
- 86% reported greater awareness of their own biases.
- 86% reported a better understanding of the prejudice and discrimination in their schools and communities.
- 80% reported greater skills in confront issues of bias in their schools and/or workplaces.
- 75% reported that they would now take active steps to confront bias in their schools.
- 88% reported that participation was somewhat or very influential to their involvement in some type of community service in their school or community.

The following are a few of the commonly expressed sentiments from peer trainers:

- "I have realized my own prejudices and am working them out with my peers."
- "I have built a stronger patience level for myself. Being a member has helped me be aware of the racial conflict around me and how to deal with situations."
- "This program showed me . . . I don't have to be like other people. I could be myself and could love who I am, for what I am. It also makes me put an emphasis on what I believe in . . . and gave me more respect for my peers."

Lessons Learned

As the Institute has grown and evolved, it has identified many factors that can foster or hinder a school's success in implementing its programs. The research findings from the University of Pennsylvania study and other studies confirmed the empirical research of ADL staff in their work with schools and other organizations across the country. In order for schools to be effective in sustaining equitable, bias-free learning environments for all students, a comprehensive training and consultation program must be developed and should incorporate the following factors:

- Anti-bias efforts within a school or district must be ongoing and include all constituents, including educators, administrators, other school staff, students, and family members.
- All members of the school community—regardless of their direct involvement—should be informed and educated about the anti-bias

initiatives undertaken by a school and the reasons for their implementation.

- Administrative leaders must be visible and active in the program planning and implementation.
- Sufficient time must be allocated for ongoing professional development for teachers and other school staff, including professional development opportunities for teaching staff to review, enhance, and modify existing curricula.
- Schools must be willing to undertake an internal assessment to determine to what extent their school's policies and procedures foster positive interactions among all of the cultural groups that constitute the school community.
- Internal mechanisms to support and sustain changes in attitudes, behaviors, and actions must be developed and implemented by schools once the ADL program has concluded.

The ADL has also learned many lessons about its approach to anti-bias work that will make Institute programs more successful and meaningful to the people and organizations with whom it works. Many of the factors related to program development, trainer training, and evaluation protocols have been identified earlier in this chapter. In 2001, the ADL's Education Division conducted an internal review of its A WORLD OF DIFFERENCE® Institute and other educational program offerings. This comprehensive review incorporated data and feedback from program participants, staff, and lay leaders in the organization. These findings are assisting the Institute in future program development, training modifications, and staff development. Four relevant recommendations include:

1. *Audience*: Maintain a focus on reaching youth (preK–12) as the primary core constituency for Institute programs. This population should be served, either through direct programming and/or through educators/youth providers/parents, in all regional offices.
2. *Depth versus breadth*: Emphasize content-rich programs that allow for meaningful and ongoing relationships with the populations served. Those programs that allow for extensive length and depth of contact will result in greater impact and long-term results.
3. *Program development*: Balance ongoing development and delivery of programs that offer preventative approaches to combating hatred and bigotry; it is also important for education programs to assist in responsive or intervention contexts.
4. *Follow-up*: Support and create programs that include follow-up programming as an essential component of their design.

CONCLUSION

The work of the ADL's A World of Difference® Institute is for all children and adults, not just for students of color or children with special needs. The programs offer an anti-bias perspective that incorporates the idea that all children have special needs, including the need to be respected for who they are and the need to learn how to work effectively with all people. The Institute seeks to help administrators, teachers, and other adults who work with children to become sources of inspiration for our nation's youth. Workshops have sometimes been life-altering events for participants. As one teacher wrote:

> The program made me face the prejudices and resentments that I felt I had a right to hold on to . . . even as a teacher. During this workshop, I ran out of excuses. I now feel an obligation to address prejudice in my class and school. For me, [the program] has been as much about my personal growth and change as it has about the skills and resources I have received.

At its core, the ADL's A World of Difference® Institute is about change. The title "A World of Difference" has multiple meanings. It reflects the reality that the United States is a country of many different and diverse people, one of this country's strengths. The title is also an acknowledgment—and a challenge—to each person to recognize the role that he or she can play in creating a fairer and more harmonious world.

Chapter 6

Facing History and Ourselves

Terry Tollefson
Dennis J. Barr
Margot Stern Strom

The 20th century demonstrated how leaders could use ancient myths and misinformation in conjunction with propaganda techniques to unleash ethnic hatred, cause neighbor to turn against neighbor, and to see "difference" as alien and threatening. The legacies of the 20th century include the horrors of humiliation, dehumanization, discrimination, and extermination, which continue to fuel confrontations among people all over the world. The challenge for educators is to create settings that can nurture the positive moral questioning of young people and foster their capacity to develop as caring, compassionate, and responsible citizens (Fein, 1979).

In the United States, the racial/ethnic diversity of students in schools continues to increase. In 1972, 15% of public school students in grades 1–12 were considered to be part of a minority group; by 1998, nearly 40% were (U.S. Department of Education, 2000). One of the lessons learned from the desegregation of schools is that intergroup contact can provide new opportunities for improving interpersonal relations but it is by no means a sufficient condition to create such improvement. In fact, it can create conditions that reinforce stereotypes and prejudices and increase intergroup tension (Allport, 1954; J. W. Schofield, 1995). A 2000 National Conference for Community and Justice (NCCJ) study substantiates this finding. The study found that, while more interracial/interethnic contact was reported than in 1993, there was an accompanying increase in racial, religious, and ethnic tensions, as experienced in neighborhoods, at work, and in schools (NCCJ, 2000).

Education Programs for Improving Intergroup Relations. ISBN 0-8077-4459-X (paper). Prior to photocopying items for classroom use, please contact the Copyright Clearance Center, Customer Service, 222 Rosewood Drive, Danvers, MA, 01923, USA, telephone (978) 750-8400.

Further, sociologists continue to find that the general population still places great reliance on ethnic stereotypes when describing others (Smith, 1990).

Studies have shown that, when provided with the proper resources and professional development, teachers can work effectively with ethnically diverse populations to create positive change (Stephan, 1999). For 27 years, Facing History and Ourselves (FHAO) has been demonstrating that education can make a positive difference in the lives of adolescents and their teachers. We can promote young people's capacities for critical thinking, understanding, tolerance, caring, and compassion. If education is truly to be preparation for life, then these are the civic lessons that cannot go untaught.

Facing History and Ourselves engages students of diverse backgrounds in an examination of racism, prejudice, and anti-Semitism in order to promote the development of student capacities to be active participants in a pluralistic, democratic society and to balance self-interest with genuine concern for the welfare of others. In an FHAO course, students first learn a framework and a vocabulary for understanding individual decision making and group behavior within a society. They then explore these issues through the historical case study of the "decades of choice" that ultimately led to the Nazi Holocaust, and they apply the lessons learned to their responsibilities as citizens in our world today. History becomes a tool to foster students' cognitive growth and critical thinking abilities. By examining the failure of democracy in the Weimar Republic, the rise of totalitarianism, and the genocide of World War II, FHAO encourages students to think critically about opportunities for prevention, citizen participation in democratic institutions, and community service. As an FHAO student wrote:

> The study of the Holocaust puts into high relief all the giant ideas we should value about America. Freedom of speech is not an abstraction. Neither is freedom of religion. Neither is the balance of powers between government branches. America, or maybe I should say the idea of America, is amazing. We still struggle with issues of hatred, racism, and social justice. That is a good thing, that we see ourselves as a nation who struggles to make things better for all our people. Sometimes it looks like we are winning—but sometimes it looks like we have a long, long way to go. (Weinstein, 1997)

ORIGINS/ HISTORY

Facing History and Ourselves was initially developed under federal funds designed to improve secondary education through the teaching of history and ethics (ESEA Title IV Part C from 1977 to 1981). At that time, the history of the breakdown of democracy in the Weimar Republic, ultimately leading to the Holocaust, was virtually untaught. Many emerging efforts were simplistic or provided little time for depth. Often they had a victim emphasis, and students could easily be left with a sense of inevitability. The FHAO model program, which linked both history and ethics, was developed to confront this 20th-century example of how neighbor was turned against neighbor.

In 1980, based on evaluation results submitted to an independent federal panel, FHAO was selected for membership in the U.S. Department of Education's National Diffusion Network (NDN) as "an exemplary program worthy of national dissemination." Under the NDN program, federal money helped to support dissemination work in more than 40 states. During the 1990s, regional offices were established in selected areas to provide local support and to focus on building in-depth programs in schools.

In 1999, FHAO launched an upgraded version of its web site, facinghistory. org, to disseminate information about the program and resources. In 2000, FHAO opened the online "campus" portion of the site for teachers in its network. Here program staff can guide discussions and provide online technical assistance, thereby increasing overall contact time with teachers. Educators can view model lesson plans, download materials, and learn best practices from one another in a virtual learning community.

Today the program annually touches more than 1 million students nationally and internationally. More than 12,000 teachers have attended FHAO institutes and workshops in the past decade, and more than 16,000 "unique visitors" come to the FHAO web site each month to view and download resources.

PROGRAM DESCRIPTION

Facing History and Ourselves works with teachers who will engage their students in the study of history and ethics in their classrooms. This adult learning model brings together teachers and scholars in seminars, institutes and workshops, where they encounter a "full scope and sequence approach" to themes that they will later use in their own classrooms with their students (Strom, 1994). While progressing from the study of identity, to a case study from history, to judgment, and ultimately to participation, they examine each theme in this sequence both in the context of history and with a view toward considering the implications for our lives today. They come to reflect on the importance of decision making and the possibilities for courage, caring, and compassion.

Facing History and Ourselves courses are typically taught to 12- to 15-year-old youth in grades 8 or 9 (although high school courses are also common). It is a time when young people struggle with issues of independence, trust, and responsibility. Life centers on relationships within their peer group. There are pressures of who is "in" and who is "out." They are beginning to understand their own motives and the motives of others. They are faced with contrasting perspectives and competing truths.

The opening sections of a typical course introduce students to the principles of human behavior and decision making. By looking at the concepts of the individual and society, students come to learn how identities are formed. They learn to recognize decision-making situations and to understand which social and cultural factors may influence the types of decisions an individual makes. They come to appreciate difference and to understand the power that labels and stereotyping may have on our decision making. At the same time, they look at times when the idea of difference has been abused, such as times where race has turned to racism, or ethnicity to ethnocentrism, or national pride to nationalism. Students investigate the themes of power, prejudice, scapegoating, obedience, and loyalty as they develop their concept of the individual as a decision maker in society. These lessons are designed to help students clarify conflict situations while introducing a process for decision making. A student's voice describes this learning process:

> During the beginning weeks, the focus was on identity. Questions like "who am I?" "where do I come from?" and "how might others see me?" We created identity charts that described ourselves. I grew up in a bilingual, biracial, multiethnic household. We came to realize that in order to have others understand us, we first need to have an idea of who we were. One of the most memorable Facing History readings for me was "Little Boxes," an essay in the Facing History resource book by Anthony Wright, a young man whose background is as mixed as my own. I was shocked to learn that I was not the only one who could identify with what he wrote. I had unwittingly placed my peers in boxes and categories. It was not until all of us in class looked carefully at our identities that I realized that there were times when we couldn't fit into a box: racially, economically, religiously, or politically. That day, we put away facades, superficial stereotypes, and imposed labels. . . . It was this shared experience that remains indelible in my mind as one of the biggest steps toward class unity, because once we were able to understand our own identities, we were able to understand those of others.

An example of an FHAO lesson is a reading written by a high school student named Eve Shalen about her experiences of exclusion in middle school, both as a victim and perpetrator. Students can view a videotape of Eve discussing her experiences with Elie Wiesel (FHAO, 1994). An FHAO teacher uses this lesson, and other resources like it, to deepen students' understanding of peer pressure. This story is a rich resource for a discussion about the various choices that individuals make—and why they make them. Students often connect this story to their own experiences when they write in their journals. A student describes how a class became engaged by this approach:

> Our Facing History class engaged us in discussions about Littleton in ways that no other class did. One of the things we learned was how in-groups and out-groups are formed, and how people feel when they are part of a group, and how it feels to be left out. We read a story entitled "The In-Group" in which an eighth-grade girl, Eve, talks about being one of two outcasts in her class. She recalls one day in the schoolyard when the "in-group" found the diary of the other outcast girl. Eve is invited to join the "in-group" to read and laugh at the other girls' private writings. Looking back, the narrator wonders how she could have participated in mocking this girl when she knew what it was like to be mocked herself. She then went on to say, "Often being accepted by others is more satisfying than being accepted by oneself, even though the satisfaction does not last. Too often our actions are determined by the moment." I agree with this statement because when you are accepted by a group, you feel better about yourself, you feel as if you belong. Yet it's hard when in order to fit into a group, you have to compromise your own principles. How can you belong and still be true to yourself? What are the consequences of being part of an in-group if that group does things that are wrong? What are the consequences of in- and out-groups on individuals and communities? These questions took on special meaning as we tried to come to grips with the tragedy of Littleton.

After the initial lessons, which explore issues of membership and the individual and society, students typically examine a particular case study in Germany in the 1920s and 1930s, where a democratic society failed and neighbor was turned against neighbor, ultimately leading to state-sponsored genocide of Jews, the mentally ill, gays, and other minority groups such as Sinti/Roma (gypsies). The focus is on individual and group behavior in a particular historical context—the many small decisions that individuals made well before the genocide while prevention was still possible. What was the role of doctors, of lawyers, of teachers? What was the role of mothers, fathers, the clergy? What choices did people have and what choices did they make? Students examine the education planned for Hitler Youth and compare it to their own. They learn the stories of a Holocaust survivor. Students begin to develop a vocabulary that identifies the actions of perpetrators, victims, and bystanders. As students learn about prejudice and discrimination in the past, they respond by thinking about the meaning of their own attitudes and behavior. These lessons elicit personal reflection, abstract thinking, and consideration of multiple points of view and cause and effect. A student reflects on how she began to connect history to her own thinking:

> By looking at some of the decisions people made in Germany in the 1930s, we begin to think about our own. Because of Facing History, I began to think about how *I* think and react and how important decision making is in *my* life. Facing History changed the way I looked at people and history. Whenever I studied history, I always thought about it as something awful to learn because I was going to be graded on it. *I never saw the people in it.* But in a Facing History class everything was different. I used my own mind and I started to ask *why* and *how*. We always got to connect back to ourselves. This was the first time I was thinking in a history class.

Students who study the rise of Nazism and the genocide of the Holocaust ask about judgment. Who is guilty? Who was punished? Using FHAO materials, students can examine not only the response of Nuremberg but also the various ways that societies have responded to past collective violence and seek to prevent it in the future, such as South Africa's Truth Commission as depicted in the 1999 video, *Facing the Truth*. Connections are made between history and the moral choices individuals confront in their own lives as democratic participants in an increasingly global society. One student struggled to express the link between individual responsibility and collective violence:

> Does anyone accept guilt for the Holocaust? Not Americans, not Roosevelt or a previous Congress or an apathetic pubic. Not Europe—the countries were too weak to oppose Germany and too caught up in their own recovery from WW I. Not the Germans— probably most would claim they knew nothing about it, or, if they did know, that they had nothing to do with it. Probably not even Hitler—doubtless he would feel no guilt, only remorse that his "final solution" didn't succeed. Then who? Who is guilty? To say that we are all—although it may very well be true—is too easy. A Holocaust can happen only because no one feels directly responsible for it. It makes it all the easier to kill by saying "You're just as responsible as I am." But that won't stop the killings. Who is guilty? The man who gives the orders or the man who carries them out? . . . I don't feel guilty for the Holocaust. The fact that I wasn't even alive at the time would

seem to prove my innocence. But mustn't we all, as members of society, take responsibility for the past, the present, and the future of the society we live in?

Finally, students consider choices and actions that can prevent the violence that results from hatred. Many examples are provided of people who have made a difference. For example, students study the case of Ida B. Wells, who launched and led a national campaign to stop the practice of lynching (FHAO, 1990). Her campaign inspired later civil rights efforts in the 1950s and 1960s. Teachers may use the case study of Ida B. Wells to show that making a difference is not simple—it may often take many years and involve many people who are willing to help. Her life, generally untaught, is an exceptional illustration of the use of the First Amendment to express outrage and advocate for needed justice and social change. It is a real case study of how advocacy, philanthropy, and journalism were used to confront the violence of lynching and to ultimately change the law—and how such change may literally take a lifetime.

John Dewey believed that schooling should be linked to the overall life of the student, with an emphasis on experience, problem solving, and community (Dewey, 1938/1963). Education stemmed from dealing with real life as opposed to curricula. Facing History and Ourselves embodies this educational philosophy in its name; the program is structured to involve real history and real connections to our lives and communities today. A student describes it well:

> This course is about examining history. It is about memory. We have to remember what happened, that is facing history. And then, if we can use that in our lives, take it in, and make it a part of our identity, individually or as a community, then we are dealing with ourselves.

As one FHAO teacher put it:

> The Facing History classroom is alive. It is a place where students, in John Dewey's words, become a community of learners. Students are encouraged to be mindful, to reflect, and to gain a deeper appreciation of the life in us and in others. And in doing all of this, Facing History and Ourselves empowers students to act, to see how each of us can make a difference to help create a more just, more compassionate society. (FHAO, 1996)

Students are encouraged to develop their own skills of reflection and judgment—critical components of what Benjamin Barber has called a "strong democracy" (Barber, 1984). By connecting real history to their lives today, students will develop an increased social concern and knowledge of their responsibility to participate as citizens in a democracy. The lessons elicit abstract thinking and consideration of multiple points of view, causes, and effects. This is the form of reflective thinking that Hannah Arendt (1977) described as being the most important protection for society from an Eichmann, who seemingly was "thoughtless" in separating his actions from meaning. One of the first FHAO students, interviewed as part of a recent study, described the impact this way:

> [The course] helped to shape not only my moral sensibilities but also gave me a healthy dose of skepticism and fear of that which is ordinary. I learned that when I see something that I know is wrong to not only trust my intuition and judgment, but to speak up. And I learned that when somebody tells you to do something that makes no sense, you stop and ask why.

PROGRAM IMPLEMENTATION STRATEGIES

In his research on school change, Fullan (1990) linked classroom improvement with staff development, demonstrating that improved learning is best achieved by first improving the knowledge and skills of teachers and administrators. Further, technical assistance will have little impact if it is not linked to collaborative working relationships (Fullan, 1991). Professional development strategies must take into account the importance of support and nurturing that includes community building among colleagues.

Facing History and Ourselves has consistently employed cutting-edge school reform and redesign strategies. To provide opportunities for continuous learning and skill building, FHAO has developed a multitiered professional development model. Once educators have learned about the FHAO program through an awareness presentation, introductory workshop, or the web, they are encouraged to attend a summer institute, an intensive 5- or 6-day professional development seminar designed to enable them to experience the program's full potential for impact. By pulling together teams of educators from particular schools—including teachers, administrators, librarians, school counselors, and so on—for its week-long institutes, FHAO has created a context for joint learning and program design. Like an FHAO class, the summer institute focuses on issues related to identity, violence, bigotry, power, and conformity. Participants explore ways to apply FHAO's content and approaches to their own teaching or school program. Throughout the institute, there are opportunities to discuss rationale, content, methodology, and assessment with FHAO staff, visiting scholars, and other participants.

Facing History and Ourselves' extensive training and follow-up classroom support for educators who use the program differentiate it from other approaches. According to Darling-Hammond & McLaughlin (1995), teachers need professional development that extends far beyond a single workshop; to teach challenging content, they need opportunities to learn how to question, analyze, and change instruction. The one-shot workshop is replaced by continuous learning together through reviewing lesson plans, comparing notes on implementation, and discussion of assessment methods. FHAO offers one-on-one support to all participants. Program staff members are available during the schoolyear in person or by telephone (or e-mail) to assist teachers and administrators with program design. FHAO continues the process of community building during the schoolyear by assembling groups of educators from within a school as well as from several schools for joint inquiry and sharing of what works and what challenges exist. Finally, FHAO encourages continued adult learning through major conferences, advanced seminar and advanced institute opportunities, online discussions, and resources provided on its online "campus."

Facing History and Ourselves' conscious decision to value the building of in-depth quality programs has paid off. Teacher surveys have indicated that teachers receiving follow-up services are more likely to build programs that exhibit more of the key elements of FHAO's approach (Lieberman, 1995). By assigning program staff to each adult learner, FHAO is able to provide assistance at the "teachable moment."

PROGRAM RESEARCH

Since its inception, the FHAO program has been the subject of both internal and external research designed to both understand and improve program effectiveness in fostering the professional development of teachers and to contribute to the field of knowledge in areas such as intergroup relations and civic education.

The program has several expected outcomes. For teachers, the FHAO program provides an opportunity to participate in professional development, to establish collegial relationships within their own school and across school lines, and to enhance their teaching skills and competencies while creating a new curriculum component for their English, history, social studies, or other courses. For students, the program provides a learning environment that promotes critical thinking, reflection, and engagement while encouraging multiple perspectives and the development of moral reasoning.

Impact on Teacher Skills and Competencies

Research has shown that FHAO's professional development activities for teachers have been successful (Lieberman, 1991, 1993, 1995, 1999, 2000). Teachers who participate in FHAO training are more confident about taking on difficult issues and questions in the classroom. They are able to utilize the methods and resources provided to create courses that address this history and its meaning for today. Consistently, when surveyed one year after an in-depth institute, 80% of these educators indicate that they are able to implement at least some of the ideas and concepts learned.

Teachers consistently report not only an initial but also a sustained increase in confidence with the subject matter, a better grasp of resources and methodologies, and an increased ability to relate history to the lives of their students. These gains are maintained over time while the teachers are actually using the program. Many teachers indicate that the professional development process revitalizes their interest in teaching and causes them to rethink their methods; they are now more likely to use questioning, classroom discussion, and examples that relate the material being studied to important issues of citizenship and individual responsibility today. In the 1993 follow-up study, a full two-thirds of the educators reported a new or revitalized understanding of their roles as teachers following their participation in the FHAO program (Lieberman, 1993).

Impact on Students

Research has shown that FHAO provides the kind of challenging, engaging material that promotes learning. In a survey, over three-fourths of teachers responding reported that the program had a large impact on their students' knowledge of history, their understanding of the origins of hatred and violence, their ability to relate history to their own lives, and their understanding of their roles and responsibilities in a democracy (Lieberman, 1995). According to one teacher, the impact was immediate at the school level: "The Facing History course has helped the school deal with issues related to culture and race relations. There is dramatically less conflict." A former FHAO student and gang member described the personal impact of the program in his case:

> Facing History showed me that there are people, teachers, and other students concerned about teenagers' well-being in this world of violence. . . . People don't have to resort to violence to solve different means of disagreements. I left the gang completely. (Chicago FHAO student, testifying in public hearings in Washington, D.C., October, 1994)

Moral reasoning and interpersonal understanding have been identified as necessary conditions for fostering such positive intergroup relations (Garcia Coll & Vasquez Garcia, 1995). Studies have found that students in the FHAO program, which uses a careful approach that first builds a framework for understanding human behavior and then ties it to real individuals and real history, demonstrate an increased understanding of these complex historical events, a greater ability to take the perspective of others, and more complex thinking about moral issues.

Lieberman used an adaptation of Selman's (1980) interpersonal understanding interview, which asks subjects to write their responses to social dilemmas in order to explore changes in student's social development. His studies (1977–1993) demonstrated that, relative to a comparison group, junior high students in FHAO classes increased significantly in the complexity of their interpersonal understanding (i.e., reasoning about psychosocial issues) as well as in their knowledge of historical content. Lieberman's studies were validated by the Program Effectiveness Panel of the U.S. Department of Education (Lieberman, 1993).

Impact on Learning Environment

The climate in which learning occurs is critical to the development of the psychosocial capacities targeted by the program. Deeply held assumptions about ourselves and others are not amenable to challenge or revision in a context of mistrust, competitiveness, or unequal status (Allport, 1954; Deutsch, 1992; Slavin, 1995c). If individuals perceive that they can manage conflict, rather than be overcome by it, they are brought closer together (Selman & Schultz, 1990). At the same time, a certain degree of conflict, or "disequilibrium," between one's own views, needs, and wishes and those of others *is* a necessary catalyst for psychosocial and moral growth (Piaget, 1970; Power, Higgins, & Kohlberg, 1989). Establishing the right balance is critical.

Qualitative research suggests that FHAO successfully encourages just such a climate through promoting personal involvement, self-reflection and prosocial awareness, and meaningful but safe grappling with differences in points of view and background among students (Bardige, 1983; Fine, 1995). Bardige sampled student journals and identified increasingly complex patterns of thinking over time that were evident in journals kept by students in FHAO classes (Bardige, 1981, 1988). Using Piagetian cognitive-developmental stages (concrete, early formal, and fully formal operations), Bardige found some developmental shifts in the journals, but the within-stage changes were especially striking: Prosocial awareness and the frequency and quality of reflective thinking increased at each stage of development. The increase in pro-social awareness included increased awareness of prejudice and a claiming of students' own experience of prejudice, daring to ask questions and raise moral issues, discomfort with the role of bystander; confronting of others and discomfort with cliques, commitment to action and generosity of spirit, and collective voice.

Melinda Fine (1991/1992, 1993a, 1993b, 1995) used the "portraiture" qualitative method (Lightfoot, 1983) to capture the processes through which moral, ethnic, religious, and political differences are managed in FHAO class discussions. Fine documented FHAO students' engagement and active involvement with ideas and complex understandings as they confronted differences in American society.

The Facing History and Ourselves–Carnegie Study

In 1996, the Carnegie Corporation of New York funded a study of FHAO as part of a major initiative to expand knowledge about intergroup relations and to identify effective approaches that foster intergroup understanding. The research was comprised of an outcome study and a qualitative case study of an FHAO classroom.

The Outcome Study

The quasi-experimental outcome study examined whether the FHAO program promotes the development of psychosocial competencies and moral reasoning, increases civic awareness and participation, and reduces racist attitudes and behavior (fighting) that put interpersonal relationships at risk (Schultz, Barr, & Selman, 2001).

Four veteran FHAO teachers and their students were chosen to participate. Two teachers taught eighth-grade social studies and two taught eighth-grade language arts. Each teacher taught a 10-week FHAO curriculum, although all four FHAO teachers integrated FHAO themes in their teaching throughout the year. They taught in public schools located in an upscale suburban town with middle-class and wealthy families, a suburb with a mix of middle-class and working-class students, and two small cities with a predominantly poor and working-class population. Four non-FHAO teachers were chosen as comparison teachers using two criteria: (1) They taught in public schools in the same communities, though not in the same schools (with one exception) as the FHAO teachers, and (2) they were also interested in and taught about issues of intergroup relations.

The sample included 246 FHAO students and 163 comparison students at pre-test (October) and 244 FHAO and 167 comparison students at post-test (May and early June of the same schoolyear). Approximately 52% of both groups were females and approximately 48% were males. Students were asked to self-report their race/ethnicity. The sample contained 62% White, 6% Black, 3.5% Hispanic, and 23% mixed/other students, with 5.5% of the students failing to report their ethnicity.

A social-developmental model guided the exploration of the impact of FHAO on psychosocial competencies (Selman, Watts, & Schultz, 1997). The model assumes that the essence of psychosocial development is the individual's developing capacity to differentiate and coordinate the social perspectives of self and others, both cognitively and emotionally (Kohlberg, 1969; Piaget, 1983; Selman, 1980; Sullivan, 1953). In this model, the individual's core operational capacity to coordinate his or her own and others' points of view about social experiences develops in interaction with three distinct—but highly related—psychosocial competencies. As applied to relationship experience, the three components of psychosocial competence are (1) *interpersonal understanding*, or the developing theoretical knowledge of the nature of relationships and group processes; (2) *interpersonal skills*, or the intimacy and autonomy strategies needed to make and maintain good relationships; and (3) *personal meaning*, or quality of the persons' connections between phenomena (e.g., historical examples of violence and courage) and the self, especially one's relationships with others (Selman et al., 1997).

The three psychosocial competencies—interpersonal understanding, skills, and meaning—develop along parallel tracks, each on a continuum from immature to mature, based on the individual's ability to differentiate and integrate perspectives. According to the theoretical model, these competencies integrate and mediate between forces of nature and nurture (i.e., biological, environmental, and sociocultural antecedents) and social behavior.

In the outcome study, the GSID Relationship Questionnaire was used to measure the interpersonal understanding, skills, and personal meaning of relationships and fighting behavior (Schultz & Selman, 1998). The composite of the various subscales on the Relationship Questionnaire is referred to as "relationship maturity" (excluding the fighting scale). Other measures included the Defining Issues Test to measure moral development (Rest, 1979), the Modern Racism Scale (McConahay, 1986), the Multigroup Ethnic Identity Measure (Phinney, 1992), and the Civic Attitudes and Participation Questionnaire (Blyth, Saito, & Berkas, 1997).

The outcome study demonstrated the efficacy of the FHAO program in promoting the development of key competencies that underlie interpersonal and intergroup relations. FHAO students showed increased relationship maturity, decreased fighting behavior and racist attitudes, and lower insular ethnic identity relative to comparison students. In terms of relationship maturity, the FHAO students gained (over and above comparison students) in their interpersonal understanding, in hypothetical and real-life interpersonal negotiation, and—most strongly—in their capacity to reflect on the personal meaning of relationships. The significant growth of FHAO students' capacity for personal meaning-making is consistent with the program's core mission to engage students in an exploration of the connections between history and their own lives in order to promote the development of a more informed and humane citizenry.

The difference between FHAO and comparison students in terms of change in the amount of self-reported fighting across the schoolyear did not reach significance but indicated a trend for the FHAO students to engage in less fighting. An analysis of an interaction among fighting, relationship maturity, and group membership (FHAO or comparison), however, revealed an important finding. The relationship maturity of students in FHAO classes who had reported fighting increased, while fighters in the comparison group continued to show large deficits in relationship maturity. The researchers interpret the findings this way: "The attenuation of the strong negative relation between relationship maturity and fighting behavior that participation in the FHAO program seems to provide suggests that the program, in building the capacity for reflection, is also promoting resiliency and preventing chronic antisocial behavior. With the FHAO program thus functioning to prevent current—and perhaps future—deficits in relationship building capacity, the FHAO students who are fighting may be more likely to refrain from fighting and other forms of violence in the future than their fellow fighters in the comparison group, who showed large deficits in relationship maturity" (Schultz et al., 2001).

Further, students participating in FHAO exhibited a decrease in racist attitudes relative to comparison students across the schoolyear. The differences between FHAO and comparison students were significant for girls. The Multigroup Ethnic Identity Measure (Phinney, 1989, 1992) was used to measure various aspects of ethnic identity as well as attitudes toward other groups and orientation. Students in the FHAO program developed more positive feelings toward, and a willingness to interact with, other ethnic groups. Finally, while Facing History students showed development in moral reasoning and increases in civic awareness and participation, these increases were not significantly greater than those of comparison students.

Findings from the Classroom Case Study

The second aspect of the FHAO–Carnegie research was a qualitative case study of an FHAO classroom (Barr et al., 1998). In addition to having an observer document the entire course, pre- and post-interviews with many of the students were used to learn about the ways in which they connected the issues explored in the course with their own lives. Analyses were conducted at the level of each student (individual cases) as well as an analysis of themes across students.

Analyses of interview data revealed that many of students felt that the "realness" or "truthfulness" of the FHAO course distinguished it from other things they had studied and provided them with the opportunity to engage deeply and personally with the material. The students responded to the course with moral outrage about history ("How could people let this happen?") and told us that the course helped them to develop greater awareness of current examples of oppression. They were able to make connections, for example, between the abuse of power in prewar Germany and the impact of negative leadership within their peer society. In addition, almost all FHAO students claimed that the FHAO course reinforced their sense that prejudice and discrimination are negative and heightened their sensitivity to their own biases. FHAO students were more able to acknowledge stereotypes after their FHAO course, and students also credited FHAO with helping people from different groups to better understand one another.

In addition, the study revealed that the students were most meaningfully engaged in issues of civic participation at the level of their own relational worlds, especially controversial incidents and dynamics within their peer society, such as ostracism, fighting, and teasing. These controversial incidents became personal frames of reference or filters as the students made meaning of the historical case study. Students were compelled to examine their actions in relation to such controversial incidents and dynamics. Their thinking was complicated by the course as they came to see that being a bystander is not a neutral stance but an active choice of disengagement that has real implications for events, relationships, and one's sense of self.

Finally, students became more aware of how their internal world—their beliefs, values, motivations, needs, and wishes—influenced their behavior. In this way, the FHAO course appears to have promoted their capacity for self-reflection, a key dimension of the "personal meaning" competency that was measured in the outcome study. Thus, while the outcome study demonstrated that FHAO promotes the competencies necessary for a thoughtful and active engagement with others in a pluralistic society, the qualitative case study provides a window into how this occurs.

CHALLENGES FOR THE FUTURE

Facing History and Ourselves is now piloting initiatives that use technology to enhance its reach to educators, students, and the community at large both nationally and internationally. The web offers new possibilities to engage with both new and current FHAO teachers in deep, long-term support and to fulfill their need for timely materials and resources, regardless of where they are geographically. Already, more than 50,000 FHAO study guides have been downloaded from the web site.

Moving forward, FHAO will continue to build the "campus" section of its web site, which allows educators who have attended our face-to-face workshops and institutes to continue their learning as a community in virtual form. Already, "hybrid" institutes have been offered that incorporate pre- and post-institute work via the web. Online courses in both facilitated and self-guided forms are also being developed and piloted. FHAO will carefully study the optimum mixture of direct and "virtual" contact that can continue to produce quality programs, while valuing and affording new opportunities to fulfill the needs of educators worldwide with resources that are available 24/7.

CONCLUSION

Democracy is at best a fragile prize that must continually be won, or what Alexis de Tocqueville called "an apprenticeship in liberty." Political science professor Benjamin Barber (1993) has noted that democracy, often taken for granted, is far from our "natural condition," but rather "the product of persistent effort and tenacious responsibility" (p. 147). The challenges posed by the new century—including the increasing diversity of our communities, issues of global human rights, and the needs of emerging democracies—may further raise the level of effort required. An early FHAO teacher described the challenge this way in 1983:

> Much is demanded of those who participate in Facing History and Ourselves: . . . to avoid the lure of easy answers and stereotypes that can easily distance us from human experience and from each other. Yet, for all the weight of the subject matter, this curriculum is strangely hopeful. By reminding us that history is largely man-made, it suggests that civilization is and what it may become is directly related to each one of us.

When young people are given the opportunity and context in which to grow as moral philosophers, they can capture the hopeful possibilities, as the following student did by connecting the broader, seemingly daunting task to our day-to-day decisions and actions:

> If one by one, hundreds of children learn the evils of hatred in history, then learn to face and change that history in their own world through art, language, and service and begin to build communities of educated committed citizens, who is to say that Facing History cannot be the catalyst for an end to prejudice, violence, and injustice? (FHAO, 1999)

Chapter 7

Forging the Chain: "Hands Across the Campus" in Action

Sharon Hicks-Bartlett

While gathering my thoughts to write this chapter, I overheard a breaking news bulletin. Bracing for some ghastly report, I followed the live images projected in a small window in one corner of the television. The announcer's unruffled voice dissolved into a soft drone as I watched petrified students and teachers dart from a school building as paramedics dashed helter-skelter. Combat-ready police lined the perimeter of the school. Cameras panned the contorted faces of dazed, wide-eyed students. "We thought he was joking, just fooling around . . . we didn't think he was serious." The killer's friend uttered these words upon learning that classmates had been wounded and killed with a gun the student had brought to school. But some of his friends had taken the young killer seriously enough to question him about the threats he had issued over the weekend. On that fatal Monday morning, just to be on the safe side, friends searched him. They found nothing. But tucked inside the backpack that everyone carries and takes for granted were weapons of vengeance the student would, only minutes after being questioned and searched, use to maim and murder fellow classmates.

Flashbacks of Littleton, Springfield, Conyers, Jonesboro, Paducah, to mention a few, flooded my mind. This time the killing field was Santee, California, where a 15-year-old ninth-grade boy from Santana High School opened fire, killing 2 students and wounding 13 others before he was cornered in a bathroom, disarmed, and apprehended. The carnage, according to news

reports, could have been worse because the boy had carried enough am-
munition to reload multiple times.

As in other school shootings, the Santana student, Andy Williams, had
revealed his plans to some of his peers. Also, at least one adult knew about
the boy's school troubles. Many students talked openly about the boy being
picked on and teased about being "skinny" and "small." But the boy seemed
to take the teasing in stride, so his friends claimed. According to some, he
laughed at himself along with them. So when he threatened to retaliate, his
friends thought he was "just joking." On March 5, 2001, Andy Williams showed
his classmates, the school, and the nation that he was not joking.

Although what transpired at Santana High and schools like it is an extreme and still-rare response to internalized marginalization, the events leading up to such violence are unfortunately neither extreme nor rare. Embedded
in the details of school shootings are stories about school cultures and environments in which intolerance, teasing, bullying, and marginalizing of others
occur daily. Too often the mistreatment and devaluation of others are permitted in schools. Some administrators downplay teasing and dismiss it as "Kids
will be kids." Many teachers feel overwhelmed, ill equipped, or unwilling to
handle anything beyond teaching their subject areas. Students, caught in the
crossfire of administrative mismanagement and teacher ambivalence, endure
as best they can. For some students, surviving in high school has as much to
do with developing a thick skin and the appropriate coping skills as it has to
do with mastering academics. Recent school violence has called into question
much of what we thought about schools, families, community, and safety.

In the search for programs to combat intergroup conflict and school violence, many schools tend to be shortsighted and reactive, sometimes im-
posing illogical zero-tolerance policies or quick-fix panaceas in hopes of
sweeping change. The interests of the school and the safety of its students
can be better served, however, by programs that promise no cure-all but
instead provide a vehicle for changing the culture of the teaching and learning environment that tolerates the marginalization of others.

This chapter contains my observations and experiences implementing and
sustaining just such a program. It is based on more than 7 years of intense,
ongoing involvement with schools, teachers, students, and parents. By presenting these experiences, it is my hope that others can learn from our successes and failures and consider them when implementing similar programs.

PROGRAM GENESIS

Hands Across the Campus™ (HAC), a program of the American Jewish
Committee, is a proactive approach to addressing tolerance, intergroup rela-

tions, and conflict issues. It focuses on the environment and school culture to understand the concerns of individual schools. Currently the program exists in a dozen suburban Chicago high schools that, while similar along some dimensions, are strikingly dissimilar along others. All the schools, however, share many common features with the high-profile school shootings. Our growing diversity, along with increasing incidents of intergroup conflict and violence, sparked discussions between the Committee and others interested in addressing pressing school problems. Out of these conversations grew efforts to create a customizable program that would serve the needs of school administrators, teachers, students, and the community.

PROGRAM PHILOSOPHY

HAC's philosophy is rooted in democratic ideals and social justice. The program maintains that while America is the most free, democratic nation on earth, historical, political, economic, social, and institutional barriers continue to constrain individuals and groups. The program aims to sensitize schools to the effects that unresolved intergroup problems have on learning and teaching and to help youth understand how intolerance, prejudice, and discrimination threaten us all. Those charged with educating students need skills and support as they learn to appreciate the diversity of their students and best prepare them to fulfill their civic responsibilities and live peacefully in our global world. HAC assists educators and students in developing leadership skills so they can actively engage self and others in building a school culture that welcomes, supports, and values differences.

OPERATING ASSUMPTIONS

The program has three components: teacher training, student leadership training, and community coalition building. Each component is based on assumptions about schools, students, teachers, and the growing demands on schools to prepare students for success after high school. These assumptions include, but are not limited to the following:

1. Schools are microcosms of society.
2. Each school has a distinct culture, which may be taken for granted and unquestioned.
3. Schools must be reflective in order to recognize the ways in which they contribute to marginalizing students and teachers.
4. Cultures can be functional and dysfunctional at the same time.

5. Teaching today makes greater demands on teachers than it did 20 years ago.
6. Americans share some basic core values, regardless of background, experiences, and culture.
7. The easy availability of guns makes bullying, and other forms of intolerance, priority matters for schools.
8. Students and teachers need skills to deal effectively with diversity and conflict resolution.
9. Students and teachers need new insights into how conscious and unconscious attitudes and behaviors shape expectations and interactions about self and others.
10. Teaching tolerance, respect for others, and the valuing of differences is important.
11. Change is sometimes difficult.

THE PROGRAM

HAC promotes tolerance by stressing the importance of building on the strength of differences. Every HAC program consists of a trio of components: teacher training, student leadership, and community coalition building. The degree to which any one component may be active in a school varies depending on the stage of the program in a particular school, its resources, and its time commitment. Eventually, however, every program incorporates all three components. To transform a school environment into one where everyone feels valued, respected, appreciated, and included and is free to learn and develop, students, teachers, administrators, parents, and people in the community must be involved in the change process. The initial goal is to create a strategy to address the intergroup relations issues in the school. The plan is formulated after careful consideration of information gathered through school meetings and workshops; it includes diversity training/workshops, custom-designed professional development sessions, facilitation, summer training opportunities, coaching, and ongoing, on-site guidance.

Component One: Teacher Training

Teacher training is the first component of the program. This training is launched with an all-day workshop conducted by diversity trainers from the American Jewish Committee. These facilitators are versed in the latest approaches to an array of topics germane to intergroup relations, including multiculturalism, cross-cultural communication, anti-bias training techniques, conflict resolution and mediation, character education, and leadership. The first workshop is designed to introduce teachers to the program and the curriculum. It is also used to initiate the ongoing dialogue and process that will be an integral feature of the HAC program. The workshops are rooted in the belief that all change begins with self, and the goal is to begin steps toward openly examining teachers' attitudes, expectations, beliefs, and frustrations with respect to intergroup relations. Teachers are introduced to basic theories, concepts, and techniques for understanding racial/cultural/class identity development and how these experiences may influence student receptivity to learning and participating in school (Tatum, 1997). We stress the importance of seeing students not only in the context of adolescent development but also in relationship to their history, family, and community. Thus, the activities, exercises, and techniques we use are designed to deepen teachers' knowledge of students' development in the context of their multiple affiliations (Ladson-Billings, 2001).

Following the first workshop, the school and teachers are engaged in an ongoing process to address those intergroup relationship issues they deem significant. Throughout the schoolyear, we are available to conduct professional development programs. In the implementation stages of the program, this ongoing interaction with teachers can range from one visit per week to two visits per month per school. To assure a quality program and to sustain the energy a new program typically engenders, we encourage the school to take advantage of the many services we offer. These services include teacher in-service training, lectures, mini-workshops, and consulting with the school on diversity management, student relationships, parent/community relations, and teacher recruitment.

HAC also offers a 3-day intensive summer program to which participating schools send teachers to learn from, and network with, other HAC schools. In addition, they learn from master teachers' creative use of the curriculum. In the summer program, teachers share their strategies for building and sustaining an HAC student club, negotiating with administrators for release time, and a host of other program-related issues. This summer gathering is an opportunity to engage in dialogues and to participate in dynamic brainstorming sessions to troubleshoot specific problems. It fosters a sense of community and models the processes that we hope teachers will continue in their home schools.

Our workshops and professional development opportunities are designed to assist teachers by sensitizing them to the cultural, racial, and class dynamics of intergroup relations; teaching them to be effective diversity managers; and equipping them with skills to help their students learn to value self and others. Our approach emphasizes democratic principles of social equity. Our goals are to raise awareness of the complex issues regarding intolerance among students and within society in general; discuss the origins of bullying, teasing, and fighting, as well as teachers' role in mentoring students and being role models for them; share with teachers the links between early childhood teasing/bullying and later racial/ethnic/gender/class prejudice and religious intolerance; discuss intervention strategies; and share resources and strategies for waging peace in our schools (Lantieri, 1998).

The American Core Values (ACV) curriculum is a set of lessons and activities that teachers can use to enrich their existing social studies materials. Teachers are discouraged from following it to the letter. Rather, it is hoped that they will use these materials selectively, as resources to supplement and strengthen their existing resources. The ACV curriculum has three primary goals: to create appreciation for America's multicultural heritage; to foster better communication among students from diverse ethnic, racial, and religious groups; and to strengthen the democratic process. The core values taught in the curriculum are personal responsibility, respect for others, fairness, cooperation with others, appreciation of cultural diversity, and community involvement. The teaching techniques involve responding to personal surveys or handouts, class discussions, reading about historical incidents, learning about cultural heroes, role playing, and team learning. Lessons cover such diverse topics as Hammurabi's legal code from ancient Babylonia, leaders who rebelled against colonialism, women's rights leaders in different countries, heroes of the Holocaust, more recent heroes (e.g., Golda Meir, Nelson Mandela), American heroes (e.g., Pocahontas, Black students at Little Rock High School), the uses of propaganda to foster stereotypes, American ethnic groups (e.g., Inupiat), stopping hate crimes, and poverty.

The Conflict Resolution curriculum consists of lesson plans and activities concerning areas of historical, social, political, and economic conflict. Like the American Core Values curriculum, it is not meant to be the last word on conflict resolution. Rather, it is hoped that these lessons and activities will generate debate, dialogue, and critical thinking among students and teachers.

Component Two: Student Leadership Training

The second feature of the HAC program is student leadership training. The first training session typically consists of a full day of activities that introduce students to concepts and skills related to race relations. Students are to learn basic concepts of diversity, prejudice, discrimination, stereotypes, and so on. They participate in a series of exercises and discussions that help them address their own conscious and unconscious prejudices and how these attitudes and behaviors limit them as well as others. Students are taught leadership skills, how to resolve conflicts effectively, and how to create action plans. Subsequent training sessions continue to focus on ways in which students can take leadership positions to address school and nonschool problems. One of the most important aspects of the student program is the "club." Following the initial training session, a core group of students is encouraged to establish a school club that focuses on developing activities, projects, and events that advance their goals and those of the program. With the help of club sponsors (i.e., teachers), this student-run organization conducts its own student outreach and seeks support from existing school clubs. When possible, club meetings are attended by an HAC representative who assists the students in their activities, project development, and ongoing student leadership skills. Rather than developing a school club, some schools embark on a schoolwide program, while others create a semester- or year-long anti-bias education course.

Component Three: Building a Community Coalition

The third part of the program is community coalition building. This component consists of sharing activities and projects with the community at large. For example, students may volunteer to perform an activity with their local middle and elementary school or a neighboring high school. If students have developed skills in conducting diversity and conflict training workshops, they may volunteer to conduct workshops for their local police department or local merchants. A workshop with parents is another example of community coalition building. The most important aspect of community coalition building is that teachers must make certain that students are well-prepared for public performances.

HAC employs these three components to facilitate changes in school culture. Our program goes beyond diversity education that thinks only in terms of a black-and-white model. We view diversity as an issue of inclusion and safety and emphasize that no one is outside of diversity, regardless of race, ethnicity, class, religion, gender, abilities, and sexual orientation. Definitions of intolerance that focus on racial/ethnic and gender groups are myopic and incomplete. A more refined definition includes *all* the ways in which individuals and groups are excluded by and exclude one another because the "other" is viewed as somehow "different." Every group is an "other" to someone. In schools, groups of "us" and "them" or "insiders" and "outsiders" are pervasive—regardless of the racial/ethnic composition or religious background of the student population. This more refined definition of intolerance includes what is often viewed as "innocent" teasing, bullying, and hurtful behavior toward others.

THE LINKS IN THE CHAIN

School Administrators: The Strongest Link

"When I think of 'diversity' I think of division, not togetherness. . . . I think of separation and that bothers me" (White female teacher).

"Being the only Black teacher here is hard . . . real hard" (Sidebar conversation with a male teacher during a workshop break).

"I don't push my Latino students much. Most of them are not going to college—it's not really valued in their families" (White male teacher during a workshop).

These quotations provide a troubling glimpse into the attitudes and feelings of some educators toward diversity initiatives. They also hint at the degree of work schools face when aiming to improve teachers' cultural competency. HAC is sometimes introduced into a school because one or more teachers have been assigned to a multicultural task force charged with researching or finding a program to address school diversity and conflict. Almost always, the schools that these teachers represent are experiencing demographic shifts that have produced "issues" and "concerns" for the school. Sometimes an administrator has heard about the program and wants to adopt it based on another school's recommendation. Often the administration has become sensitive to a changing student population and a lack of diversity in the school's faculty. In some instances, a school has been accused by students, parents— and sometimes even faculty—of being racist, homophobic, or simply indifferent. On rare occasions, a parent has discovered the program, requested literature, observed a student performance, or heard a presentation given to a parents' group.

Prior to adopting the program, we require that the school and its administration make an unequivocal commitment to this labor-intensive program. Even in the most welcoming school, with full administration and majority teacher support, HAC encounters challenges. One of the first problems administrators experience is the exacting work of winning the hearts and minds of their faculty, some of whom may be resistant to change. School administrators must openly demonstrate their commitment to the program if they are to sell it to those inside and outside the school. This requires developing appropriate language to communicate the goals of the program and a way of packaging the program that works in the community. In some communities, talking about race relations simply does not work. The same program, couched in the language of democratic principles, may work easily. Administrators are helped by HAC personnel to anticipate and identify problems in program acceptance by the local community and how to work around them.

School decision makers must be willing to make unpopular decisions. For instance, in one suburban school, the principal mandated that every adult in his building, including support staff and maintenance crew, participate in a full-day diversity workshop. It had become evident to him that voluntary workshops tended to attract a self-selected group already predisposed to discussing tolerance issues. To ensure that "everyone was on the same page," this principal mandated participation. The immediate response was mixed. Some individuals welcomed the opportunity to learn about these issues. Others adopted a defensive stance and resented the implication that they needed such a workshop.

Administrators sometimes require assistance in matters of community outreach and teacher recruitment. Most principals don't fully comprehend the array of factors that make attracting teachers of color arduous. Schools often fail to present an attractive package to minority candidates, one that includes information on local housing, churches, and the quality of life in the community. In addition, some teachers of color may not want to be pioneers, knowing well that such situations demand an understanding support system, mentors, and an environment that is sensitive to racial/ethnic and religious differences.

Strong leadership, support, and modeling are the three keys to fostering school change. Strong leadership is the willingness to embrace change, however unpopular or controversial. More than advancing a vision of school transformation, it requires adopting a collaborative approach and assembling a faculty committed to working together. Successful leaders understand that inclusion and feeling safe in the school are inextricably related to educational success. By keeping communication open, encouraging the dissemination of program information among faculty, and confronting resistance, school administrators come to be seen as unequivocally supporting the program. By modeling effective intergroup conflict resolution, administrators convey a message to teachers and students that such conflicts are resolvable.

Students: The Pivotal Link

"Just because I'm the only Black person in class, my teacher calls on me for everything that has to do with Black people. It's so stupid! I've only been alive 15 years—how am I supposed to know everything! I hate that class!"

"My driver's education teacher told me that Blacks are better than Whites at sports because of natural selection. He said that the biggest and strongest survived slavery and that their children inherited their strong genes and each group got stronger until now Blacks are better athletes than Whites."

"The White kids here make fun of me and call me 'wigger' [derogatory term used by Whites for a White person who is labeled as acting Black] because I hang out with Blacks and date Black guys and dress hip-hop."

"People tease each other all the time, especially if they're friends or if someone is different, say a nerd or weird or something."

Anyone who works with adolescents knows that it is highly emotional work. Developmentally, they may be overly sensitive and critical, self-conscious, moody, passionate, and dramatic. Teachers who connect with students understand this. Today, adolescents manage lives far more complex than did their parents. For many, school is hectic, demanding, and competitive (Pope, 2001). In addition, some juggle work (sometimes full-time) and some are parents themselves. Often they manage their life devoid of the community and familial support that students in past generations could count on.

HAC student leadership workshops are designed to create a safe space for students to discuss their lives both in and out of school. Some students detest school, others love it, and a larger group navigates the vast middle regions. Regardless of a student's orientation toward school, HAC workshops reveal that many students attend all 4 years yet never feel safe or connected to it. Multiple factors contribute to being part of one's school. The workshop is designed to unearth those forces and create the connections between and among students and their teachers that contribute to building a caring community of teachers and learners.

A typical full-day workshop includes from 35 to 45 freshmen- to junior-level students; they are guided through various exercises, dialogues, and activities that are all designed to take them from the general to the highly specific work of examining self, others, and their beliefs and attitudes about differences. Students come with some trepidation, particularly those unaccustomed to participating in school activities. Although the workshop participants know that they have been "selected" from the student body to provide feedback and insights into the school, they remain suspicious and wonder about the real reason they have been summoned. They are told that their selection is due to others having recognized their leadership potential. We emphasize that selection should reflect the diversity in the student body. This includes both traditional and nontraditional students (e.g., students labeled as troublemakers, alleged gang members, outcasts, etc.). Nontraditional students tend to know better than most what it is like to be labeled and marginalized. Rarely have these students participated fully in school. Often they arrive at the workshop apprehensive about their inclusion. It is our goal that the students emerge with a sense of responsibility and commitment to helping their school and to working toward positive change.

To prepare the group for the workshop, considerable time is devoted at the outset to establishing reciprocal rapport. This not only creates a safe environment for discussion but also establishes important ground rules and allows time to calm nerves. Particular care is given to explaining the purpose of the gathering. Students are told that they are on the front-line of a new school program and that without their involvement and support, the success of program cannot occur.

Every student has had at least one experience of being excluded; nearly everyone has been on either the giving or receiving end of hurtful behavior. These shared experiences become the common ground on which to explore feelings of safety and the individual's role in creating a school atmosphere that is inclusive or exclusive, marginalizing or mattering. Comments such as those shared in the quotes above are frequently made. Many are woefully misinformed about the historical contributions to America of their own and other groups. Most have been taught to steer clear of entire categories of people, although personal experiences at school may counter these parental caveats. Students enter the workshop confused about the information they have been taught, heard, and observed regarding cross-cultural relationships. It is important to assist them in identifying the origins of this (mis)information and to teach them how to transcend such divisive dispositions, while at the same time helping them deal with the contrary views parents and significant others may possess.

To help students unburden themselves of the messages learned within the family, neighborhood, and church, as well as from media and friends, they participate in exercises that identify where these messages originate and how best to counteract their inevitable influences on us all. Divesting themselves of these pressures is exacting. It is important for students to understand that, regardless of their backgrounds, most of them consciously or unconsciously carry messages about others that constrain intergroup relationships. They are helped to understand that, to varying degrees, they are products of a complex interplay of family, group history, personal experiences, peer relationships, and religion, among other factors. Analyzing these forces is new to most students. The message we underscore that it is possible, in spite of everything else, to learn to constructively defend more inclusive beliefs in a way that does not require the rejection of family or friends.

Students readily talk about personal feelings of being excluded, teased, and bullied. A show of hands always reveals that these experiences are common. Feeling unsafe transcends fear for one's physical safety; it includes feeling disconnected from a community of support (Maeroff, 1999; Sizer & Sizer, 1999). Feeling safe at school means being validated and affirmed by others. The classroom is an ideal setting for this to occur; yet too often it does not.

Racial and ethnic differences are salient distinctions in school. So, too, is membership in any identifiable school group, such as those whose religion requires the donning of a particular style of dress. Sometimes actual group membership is irrelevant. A student may be marginalized because he is given the label "faggot," a term I have overheard in every school in which

I've worked. When students hear the painful stories of students who have been so labeled, the reaction is often visceral. The emotions expressed in storytelling convey to the listeners that the pain of being different extends beyond race and ethnicity. Eventually, students learn that no one is outside of diversity. These stories come out after hours of working, sharing, and listening to each other—at a point when defenses have finally been lowered and students can see themselves in the details of other's experiences. Except for the most hardened, almost all students experience a point in the workshop when they are sufficiently moved to listen with their heart, not just with their ears.

At this point, Black students begin to understand that they do not have a monopoly on pain and suffering. White students feel that they, too, can freely contribute their stories of discrimination and exclusion, however uncomfortable or novel the experience of sharing may feel. They also begin to understand why it is not always easy for students of color to "just get over it." The input from Asian American and Latino students challenges everyone to think beyond the Black–White dichotomy that preoccupies so much of the discourse on race.

Part of the workshop focuses on penetrating the "isms" and the variety of forms they can take. Once students have been exposed to these issues, they are taught strategies and suggestions for monitoring themselves and others along the journey toward healing intergroup conflicts. Students discover that it is avoiding discussions of controversial issues concerning tolerance or intergroup conflict that causes the most pain—it is the silence, the feelings that come from being ignored, devalued, and excluded that are most painful. By the workshop's end, students have participated in many critical thinking exercises, shared countless personal stories, actively listened to each other, disagreed and agreed on many things. The tightly controlled, reserved demeanor that some students bring to the workshop has now vanished, replaced by a heightened awareness and new understanding. The racial and clique divisions manifested in the seating choices, for example, have now disappeared. During the closing exercises students say that, for the first time, they have really talked to each other and have heard from students they would never have listened to beyond superficial conversations. Considerable attention is also given to inculcating in students the importance of developing leadership skills and to their individual and collective responsibilities in creating a safe, inclusive school.

A major goal of the workshop is to create an "ah-ha!" experience, a paradigm shift, a palpable feeling within each student regarding diversity issues. When this type of awareness emerges, it is often visible, if not verbally shared. To create these insights requires care in creating a sense of community within the group. We spend time talking about respect, perceptions of others, and how we are all to some extent ignorant of one another. We discuss the value of hearing multiple viewpoints and how active listening to others not only reveals the gaps in our information but also allows us to build on what we have in common. We follow Stephen Covey's habit of "seek first to understand, then to be understood," which is conveyed effectively through the storytelling exercises (Covey, 1990).

Teachers: The Crucial Link

> Teaching is an interactive practice that begins and ends with seeing the student.
> —Ayers, 1993, p. 25

This quotation calls for deepening the relationship between teachers and students. Ayers is not alone in stressing the importance of seeing students as unique, multidimensional individuals who, regardless of their backgrounds, bring valuable experiences, skills, and talents to the learning situation. Like Ayers, Ladson-Billings (2001) recommends that teachers develop "cultural competence" to draw on students' cultures as a basis for learning about them and where they come from. Lisa Delpit (1996), long an advocate of teachers' communicating across cultures, underscores the need to understand and appreciate the "affiliations" that students bring to school. If student learning is to improve, teachers must play a critical role in changing the school's culture. They must learn to effectively teach "other people's children" with the same sensitivity and regard they want for their children. When it comes to issues of diversity, these scholars recognize that teaching beyond the basics is essential. For today's multicultural classroom, learning is greatest when students feel included and valued and know that they are expected to learn.

Helping teachers develop a deeper understanding of culture and its role in learning requires training that consists of ongoing involvement in and support for professional development. Many teachers have completed college without any substantive knowledge of racial identity development, multicultural education, or cross-cultural communication skills. Those few educational opportunities to explore these areas are typically offered as electives, thus leading only the most motivated to take the courses.

Forty years ago, racial and ethnic issues dominated multiculturalists' concerns (Ladson-Billings, 2001). Today, along with the interest in racial and ethnic groups, there are significant religious, socioeconomic, ethnic-identity, and multilinguistic issues that render diversity a more complicated matter than ever before. Students may bring to the class multiple associations that need to be recognized for their influence on learning. Unfortunately, the reality is that teachers are becoming Whiter and Whiter, while students are becoming Browner and Browner. In addition, minority teachers are scarce commodities. Approximately 42% of all public schools have no minority teachers—a fact that precludes most nonminority teachers from learning from their colleagues of color. Students, both minority and nonminority, are disadvantaged by not having a diverse teaching staff. A diverse staff allows minority students an opportunity to see people in positions of authority who look like they do. Nonminority students get to interact with and learn from those who do not look like them. The presence of a diverse teaching staff can challenge the assumptions and stereotypes that growing up and working in homogeneous communities can engender.

Barth (1990) maintains that a school builds a "community of learners" by changing the school culture. Like Ayers, Barth believes that this process begins with valuing others, valuing learning, and valuing community. This is no easy task. Teachers, the most overworked people in the school, need time for reflection on self and practice. Sadly, many teachers, regardless of their tenure, "are uncomfortable acknowledging any student differences and particularly, racial differences" (Ladson-Billings, 2001, p. 31). Many prefer not to see color, deluding themselves into believing that ignoring the obvious is evidence of a personal lack of prejudice. In reality, being colorblind serves only to diminish others. Learning about their students' diverse backgrounds helps them uncover their own false views and assumptions. Many teachers have to be convinced that such an exploration is worthwhile and can improve teaching and learning. A school's health rests in part on being able to address its "nondiscussables," those topics that, while important, are replete with so much taboo and fear that they remain buried and unexamined (Barth, 1990). Race, diversity, and the meanings associated with shifting school demographics are among the nondiscussables that some schools avoid.

Our strategy for helping teachers investigate the cultural journeys of their students is to engage teachers in constructive dialogues about their own culture and intergroup differences and the role these factors played in their own education. HAC workshops, along with the ongoing training opportunities for studying these issues, fill a void that is often not well addressed in teacher education courses. Critical self-reflection, reflection on practice, decoding assumptions, and addressing controversial issues are precisely those areas that are central to HAC's work with teachers. Ideally, the workshops and training opportunities not only allow teachers to voice their fears and concerns but also provide a chance to learn about how culture and other types of difference matter in the classroom (Ladson-Billings, 2001). Once teachers are introduced to these issues, many will desire additional resources and materials to use in the classroom. The American Core Values curriculum addresses this wish.

The first workshop must proceed with extreme care and patience because it establishes the tone for subsequent work at the school. Even when the initial group is voluntary and enthusiastic, challenges arise. Some resistance can be explained by the relative lack of real knowledge about the workshop and perceptions about what is expected from such workshops. Frequently, at the end of a workshop someone will utter a sigh of relief and voice surprise that the workshop wasn't "angry." Some of this after-workshop relief derives from "White guilt" and fear. The overwhelming majority of Americans attend schools, live in neighborhoods, and participate in social activities with people who look like they do. Lives marked by deep interactions and contacts with others who are different are still rare. While many teachers profess to want friends from different racial and ethnic backgrounds, most admit that they do not have any. In these workshops, we explore how our perceptions of others and the world are challenged when we learn and work in a diverse environment. Lacking this diversity makes developing cultural competency skills difficult.

Here again is one teacher's spin on Latino students, whom he felt attended school primarily because it was required: "I don't push my Latino students much. Most of them are not going to college. It's not really valued in their families." This teacher had no concrete evidence for his views; instead, they were based on his stereotype about Latino students. At no point did the teacher consider that his low expectations had any influence on his students' performance. Such viewpoints become part of the ongoing dialogue that troubles students. In these workshops, teachers must be encouraged to consider alternative explanations for poor student performance. Perhaps in a more diverse setting such perspectives might encounter challenges in interactions with colleagues.

While many teachers understand Ayers's recommendation that teachers see students as multidimensional, they are often ill equipped to do so. Too many are fearful and unsure of the appropriate methods for addressing potentially controversial racial and other intergroup issues. Some prefer to remain silent. Those who have had positive experiences with others, and have successfully worked through intergroup communication conflicts, will likely embrace the changing demographics of their school and not assume it signals cause for alarm.

Resistance to diversity workshops is sometimes widespread among participants, particularly if attendance is mandatory. This resistance may range from verbal objections at being "told what to do" to carefully worded disclaimers that one doesn't need such a workshop or that such programs create problems where none exist. In some cases, feelings are expressed that minorities and other oppressed or disadvantaged groups "really ought to learn to get over it and move on." As one White male teacher put it, "I understand that you're trying to teach us to be more sensitive, but I think that's the whole problem—people are *too* sensitive! Minorities should learn to let things go . . . just let it roll off their backs. People teased me when I was growing up all the time . . . about my last name. They should do like I did. Just let it roll off their backs . . . stop taking things so seriously. You need to do *de-sensitivity* training, where you teach people to be less sensitive, not more sensitive."

Sometimes resistance masks anger and denial. Those steeped in denial do not listen with open ears, but rather with a closed mind and heart. Sometimes those in denial feel that things have improved enough that discrimination is a relic of the past. Even when faced with indisputable evidence of discrimination, those in denial dismiss the evidence as "exceptions" to the rule or too anecdotal to be reliable. They see sexism, racism, homophobia, and other forms of discrimination as little more than the acts of individuals behaving badly. They remain unconvinced discrimination is pervasive in society. That these "isms" are embedded in our institutions and continue to have a powerful, enduring effect on people's lives is difficult for some to grasp. They explain away their students' racial insensitivity toward each other, denying their own responsibility to help students repudiate marginalizing attitudes and behaviors. Teachers also face difficulties stepping outside their role as teachers. Part of the problem is that admitting their ignorance of the diversity issues places them in an uncomfortable position, where they may know less than their students. Teachers may need to take a backseat to students whose culture the teacher is attempting to learn more about. Diversity teaching demands that teachers not portray themselves as experts, that they put themselves in the role of the learner (Gallos & Ramsey, 1997). For some, relinquishing their position may contradict how they see their role as educators.

It is important to point out that the diversity or lack thereof in the workshop will shape the workshop's dynamics. When teachers of color are present in workshops, White teachers, in general, tend to be rather quiet and reserved. Some admit nervousness and worry that Black teachers will get angry over their historical mistreatment (Howard, 1999; Ladson-Billings, 1997). One goal of the workshops is to poke, probe, and provoke thoughtful discourse among teachers. When participants come from diverse backgrounds, the workshop can build on that richness. Sharing stories and experiences creates linkages of understanding and empathy. Unfortunately, issues and challenges that might inevitably arise in a diverse setting sometimes remain unaddressed in relatively nondiverse groups.

Enduring change cannot occur if teachers are omitted from the school-change equation. As many schools eventually learn, if primacy is given to any one component of the program, it ought to be given to the work done with teachers, for they possess great power with students and have considerable influence over what transpires in the classroom. Teachers create emotional memories that students will never forget (Bluestein, 2001).

SUMMARY: FORGING THE CHAINS

Hands Across the Campus™ is a flexible, customizable, curriculum-based tolerance and prejudice-reduction program aimed at creating caring, inclusive school communities that see diversity as a strength, not a weakness. This labor-intensive program requires all the key players in a school to think, work, and play together to create and sustain an environment in which conflict is resolved through peaceful means and where communication across groups is viewed as an opportunity to learn from others (Lantieri, 1998). With important shifts in urban and suburban demographics, communicating with a wide variety of different people is unavoidable. Communicating effectively across groups necessitates intergroup skills and, above all, a commitment to a sense of discovery about others and a belief that people should be respected, treated fairly, and appreciated. HAC assists schools in critically examining the ways in which past and present practices and policies include some while excluding others. It provides ongoing support that allows schools to change by revisiting policies and practices that may no longer suit current realities.

HAC is a program that makes linkages between and among those who interact together for the purpose of teaching and learning. Each link is necessary; each link is inextricably coupled with the others. Each contributes to the formation of the whole school. This chapter identifies three essential relations in schools that are the focus of the HAC program and discusses some of the ways in which each adds to the goals of prejudice reduction, tolerance, and conflict resolution.

Administrators and other school officials are the first link. The support and leadership they provide are critical. The journey to becoming a school that demonstrates—in its policies, treatment, and care—that it values and respects others is not easy. Leaders must not only convince those below them to support a new program they must also believe in the program's merit. Leaders must carefully create alliances with others who are essential to the successful implementation of the proposed changes. These intrepid decision makers must also stand firm when necessary. Both conflict and controversy are unavoidable. These individuals serve as models to their faculty and students. Are they effective diversity managers? Do they resolve conflicts with teachers, students, and staff in ways that build rather than destroy relations? Leaders must convincingly demonstrate that they demand and expect the best from themselves and others. Only by so doing can HAC successfully forge the first link toward creating a caring and safe school where differences are valued.

Teachers are the second link. Our approach is to provide them with continuing opportunities to reflect on self and practice. Increasing racial, ethnic, religious, and socioeconomic diversity, along with variations in family structure, are reflected in schools and contribute to the many challenges in communication and styles of conflict resolution. As a result, teachers are expected to go beyond teaching subject matter to understanding racial- and ethnic-identity development and how it influences learning. Our approach is to help teachers examine how they and their profession are shaped by both macro and micro societal transformations. Teaching now requires the ability to create cross-cultural trust and respect (Freire, 1998). Teachers not only play a critical role in the lives of students; they are also tied to collegial relationships that help set the tone for the life of the school.

In the end, our work and that of schools hinge on students. They are the third essential link in the chain. The manifest function of school is to educate students. Students now need new skills and dispositions that transcend book knowledge. The very definition of an educated person has expanded to include the acquisition of social skills and emotional intelligence. The ability to get along with others, the capacity to resolve conflicts and work together with others, is essential in today's workplace (Goleman, 1998).

In working with students, we challenge them to go beyond the confines of their community, to think about their obligation not only to make their school a better place but also to make the world a better place in which to live. Much of our work with students involves developing and honing leadership skills. We assist students in creating and implementing projects, activities, and other events to encourage leadership development that will prepare students for the changes that will occur in society.

This chapter has sought to highlight the challenges and barriers of adopting, implementing, and sustaining a tolerance program in high schools. It emphasizes that even with a well-thought-out program, even one that has anticipated the pitfalls along the way, the program's success is not guaranteed. Rather, the program is part of a chain of people, activities, and events that come together to engage in a process of change that, while taxing at times, leads to new ways of thinking, learning, and living in a changing world.

PART III

PROGRAMS IN COLLEGES AND UNIVERSITIES

The three programs presented in this section are all oriented toward college students. These programs are more intellectually ambitious and challenging to the participants than the programs for younger students. They take advantage of the more fully developed intellectual, social, and emotional skills of college students. In some respects, they face greater challenges than programs with younger students. If students have not previously experienced training in intergroup relations, biased attitudes and behaviors may have become well entrenched by the college years. Also, these young adults will have been subjected to many more of the biased messages conveyed by the mass media. They are also likely to be more defensive about their intergroup attitudes and behaviors. This will make some of them more resistant to change than younger students. The majority of students will have had few experiences interacting across group boundaries, and many will be even more apprehensive about doing so than younger students. On the other hand, these programs are presented in an educational context with self-selected individuals who are motivated to learn and often want to overcome their biases. They may be willing to embrace change, despite the discomfort it can initially cause. They often realize, in a way that younger students do not, that they will be entering an increasingly diversified society and that, if they are to function effectively in that society, they need to acquire the skills and knowledge about intergroup relations that will enable them to do so.

Chapter 8, written by Biren (Ratnesh) Nagda and Amelia Derr, presents one of the most daring programs currently being conducted on intergroup relations. It is based on the premise that intergroup dialogues, and the direct confrontation of sensitive issues they entail, are a highly effective way of improving intergroup relations. In this program, equal numbers of members of two groups with a history of conflict meet together to hold facilitated dialogues about issues of contention between the groups. The facilitators have typically been through the program themselves and received additional training. The program attempts to instill an ethos of social justice, create intergroup competencies, and promote social activism. In practice, students from the two groups are initially introduced to the dialogue process by engaging in structured interactions. The dialogues then focus on commonalities and differences between the groups and structural inequalities in society. The dialogues proceed to an examination of controversial issues and intergroup conflicts, exploring both microlevel processes within the dialogue group and macrolevel processes within society. Videos, readings, fact sheets, and other supplementary information may be introduced to stimulate the dialogues. During the final stages of the program, attention shifts to coalition building across group lines and social action in the larger community.

The next program for college students is described in Chapter 9, by Donald Biggs and Robert Colesante. It deals with an approach that is broader than most of the others covered in this book. Their interest is in social morality in a pluralistic society. They are concerned with teaching students about their collective responsibilities in such societies. Their approach is steeped in the insights of Lawrence Kohlberg about moral education. They try to teach students to be more tolerant, less authoritarian, and more principled in their moral thinking and decision making. Their approach in the classroom emphasizes the analysis of collective moral dilemmas, a concern for social responsibility, fostering empathic concern, and taking social action. There is a strong emphasis on becoming involved on the campus and in the community to address issues of social injustice. Unlike the dialogue groups described in the previous chapter, this program's approach to the "moral education of citizens" puts little emphasis on group differences. Rather, it stresses the common goals and values that citizens of a diverse democratic community share. These goals and values are as likely to be decided upon by voting as by more informal means of reaching consensus. Finally, the program proceeds by trying to change the classroom into a pluralistic community where the students/citizens can structure their own studies through democratic participation.

The third approach to intergroup relations in colleges and universities is described by Cynthia Cohen, with Marci McPhee, in Chapter 10. These authors discuss an ambitious project undertaken by Brandeis University to promote intercommunal coexistence across the campus. The overall goals are to increase intergroup understanding, empathy, and cooperation. The most fascinating aspect of this initiative is the range of activities involved. The activities include faculty work groups, courses, student internships, public events for the university community, fellowships, research projects, conversation groups, international outreach, and projects in the community. The initiative operates simultaneously along three strands: engaging faculty, enhancing coexistence on campus, and promoting international partnerships. The people involved in this initiative are very interested in having it serve as an example for other universities that wish to transform themselves in similar ways. Their approach tends to place a greater emphasis on the arts and humanities than most intergroup relations programs, which find their disciplinary homes in the social sciences or education. As Cohen and McPhee report, the people involved have found promoting the initiative to be challenging both personally and in terms of creating changes in a larger educational community where some segments of that community are not favorably disposed to these changes.

As was true in our earlier chapters, here, too, the authors provide empirical evidence that the programs described have positive effects on participants. The methods of evaluation vary widely because the programs are varied in approach and scope, ranging from special training sessions, to academic courses, through universitywide initiatives. These program evaluations illustrate that, just as there is no one best way to address improving intergroup relations, there is no universally valid method of evaluating such programs.

Chapter 8

Intergroup Dialogue: Embracing Difference and Conflict, Engendering Community

Biren (Ratnesh) A. Nagda
Amelia Seraphia Derr

It is not the mere fact of living together that is decisive. It is the form of resulting communications that matter.

—Allport, 1954, p. 272

Racial and ethnic tensions on college campuses in the United States in the mid- to late 1980s propelled many efforts to address issues of diversity through recruitment of students and faculty of color, multicultural curriculum transformation, and institutional change. Increasing racial and ethnic diversity on campuses, and the consequent challenges, are reminiscent of the changes following the school desegregation efforts supported by the 1954 *Brown v. Board of Education* decision. In their Social Science Statement concerning the benefits of desegregation, Stuart Cook and colleagues relied heavily on the contact hypothesis: Interactions among individuals from different groups can reduce intergroup prejudice and tensions. In reality, however, such benefits were not always actualized because of conditions counter to positive contact—competition, unequal status, and lack of support from authorities (Stephan & Brigham, 1985).

Fifty years after *Brown*, the U.S. Supreme Court in 2003 reaffirmed the compelling interest of diversity in education by upholding affirmative action and race-conscious university admission policies. Patricia Gurin (1999),

Education Programs for Improving Intergroup Relations. ISBN 0-8077-4459-X (paper). Prior to photocopying items for classroom use, please contact the Copyright Clearance Center, Customer Service, 222 Rosewood Drive, Danvers, MA, 01923, USA, telephone (978) 750-8400.

in her expert testimony in this case, offered a tripartite model of diversity in higher education. Concurring with Pettigrew (1998), Gurin emphasized going beyond mere desegregation or structural diversity—the representation of different racial and ethnic groups on the college campus—to fulfill the promise of educational benefits for all students. She argued that two additional considerations are critical for institutions to move toward integration: classroom diversity, that is, incorporation of knowledge about diverse groups in the content of a course; and informal interactional diversity, that is, opportunities for substantive interactions among students from diverse backgrounds. These two forms of diversity influence students' critical thinking, perspective taking, and other skills important in fostering active citizenry in diverse democracies (Gurin, Dey, Hurtado, & Gurin, 2002).

Theoretical development and research findings provide impetus for educators and social scientists to consider ways in which the benefits of intergroup contact can be meaningfully articulated and operationalized. In this chapter, we describe one such effort: college-based intergroup dialogues aimed at engaging participants from diverse backgrounds to explore commonalities and differences in their social identities, learn about social inequalities, and envision multicultural communities that are socially just. We first describe the history and scope of intergroup dialogues. We then discuss the foundational assumptions guiding the design and application of intergroup dialogue. Next, we describe an academic program at the University of Washington School of Social Work in which intergroup dialogues are incorporated into a required course. We present an education curriculum with illustrative excerpts from students. Finally, we discuss research findings about the impact of intergroup dialogues on college students.

HISTORY AND SCOPE OF INTERGROUP DIALOGUES

Within the higher education arena, intergroup dialogues are defined as facilitated, face-to-face encounters between two or more social identity groups that have a history of conflict or the potential thereof (Zúñiga & Nagda, 1993). These encounters engage students in substantive, sustained, and conceptually integrated learning experiences (Zúñiga, Nagda, & Sevig, 2002). In the open and inclusive dialogue environment, students may engage honestly with others to explore issues that they may not easily address elsewhere. Trained facilitators use experiential activities and other simulations as well as reflections and dialogues in pairs as well as small and large groups. Participants may also be involved in action projects outside the dialogue group. This model, originally implemented at the University of Michigan in 1989, has been adapted at universities across the United States: the University of

Illinois at Urbana–Champaign, University of Maryland, University of Massachusetts at Amherst, University of Washington, Arizona State University, and Mount Holyoke College (see Schoem & Hurtado, 2001, for descriptions of select programs).

The intergroup dialogue effort at the University of Washington School of Social Work began in 1996 as a response to the urgent challenge for social work educators to prepare practitioners to work effectively with an increasingly diverse clientele and to embrace the profession's mission of social justice. While drawing upon the many principles that parallel the vision and practice of other programs, intergroup dialogues in social work education go beyond engaging citizens in a diverse democracy. They are centrally concerned with developing an ethos of social justice and competencies for interacting with people across differences and responding to social inequalities that impact on human life.

In 2000, the University of Washington provided permanent funding to establish the Intergroup Dialogue, Education and Action (IDEA) Training and Resource Institute. The institute's mission is to develop and support intergroup dialogue efforts in the School of Social Work and in other departments at the university and to collaborate with local and national community organizations. The broad goals of intergroup dialogue—developing capacities for sustained dialogue, raising critical consciousness, building community across differences, and fostering empowerment for constructive personal and social action—guide all its efforts. Both introductory and advanced social work courses incorporating intergroup dialogues are offered at the undergraduate and graduate levels. Facilitator development and support as well as building alliances with other college-based intergroup dialogues programs and organizations that emphasize civic engagement and citizen empowerment for community change are important functions of the institute, as are research and evaluation.

THEORETICAL BACKGROUND FOR INTERGROUP DIALOGUES

Intergroup dialogues, while associated with a long tradition of efforts to improve relations among diverse groups of people, are a distinct approach. Traditional efforts to generate social bonds between estranged groups emphasized cooperative interactions and similarities among groups (e.g., Sherif, 1966). However, when intergroup encounters occur in contexts of power inequalities, a focus on similarities may be perceived to serve the interests of the dominant group as an instrument of social control to maintain the status quo (Abu-Nimer, 1999). Intergroup dialogue emphasizes both commonalities and differences.

Dialogue aims to discern understanding and insights through the generative power of conversation (Bohm, 1996). Intergroup dialogue is a social justice approach to dialogue that centers on issues of social-group memberships and social inequalities manifested in oppression–privilege dynamics. The intergroup encounters are structured to build a sense of connectedness among people from different groups who are identified by their social group identities (e.g., race, ethnicity, gender, sexual orientation). The dialogues address intractable conflict issues (e.g., racism, sexism) and may not lead to immediate resolutions. Through conflict exploration, however, dialogue participants may more deeply understand social tensions while at the same time redefining ways in which they collude in and challenge social injustice. Such an approach is desirable "because the contact hypothesis model is based on individual and interpersonal encounter, [and] it lacks the ability and potential to address inter-ethnic conflict and asymmetric power relations" (Abu-Nimer, 1999, pp. 8–9). Our conception of intergroup dialogue is drawn in part from what others have called a conflict-oriented approach (Abu-Nimer, 1999; Chesler, 2001) and in part from the potentiality of community across differences, coexistence, and coalition (Ury, 1999). Thus, we refer to our approach to intergroup dialogues as a *conflict–community* approach. Integral to this approach—embracing difference and conflict while engendering community—are the foundational assumptions elaborated below.

1. Conceptualization of Intergroup Relations as a Multicultural Mosaic. Campus intergroup relations are situated within the larger context of societal relations. While society becomes more diverse through population growth and immigration, traditional conceptualizations of intergroup relations in the United States—the assimilation and melting pot models—have been summarily rejected in favor of ideals that allow for a pluralistic appreciation of diverse cultures. A salad bowl, or cultural diversity, approach allows for the recognition of differences but may recognize culture as exotic and existing only for those who are different from the dominant groups. Moreover, this model neither acknowledges the social power relationships that form the backdrop for intergroup interactions nor does it account for the ways in which substantive and communicative interactions occur among people. A newer model, the mosaic, recognizes the tensions and differences in interactional exchanges that are inherent in intergroup relations (Alperin, 1990; Fredrickson, 1999). The mosaic model, while respecting the uniqueness of different cultures, engages people in discovering or constructing a shared wholeness through interaction. One can imagine a quilt emerging from the active, intentional gathering and sewing together of different pieces of cloth. It is in this interweaving that meaningful intergroup contact is made possible and enacted.

2. Acknowledgment of Difference, Conflict, and Possibilities for Community. The emphasis on social justice in intergroup dialogue has profound implications for rethinking approaches to positive intergroup relations. Particularly, long-valued beliefs about intergroup contact (Allport, 1954) and more recent revisions (Pettigrew, 1998) need to be reexamined when differences in social identities and access to societal power are explicitly recognized, discussed, and challenged. Intergroup dialogues situate themselves fully in existent societal power relations yet challenge them. They provide engagement spaces for participants to build connective ties that honor their different experiences in society, allow for critical social inquiry, and enable them to define the similar and unique responsibilities they hold in forging community across these differences.

The multicultural mosaic model underscores community. While social conflict is the background and content of many discussions, the engagement process facilitates an emerging "whole-ness" that is more just and inclusive. bell hooks (1995), in her interpretation of Martin Luther King Jr.'s ideal of a beloved community, wrote:

> The beloved community is not formed by the eradication of difference but by its affirmation, by each of claiming the identities and cultural legacies that shape who we are and how we live in the world. . . . We do not surrender ties to precious origins. We deepen those bondings by connecting them with an anti-racist struggle. . . . The notion that differences of skin color, class background, and cultural heritage must be erased for justice and equality to prevail is a brand of popular false consciousness that helps keep racist thinking and action intact. (p. 265)

When issues of difference and power imbalances are constructively recognized in forging cooperation, alliances or coalitions can result. The intergroup dialogue can become a nexus for experimenting with such new frames, perspectives, and actions as well as a place for nurturing possibilities and cultivating hope for change (Lederach, 1997).

3. Contextualization of Group Differences and Intergroup Issues in Social Power Relations. The mosaic model holds an implication about the societal context of group differences: Interpersonal and intergroup conflicts and issues are situated within the community and society as a whole. Intergroup dialogues connect individual and interpersonal relations with structural issues in society. Peace researchers and practitioners use the "Nested Paradigm of Conflict Foci" as a way of situating issues in larger systems. The first two analytical levels of this model—*immediate issue* and *relationship*—articulate conflict issues and their resolution in interpersonal terms. The latter two levels—*subsystem* and *system*—broaden the focus to the proximal context of the conflict (e.g., school or organization) and to the societal system level. In intergroup dialogues, issues of estrangement between groups are examined through the lens of power inequalities, rather than simply conceptualized as miscommunications or misperceptions. Group identities and differences, and interpersonal and intergroup relationships, are marred by stereotypes and prejudices resident in the institutional, social, and political structures that perpetuate them. Such an approach "underscores the need to look consistently at the broader context of systemic issues. It suggests . . . that at the subsystem level we can experiment with various actions that promise to connect 'systemic' and immediate 'issue' concerns" (Lederach, 1997, p. 59).

4. Formation of Connective Ties Across Differences. Weaving the multicultural mosaic requires building connections across different threads. William Ury (1999), renowned scholar and practitioner of conflict resolution, reflects on the possibilities of intergroup contact and the dearth of ideas concerning the process and form of intergroup communication: "Do we know what to say? . . . No more daunting challenge faces us than learning to live together. How can we deal with our differences without either suppressing them or going to war over them?" (p. 197). Dominant communicative ways of dealing with differences are through debate, justification, and defense of one particular viewpoint, worldview, or status. In intergroup dialogue, affective ties are fostered through dialogue, a horizontal communication process that can lead to greater synergy and understanding. As opposed to debate, with its emphasis on a single position, dialogue enables participants to listen and appreciate the validity of different perspectives, even when these may be radically divergent from one's own. The spirit of dialogue is building a greater wholeness. Debaters engage in critiquing and deconstructing arguments while dialoguers inquire about feelings, perspectives, and frames of analyses in an attempt to expand understanding, which helps to clarify assumptions and barriers. Dialogue encourages a critically self-reflective process about one's own experiences and circumstances and fosters deeper inquiry that helps to reframe viewpoints. Dialogue enables trust to develop in relationships otherwise marred by estrangement.

Whereas traditional intergroup efforts call for common goals and a need for interdependence in achieving these goals, dialogue also offers a commonality of process and relations. Pettigrew (1998) referred to friendship potential in intergroup situations as the core element for positive interactions. Intergroup dialogue engenders the qualities of friendliness—sharing, listening, engaging, questioning, supporting, challenging, joining—across differences. Participants talk about life stories, share perspectives on different issues, listen to and ask one another questions, and engage in other meaningful ways.

5. Creation of a Facilitative and Supportive Structure. When intergroup encounters and sustained dialogue are incorporated into educational settings, educators have an ethical responsibility to facilitate and support these endeavors in ways that promote student well-being and enhance their preparation to be active and productive citizens. Transformative learning scholars point to the importance of a supportive, facilitated structure in which the conditions of social democracy are fostered (Mezirow, 2000) in "an ecology of relationships with people who value diversity and transformative discourse." The facilitated structure of intergroup dialogue, focusing on the interactive engagement process, goes beyond the conditions of intergroup contact specified in the contact hypothesis. It is a subsystem that supports group transformative learning of both participants and facilitators.

Educators, as authorities for students, can support participants' active learning in intergroup dialogues by sanctioning the dialogues in a variety of ways: public announcements, rewards and recognition for efforts, requiring coursework for students, and participation of faculty. To further promote student learning, organizers must attend to how experiences of members in an intergroup dialogue impact on situations and people outside the group (Pettigrew, 1998). Structured opportunities following the intergroup immersion experience that help participants build on their learning and gain a greater repertoire of knowledge, skills, and values can greatly increase the benefits of intergroup dialogues.

The five foundational assumptions discussed above outline the manner in which intergroup dialogue offers a new way of conceiving intergroup contact opportunities and guide implementation of intergroup dialogue programs. Beyond a focus on either similarities or differences, intergroup dialogue aims to expand awareness of the greater social context, particularly social conflicts, that influences intergroup relationships. Ultimately, the focus of intergroup dialogues is to enhance understanding across differences and possibility for collaborative actions that promote greater social justice.

INTERGROUP DIALOGUES IN PRACTICE

Intergroup dialogue, heralding perhaps a new generation of intergroup relations efforts, holds promise for many settings in addition to higher education. In fact, various intergroup dialogue programs are currently used in K–12 schools, workplaces, and community settings (Schoem & Hurtado, 2001). In the undergraduate social work curriculum at the University of Washington, intergroup dialogues are incorporated into a required junior-year course, Cultural Diversity and Social Justice. Students meet weekly for a 2½-hour lecture–

discussion session in which they are presented with theoretical and conceptual information related to a broad range of diversity and justice issues—race, ethnicity, gender, age, sexual orientation, religion, national origin, ability, and socioeconomic status. The course begins by examining group identities and group differences, followed by theoretical consideration of the dynamics of oppression and privilege at institutional, intergroup, interpersonal, and individual levels. We then examine specific dominant–subordinated relations such as racism, sexism, classism, and heterosexism. The course concludes with envisioning change, social action, and alliance building.

Students also participate in 9 or 10 weekly 2-hour interracial/interethnic dialogue groups of about 12 students each, led by facilitators. The intergroup dialogues provide an in vivo opportunity to apply and experientially understand the theoretical and conceptual information covered in the lecture–discussion sessions. Students engage in dialogue through participating in experiential activities, reflecting on assigned readings, and learning about current intergroup issues. Each week, they write reflection papers based on their learning.

Peer Facilitation and Training

Senior undergraduates in social work undergo intensive training to facilitate the intergroup dialogues. Facilitators work in two- or three-person teams. To support the principle of equal status, the co-facilitators of each team are representatives of the different identity groups participating in the dialogue group. Such a co-facilitation approach also models for students how collaborations and coalitions may be forged across differences. The facilitators act as peer guides, leading students through learning processes that they themselves have gone through previously as juniors.

Intergroup dialogue facilitators are trained through a two-quarter course sequence that provides them with foundational knowledge and skills for working with diverse teams and small groups in educational settings. The first-quarter course extends students' knowledge about intergroup relations and conflicts and builds their skills as facilitators of intergroup dialogues. Topics covered include philosophy and principles of dialogic education and dialogic communication; intergroup communication; social identity development; principles of working with conflict; group dynamics, group observation, and facilitation; team building among cofacilitators; and creating a support system among instructors and facilitators.

Course instructors closely monitor the progress of students throughout the first-quarter course and select facilitators for the next quarter's intergroup dialogues. The second-quarter facilitation course is designed as a practice seminar while the facilitators are actually leading the dialogues. Class sessions focus on comparison of facilitation experiences, troubleshooting, co-facilitator team building, and planning for upcoming dialogue sessions. Co-facilitators also meet weekly outside the seminar to prepare for their dialogue sessions.

The Intergroup Dialogue Curriculum

The curriculum, drawn from scholars and practitioners from many disciplines who have specified components and conditions for fostering positive group interactions, is guided by the following assumptions: Intergroup dialogue is sustained contact over time (not a one-time intervention); an ongoing process of development (not an ultimate outcome); a differential learning process for students from dominant and subordinated groups (rather than "one size fits all"); a combination of dialogue, reflection, and action (as opposed to separate curricular elements); and one part of a continuing learning process in which one experience builds on others or serves as a springboard for more learning.

The intergroup dialogue model is comprised of four stages: (1) group beginnings, (2) learning about commonalities and differences in experiences, (3) working with controversial issues and intergroup conflicts, and (4) envisioning change and taking action (Zúñiga et al., 2002). We discuss each stage below and include excerpts from students' reflection papers to illustrate their experiences in the weekly intergroup dialogues that correspond with these stages (for a curriculum guide, see Nagda, 2001).

Group beginnings (stage 1) prepares the group as a whole for engaging in dialogue across differences. The critical tacit questions for students and facilitators that guide this stage are: What is the nature of the learning community that we want to create? What do I bring to this learning community?

Together with the entire cohort of students, we convene all facilitation course instructors, cultural diversity and social justice course instructors, and dialogue facilitators for an initial orientation session. We emphasize the importance of intergroup dialogues to social work values and the ethics of diversity and social justice. We speak of the origins and philosophy of intergroup dialogue, the nature of the developmental process and student engagement, and the connection between the intergroup dialogue sessions and the lecture–discussion sessions. This session provides the sanction of authority by placing intergroup dialogues in the larger context of social work education and the university. Having all the students together also conveys a sense of a collective educational experience.

I was happy to find out that the issue of racism will be central to our dialogues. Racism is something that I have witnessed and experienced throughout my life. . . . I know for myself that racism dwells within and around each of us and is certainly an issue worth talking about. . . . I do not recall ever discussing my own experiences of racism to the extent to which I shared my [own] feelings and how the experiences had affected my perceptions of others. Especially in high school, nobody wanted to talk about racism and its effects. (student of color)

Within the separate dialogue groups, three activities help set the stage for learning. First, as a way of personal introductions, students engage in a "wheel exercise." Students take a piece of paper, draw a circle, and divide it into four parts. Each quarter represents one of the following questions:

- How racially and ethnically diverse was your neighborhood when you were growing up?
- What are your hopes and fears about participating in intergroup dialogue?
- Who inspires you?
- What is your vision of a just, multiracial community?

Students depict their responses to these questions in images and then share them in small- and large-group discussions. This activity enables students to begin to define their role in participating in multicultural communities. Through their sharing, students begin forming connections with one another. While some of them may already know each other, they may not have shared these parts of their lives.

Second, facilitators and students together explore the differences between dialogue and debate (see Berman, nd). Facilitators share their experiences and talk about dialogue as a communication process that honors differences and encourages connection. Students may reflect on times in their lives when they experienced dialogue and times when they were in debate, their feelings in each of these situations, and the conditions and elements of the situation that enabled dialogue to occur. The group generates its own guidelines for engagement that foster respectful and optimal learning. Guidelines often include honoring confidentiality, using "I" statements, active listening, asking for clarification, and taking responsibility for one's statements.

Third (usually in the second session of the dialogue), students and facilitators engage in the "cultural chest exercise." This activity contributes to the relationship- and trust-building process by encouraging students to share aspects of themselves that are personally important or socially imposed. Students place meaningful objects that represent their cultural/social identities (e.g., race, ethnicity, class, gender, sexual orientation, national origin, spirituality/religion, age, ability) in the inside of these "chests" (a box, bag, or another container). They decorate the outside of these "chests" with words, pictures, or other ways of depicting the stereotypes, prejudices, or assumptions that others make about them based on their social identities. As students share their chests with the whole group, the dialogue processes of listening, sharing, and asking questions are critical. This activity enables students to see both the individual and collective parts of each other; it deepens students' capacity for sharing in ways they may never have experienced before; for some, it is a first opportunity to think about themselves as cultural beings.

> The sharing of cultural chests allowed our group to find both the similarities and differences amongst each other. . . . We are creating an environment that permits us to feel more comfortable in expressing ourselves. (student of color)

> I found this was a difficult assignment. I realized that I have never really identified with a culture, and it took me a long time and talking to my family to find the object to put into my chest. I never thought of myself as being a member of any culture but the American culture. What is that? (White student)

Without making a judgment about this phenomenon, facilitators note that students who are aware of themselves as members of oppressed groups are likely to share items related to social identities (historical or cultural narratives, significant symbols, or pictures of cultural role models), while those from privileged backgrounds share about themselves as individuals (pictures of friends, hobbies, or personal histories). Facilitators ask students for their own observations and reflections on the similarities and differences emerging from their sharing. Stage 1 begins the personalizing process of the intergroup context for students; while students are still interacting with others interpersonally, their basis for interaction is a self-defined social identity perspective.

Learning about commonalities and differences in experiences (stage 2) among groups focuses specifically on racial and ethnic identities. This stage encourages personalized understanding of how social differences (race and ethnicity) and social conflicts (racism and ethnocentrism) impact on individual and communal life. The critical tacit questions are: What have we learned about what it means to be persons of our racial- and ethnic-identity groups? How do we locate ourselves in our socialization experiences and in societal dynamics of oppression and privilege? What does this mean for our relationships with one another?

Students begin to reflect on their experiences as racial and ethnic beings, share their perspectives, and ask one another questions based on these memberships. Opportunities for both intergroup and intragroup dialogues are essential here. Intergroup formats allow for learning across groups while intragroup formats enable certain questions to be addressed among people who share their experiences.

The "concentric circles" activity (Myers & Zúñiga, 1993) engages students in one-on-one sharing and listening using questions such as:

• Describe a time when you felt different from the people around you.
• When and what did you first notice about people who were different from you?
• Describe a time when you felt proud of your racial/ethnic identity(ies).

Each student responds, without interruption, to each question for 2 to 3 minutes with a partner. When both partners have had an opportunity to answer the questions, they engage with new partners. They share their ideas with and hear from a few different people in a short span of time, which promotes simultaneous relationship building as well as reflection about one's own location in societal relationships of domination–subordination.

The reflection questions helped us to begin to see how different many of our individual experiences with race and ethnicity have been. . . . It was moving to hear the childhood memories some of our fellow students had of hurtful things that were said to them concerning their race or ethnicity. For White students in the class, the memories of first impressions of racial difference are often vague and indistinct. For students of color, the memories are frequently vivid and painful. (White student)

While listening to my classmates, I realized that in my past I have even been a victim of racism and prejudice, although at the time I had not realized that I was. (student of color)

Next, students participate in intragroup dialogues (people of color, White people, and when necessary, bi/multiracial people), also known as caucus groups. Care is given to explain that the purpose is to help deepen the dialogue and address issues that may be difficult to put forth in a mixed group. Within the separate groups, the facilitator will ask the students for their emotional reactions to being separated into social-identity groups. They then pursue and list their responses to the following questions, which are brought back to enrich dialogue in the larger group:

- What are the advantages and disadvantages we experience in society as members of our racial/ethnic group(s)?
- What are the advantages and disadvantages we experience in this department/college as members of our racial/ethnic group(s)?

The lists from different groups convey much about students' understanding of societal power relations. For people who have been marginalized, the lists are often quite explicit and long. For people from subordinated groups, the advantages list usually shows the strength of family, cultural, and community ties. For privileged groups, the lists may be shorter and convey a lack of clarity regarding what constitutes individual- and group-based advantages and disadvantages. All these issues provide content for the ensuing dialogue.

> The differences between these two groups and the oppression of the people of color were so blatant that it was hard to process them as realities. That is probably what most of us tend to do—we know that these realities are out there, but we do not want to believe that they are right in front of our faces. (White student)

Facilitators also ask students about their engagement on an emotional level. Again and again, facilitators report that some White students are uncomfortable sharing in the intragroup settings. Be it guilt, shame, or a feeling of separation, some White students experience great anxiety in engaging in these homogeneous settings. Having the presence of a White facilitator, who can help students reflect on why they may be having these emotional reactions, is helpful.

> I learned from this interaction that this separation only affected the White students and had no effect on the students of color. When we came back together as a group, I think that we (the White students) realized that the separation bugged us so much because of the possible guilt we have due to our association with a societal group that has discriminated people of color in the past. (White student)

For students of color and bi/mutiracial students, these intragroup settings are powerfully engaging and lively; they are able to feel less isolated and can articulate many issues that may perhaps have not come up in the large group.

> Having to discuss issues of oppression, I felt more comfortable speaking with other students of color. . . . In writing out the disadvan-

tages, the exercise served as a tool of empowerment. I learned that even though we have faced many barriers, we have beaten the odds against us. We can be recognized as strong individuals who have persevered against life's many challenges. (student of color)

Similarities and differences in perspectives, disbelief of a perspective that is opposite from one's own, and disagreement with certain analyses are typical of the process in stage 2. In addition, facilitators stay attuned to opportunities to push the students to contextualize the emergent dynamics—attitudinal, intellectual, emotional—from the individual and group levels to the structural dynamics of inequality. This calls for using group processes as content for illuminating and understanding the issues of social conflict under discussion.

Working with controversial issues and intergroup conflicts (stage 3) focuses on selecting a few critical and current issues that highlight intergroup conflicts. The critical tacit questions are: What is our current knowledge and understanding about these issues? How are the issues manifested from the personal to the societal level, historically to the present? What do we need to do to continue learning as well as having an impact on personal and social change concerning these issues?

Dialogue sessions in stages 1 and 2 involve much reflection and content based on individual experiences drawn from life stories of students. In stage 3, other learning modes are used for generating dialogue—simulations, readings, videos, speakers. This stage is directed toward understanding how social conflicts such as racism manifest in different issues that all have macro (historical, political, and structural) implications. The contextualization of individual experiences, perspectives, and group processes to macrolevel issues that was begun in stage 2 is extended in stage 3. Political content and social issues are explicitly introduced for dialogue. It is critical to practice the dialogue skills students have learned because disagreements and conflicts are likely to result from different levels of knowledge and experiential understanding of the issues in stage 3. Facilitators are advised not to endorse one way of thinking about the issues but rather to probe the reasons—personal, cultural, institutional, historical—that inform the students' different perspectives.

The dialogue format for these sessions includes a selected topic for discussion and a generic format that includes (1) a stimulus for dialogue—such as a video, (2) conceptual and informational input—such as fact sheets and readings, and (3) structure—small groups, dyads, and 1-minute papers (quick reflections). One topic is selected for each session of stage 3 (e.g., interracial relationships, affirmative action, and hate crimes after 9/11). In the session on interracial relationships, facilitators engage the students in dialogue by first asking them about their reactions to a video and issues raised in readings on such things as miscegenation laws and then asking them to compare their own understandings of interracial relationships. A variety of perspectives usually emerge that lead to questions such as:

- How are we personally impacted by this issue?
- What does it imply for continuing cultural traditions and heritage?
- How do race and gender dynamics interact in this issue?

In the session on affirmative action, facilitators may adapt the "take-a-stand" exercise in which students physically take a stand on a comfortable–uncomfortable or agree–disagree continuum in response to a number of statements such as:

- Because discrimination is a thing of the past, affirmative action should be abolished.
- Affirmative action policies are important in "leveling the playing field" for groups that have been historically oppressed.
- Affirmative action creates self-doubt and feelings of inadequacy in those who benefit from it.

As students stand on different or similar sides of the room, they are asked to share their perspectives. A mini-dialogue after each statement helps to build momentum for the next statement and sustains dialogue. Such issues as resistance, pain, anger, or challenge that arise can sometimes be worked out more constructively in small groups than in the large group. Differences and conflicts provide potential for new understandings to emerge. Even when all students may be "on the same side," they discover that their reasons for agreement are very different. Many related issues may emerge and can be probed further in the large group.

For all issues, we promote systems-level thinking that illuminates the interconnection of levels ranging from the personal to the political. We also want students to engage in difficult conversations that can lead to reframing the issues or lenses that inform their perspectives.

> The discussion as well and the readings were very useful in helping me understand an issue that I am not really familiar with. Over the years, what affirmative action has meant to me was that I would be receiving a little help to achieve what I wanted. In a way I did feel like it was a privilege. However, I now know that affirmative action is an equal right, not a special right. It concerns me that myself and

other ethnic minorities do not realize that things like affirmative
action have an effect on each of us, either directly or indirectly. I
want to learn more, so that I will be able to make clear and valid
arguments. . . . The sessions have made me realize my own prejudices, and at the same time, I feel empowered to fight oppression at
al levels. (student of color)

Envisioning change and taking action (*stage 4*) more specifically engages students in thinking about their sense of agency in affecting unjust
incidents and conditions outside the dialogue group. The tacit questions here
are: What are our commitments and responsibilities to bring about a more
just society? How do we have a constructive impact on the social inequalities and conflicts we experience, know of, and see? How do we continue
our learning?

While critical reflection and dialogue are pillars of dialogic learning
process, they are only part of the process. Envisioning change and taking
action is the final step that enables students to incorporate a new identity as
social change agents. As bell hooks (1995) emphasized, this new identity
neither denies students' racial/cultural identities nor tries to enforce a similarity on everyone. Taking social action that honors and integrates the racial/
ethnic identities and connections into dimensions of anti-racist action and
coalition building across differences involves understanding how to be an
ally. An ally is more than a friend or an acquaintance; an ally carries a
commitment to actively intervene in oppressive incidents and to promote
conditions for greater justice in support of or on behalf of people who are
discriminated against or marginalized (Wijeyisinghe, Griffin, & Love, 1997).
Facilitators invite students to reflect in one-on-one dialogues on experiences in their lives in which they felt someone was an ally. Students then
generate a list of characteristics of an ally.

Another important cognitive input is the action continuum (Wijeyisinghe
et al., 1997). Some students may feel intimidated by social action. Many students
believe that action is comprised only of protests and lobbying. Understanding
that the action continuum includes different levels of readiness—from ignorance and perpetuating injustice to recognition, and from no action to education to prevention—clarifies social action and empowers students to engage
in actions that are doable. The "spheres of influence" activity (Goodman &
Shapiro, 1997) involves students in brainstorming possible actions in multiple
spheres—self, family and friends, schools/workplaces, community—in response
to certain incidents culled from students' own experiences or presented by
the facilitators. Some examples are: "You are with a group of friends and one
of your friends refers to someone as poor White trash" or "Your state representative says that we shouldn't accept any more immigration by people of

color because those already here make the government spend too much tax-payer money on welfare." Students also reflect on the reasons for the level of ease or difficulty in taking action in the different spheres. At the end of the first session in this stage, students identify an action that they would like to take before the next session.

The beginning of the next session involves a sharing and dialogue around the actions students took. They talk about their feelings in taking the action, assess the situation had they not taken the action, and broaden the discussion to the challenges and successes of interrupting injustices.

> I want to help create social change and one way I can take action, right now, is to be aware of language I use when speaking about groups that I may not be associated with. I never realized that I tend to separate myself from others. By saying things like, "Those people" or "They" and "That group." When a facilitator brought that to my attention, I could not believe I was doing it! . . . I have decided to start using first-person language. (White student)

The second half of the session picks up on one or two of these incidents. Students role-play elaborated scenarios. Some act out the actual incident; others intervene with actions and then invite other students in the audience to engage in taking action. These activities are designed to enhance knowledge about different actions, critical understanding of both the risks and benefits of actions, confidence in taking action, and possibilities for building alliances. The role play makes learning more lively and taps into students' creative dimensions.

Group closure is an important part of stage 4. Students express their learning and affirmation of the different people in their dialogue group. They share reflections about ways in which they would like to build on the learning.

> Looking back at the beginning of class I thought that this class would be like others, but it is so different. Now, after such painful experiences, I wish in one way that I did not take this class. But after the last dialogue meeting I think that, painful or not, it is time to open my eyes to what is happening around me. It is time to take action, and help others like me suffering discrimination or other forms of oppression. . . . I need to assist in meetings, organizations, and talk with my friends and co-workers. Expressing my feelings and thoughts will be hard, but I will work on doing that. (student of color)

During the first part of the last session, the separate dialogue groups meet to create a representation—such as a collage, an active portrayal, or a group narrative—of their collective experience for an all-cohort celebration of the learning. In the second part, each group shares its representation with the whole class. This experience reconnects all the students and enhances the collective experience across all members of the class. In the wrap-up of the encounters, we also share with students different ways in which they can continue their learning, including becoming trained to facilitate intergroup dialogues the following year. Facilitators share how their own learning in the intergroup dialogue affected their experiences in social work internships and elsewhere. Some have noted that they didn't realize the full extent of their learning until they were working with clients. Others have said that the learning takes time to unfold.

The intergroup dialogue curriculum, organized in a developmental sequence, allows students to move through different phases of creating an inclusive learning climate, sharing personal experiences as racial/ethnic beings, contextualizing experiences in pertinent intergroup issues and social conflicts, and exploring actions toward greater justice. The students' learning, as illustrated in the quotations, includes newer ways of thinking about themselves and others, of feeling the impact of race and racism, and of relating to others and the larger society. We now turn to the research emerging on intergroup dialogue that looks at these learning outcomes and processes more systematically.

RESEARCH ON COLLEGE-BASED INTERGROUP DIALOGUES

Intergroup dialogue, as defined here, is a relatively new field. Whether in education or other settings, a body of research is only now emerging. Qualitative research shows that intergroup dialogues offer students new, and sometimes their first, opportunities to engage meaningfully with others who come from different backgrounds. Students report challenging their own ignorance, learning about experiences of people from different social groups, and developing a more structural understanding of social inequalities (Nagda et al., 1999; Zúñiga & Nagda, 1993). Yeakley (1998) found that the opportunity to share personal experiences as a part of the intergroup dialogues distinguished students who reported positive changes from those who reported negative ones.

Quantitative studies also show promising results. A pre-test/post-test study on intergroup dialogue outcomes showed significant positive differences for all students in four areas: (1) sustaining dialogue (e.g., communicating across differences), (2) raising consciousness (e.g., importance of racial group membership, critical social awareness), (3) fostering community (e.g., building bridges), and (4) envisioning change and taking action (e.g., increasing confidence in changing themselves and society) (Nagda & Moise-Swanson, 2001). Other studies have also illuminated the importance of learning processes in intergroup dialogue. Lopez, Gurin, and Nagda (1998) found that active learning pedagogy, such as in the dialogues, was correlated to students' thinking about structural targets of action (the larger society and university climate) while content—lectures and readings—was not. Nagda and Zúñiga (2003), focusing on students' dialogic engagement processes (e.g., sharing views and experiences, being able to disagree, working through disagreements and conflicts), found that such engagement predicted increased perspective-taking ability, comfort in communicating across differences, and ability to bridge differences. Finally, Nagda, Kim, and Truelove (2004) found that motivation to engage in an intergroup learning community mediated the impact of enlightenment (lecture and readings) and encounter (intergroup dialogues) aspects on students' confidence for self-prejudice reduction and promoting diversity.

CONCLUSION

In the midst of multicultural change as a society, there are no clear norms for interacting in intergroup situations. Random contact among people from diverse backgrounds may generate conflicting or contradictory norms. Constructive communication processes are necessary to actualize the promise of multicultural coexistence and community. Intergroup dialogue offers such a space of hope and possibility wherein all participants can engage meaningfully in joint exploration about what it means to collaborate, coexist, and act in coalition. This joint engagement and action occurs in the spirit of learning about one another and forging harmonious relations; it also emphasizes actions that can promote social justice. Grounding the generative power of dialogue in the content of both participants' own experiences and other sources of knowledge fosters solid, integrated learning. The intentional facilitation and the learning structure provide an interactive and behavioral milieu in which an individual's ideas, actions, hopes, and desires are put forth to interface with those of others. It is in this encounter—honest and sometimes painful—and the ensuing reflection and dialogue that the creative forces of human connectedness and possibilities emerge. It is, therefore, imperative that the contextual conditions for intergroup dialogue provide a strong support system for both participants and facilitators. It is critical that intergroup dialogue have the sanction of authorities, be it through advocacy by leaders, recognition as being essential to a community experience, or provision of continuing opportunities for learning, involvement, and action.

Chapter 9

The Moral Education of Citizens: Explorations and Outcomes with College Students

Donald A. Biggs
Robert J. Colesante

This chapter describes a journey that began in 1991 with the initiation of a course designed to promote an understanding of the role of schools in a pluralistic society. We, like many other educators, were intrigued by "multiculturalism" and the promise that "celebrating diversity" could improve intergroup relations in society and in particular on our campus. Our initial efforts focused on the need for schools to increase knowledge about group differences among citizens in the United States.

In these early years, we observed that students from different groups consistently avoided contact with one another before, during, and after class sessions. They sat and talked in different camps with others like "themselves." When asked "Why?" they told us it was their right to hang around with people like themselves, and they reminded us of the commonsense adage that "birds of a feather flock together." They thought they had nothing in common with those "other" people and that it was not "normal" to associate with people who were different from them. When discussing the deteriorating conditions in the public lives of citizens in the United States, students often favored solutions that involved segregation and abandonment of common spaces in their communities. At the conclusion of the course, they cited research about group differences to support their segregated lifestyles.

This course was very popular among students. Most were satisfied with it and felt they had gained from it. Still, we were convinced that we had

Education Programs for Improving Intergroup Relations. ISBN 0-8077-4459-X (paper). Prior to photocopying items for classroom use, please contact the Copyright Clearance Center, Customer Service, 222 Rosewood Drive, Danvers, MA, 01923, USA, telephone (978) 750-8400.

gone "overboard" with diversity and individualism. Although we began our journey by asking whether multicultural education courses would be effective in promoting better relations among racial and ethnic groups, our observations convinced us that these courses were not helping students learn how to live together in a pluralistic society. We needed to prepare students to play a more active role in maintaining a common public life that respects the rights and welfare of all citizens. So we created a second course that focused on the collective responsibilities of citizens to deal with issues of social morality in a pluralistic society. About the same time, we also added a supplementary course for training peer discussion leaders with the goal of increasing the quality of student participation in our classes. Recently we have introduced a web site component and are assessing its effects on involvement, participation, and cohesiveness.

This journey has involved a weaving back and forth through periods of theoretical reflection, systematic evaluation, and instructional experimentation. Where are we now? We assume that intergroup relations in our society are basically issues of public morality and that citizens are responsible for resolving such issues. However, they must be prepared to identify these issues and participate in the democratic processes that will provide a just and fair resolution to them. They must be able to figure out the causes of events, assess responsibilities, and evaluate actions of those involved. Although citizenship education does not necessarily provide a quick approach for solving problems in intergroup relations, it may have the most long-term impact.

A brief analysis of a recent event makes clear the pressing need for education that prepares citizens to identify collective responses to issues of public morality. In response to the terrorist attacks on the World Trade Center and Pentagon, citizens had to consider the rights of individuals and the public good. Following these events, citizens have seen some of their cherished individual rights sacrificed in the name of the public good. Many searched for flags to reaffirm their commitment to the public good. Still others discouraged the president from "waging war" on terrorism.

The press as well as political leaders fueled a moral climate in the United States that was egocentric and chauvinistic. Our government "right or wrong" was a mantra for some politicians. Following the terrorist attacks, the question of what moral principles should guide our responses to these criminals became part of a national dialogue enacted in the media and in government chambers. We had been treated "unjustly," but does that mean that we can treat others "unjustly"? President Bush articulated a simplistic moral principle that others in the world were either with us or against us. Following the 9/11 terrorist attacks, the country was facing challenging "moral issues" without the prerequisite moral and civic knowledge that would allow them to make responsible decisions about these issues.

We will argue that civic education should prepare citizens to make thoughtful decisions about the moral issues in their public lives. First, we describe the responsibilities of citizens for maintaining a moral climate that respects the principles in the U.S. Constitution and Bill of Rights. Next, we briefly discuss the divisions between moral and civic education in the United States. Then we present an argument for an integrated approach to civic education that prepares students to be responsible caretakers of public morality in a democratic society. Finally, we describe examples of two courses in civic education for university students that provide thoughtful classroom experiences in which they are challenged to make such decisions.

A RATIONALE FOR CITIZENSHIP EDUCATION

Our efforts have been guided by Kohlberg's (1976) admonition that there is no clear line between effective social studies education and moral education. Participation in the social process is a sign of effective moral and civic education. In our classes, we discuss those moral values that are important for creating a "public conscience" on our campus. The encouragement of "participation" or "involvement" in our classes is not just "talking about" moral issues in the abstract. It is participation in a collective decision-making process about real issues in the lives of students (see Kohlberg, 1985; Power, Higgins, & Kohlberg, 1989).

We emphasize active participation and role-taking opportunities in which students assume the public role of "citizen" rather than the private role of "individual." The participation process is democratic in the sense that it is based on the assumptions that (1) discussions by citizens in a pluralistic society will give rise to improved insights for solving their shared problems and (2) individual roles in these discussions are dictated by their interest in the common good (Pratte, 1988). It is moral in that students are engaged in formulating a sense of public conscience as well as collective norms to guide their decisions about what is best for citizens. We expect that students who complete these courses are more tolerant, less authoritarian, and more principled in their moral thinking.

We neither celebrate differences nor try to obliterate them in a melting pot. We ask students how their stereotypes about ethnic groups affect them in their public role as citizens. This is a tough task because stereotypes about groups often have more to do with "common sense" than propositional knowledge (see Bruner, 1986). Stereotypes are assumed to be true because they are "ordinary knowledge" or just the "way things are."

The "citizenship transmission" model, popular since the founding of the country, represents the oldest and most powerful tradition of citizenship education in the United States (Giroux, 1983). The primary goal was nation building or the creation of a united society of citizens who supported their government. Like Galston's (1989) concept of civic education, it placed less emphasis on critical reasoning than political socialization.

In the early years of the 20th century, *The Melting Pot*, a melodrama by Israel Zangwill, likened the United States to a cauldron that melts away differences among immigrants so that they can become "real Americans." This metaphor was used by politicians to justify civic education programs that emphasized the importance of immigrants dropping their "foreign ways" and taking on the ways of "Americans."

Still, the proverbial melting pot did not include all citizens. After the *Plessy v. Ferguson* Supreme Court decision of 1896, it was clear that the United States had two classes of citizens. Persons of color could not expect to enter the same cauldron as Whites. They were to know their place and adhere to racist laws that restricted their freedom to drink public water, use public bathrooms, attend public schools, and be treated in public hospitals (for a discussion of these "Two Tracks to Citizenship," see Biggs, Colesante, & Smith, 2000).

The *Brown v. Board of Education* Supreme Court ruling put an end to the idea of "separate but equal" services for African American citizens. However, educational institutions were unprepared to educate White and Black students to live in an integrated society (Darling-Hammond, 1995). The traditional curriculum focused on the achievements of White persons, with very little mention of the contributions of people of color. Segregation in local communities and systems for funding schools based on the income level of neighborhoods also proved to be barriers to integration. It was at about this time that multicultural education was advocated as a means of educating citizens for life in a pluralistic society. It highlighted the public sins of our country, our civic obligation to recognize them, and the necessity of taking actions to prevent their recurrence. It was an impetus for more inclusive accounts of history and global studies as well as the development of specialized courses that highlighted the role of diverse groups in shaping American life.

During the 20th century, the liberal tradition, with its emphasis on enhancing the individual freedoms of citizens, served the United States well in that it fostered individual enterprise, hard work, and economic prosperity. Still, this tradition can be faulted for its role in contributing to public malaise and the deterioration of public life (James, 1981; Pratte, 1988). What seemed to be missing was an agreed-upon concept of public morality that could provide standards for making decisions about moral issues in the lives of citizens. The obvious source of such standards is in the moral compact found in the Constitution. However, because of the American tradition of focusing on individual morality with religious overtones, the search for public moral standards has often been immersed in a quagmire of church–state debates (McClellan, 1999).

MORAL EDUCATION APPROACHES

The moral education of youth in the United States was given a boost by 1975 and 1980 Gallup polls in which 75% of the respondents advocated instruction in the public schools dealing with morals and moral behavior. A number of high-profile school shootings during the 1990s brought even greater attention to the moral development of youth. Still, educators continue to ponder questions related to moral education: What is meant by "morality" and "moral behavior"? What can schools do to foster moral behavior?

We will discuss two major traditions in moral education. The first, referred to as character education, reflects the intentional and proactive effort of a school to teach the content of those moral values deemed important in society. The second is based on Kohlberg's stages of moral reasoning and the goal is to stimulate the development of principled moral reasoning and promote a sense of justice.

Character Education

In the early 20th century, character education was associated with codes of conduct and courses of study in school. They were designed to transmit certain core ethical values and desirable habits in all facets of school life (McClellan, 1999). The Children's Morality Code, published in 1917 by William Hutchins, identified self-control, good health, kindness, sportsmanship, self-reliance, duty, reliability, truth, good workmanship, and teamwork as "ten laws of right living." Often these values were infused into the curriculum through assigned readings, group projects, and class discussion.

A major evaluation of these efforts took place in the 1920s and 1930s. Hartshorne and May (1928–1930) concluded that enrollment in character education programs had little or no relationship to whether students exhibited honesty, altruism, or self-control. In fact, situational factors, such as the presence or absence of supervision during a testing situation, seemed to play a far greater role than any character trait. These were highly influential reports that stifled innovation among character educators and decreased confidence in the capacity of school to influence moral behavior (Wynne, 1985/1986). As early as 1934, Maller argued that aggregate data in the Hartshorne and May studies actually did show consistency in behavior and the presence of a general trait which could be called "character." Burton (1963) agreed with this conclusion: "There is an underlying trait of honesty which a person brings with him to a resistance situation" (p. 492). Rushton (1981) later questioned Hartshorne and May's conclusions because they were based on low correlations among *individual* tests rather than on the higher correlations of *aggregate* scores based on measures of a similar behavior.

Social learning theory is used as a rationale for character education (Burton & Kunce, 1995). Children learn to be "good" by imitating models of good behavior. Very often students are involved in observational and vicarious learning experiences, such as watching adults, reading stories, or listening to friends. A substantial body of research relating socialization processes to character development has assessed adult influences on the formation of a moral disposition in children (e.g., Grusec, 1981; Staub, 1979, 1981). One persistent finding is that direct messages, like telling a child that sharing is good or cheating is bad, usually do not have a positive impact on their behavior.

In the 1980s and 1990s, there was a renewed interest in character education as a basis for schoolwide efforts to shape the behavior of young people. Leming (1997) reviewed 10 programs in character education and found that all of them included some list of core ethical values similar to those identified at the beginning of the 20th century. The Josephson Institute of Ethics identified trustworthiness, respect, responsibility, fairness, caring, and citizenship as the six pillars of character. The Community of Caring Curriculum identified caring, respect, trust, responsibility, and family as values the American people hold in common.

Moral Development

A second major tradition in moral education derived from Lawrence Kohlberg's (1984) six stages of moral reasoning.

Many critiques have been offered to discount Kohlberg's model of moral development (for an overview of some of these, see Kohlberg, Levine, & Hewer, 1983). None has received as much attention as Carol Gilligan's claim that Kohlberg neglected the important role of gender socialization in moral development (Gilligan, 1982; Jaffee & Hyde, 2000). However, more often than not, her claims have been overstated, misunderstood, or misrepresented (Gilligan, 1998; Vogt, 1997).

Research on moral education based on Kohlberg's model of moral development began when Moshe Blatt (1969) exposed sixth graders in a Jewish Sunday School to weekly discussions of moral dilemmas over a 12-week period. The results surprised even Kohlberg! A substantial percentage of the students (64%) advanced in their moral reasoning, compared to about 10% in a control group. The positive effects of discussing moral dilemmas on the moral reasoning of students have been replicated many times. Schlaefli, Rest, and Thoma (1985) reviewed 55 studies to measure changes in moral reasoning; 29 involved discussions of moral dilemmas, 19 were deliberate psychological education programs (see Mosher & Sprinthall, 1970), and 7 were academic courses such as social studies or the humanities. They reported significant changes for college students involved in discussions of moral dilemmas lasting longer than 3 weeks.

Closer inspection of the studies identified several conditions that differentiate effective from ineffective programs involving moral discussions. Discussions of moral dilemmas are unlikely to be successful unless students have certain cognitive and perspective-taking skills. They must have acquired capabilities for formal operational thinking to progress from preconventional to conventional moral reasoning (Faust & Arbuthnot, 1978; Rowe & Marcia, 1980; Walker, 1980).

Teachers must be willing to discuss controversial topics in a "caring" context where disputants consider their personal relationships as more important than winning arguments (Noddings, 1994). Willingness to talk with those we disagree with is the hallmark of moral maturity and an important part of principled moral thinking (Berkowitz, 1988; Vogt, 1997). A consensus about the "right thing to do" may not evolve out of moral conversation. Students progress most in their reasoning when confronted with opposing arguments and with reasons that are one stage above their own stage (Walker, 1983).

Recent studies (Colesante & Biggs, 1999; Lim, Biggs, & Colesante, 1998) have investigated responses to methods of teaching about controversial issues. A male teacher who used stories was rated as more appealing than a teacher who used a more formal didactic approach when discussing conflicting views about the rights of homosexuals and the rights of those who engage in "hate speech." In the other case, students rated instruction about the reproductive rights of women as more effective when based on a care rather than a justice orientation. In both studies, students were influenced as much by the method of presenting conflicting views as they were by the position of the teacher. One implication is that there are inherent difficulties in trying to take a so-called objective or neutral approach to teaching about controversial issues (Jaffee & Hyde, 2000; Wark & Krebs, 1996).

Role-taking opportunities are important in promoting the development of moral reasoning (Day, 1991; Lind, 2000). This activity involves putting oneself in the shoes of another and seeing a situation from his or her point of view. It includes awareness of what others are thinking and feeling as well as speculation about how a situation could impact on their lives. Students who are exposed to more role-taking opportunities in their courses had greater gains in their moral competence (Lind, 2000).

Classrooms that include instances of "transactive discourse" are more effective in promoting moral development (Berkowitz & Gibbs, 1983). Transacts are student-to-student comments that transform, extend, or summarize the reasoning of another person; they are more common in effective moral discussions. Even a modest effort at preparing students to encourage transactive discourse could have a considerable payoff for a moral education program (Berkowitz, 1985).

Discussions of moral dilemmas have been criticized because there is no evidence documenting their effect on moral behavior (Leming, 1993). Moral behavior includes at least four processes: moral sensitivity, moral judgment, moral motivation, and moral action (see Rest, 1983). Kohlberg (1985) himself was skeptical about the effectiveness of the moral discussion method to impact moral behavior: "We have not . . . felt that stimulating the development of justice reasoning through moral dilemma discussion is in itself a sufficient approach to affecting moral actions such as cheating" (p. 60). In fact, the first study of the moral dilemma approach found the program to increase moral reasoning but not to reduce cheating behavior (Blatt & Kohlberg, 1975).

The Just Community Approach

The Just Community approach provides democratic structures for students to participate in the management of schools. Students learn how to make collective decisions that balance self-interests with those of the school, the city or state, and society at large. In this process, they also learn to take the perspective of others, to respect the rules of a community, and become identified with the achievement of its goals.

Durkheim's model of moral education is used as a rationale for the just community approach (Kohlberg, 1970). Moral values are important because they contribute to the social climate (Durkheim, 1925/1973; Power et al., 1989). Durkheim identified three basic dispositions of morality as discipline, altruism, and rational autonomy. Most importantly, he proposed that the "common life" of the classroom and school should become the content for moral education. While inspired by Durkheim's theory, Kohlberg was uncomfortable with its indoctrinating aspects. He looked to Dewey (1916/1966) for a model that could allow authority to rest with the community rather than one individual. In doing so, he defined the teacher as an advocate for the interests of the community, thus fusing Durkheim's emphasis on the power of a group to bring about conformity to moral rules with Dewey's "democratic community" which provides a mechanism to balance the rights of individuals against the common good of the community.

Most of the research on the Just Community approach occurred during the 1970s, with major summaries published in the 1980s. Several reports showed that Just Community schools were successful in promoting moral reasoning and the development of a sense of community. Those schools that emphasized Kohlberg's theory of moral development and stressed the importance of community over the individual rights of students were particularly effective (Power et al., 1989). Just Community programs were successful in reducing theft, promoting racial tolerance, increasing student participation, and reducing drug and alcohol use in the school (Power, 1985).

THE MORAL EDUCATION OF CITIZENS

The moral education of citizens provides school and community experiences that foster the development of a public conscience and a sense of altruistic caring that can guide their collective decisions about moral issues in their public lives. We, like Kohlberg (1976), assume that "social education is moral education and moral education is preparation for citizenship" (p. 213). Our approach is identified with the tradition of philosophical civic republicanism and stresses the importance of maintaining a moral compact among citizens in a democracy (Pratte, 1988).

Students learn about the public good and those civic virtues that are necessary but not sufficient conditions for a moral society. They are prepared to accept with informed consent the social contract of the Constitution (Kohlberg, 1967) and recognize the need to construct a campus community that upholds these moral values. Still, our approach involves more than teaching students about the content of these values; it encourages the development of principled reasoning about moral issues in their campus lives.

Our classes provide collective experiences in making decisions about conflicts over issues of public morality on campus. The underlying model of moral behavior, described by Rest (1983), involves four processes that we use as a format for our student discussions. The goal is to increase their understanding of conventional moral standards on campus and the importance of principled moral reasoning in making decisions about those students who are accused of violating the standards. First, they must assess whether a violation is due to a lack of moral sensitivity or a lack of understanding of the campus standards of public morality. In some cases a student may be unaware of how his or her actions negatively impacted the lives of others, while in other cases the student may not be aware of conventional standards of public morality on campus. Next, they identify the role of conflicting values in the student's decision making. Were there economic, social, or health factors that interfered with student decision making? Next, they examine the role of preconventional, conventional, and postconventional standards in resolving the conflict. Finally, they make a decision about how the conflict should be resolved and provide a rationale to support it.

Our view of the moral education of citizens is based on a concept of the public virtues or moral standards that are identified through democratic processes (see Habermas, 1983/1990; McLaughlin, 1992). The task for students is to apply public standards of morality to make collective decisions that improve the campus community. The message to students is that their humanity is inextricably linked to the quality of their public lives. For guidance, students are provided with copies of documents that articulate the rights and responsibilities of students. The teacher advocates for the virtuous campus community and the virtues of students as a whole and presents reasons, logic, and evidence to support civic virtues and the public good. Civic virtue is a disposition on the part of students to act on behalf of the student university community while being considerate of the rights and welfare of individuals.

We provide students with experiences in creating democratic communities. They elect class officers and establish norms for appropriate behavior. Students are expected to take their role as citizen in the democratic process seriously and prepare questions or comments for their web site, make presentations at town meetings, and act as class officers.

Social Morality and Citizenship in a Pluralistic Society

Our first course in citizenship education provides opportunities for students to make collective decisions about cases in which their peers are accused of infringing on the rights and welfare of others. In their small groups, they make decisions about the merits of a case and formulate their recommendations.

The course began in September 1993 with approximately 60 students. Initially, they heard lectures on community, democracy, and social morality and then met in small groups to discuss the content of the lectures and their readings. The feedback suggested that the course was too "abstract" and "alien" to their life experiences. They could not recognize how the concept of the public good should influence discussions about issues of public morality on campus. Consequently, we restructured the course to provide experiences in democratic living and collective decision making about real issues of public morality that have arisen on the campus.

Students are given reports that describe people who have been accused of violating the campus code of conduct. The cases are real, but the identifying data is removed. They answer the following questions:

1. Were the standards for student conduct violated in this case? What were they?
2. Were these standards known and agreed upon by all of the parties in the case?
3. What were the consequences of the actions described in the case?
4. What, if any, obligations or responsibilities were not met? By whom?
5. Did persons in the case intend to violate the rights and/or the welfare of others?
6. Should the case be resolved through mediation or arbitration?
7. What criteria did you use to judge the actions of the students in the case? State your recommendations and your rationale.

Students meet as campus ethics committees to develop these recommendations. Peer discussion leaders provide information, offer suggestions, and identify sources of information regarding the issues in the case. In a town meeting of the whole class, these committees present their recommendations, then vote and have opportunities to introduce amendments. At the conclusion, they adopt a set of recommendations that reflect the consensus of the town meeting. Faculty and administrators provide feedback about the process used in the town meeting.

One case that garnered interest among students occurred when a male undergraduate football player sexually assaulted a female undergraduate. The football player had arrived at the woman's suite with her suitemate after being out at local bars that evening. The woman's suitemate left him and two of his friends while she assisted another friend who was ill in the bathroom. The man entered the woman's bedroom, approached her bed, and proceeded to kiss and fondle her. She awoke afraid and confused, with the man climbing on top of her. She told him to get out of her room and went to an adjoining room and told her version of the events. The next morning, she reported the incident to residence hall staff and initiated a judicial referral charging the man with sexual assault and sexual harassment.

Through the process of collecting information, discussing the central issues, and describing how the students and the campus community were affected, students in their ethics committees were asked to assume the role of a citizen judging the severity of the events and to suggest appropriate responses.

Social Responsibility and Citizenship in a Pluralistic Society

Our second course in the moral education of citizens deals with issues that involve a conflict between individual rights and the common good. These range from destruction of public areas on campus to cases in which a multinational corporation is accused of destroying natural resources in the state.

Students learn about two characteristics of socially responsible citizens. The first is their moral sensitivity, or their ability to consider the impact of anticipated actions on the rights and welfare of individuals and the community. These citizens are able to interpret situations in their public lives in terms of possible actions, their impact on the community, and how others might react to the outcomes of different actions (Rest, 1983). An important part of moral sensitivity is altruistic caring that is based on a sense of empathy for others (Batson, 1990). When empathy for others is low, our actions are more likely to reflect self-interest rather than the interest of others. Still, moral sensitivity or empathic concern does not always lead to responsible actions (Rest, 1983).

To promote higher levels of moral sensitivity and empathic concern, we use texts that describe individual differences in the life stories of citizens from different racial and ethnic groups in the United States (see Vitz, 1990). Students also see films and read research that question the validity of stereotypes about citizens and provide an understanding of individual differences within ethnic and racial groups.

The second characteristic of socially responsible citizens is their social competence, or their ability to cooperate with others within a framework of democratic norms and laws. They respect the collective norms of a democratic, pluralistic society that permits them to live together and solve their common problems (Wentzel, 1991). But most of all, they are willing to actively engage in democratic processes and support the outcomes of those processes.

Students are divided into "campus study groups" that meet once a week under the direction of an undergraduate intern who facilitates discussions and makes sure that the group accomplishes the assigned tasks. Their first task is to define social responsibility and identify individual or group actions that compromise the rights or welfare of the community. We suggest that they focus their attention on those issues that involve conflicts between individual rights and the rights of the community.

Study groups identify specific standards of social responsibility based on their sense of public conscience. Then they report their recommendations to a forum meeting of the class as a whole. At this time, the class considers the merits of the reports and makes recommendations that lead to a consensus of the class.

In their campus study groups, students examine four questions:

1. How is social responsibility defined on this campus and by whom? What are examples of individual and collective perspectives on social responsibility?
2. Are there good reasons to believe that increasing the level of social responsibility on campus would improve the quality of campus life

as well as positively affect relationships among students from different ethnic groups?

3. Which standards would you use to assess the present level of social responsibility on campus? What are the major issues regarding social responsibility on this campus?

4. What kinds of programs and/or activities would promote socially responsible citizenship on the campus? Design either a classroom or out-of-classroom program that would encourage socially responsible citizenship on campus.

This class also uses a moral discussion format (Lind, 2000) that aims to improve the quality of reasoning about pro and con positions. Students study issues of campus morality in which the rights of individuals were in conflict with the rights of the campus community. A very dramatic incident involved an emotionally disturbed student who entered a classroom with a gun, holding the students and professor hostage for more than an hour. A group overcame the student holding the gun, and he fired a bullet into the groin of one of the students. He and his family later sued the university for damages. They lost their case. The court ruled that "the state was not an insurer or guarantor of the safety of students and had no legal duty to shield students from the criminal actions of others or to prevent such attacks."

The study groups were asked the following questions:

1. What is the proper role of each of the key actors involved in this incident?

2. Was the safety and security of the public threatened by the actions of the culprit?

3. Does the state have any obligation to support the collective actions of the students and provide reimbursement for damages that they may have suffered?

Evaluations of the Courses

We have relied on two strategies for evaluating these courses. The first compares changes in different aspects of personal development relevant to the goals of the course. We examined changes in such factors as tolerance, empathy, support for democratic norms, and self-esteem (Avery, Bird, Johnstone, Sullivan, & Thalhammer, 1992; Bryant, 1982; Rosenberg, 1965; Sullivan, Piereson, & Marcus, 1982). Of these, we found changes in tolerance at the conclusion of the course. The effect size (Cohen's d) for the increase in tolerance was .75, $p < .001$.

Our primary evaluation strategies have asked whether level of participation or identification with the course was positively related to students' satisfaction and their estimate of gains. We look at involvement as both participation in course activities and identification with the course (for a discussion of involvement as both participation and identification, see Finn, 1989). We predicted that those students who get more involved by taking notes, listening to what people had to say, actively engaging in discussion, and identifying with the goals of the courses would experience more satisfaction and report learning more in the classes. We asked three questions regarding the relationship of involvement to course satisfaction and gains from these classes.

Question 1: How Satisfied Were Students with Their Experiences in These Courses and What Did They Gain from Them? Data were collected over six semesters and included more than 600 students. Each semester, 75% to 80% reported that they were satisfied with the courses as a whole, and a similar percentage reported that they gained from them (75% to 80%). Students were most satisfied with the topics they discussed, small-group discussions, and opportunities to present their views. They gained most in their ability to form their own views; to see similarities, differences, and relationships among people; to function as members of teams; and to get along with others. Since we stress cooperation, collective activities, and interdependence, we have been pleased that students report gains in these areas. Given the importance placed on conversation and dialogue in moral education (Berkowitz & Gibbs, 1983; Noddings, 1994; Chapter 8, this volume), we find it particularly important that they were satisfied with the opportunities they had to present and discuss their views.

Question 2: What Is the Relationship between Student Level of Involvement and Evaluations of the Courses? Students were more likely to participate in small- rather than large-group discussions, and they often listened to what others had to say. They tried to see how facts or ideas fit together and to identify practical applications in their daily lives. They were less likely to take notes, make outlines, or do additional readings.

Throughout the years of our data collection, involvement has been the best predictor of students' satisfaction and estimate of gains from these courses. Depending on how it is measured, involvement explains between 12% and 25% of the variance in students' satisfaction and estimate of gains. When we combine multiple ways of assessing it, involvement explains up to 50% of the variance in course satisfaction and estimate of gains (contact the authors for data).

Question 3: What Experiences or Characteristics of Students Were Related to Their Involvement in the Courses? We assume that those students who are more strongly identified with these courses and those who are more active participants will be more satisfied and feel that they gained more from them. Highly involved students were more apt to be younger female students with higher levels of self-esteem. They were more apt to have friends from diverse backgrounds and to have more frequent conversations about issues of diversity.

CONCLUDING COMMENTS

What is private morality? Ask college students this question and you will get a host of answers. Some will say it is the same as a person's religious beliefs. Others will suggest that it is how we treat each other. Still others may say it is what one does while no one is looking. Ask a slightly different question—"What is public morality?"—and you get puzzled looks! In the United States, with its historic commitment to individualism, citizens don't often think about the public consequences of their behaviors. Still, citizens in this country are faced with serious issues involving public morality in their daily lives, and educators need to prepare future citizens to make decisions that protect the quality of the public spaces and institutions in their communities.

We believe that students need experiences that prepare them to cooperate with others in defining standards of public morality. Our courses challenge students to make collective decisions about controversial moral issues on a college campus. They study cases in which students are accused of impinging on the rights of others or the rights of the campus community. They learn to use democratic procedures to make collective decisions about which standards of good citizenship have been violated and what should be the consequences for the student. We learned that students recognize the problems of public morality but think that it is not the responsibility of ordinary citizens to resolve them.

This chapter tells the story of a journey from "multiculturalism" and our initial attempts to better prepare students to live in a pluralistic society to our most recent attempts to prepare students to be good citizens of such a pluralistic society. Good citizens are morally decent persons who understand our common social contract and advocate for the values it reflects. They take responsibility for the quality of the moral climate of their campus, city, state, and nation.

Good citizens do not tolerate conditions in their public lives that rob anyone of their inalienable rights as Americans. They are outraged when the rights or welfare of others are abused because they do not want to live in a community in which such actions are acceptable. We believe that our students are more apt to become good citizens when they assume their responsibility for the moral climate of their campus. If we want them to be citizens who can improve the moral climate of cities, we must provide them with opportunities to learn the skills they will need to do so.

We would like to close the chapter by listing some practical tips for others who may want to go where we have gone. We do so with the caveat, found in most other chapters in this volume, that a quick-fix or cookie-cutter approach to improving intergroup relations does not exist. Moreover, development is more likely a result of an accumulation of diverse personal and instructional experiences than one "magic bullet" (Astin, 1996; Pascarella & Terenzini, 1991). What are needed are multiple approaches that are guided by research and grounded in sound theory. With that said, here are some hurdles we encountered along the path from multiculturalism to the moral education of citizens and what we did to get over them.

1. *Hurdle A*: Students would talk about democracy but did not know how to make it a part of their class. *Resolution*: We simplified the task of creating democratic structures by focusing on concrete and recognizable aspects of democracy, such as electing class officers, debating proposals, voting to identify support for a proposal, and so on.
2. *Hurdle B*: During debates, students would often arrive at a roadblock, which occasionally led them to attack persons rather than arguments. *Resolution*: We enforced class rules regarding personal attacks and suggested alternatives for how elected officials could resolve the difference through negotiation or mediation. We did not resolve the problem for the students.
3. *Hurdle C*: Students would often debate issues but not come to a decision about what to do. *Resolution*: We coached the elected officials and discussion leaders to push the group to recommend actions and vote on them.
4. *Hurdle D*: Discussion leaders were not prepared to cooperate with each other or to lead democratic discussions. *Resolution*: We required a course in peer teaching. It included workshops on team building, discussion of moral dilemmas, and democratic decision making.
5. *Hurdle E*: Students were "bored" discussing cases that were not "real" to them. *Resolution*: We gathered real-life cases that involved intergroup relations on campus and invited officials of the university into the classes to hear students' analysis of them and to respond to their recommendations.

Other educators will encounter different hurdles and different configurations of obstacles to effective teaching. But we think the broad outlines of our general approach will be useful for many educators in many settings. This approach undertakes the moral education of citizens by transforming the classroom into a pluralistic community in which citizens organize their problem-solving experience through democratic participation. They (and we) try to practice what we teach, and by practicing democratic decision making, we learn from one another.

Chapter 10

The Brandeis Initiative in Intercommunal Coexistence: A Multifaceted, Comprehensive Approach to Improving Intergroup Relations

Cynthia Cohen
with Marci McPhee

> I believe that coexistence will not flourish on campus unless we undertake activities that involve every segment of our campus community. It is not just about research, or training, or conferences. Coexistence education develops capacities among faculty, students, and staff. It looks inward as well as outward, focusing on coexistence issues in our own community as well as learning about conflicts in Sri Lanka and Sierra Leone. At Brandeis University, "coexistence" involves a comprehensive approach to learning and action.
>
> —From a speech by Brandeis University President Jehuda Reinharz, November 1999.

Coexistence, as understood within the Brandeis Initiative in Intercommunal Coexistence, refers both to a quality of intergroup relations and an approach to improving them. To understand coexistence, it helps to imagine relationships between groups falling on a continuum that ranges from genocide, sustained oppression, and violence to harmonious relations, reconcilia-

Education Programs for Improving Intergroup Relations. ISBN 0-8077-4459-X (paper). Prior to photocopying items for classroom use, please contact the Copyright Clearance Center, Customer Service, 222 Rosewood Drive, Danvers, MA, 01923, USA, telephone (978) 750-8400.

tion, and cooperation. Coexistence at its most minimal level refers to that point on the continuum where violence has ceased and parties accord each other the most basic, even if begrudging, respect. It also embraces all of the points beyond—greater understanding, empathy, and cooperation. Recognizing that relations between groups can as easily cascade backward toward violence as inch forward to recognition of interdependence, we believe that sustainable coexistence requires increasing former enemies' capacities to understand each other's suffering and to address inequities in their relationship.

This chapter describes the methods we use to promote the theory and practice of coexistence, both at Brandeis and with partners throughout the world. These methods include activities familiar in university settings—courses, seminars, student internship programs, public events, fellowships, and research projects—as well as less conventional formats such as conversation groups, oral history projects, concerts, residencies, and collaborative projects in historically divided communities. The chapter describes the Initiative when it had been up and running for 2 years, and it has been fascinating to watch its various segments unfold. Coexistence has now become a permanent part of Brandeis's curriculum and community life, with ongoing efforts in research and international collaborations, an expanded undergraduate program, and a master's program scheduled to begin in the fall of 2004.[1]

THE PROGRAM AT A GLANCE

In 1999, with support from the Alan B. Slifka Foundation, Brandeis launched a 3-year Initiative in Intercommunal Coexistence (BIIC), a program of the International Center for Ethics, Justice and Public Life. The Initiative is designed to engage students, faculty, and staff in the theory and practice of coexistence. We also hope to provide leadership to the emerging professional field by linking practitioners and scholars so they can jointly develop and disseminate new and useful knowledge. In so doing, we build on the university's long-standing traditions of academic excellence and commitment to social justice.

The Initiative is comprised of three strands of work:

- *Strand 1*: Engaging the university faculty in developing scholarly approaches to the emerging field of coexistence
- *Strand 2*: Enhancing coexistence within the university community through an on-campus project designed to strengthen intergroup relations
- *Strand 3*: Promoting international partnerships and collaborations

We seek opportunities to link these strands of work in a mutually reinforcing relationship. In general, our approach emphasizes the role of the arts and humanities in coexistence theory and practice, and focuses on the ethical challenges inherent in efforts to improve intergroup relations. Another important component of our work includes rigorous quantitative and qualitative evaluation, particularly of the on-campus project, which will contribute knowledge about assessment that will be useful to the field of coexistence. This chapter focuses on those aspects of each strand that are most useful to readers interested in programs to improve intergroup relations. We have emphasized strand 2, the on-campus project, as it deals directly with related issues.

The Contexts That Inform Our Goals

The approach of the BIIC emerged from the historical and institutional contexts of Brandeis and the world in which we live. The Initiative responds to the worldwide rise in intrastate ethnic conflict, especially to the increase in nongovernmental initiatives designed to prevent and transform the violent expression of those conflicts. In places as widespread as Boston and Sarajevo, Jerusalem and Cape Town, Belfast and Colombo, teachers, journalists, clergy, artists, and recreation workers find themselves designing programs to reduce stereotypes and help former enemies discover the humanity of their adversaries, sometimes with little or no training.

The BIIC grew out of a recognition of the need for theory that is both informed by and can strengthen the methods used by these coexistence practitioners. Our intention is to create opportunities for cross-regional sharing and critical reflection. We have begun, in modest ways, to facilitate such processes and to bring the questions and insights of scholars and practitioners into generative relationship.

The Initiative also stems from the unique questions about coexistence that arise at Brandeis. A nonsectarian university founded by the American Jewish community, Brandeis has a commitment to social justice rooted in the legacy of our namesake, Supreme Court Justice Louis Brandeis. The university's dual commitment—to its Jewish roots and to pluralism—makes it a unique laboratory for exploring questions of majority/minority relations. A formerly oppressed Jewish minority assumes the status of majority within this institution, with the privileges and responsibilities associated with organizational leadership and power. We are hopeful that addressing majority/minority relations in this nonsectarian Jewish-sponsored university in America may result in insights that will be of use to Israelis who are grappling with the paradoxes of governing a state that strives to maintain its character as both Jewish and democratic. These insights are applicable in other institutions and societies addressing majority/minority issues.

Within Brandeis, the Initiative is a program of the International Center for Ethics, Justice and Public Life. The Center exists to illuminate the ethical dilemmas and obligations inherent in global and professional leadership, with particular focus on the challenges of racial, ethnic, and religious pluralism. Its programs, publications, and projects have several underlying principles that are also hallmarks of the work of the Initiative: bridging scholarship and practice, integrating the perspective of the arts, focusing on the ethical dimension of theory and practice, and involving a variety of academic perspectives in an interdisciplinary way.

Goals

Informed by these historical and institutional contexts, the Initiative has several goals:

- Develop a solid and sophisticated academic approach to the coexistence field through interdisciplinary faculty involvement in teaching, research, creative work, and reflective practice
- Enhance the coexistence-related capacities of Brandeis students by engaging them in coursework, campus activities, and field placements
- Strengthen intergroup relations at Brandeis while generating knowledge about the effectiveness of coexistence practices by implementing specific coexistence projects within the Brandeis community
- Initiate a long-term research project on the impact of this campuswide coexistence initiative on students and the campus community
- Enhance specific coexistence efforts around the world through partnerships between the university and community-based groups in several countries
- Promote the emergence of the field of "coexistence" nationally and internationally as a legitimate focus for interdisciplinary scholarship and creative inquiry.

Unique Qualities

The BIIC benefits from the intellectual resources and the articulated values of the university. Projects are informed by diverse disciplinary perspectives and by the imaginative energy of our students. Even among other programs based in academic institutions, we are unique—if not by virtue of each of the following elements, then certainly by virtue of their combination into one initiative:

- Our focus on coexistence as a conceptual framework (as distinct from conflict resolution/transformation, peace studies, diversity training, or multicultural education)
- Our simultaneous commitments to the development of theory and practice in interdisciplinary, cross-cultural perspective
- Our commitment to engage with issues of intergroup relations in conflict regions throughout the world and on campus
- Our emphasis on the arts and humanities
- Our focus on the ethical dimension of coexistence practice, addressing especially ethical challenges and tensions as experienced by practitioners

These qualities define the Initiative. However, we believe that any institution could develop a rich program by combining theoretical work with practical application and by addressing local issues and linking them to conflict regions internationally. Most programs would be strengthened by creating space to address ethical issues as they arise in the practice of coexistence work and by incorporating the arts.

STRAND 1: DEVELOPING SCHOLARLY APPROACHES TO COEXISTENCE

How does an institution develop a coherent approach to an emerging professional field whose boundaries and principles are still evolving? It was tempting at first to prescribe a set of definitions and practices that would become hallmarks of "the Brandeis approach." However, coexistence theories and practices are filled with rich conceptual, ethical, and pragmatic questions and dilemmas. Brandeis has a 50-year tradition of critical, interdisciplinary inquiry. So we began by working toward consensus among the faculty on overarching questions and principles through a year-long planning process in 1998, before we made any extensive commitments to program development. These principles, articulated in a planning document presented to the president of the university, include commitments to reflective practice, cross-cultural perspectives, integration of theory and practice, interdisciplinarity, and attention to the ethical dimension.

Following this planning process, we were able to secure financial support for the Initiative for 3 years (1999–2002), with a strong possibility for longer-term funding after the initial period. We decided to focus many of our initial resources on programs and courses that invited students, faculty, staff, and affiliated practitioners to bring their intellectual and creative resources to bear on questions that are among the most challenging in the field. These questions include: how to address the need for justice without fueling cycles of violence and revenge, how to respect different cultures' value systems without falling into the trap of relativism, and how to maintain a realistic view of prospects for peace without losing a sense of hope.

Faculty Seminar Series

During its first year, the Initiative sponsored a seminar series to examine the key concepts, values, and beliefs embedded in both human rights and conflict resolution paradigms. In conflict regions throughout the world, human rights advocates and peace-workers using methods of conflict resolution often find themselves at odds. Some human rights activists suspect that those engaged in conflict resolution are inattentive to concerns about justice; some advocates of conflict resolution see human rights activists as self-righteous and unnecessarily adversarial.

Members of the Brandeis faculty and administration participated in seminars with distinguished scholars and practitioners who brought to our inquiry perspectives from jurisprudence, philosophy, theology, sociology, and folklore; as well as from coexistence practice in Africa, Asia, Europe, and the United States. To illustrate the dynamic conversation that took place in this faculty seminar series, listen in on this brief interchange between Martha Minow, Harvard Law School professor and author of *Between Vengeance and Forgiveness*, and Jane Hale, Brandeis faculty member:

> *Martha Minow:* Some say if the victimized forgives, it can start the chain [of repentance] for the perpetrator. That is too much to ask. Why should the victim have this new burden—to have this extraordinary capacity to let go of resentment or to include the other?

> *Jane Hale:* "Letting go of resentment" and "forgiveness" are not synonyms. If we understand resentment as from the French word *ressentir,* it means "to feel again." If I have resentment, I am hurting myself. I am feeling what the perpetrator did, and that is what I need to let go of. Between forgiveness and vengeance there is a point of letting go of the resentment. You are not hurting yourself anymore, and you are not letting the perpetrator hurt you.

This theme was developed in faculty seminars led by African peace-builder Dr. Hizkias Assefa and human rights journalist Michael Ignatieff. Assefa argued that forgiveness should be understood as a decision on the part of a victim to let go of bitterness, distinct from any assessment of the perpetrator's moral trustworthiness or degree of repentance. Ignatieff challenged faculty members to acknowledge the positive dimension of revenge, however problematic it is in perpetuating cycles of violence. Unlike forgiveness, revenge can be understood as an expression of loyalty to the memory of lost loved ones and comrades. Related questions about addressing past abuses and injustices are weaving themselves into subsequent research projects, courses, colloquia, and collaborative projects in historically divided communities.

Support for Coexistence Research

In addition to the faculty seminar series, eight professors were given modest support to conduct research projects that bring the resources of their disciplines to bear on questions central to the field of intercommunal coexistence. The projects emerged from the disciplines of biology, fine arts, Near Eastern and Judaic Studies, philosophy, politics, sociology, and sustainable development. These research projects are contributing to publications, new courses and modules, a video dialogue project, and an art exhibition.

Courses and Related Campus Events

In a university, courses are a primary site for engaging students in the development and organization of knowledge. At Brandeis, we have been refining a fundamental course, Introduction to Coexistence, for several years. During the second year of the Initiative, the course was redesigned to incorporate a six-session international documentary film series entitled *Moving Pictures: Framing Coexistence*. Classes were public events, with the campus community attending these film screenings and participating in conversations about coexistence efforts in Sri Lanka, South Africa, the Middle East, the former Yugoslavia, and Northern Ireland. The series was designed to explore both the possibilities and limitations of documentary-making as a resource for coexistence education. Students from the class produced a web site based on the series.

Several courses related to coexistence were supported by the BIIC. Dr. Pumla Gobodo-Madikizela, former member of South Africa's Truth and Reconciliation Commission, offered an outstanding class, The Rupture of Silence: the Truth and Reconciliation Commission in South Africa, which examined memory and the language of trauma from the perspectives of victims, perpetrators, and bystanders of apartheid. Students viewed actual testimony presented to the Commission. In a public presentation, Gobodo-Madikizela described her first encounter with Eugene de Kock, the architect of some of the most brutal violence perpetrated by the apartheid regime:

When I asked him to tell me about the meeting with the women whose husbands were killed by a bomb put together through his instructions, his face immediately dropped. Sitting directly across from me, his heavy glasses on the table that separated us, he shifted his eyes uncomfortably. His feet shuffled, and I could hear the clatter of his leg chains. His mouth quivered, and there were tears in his eyes. As he started to speak his hand trembled, and he became visibly distressed. With a breaking voice he said, "I wish I could do more than just say I'm sorry. I wish there were a way of bringing their bodies back alive. I wish I could say, 'Here are your husbands.'" As he said this, the table between us seemed to collapse. And reaching to him the only way one does in such human circumstances seemed natural.

When I touched his clenched hand, it was cold and rigid. It felt as if he were holding back. This caused me to recoil for a moment and to reflect on the spontaneous act of humanity as something incompatible with a circumstance with a perpetrator of such serious atrocities. However, other than his clenched fist, I could find nothing incongruous between his show of emotion and my response.

I had held back tears but let go of them the moment I entered the car for the drive back to Johannesburg. I was angry, but it wasn't de Kock who was the object of my anger, but White people. Why did they continue to enjoy the fruits of apartheid and the oppression of Black people, instead of speaking out against it? Why did they allow humanity to be destroyed in the way that de Kock's was? That moment of shared humanity between de Kock and myself seemed to open up a window into the kinds of human possibility that would have been possible for de Kock had he not been brought up under a system that encouraged human corruption. Throughout the drive, frightened, angry, and confused, I blamed White society. I put myself in de Kock's shoes and turned his experience in my head over and over again, and wondered where I would be, had our roles been reversed.[2]

Conversation Groups

As an alternative to formal faculty seminars, we have experimented with the conversation group as a format for building a community of inquirers and engaging scholars and practitioners in questions related to coexistence. In the fall of our second year (2000), we convened a three-session conversation series to explore the relationship of art and aesthetics with coexistence and reconciliation. The impetus for this series was the preliminary research report from fine arts Professor Pamela Allara, a Fulbright Scholar who went to South Africa to document art related to post-apartheid reconciliation. She discovered that the new government's policy was to support cultural production (including crafts) as a form of economic development, rather than to fund art per se. She found that intergroup relations were characterized by a minimal form of coexistence rather than reconciliation. Members from Brandeis's philosophy department, English department, and the Center prepared papers responding to questions raised in her research. These papers became the basis for planning programs that will accompany an exhibition of South African artwork.

Residencies

Several outstanding scholars and practitioners have added their experience and perspective to this inquiry during residencies at Brandeis. Dr. Hizkias Assefa—scholar, author, mediator, and international peace-building practitioner—coordinates the African Peace-Building and Reconciliation Network in Nairobi and is a Distinguished Fellow at the Institute of Conflict Analysis and Resolution at George Mason University in Virginia. In November 1999, Assefa spent a week at Brandeis giving lectures, holding faculty seminars and student discussions, planning future publications, and working with local Eritrean/Ethiopian communities. His residency was entitled "Doing Justice *and* Loving Mercy: Perspectives on Coexistence and Reconciliation from an African Peacebuilder."

Dr. Lawrence Pitkethly, a documentary-maker and former BBC journalist originally from Belfast, Northern Ireland, spent 10 days at Brandeis in spring 2001. The highlight of his residency was the American premiere of *Belfast My Love*, Pitkethly's documentary film that highlights the voices of "ordinary citizens" of Belfast as they reveal the complexities of a society transforming itself from violence to coexistence and democratic decision making. Pitkethly worked with students on the web site related to filmmaking and coexistence, led a faculty seminar, visited classes, and met with various members of the Boston Irish community and others interested in ethnic conflict, coexistence, and documentary-making.

Jane Sapp, an African American singer, songwriter, educator, and cultural worker, has been doing coexistence work for many years in communities throughout the United States and abroad. She is a Senior Fellow at MIT's Center for Reflective Community Practice and leads several community choruses. She has worked with the Initiative in many ways, serving as consulting artist to the on-campus Coexistence Leadership Team, leading "community sings," performing in an on-campus concert, and providing intellectual and artistic direction to BIIC programs.

STRAND 2: ENHANCING COEXISTENCE
AT BRANDEIS UNIVERSITY

At Brandeis, we believe that for an institution to make a credible contribution to the professional and intellectual work of coexistence, it must also
be prepared to look inward. It must address the interethnic, interreligious,
and interracial possibilities and tensions within its own ranks.

Because of its simultaneous commitment to its Jewish roots and to pluralism, these questions are particularly compelling at Brandeis. About two-
thirds of the student body is Jewish, with significant international, minority,
and non-Jewish White American populations as well. At Brandeis we asked
ourselves: *How can the sense of community here be strengthened? How can
people make more meaningful connections across differences in religion, race,
and nationality? Can we find more constructive ways to deal with tensions
that seem to reside beneath the surface of our polite interactions?* We present
this as a case study in hopes that insights might be useful to others addressing intergroup relations in their own institutions.

Campus Coexistence Leadership Team: Year 1

In order to address these questions, the Initiative recruited a Campus
Coexistence Leadership Team. Although other programs on campus have
looked at various aspects of pluralism and diversity over Brandeis's 50-year
existence, the team was the first sustained effort involving faculty, staff, and
undergraduate and graduate students. A diverse core group of 16 members
was selected through a universitywide application process. Members of the
team represented different ethnic backgrounds, religious traditions, and roles
within the university.

Members of the team made a 2-year commitment, meeting weekly from
December 1999 through May 2000, starting with a weekend retreat to im-
merse themselves in the processes of creating relationships and building trust.
The group was joined by two facilitators, a consulting artist (Jane Sapp), an
independent evaluator, and a student coordinator. The primary activities of
the team included sharing life stories, creating artwork, and exploring the
dynamics within subgroups. In addition to working toward greater understanding of one another's experiences—both in the world at large and at
Brandeis—the group spent time envisioning the Brandeis they hoped for
and creating an action plan to make that future more likely.

Through the methods of oral history and artistic exploration, the team
worked toward building leadership capacities at the intrapersonal, interpersonal, and institutional levels. We emphasized *listening* as key to respectful

intergroup relations. We shared stories as a mode of personal reflection, a way of facilitating interpersonal communication, and a method of enhancing intercultural awareness. We used the arts to stimulate creativity and to generate imaginative ideas. And we explored issues of power to create an effective working group and to prepare members for working on majority/minority issues and questions of diversity on campus.

The character of the weekly meetings took on various configurations: meeting as an entire group, in pairs, in groups of Jews and non-Jews, and in subgroups separated according to position within the university. Members of the team collaboratively wrote a description of this process. The following are excerpts from this text:

> We listened to each other's stories. . . . Our stories affirmed that we are enriched by the particularities of each other's lives: the Irish lace that adorned the windows of a childhood family home; a mother's lessons for making Puerto Rican rice; the traditional "garb" worn as a child at home in Africa but kept locked in a suitcase here at Brandeis; the hand gestures and facial expressions that allowed for communication with an aging Jewish grandmother, even as she grew unable to speak. Coming to appreciate the particularities of each other's aesthetic inheritances led us to envision a Brandeis where people . . . could find places where they feel at home—where each distinct group can express and develop its own culture.

One member's story was particularly poignant, containing a reference that became the unifying symbol of the group. When he arrived from Senegal to begin his graduate studies at Brandeis, he brought his traditional African garb with him but left it locked in his suitcase. Although he seldom wore it, it gave him comfort to know he had it with him. He told his story:

> I always wore this big garb, the Fulani clothing.
> And my classmates always made fun of me.
> My mother would say, You're the first in the class,
> Why should you complain about your garb?
> When my father died, I learned more about him
> And the small case on the garb where he put his Koran.
> How do I fit into the Brandeis community?
> I can't lose my identity or myself
> I have my garb in my suitcase
> and I can take it out whenever I want.
> —Moussa Sow, Ph.D. student

Other members also felt that they had brought some treasured part of home that was kept safely locked away, either literally or figuratively. As the semester-long intensive process concluded, the team turned its attention from its own dynamics to developing an action plan for Brandeis.

Campus Coexistence Leadership Team: Year 2

During Initiative's second year (2000–2001), the Team engaged the university in its vision and worked with community members to catalyze institutional change.

"Building Community Through Songs of Social Justice" Implementing the action plan in the second year meant creating moments when a larger circle within the campus community could experience the "vision" for Brandeis's future. We focused on creating an event that would have an impact both far-reaching and deep. In January 2001 folksinger and activist Pete Seeger teamed up with Jane Sapp. Months of cross-cultural community-building work, using music as a means of bringing people together, culminated in a concert entitled "Building Community Through Songs of Social Justice: Pete Seeger and Jane Sapp in Concert."

The preparation began early in September, when participants from across the university came together for three "community sings" with Sapp. Students, faculty, staff, and children joined to sing songs of social justice. Participants shared songs from their own cultural heritage. New lyrics sprang from the group as they worked together to write verses responding to current injustices, sung to traditional tunes from the civil rights movement.

Members of the junior class responded to this opportunity, meeting with Sapp to write their own song. Three campus vocal groups—gospel, Jewish, secular—met with Sapp and Seeger to perform and discuss the meaning of music in their lives and their communities. During their 2-day residency, Seeger and Sapp met in small-group discussions with faculty and students to reflect on the use of music in community building across difference and on their own participation as artists and organizers in movements for social justice.

In honor of Seeger's residency, the vice president of human resources and member of the team coordinated an exhibition of images and stories, entitled "Faces of Work at Brandeis." Designed to honor the often-unseen workers at Brandeis, the exhibition was comprised of photographs and excerpts from oral history interviews with 15 workers about their backgrounds, work, Brandeis experience, and hopes for the university. During the opening reception, members of the Brandeis community honored the workers. A student who interviewed several of the workers commented, "Not all of the wisdom at this institution is spoken from behind a podium in front of a classroom."

The concert began with members of the team reading Sapp's poem "Can Brandeis Be This Place?" It concluded with Seeger singing one of his signature songs, "Turn, Turn, Turn," ending with the words "A time for peace/I swear it's not too late."

The buildup of all of these various events, culminating in the electrifying concert to a packed house of Brandeisians and friends, was an experience of connection across various boundaries of race, ethnicity, religion, and status in the university community. It allowed members of the university to experience, for a few moments, the team's vision of meaningful connection and an engaging public life.

"A Call to Conversation" The second major initiative undertaken by the team during its second year was to engage the campus community in a series of conversations about majority/minority relations on our campus. We initiated these discussions by issuing "A Call to Conversation," published as an insert in our campus newspaper. The call includes stories about how different members of the Brandeis community actually experience the university's simultaneous commitment to its Jewish roots and to pluralism:

- A student from East Africa shared her experience of going to the cafeteria for the first time after arriving on campus, only to be yelled at by several students not to mix food from the kosher kitchen with food from the nonkosher kitchen. "No, no, don't do that! Don't put that there: It's kosher!" She did not know what *kosher* meant and was too embarrassed to ask.
- A non-Jewish student spoke about how "empty and deserted" the campus felt during a major Jewish holiday. She wished she knew more about Judaism and she wanted to attend a Passover seder or Shabbat dinner.
- An Orthodox Jewish student empathized with the isolation that a non-Jewish student might experience on the Jewish holidays—but said that she would never invite someone who was not Jewish to a Shabbat dinner.
- During her 9 years as a Brandeis employee, an administrator had never been invited to a Jewish religious or cultural event. Several students asked her to come to the Purim party. Moved by their invitation, she thanked them profusely.
- Several minority students described incidents in which they believed that their professors, their White classmates, and other students of color related to them as less than fully qualified to be at Brandeis.
- A Jewish graduate student, sympathetic to the development of more inclusive social spaces on campus, hoped that non-Jewish members

of the Brandeis community would understand, in historical and cultural terms, the importance of an institution committed to the development of various strands of Jewish religious and communal life.

Using these stories and others as prompts, the "Call to Conversation" invites members of the university to address the tension between Brandeis's commitment to its Jewish roots and its commitments to diversity and pluralism. We are now in the process of convening small, relatively homogeneous conversations among student, staff, and faculty groups on campus to address these questions. We have chosen homogeneous groupings as a first step in order to create the context most conducive to honest discussion and self-reflection. Our intention is to extend this process to the point where people are able to address these issues honestly and openly in diverse groups—including in campuswide conversations. To this end, we are convening a series of facilitated dialogues or encounter groups, where key campus leaders work to deepen their understanding of majority/minority issues on campus and to enhance their own capacities to relate respectfully but openly across differences in religion, ethnicity, race, and economic class.

We undertake these actions in the belief that changes in the campus culture will result from many small efforts initiated from different locations within the university's social and institutional structure. We count on participants in the facilitated dialogues and the team to use their deeper understandings and insights to make policy changes from the positions they hold within the university.

Following the conversation groups and facilitated dialogues, we will share what we have learned with the university. We will present a more complete picture of how various groups within our community understand, experience, and envision Brandeis's simultaneous commitments to its Jewish roots and to pluralism and diversity. We are confident that over time, as people on campus understand more fully one another's hopes and fears, disappointments and vulnerabilities, intergroup relations will improve and will be supported by more nuanced institutional policies. Our hope is that Brandeis will continually seek more creative ways to address the tensions and possibilities inherent in its commitments to its Jewish roots and to pluralism.

Evaluation of Strand 2

The evaluation component of the project was initiated not only to gain insights about the effectiveness of the particular approaches used but also to contribute to the broader field of coexistence by assessing the impact of our methods and reflecting on the evaluation process itself.

Using a theory-based approach, we invited stakeholders to develop a model that demonstrates the relationships among *assumptions* about the problems relating to coexistence on campus, *activities* to address these problems, and *outcomes* from effectively carrying out the activities.

In order to address these questions, the evaluator is using several methods. During the first year, she attended all team meetings and took extensive notes; interviewed the facilitators and team members at different points in the year; collected information from advisory group members on coexistence; analyzed various student surveys; and collected information about other campus initiatives related to coexistence. In addition, the evaluator continues to gather campuswide data by surveying incoming students during orientation and assessing data generated from a survey of graduating seniors. Finally, our evaluator is working to establish a database of coexistence-related groups on campus. This effort assesses the climate, and we hope that it will also help organizations identify other groups on campus working toward similar goals.

Although the evaluation is still in process, examples from our preliminary findings may be useful. They derive from our attempts to answer three kinds of questions. The first set of questions relates to the current status of coexistence at Brandeis. This "baseline data" will be used to measure change in the quality of intergroup relations over time. We used surveys and focus groups to collect this information. We asked people to respond to statements such as: "I feel treated equally by others at Brandeis," "I feel comfortable expressing my true identity," "I felt judged or stereotyped by members of my own group," and "I participated in discussions related to getting along with people from different racial, ethnic, religious, or national backgrounds." We disaggregated responses to these statements by race and religion, and we uncovered some useful patterns. In response to the statement "I feel treated equally by others," 67% of Jewish seniors and 39% of non-Jewish seniors responded "very true" and 58% of White seniors and 34% of non-White seniors responded "very true." In another example, in response to the statement "I feel judged and stereotyped by members of my own group," 75% of Jewish freshmen and 60% of non-Jewish freshmen and 69% of White freshmen and 62% of non-White freshmen responded "very true."

In addition to using baseline data to assess change over time, we are also using it to answer a second set of questions: How can we improve the Initiative as it progresses? For instance, because these data suggest that religion is a more salient factor than race in students' feelings of comfort at Brandeis, we have fashioned a series of dialogues to focus on Jewish/non-Jewish relations here, with race being addressed as an integral secondary issue. We have also used other methods to assess the program, including interviews with participants and observational notes on sessions. The insights gained through these methods allowed us to restructure the campus project during its third year. For instance, it was very difficult for the team, as a mixed group of students, administrators, and faculty, to implement group projects due to scheduling conflicts. However, we discovered that members integrated their learning into their other roles at Brandeis. Therefore, in the third year of the project, we facilitated separate dialogue groups for students, faculty, and administrators. In these groupings, the interreligious and inter-racial issues can be engaged without the distraction of differences based on university status, allowing the group to go deeper into majority/minority relations. We also chose participants based in part on their ability to cata-lyze institutional change by incorporating insights from the dialogue pro-cess into the programs they design in their ongoing campus leadership roles. Thus the project's impact on the larger campus community is not dependent on additional projects conducted by this group.

We are using data gathered from the evaluation to help answer ques-tions addressing the range of perceptions that exist about intergroup rela-tions at Brandeis: How do different members of our community perceive and experience Brandeis's simultaneous commitment to its Jewish roots and to pluralism? How would they like Brandeis to manifest its commitments to these two imperatives in the future? What sorts of resistance do members of the community express to addressing these questions and to making change? These are the central questions of the on-campus part of the initiative. We are addressing them by analyzing transcripts of conversations and dialogues, data from surveys, and our notes documenting the process itself. We intend at the culmination of the initiative to present to the Brandeis community a complex picture of itself based on what we have elicited, seen, and heard.

Complexities Encountered Activating Strand 2

The complexities of working on coexistence issues on campus emerged immediately. The first challenge was to recruit a diverse team from across the university that could make the intensive, unpaid 2-year commitment necessary to undertake this kind of project. Unfortunately, the time commit-ment precluded many strong leaders on campus from applying. Also, fac-ulty and staff preferred meeting at different times than did students.

Particular challenges emerged in creating trust among the diverse group. On a small campus, such a mixed group contains hierarchical relationships, making personal connections awkward. The dynamics of power related to status demanded ongoing attention that sometimes superseded the core is-sues of racial, religious, and ethnic differences that the group was designed to address. Members of the group found it challenging to be vulnerable to each other at the level that was required for the sharing of life stories. Once this level of trust was achieved—and it was achieved—it became difficult for the group to refocus its attention away from the personal onto campus issues to develop an action plan.

Furthermore, Brandeis includes subgroups that are not particularly interested in strengthening intergroup relations. Some team members faced pressures from their own communities for participating in this project. Many institutions have a strong cultural norm against direct expressions of conflict or acknowledgment of differences. We encountered resistance in convening homogeneous groups identified by religion, race, or ethnicity—both within the team itself and across campus. Resistance to confronting these painful issues can be found within individuals, group, and institutions. At Brandeis this resistance was most strongly expressed when the team divided into Jewish and non-Jewish subgroups. The painful history of anti-Semitism was evoked for both Jews and non-Jews. Members feared that the trust they worked so hard to establish would be undermined.

Addressing these instances of resistance effectively requires tact, persistence, and insight. This is especially important when attempting to facilitate change in an institution of which one is a part. The Initiative simultaneously seeks to secure support for all three strands of its work while challenging the community to engage in conversations that are uncomfortable. Through the persistence and courage of members of the team, we have been able to address these issues productively in small-group settings. As we write this chapter, we are working to use these insights to engage the community as a whole. Time will tell whether we have been able to address these challenges in a way that will enable Brandeis to grapple productively with coexistence issues. Ultimately, we hope to learn how to address majority/minority relationships in constructive ways and to document that learning for use in divided societies worldwide.

STRAND 3: NATIONAL COLLABORATIONS AND INTERNATIONAL PARTNERSHIPS

The Initiative cultivates collaborative relationships with scholars and practitioners in the United States and internationally. These relationships are sustained through fellowship programs, exchanges, joint projects, and correspondence.

The Ethics and Coexistence Student Fellowship

Now in its fourth year, the Ethics and Coexistence Student Fellowship is a program jointly administered by the BIIC and the Center. The program provides Brandeis undergraduates with support for summer internships in grassroots coexistence organizations in the United States and abroad. In summer 2000 we identified internship sites in partner organizations with which we are building lasting relationships.

The program consists of three phases. After being selected through a competitive application process, students take Introduction to Coexistence, a spring-semester course introducing them to key coexistence concepts and practices. Fellows spend at least 8 weeks working in grassroots coexistence organizations over the summer. In the fall, students complete an independent study with a mentor, integrating their internship experience and academic studies. The mentorship experience, designed primarily to enhance student learning, also allows us to connect with faculty members throughout the university, engaging them in coexistence questions and issues.

Nikki Evans wrote a particularly introspective reflection during her internship during the summer of 2000 in South Africa:

> I've come to realize that my status as an American or as Black here isn't as important as my being both Black *and* American. Black South Africans first recognize me as a Black person like them, who also happens to be American. For White South Africans, it is different: They connect with me as an American who also happens to be Black. I like the first one better, because this is one of the few times in my life where I feel this comfortable in my Black skin. However, I can't deny the privileges that my American status awards me—an oceanfront apartment, certain financial security, and a more tolerant attitude among White people when they hear my accent. Funny, I used to always talk about privilege as something that is so removed from my life, but now I must face the fact that simply because of my citizenship, I am ahead of most Black people living here. I am not sure how I feel about this.

Like Evans, many Student Fellows come home with more questions than answers. But they return with horizons expanded, minds stretched, and their commitment to coexistence strengthened.

Since the program's inception in 1998, 20 undergraduates have worked in Argentina, Bosnia-Herzegovina, Bulgaria, China, Ecuador, Israel, Gambia, Grenada, Mozambique, Northern Ireland, the Palestinian Territory, Pakistan, South Africa, Tanzania, and the United States. Four Fellowship alumni have won Hart Fellowships from Duke University, and one alumna is a Truman Fellow.

The "ripple effect" of the Student Fellowship experience is felt throughout the campus. Each student gives a campus presentation on his or her work in the fall, sharing dilemmas as well as learnings. The students become campus resources. Several Fellows served as panelists in the sessions for the international documentary film series *Moving Pictures: Framing Coexistence.*

Brandeis International Fellows

In 1998 the Center explored the theme "Coexistence and the Quest for Justice." The centerpiece of the exploration was the Brandeis International Fellows Program, in which 16 coexistence scholars and practitioners—from Sri Lanka, South Africa, the former Yugoslavia, and the Middle East—came to Brandeis for two institutes and conducted modest coexistence projects in their home regions between institutes.

We interviewed the Fellows to learn about the ethical questions and dilemmas they faced in their work. We are studying their narratives to create a set of teaching materials to be used in professional development workshops with coexistence practitioners. The following excerpts from their oral history interviews illustrate the topics we will address in these teaching materials:

• An Israeli Palestinian facilitator leads coexistence sessions with Israeli, Palestinian, and other Arab young people in a summer camp in the United States. Reflecting on his work, he asks: "Am I asking the occupied people to understand their occupiers? Yes, they have to understand them. They must understand their situation, and why they are so afraid, and what are their needs. But does this mean I am supporting the status quo? This is my dilemma."

• A Muslim Bosnian woman worked for an international aid agency setting up playrooms for Muslim, Croatian, and Serbian children traumatized during the war. Reflecting on that project, she says: "It was during wartime, and my dilemma was personal. Maybe some crazy person in my town would hear that I had worked in Serbska with some Croats, and who know what my future would be? I was asking, why am I risking my life? Why would I do that to myself?"

• The Sri Lankan Sinhalese media director of the National Peace Council is based in Colombo. He acknowledges the following dilemma: "When [my Tamil friend and colleague] talks, I get a sense of how the people in the Northeast feel. They will not grumble if the LTTE [Tamil Tiger organization] kills mayors, because they see these mayors as agents of the army, and the army is occupying them and they are fighting a war. I have a better sense of how people in the Northeast feel. But I have a problem if I tell this story to people in my office or family. They can't accept this, and get upset. They say that I'm supporting the LTTE, which to them is a very bad thing. But then I have to say, 'Those are the people we are trying to make peace with.'

I start losing my sense of what is acceptable, of what is right and what is wrong. That is the type of dilemma I face."

In keeping with the format successfully tested by the Center's ongoing Humanities and the Professions programs, we will link the Fellows' narratives with literature that examines similar ethical questions. Practitioners' stories and literature will be linked with essays drawing on scholarship in the field of moral philosophy to create teaching materials for professionals in day-long seminars, designed to support practitioners to reflect on ethical tensions and questions in ways that strengthen their practice.[3]

CHALLENGES WE FACE

The work of the BIIC is multifaceted and requires a varied set of skills and capacities, some of which appear to conflict with each other. One of the tensions involves linking the perspectives of scholars and practitioners. The work of a scholar involves reading, theory building, abstract thinking, writing; the energy required is reflective. The work of a practitioner involves action and interaction, coordination, and relationship building. The energy required is dynamic and engaged. It's difficult to meld the two in a complementary style. This tension is familiar to many people who reflect on their practice or who seek to generate theory based on experience in the field. But it is made more extreme in coexistence because both poles of this tension can be particularly demanding. The pole of scholarly work is highly interdisciplinary, drawing on fields as diverse as politics, theology, economics, and the arts. The pole of practitioner work addresses sensitive issues, often taking place in relation to violent conflict. Coexistence practice can incorporate elements of human rights advocacy, economic development, mediation, spiritual counseling, therapy, artistic expression, and journalism, as well as direct facilitation of encounters, dialogues, and exchanges.

Another source of tension for the BIIC is to sustain accountability to on-campus constituencies, professional relationships with Boston-area and national institutions, and an international network of community-based organizations. To simultaneously hold in view very different interests requires both intensive engagement and flexibility. In building the capacity of Brandeis and informing people about the field of coexistence, we've sought to work broadly throughout Brandeis, allowing depth of some projects and inquiries to suffer.

Many of the challenges inherent in this work stem from our status as a small, young effort with a large vision and broad mandate. Any one strand could be a full-time effort. Managing all three with a small staff requires careful judgment. The aim is to bring these strands together into synergistic relationship rather than competing for limited resources. When it works, the strands weave together beautifully and build on each other. When various facets of the project don't jibe, the work becomes scattered and overwhelming.

CONCLUSION

The BIIC, while unique, has many elements that are found in other programs designed to strengthen intergroup relations. Like other groups, we engage in interventions designed to facilitate communication across differences, to address painful histories, and to help diverse communities envision a more just future. We reflect on these interventions to generate new insights and use these insights as the basis for education, training, and publications. The institution in which we work, the students we teach, and the participants in our training and educational programs invite us to plan and conduct new interventions. And so cycles of action and reflection continue and develop.

For us, the usual cycle of action and reflection is shaped by our commitments to support scholarly work (strand 1), to improve intergroup relations on campus (strand 2), and to develop and strengthen meaningful international partnerships (strand 3). As we hoped, working with all three strands is revealing rich synergy.

It is our hope that this description of our work, our ideas for the future, and self-assessment of strengths and limitations will be useful to others involved in projects designed to strengthen intergroup relations.

NOTES

1. For updated information about the Alan B. Slifka Program in Intercommunal Coexistence, please visit http://www.brandeis.edu/coexistence. An archive documenting the 3-year Brandeis Initiative in Intercommunal Coexistence can be found at http://www.brandeis.edu/ethics/coexistence_initiative/index_archive.html.

2. See "Working with Integrity: A Guidebook for Peacebuilders Asking Ethical Questions" by Cynthia E. Cohen, available at http://www.brandeis.edu/ethics/publications_resources/index.html.

3. This story features centrally in Dr. Gobodo-Madikizela book *A Human Being Died that Night: A South African Story of Forgiveness*.

SCHOOL CONTEXTS AND PROGRAM EVALUATIONS

Part IV is quite distinct from the other sections of the book. And its four chapters are themselves also more distinct from one another. In the first three parts of this book we have been presenting descriptions of intergroup relations programs. By contrast, the authors of the following four chapters stand back from these programs and try to understand why they are needed, how effective they are, and why they work. Chapters 11 and 12 examine the condition of schooling, both cognitive and organizational; Chapters 13 and 14 systematically review what we know about program effectiveness.

In the first of these discussions, in Chapter 11, Patricia Avery and Carol Hahn review the results of a large-scale survey of the impact of civics education courses in middle schools. This nationally representative survey provides an indication of the status quo with respect to knowledge of diversity in our society. It also provides evidence about what intergroup relations programs can add to the basic knowledge that is already being conveyed in schools. In Chapter 12, Kenneth Cushner discusses organizational aspects of educational institutions that affect intergroup relations, including factors that facilitate positive relations and factors that hinder positive relations. Published studies on the effectiveness of intergroup relations programs are reviewed in Chapter 13 by Cookie White Stephan, Lausanne Renfro, and Walter Stephan. And the psychological processes that intergroup relations programs use to bring about changes in beliefs, attitudes, values, and behaviors are discussed by John Dovidio, Samuel Gaertner, Tracie L. Stewart, Victoria Esses, Marleen ten Vergert and Gordon Hodson in Chapter 14. Together, these four chapters provide readers with a greater understanding of what intergroup relations programs need to accomplish, the institutional obstacles that stand in the way of making progress in intergroup relations, the effectiveness of intergroup relations programs, and the processes responsible for their effectiveness. In the next several paragraphs, these chapters are previewed in more detail.

Avery and Hahn summarize the results of the Civic Education Study, a representative national survey of 14-year-olds that tapped their attitudes and knowledge regarding diversity and democracy. Related studies examined the content of civics textbooks and gathered information from teachers and students using focus groups. Avery and Hahn's basic premise in Chapter 11 is that an appreciation of diversity is essential to the functioning of democratic societies because it informs decisions concerning the common good. Their studies indicate, for instance, that while whole ethnic groups are frequently mentioned in civics texts, individuals from those groups are not. The result is that White, European males are the most frequently cited and discussed *as individuals* in these texts. The teachers reported that little attention was paid to Hispanics or Asian Americans in their civics courses. Many teachers also admitted feeling uncomfortable dealing with controversial issues related to diversity. Avery and Hahn find that students' "knowledge of diverse groups is episodic and incomplete." Their knowledge of other countries appears to be even sketchier. Nonetheless, the students' attitudes toward immigrants and women's rights are generally positive. Also, support for democratic principles in general is high, but it weakens where specific issues, such as the free-speech rights of groups that disagree with public opinion, are concerned.

Cushner, in Chapter 12, examines the organizational contexts in which intergroup relations programs function. An array of social-climate factors can make schools more or less hospitable to positive intergroup relations and to programs aiming to encourage them. Cushner organizes these social factors into those that hinder change in intergroup relations and those that promote it. Among the factors inhibiting change are, at the individual level, a lack of diversity among teachers and students and ethnocentrism among teachers. At the organizational level, barriers to changes that would improve intergroup relations include nondemocratic administrative practices, communities that are unreceptive to change, and within-school segregation. The author provides an equally impressive roster of factors that can lead to positive changes in intergroup relations. Among the most salient are strong leadership, sensitivity to the local community, clear policies that promote intergroup relations, staff training and support, effective role models, an emphasis on diversity across the curriculum, and a diverse faculty and administration. Cushner also stresses the importance of evaluation as a tool to monitor the effectiveness of change programs.

In Chapter 13, Stephan and her colleagues discuss the basic types of designs that can be used to evaluate the effectiveness of intergroup relations programs. Then they present a systematic analysis of 35 empirical studies of the effectiveness of intergroup relations programs. These programs varied from short term to longer term (a semester) and were conducted with students of different ages in various parts of the country. The results of these studies indicate that intergroup relations programs are generally moderately effective, but many do not fully achieve their goals. Both attitudes and behaviors were successfully changed in these programs, and there was some evidence that these programs produce relatively enduring changes. The multifaceted nature of most programs makes it difficult to determine what specific techniques are associated with the greatest success. It appears that many different types of programs can be successful and that success may depend as much on how the programs are presented as on the specific techniques that are employed. The authors end with a call for further research to facilitate the strengthening of intergroup relations programs.

Dovidio and his colleagues, in Chapter 14, examine and categorize the psychological processes responsible for reducing bias in intergroup relations programs. They argue that, although there are differences in technique and content, a number of common processes underlie change in such programs. They divide these processes into those that bring about enlightenment within individuals directly and those that produce change through the indirect processes associated with intergroup contact. After defining the nature of bias, they analyze a series of processes that underlie change. Among the cognitive processes leading to improvement are changing categorization processes, adding to social knowledge, and altering standards for intergroup behavior. Emotional processes include creating affective connections to other groups, reducing negative affect associated with other groups, and arousing self-directed negative affect concerning inappropriate intergroup cognitions and behavior. The authors also discuss the operation of these processes within various types of programs and review the implications of these findings about psychological processes for program design and evaluation.

Together these four chapters attempt to move from specific programs to a more general explanatory level. The authors discuss the "state of nature" (before interventions) in schools and catalogue what we know in general about how programs manage to alter the conditions that prevail in schools. Building on this general knowledge can help those designing or implementing programs to improve their chances of being effective.

Chapter 11

Diversity and U.S. 14-Year-Olds' Knowledge, Attitudes, and Experiences

Patricia G. Avery
Carole L. Hahn

This chapter draws from an international study on civic education to provide a picture of U.S. students' attitudes toward and experiences with diversity (Baldi, Perie, Skidmore, Greenberg, & Hahn, 2001; Torney-Purta, Lehmann, Oswald, & Schulz, 2001; Torney-Purta, Schwille, & Amadeo, 1999). The nationally representative sample of U.S. students helps us better understand the context within which programs to improve intergroup relations take place. The results of the International Association for the Evaluation of Educational Achievement's (IEA) Civic Education Study (CivEd) give us a picture of the varied experiences—planned and unplanned—students in the United States typically have that may influence their orientations toward diversity. Some students have presumably participated in anti-bias programs in their classes or extracurricular activities, but it is likely that many have not. In other words, in this chapter we ask: "What is the status of young people's orientations toward diversity today?"

Before we examine the CivEd results, however, it is important to consider the significance of students' attitudes toward diversity. That is, why is it important to study young people's orientations toward diversity? What difference does it make?

Education Programs for Improving Intergroup Relations. ISBN 0-8077-4459-X (paper). Prior to photocopying items for classroom use, please contact the Copyright Clearance Center, Customer Service, 222 Rosewood Drive, Danvers, MA, 01923, USA, telephone (978) 750-8400.

DIVERSITY AND DEMOCRACY

The most obvious answer to the question "What difference do young people's attitudes toward diversity make?" is that a society in which people are not hostile toward one another on the basis of differing ethnic backgrounds or religious beliefs, for example, is probably a safer, more "livable" society than is one in which groups are in constant conflict. Surely it is a worthy goal to create a society in which people live without biases against one another. More importantly, however, the level of active prejudice and discrimination in a society is intimately connected with the quality of that democracy. To the degree that citizens are unable to understand others' perspectives or think of the common good, democracy is in peril.

We believe that young people's orientations toward diversity is one indicator of the health of a democracy. First, democracies revolve around "majority rule with respect for minority rights." Kindergartners can quickly grasp the notion of "majority rule" (the choice with the most hands raised wins), but the concept of respect for the fundamental rights for all persons can be difficult for many adults to comprehend. What is to prevent the majority from denying the minority basic civil liberties? Would it be all right to vote on whether children of the Mormon faith can attend public schools? Presumably not, because the U.S. Constitution guarantees certain freedoms to all and acts to prevent tyranny of the majority. But the concept of fairness has evolved over time, and it is always fragile. There have been many times throughout U.S. history when basic civil liberties have been denied to groups—African Americans under slavery, Japanese Americans during World War II, and American Communist party members during the McCarthy era. Although the U.S. Constitution may protect citizens from some of the majority's intolerance, ultimately the sustenance of the democracy depends on the people's belief in a sense of fairness and the fundamental rights of the minority. Young people's attitudes toward differences—be they ethnic, national, cultural, or religious differences—therefore become a barometer of society's ability to withstand the capriciousness of the majority will.

The second way in which attitudes toward diversity affect the quality of a democracy lies in the degree to which individuals can engage in deliberation about significant public issues. Political philosopher Amy Guttman (2000) identifies deliberation as one of the primary ways in which citizens resolve conflicts, describing it as "public discussion and decision making that aim to reach a justifiable resolution, where possible, and to live respectfully with those reasonable disagreements that remain unresolveable" (p. 75). To engage in deliberation, citizens must be willing to suspend judgment and listen to perspectives other than their own. This requires an appreciation of the way in which diverse beliefs and perspectives enlarge one's understanding of public issues. As Guttman notes, it is desirable for voters to have engaged in careful deliberation and considered multiple perspectives on public issues.

The ability to adopt multiple perspectives is central to the ability to consider the "common good." This is the third reason young people's attitudes toward diversity are important to democracy. Americans are traditionally known for their sense of rugged individualism and their tendency to focus on their own self-interest. Every school system that has tried to pass a school bond referendum knows the difficulty of persuading adults who do not have children in the schools to support increased school funding, and hence higher taxes. The elderly couple that votes for the bond must have a sense of the common good. But if that common good is to extend beyond those with whom one shares much in common, citizens' conception of "community" must encompass those who differ from themselves in terms of race, ethnicity, religion, belief, and so on. Suppose, for example, the elderly couple is able to move beyond their own self-interest to support increased taxes for schools, but only insofar as those schools enroll children who look and believe as they do. It is virtually impossible to identify, much less support, the common good if one cannot assume the perspectives of those who differ from oneself.

How do young people's attitudes toward and experiences with diversity portend the strength of our democracy? Students' understanding of diversity is an indicator of the degree to which they will be willing to support minority rights, to engage in deliberation about public issues, and to consider the common good when making judgments about public issues. Each of these areas—minority rights, deliberation, and the common good—requires an appreciation of the way in which people of differing ethnicities, religions, colors, beliefs, and cultures contribute to democratic societies. With this in mind, we turn now to the CivEd study, one of the most recent and comprehensive attempts to capture young people's knowledge, attitudes, and experiences with diversity.

THE CIVED PROJECT

The CivEd project is a two-phase study designed to assess the way in which young people are prepared for their roles in a democratic society. The first phase of the study, conducted in the mid-1990s, culminated in narrative case studies that describe the status of civic education in each of 24 countries (see Torney-Purta et al., 1999). The description of civic education in the United States is based on a comprehensive literature review, a survey of 50 state curriculum specialists, focus groups with students and teachers, and civics and history textbook analyses (Hahn, 1999). The second phase of the study consists of the results of a survey administered to nationally representative samples of 14-year-olds in 28 countries, including the United States. The U.S. sample consisted of 2,811 ninth graders from 124 schools. Because the survey was developed for cross-national comparisons, it does not tap students' knowledge of specific institutions in the United States (e.g., How many senators represent one state in the U.S. Congress?) but assesses their understanding of essential democratic principles. Both phases of the CivEd study focus on three central concepts and sets of questions:

> *Democracy*: Given that democracy is a central concept, what does it mean in the national context, and what are young people expected or likely to learn about it by age 14 or 15? What do students learn about democratic institutions and the rights and responsibilities of governments?
>
> *National identity*: What are young people expected to or likely to have acquired as a sense of national identity or national loyalty by age 14 to 15? What are they likely to learn about relations with other nations and international organizations?
>
> *Diversity*: What are young people expected to or likely to have learned by age 14 to 15 about those belonging to groups that are seen as set apart or discriminated against (as defined, for example, by ethnicity, race, immigrant status, mother tongue, social class, religion, or gender)?

Items on the student questionnaire assessed five areas: civic content knowledge; civic skills; conceptions of democracy, citizenship, and government; attitudes toward civic issues; and political participation (experienced and expected). Although the CivEd study was concerned with a much broader area than diversity, diversity was a prominent theme. Many of the findings of the study—in the narrative case study in phase 1 and the student survey in phase 2—suggest a picture of students' experiences with and understanding of diversity.

The term *diversity* is often associated with race or ethnicity in the United States. The CivEd study, however, views diversity from several perspectives. Phase 1 consisted of a textbook analysis and focus group research. In the textbook study, the content of six of the most widely used U.S. history and civics texts for grades 7–9 were analyzed (Avery & Simmons, 2000/2001). Students and teachers participated in the focus groups, where issues of democracy and diversity were examined (Hahn, 1999). These two studies provide data specific to groups in the United States. However, because in phase 2 the same questionnaire items were used in all 28 countries, attitudes toward groups that might have special significance in one country (e.g., the Pakistanis in England, the Romany in the Czech Republic, the Sami in Norway, or African Americans in the United States) could not be included on the survey that was used across countries. As such, the survey assessed attitudes toward "immigrants," a "group" that is generally perceived as an "outsider" in every country. Students were also asked to share their attitudes toward women's political rights, another "group" that has traditionally been less powerful across countries.

Students can also be exposed to diversity by studying countries and governments other than their own; several clusters of items assessed students' interest in other countries as well as their exposure to information about other countries in school. Another set of items assessed students' support for a diversity of ideas as well as their understanding of its effect on democracy. Students were also asked about the way in which they *experience* a diversity of ideas in the classroom. To what degree does the classroom climate support students' expression of different viewpoints? Thus, we look at diversity in terms of ethnicity, immigrant status, gender, nations and governments, and ideas.

Ethnic Diversity

The textbook analysis and the teacher and student focus groups shed some light on what U.S. students learn about ethnic diversity in school. The textbook analysis suggested that while ethnic *groups* are often mentioned (e.g., African Americans, Chinese immigrants), *individuals* from ethnic-minority groups are much less likely to be mentioned. The individuals cited most frequently in the civics and history texts are White, European American males (Avery & Simmons, 2000/2001).

In the focus groups, most teachers and students reported that U.S. history courses included information on the treatment of Native Americans and African Americans under slavery and segregation as well as the civil rights movement. Few mentioned any attention to Hispanics or Asian Americans in U.S. history courses. One teacher in the Pacific Northwest explained:

> We usually start with our state history and discuss the people who populate our region. We discuss who was in our state first . . . we look at the Native Americans, and then we begin to look at the people who came later. . . . If we are talking about the building of railroads we discuss the arrival of the Chinese. When we talk about the expansion of our farmlands we discuss the Japanese arrival and involvement with the expansion. We talk about the arrival of African Americans into our region.

Several teachers said that they talked about discrimination against religious minorities in their history classes. The students in the focus groups made mention of that, but without elaborating. They were more likely to describe what they had learned about the treatment of Native Americans in the 1800s and about African Americans under slavery, during segregation, and in the civil rights movement. In one focus group in Texas, which contained several Mexican American students, students also cited discrimination against Mexicans.

In addition to learning about ethnic diversity in the context of U.S. history lessons, students in the various focus groups mentioned studying about discrimination in conjunction with Martin Luther King Jr.'s birthday and with Black History Month. The history education expert we interviewed echoed the students' observations. She said that in her research on students' historical understanding, by the end of eighth grade "all of the kids knew there was prejudice" and that "race, class, and gender were problematic" in the history of the United States.

None of the students in the focus groups mentioned specific extracurricular activities per se that contributed to their knowledge of diverse ethnic groups. Rather, most students reported that the act of participating in extracurricular activities with members of ethnic groups different from their own contributed to their understanding of ethnic diversity. This was especially true for students who attended schools in which members of ethnic-minority groups made up a substantial part of the student population. These personal experiences taught young people about diversity in the contemporary context while their history lessons taught them about social diversity in the past.

Overall, it seems that students learn about the contributions of some groups to the history of the nation and they are aware of inequities of the past and the present. However, their knowledge of diverse groups is episodic and incomplete. That is, they associate Native American experiences with the period of "the westward movement" and African Americans with segregation, rather than learning about the experiences of diverse groups in a multicultural society throughout history. Most students seem to learn little about the historical experiences of Hispanics and Asians in the United States. Unfortunately, we were not able to learn more about attitudes toward these particular groups from the phase 2 student survey because such questions would not have been meaningful in the other 27 countries where students were assessed.

Attitudes Toward Immigrants

U.S. 14-year-olds expressed very positive attitudes toward immigrants' rights on the phase 2 survey. For example:

- 91% said that immigrant children should have the same opportunities for education as nonimmigrants;
- 84% agreed that immigrants should have the same rights as everyone else in the country;
- 84% expressed support for immigrants choosing to keep their own customs and lifestyle;
- 83% agreed that after several years, immigrants should be able to vote; and
- 79% reported that immigrants should be able to keep their own language. (Baldi et al., 2001, p. 81)

In comparison to students from most other countries, U.S. students scored above the international mean in terms of their positive attitudes toward immigrants (Torney-Purta et al., 2001).

A persistent image throughout the six U.S. history and civics textbooks analyzed in phase 1 of the CivEd study was the United States as "a nation of immigrants" (Avery & Simmons, 2001; Hahn, 1999). In the history texts, immigration is viewed as an integral part of American history. The civics texts describe the naturalization process as well as past and present immigration policies. Evidence of past intolerance toward immigrants is presented, such as the Know Nothing party (anti-Catholic) and the Chinese Exclusion Act of 1882, but, in general, the textbooks present the United States as a country that is a haven for others, one that beckons: "Give me your tired, your poor, your huddled masses yearning to be free." Given the image presented in the texts, it is not too surprising that in the focus groups both teachers and students briefly mentioned teaching and learning about immigrants in history lessons.

It is important to realize that although U.S. ninth graders overall appear to have fairly positive attitudes toward rights for immigrants, that is not true for all students. Ninth graders born outside the United States were more supportive than those born in the country; Hispanic, Asian, and multiracial students were more supportive than White students; and females reported more positive attitudes than did males. There were no statistically significant differences among students from different socioeconomic backgrounds.[1]

Attitudes Toward Women's Political Rights

In the first international study of young people's civic knowledge and attitudes conducted in 1971, the United States was last among the eight countries participating in terms of support for women's political rights (Torney, Oppenheim, & Farnen, 1975). Given the significant changes in U.S. women's roles in the past 30 years, it is heartening to find that in 2000, the majority of students' attitudes reflect those changes. For example:

- 91% of U.S. students agreed that women should have the same rights as men and should be able to run for public office as men do:
- 90% said that women should get equal pay for equal work.

Nevertheless, 11% of the students said that women should stay out of politics, and 17% reported that men are better qualified to be political leaders (Baldi et al., 2001). This last finding is somewhat disturbing. Although the vast majority of students said women should be able to run for public office, almost one-fifth also said that men are better qualified for public office.

There are also striking gender differences in response to the set of statements related to women's political rights. Across all 28 countries, including the United States, females are significantly more supportive of women's political rights than are males (Torney-Purta et al., 2001). Similar findings were obtained in another recent cross-national study of student political attitudes (Hahn, 1998).

The U.S. textbook analysis suggests another cause for concern (see Avery & Simmons, 2000/2001). Males outnumber females in U.S. history texts by a ratio of 14:1 and in civics textbooks by a ratio of 16:1. Further, across texts there is a high level of consensus around the males who deserved mention (e.g., George Washington, Andrew Jackson, Abraham Lincoln, Richard Nixon), but the only woman cited in all three civics textbooks was Supreme Court Justice Sandra Day O'Connor, and the only woman mentioned across the three U.S. history textbooks was Anne Hutchinson. It might be argued that the textbooks are merely reflecting the fact that the political sphere has been (and continues to be) dominated by men, and yet the disparity in representation should itself be a topic for discussion within the texts. But only one of the texts directly discussed the disparity between men and women in politics. In this text, a table shows the number of members of the 99th Congress according to party, sex, race, religion, and educational background. Written to the side of the table is the following:

> . . . as the chart . . . shows, members of Congress have more in common than legal qualifications. Note that most members are white, male, and belong to one of the two major political parties. What does the chart show you about the educational level and occupational background of congressional members? (Avery & Simmons, 2001, p. 123)

The disparity is treated as an interesting observation rather than a problem to be investigated. It is thus doubtful that civics texts will be a source of inspiration for young women interested in politics. These findings are reinforced by the results of a case study of ninth-grade civics classes in which there was virtually no mention of gender or women in the political sphere. The mentions of women in the textbook tended to be in separate sections that were ignored by teachers (Hahn, 1996).

In the focus groups, teachers and students alike mentioned teaching and learning about women in the colonial period and during the suffragist movement. Again, students seem to be associating women with particular time periods, rather than being conscious of women's experiences throughout the country's history. Additionally, when asked about the people they had learned about in school, students tended to name men. Men who had been presidents, war heroes, and activists in the civil rights movement were the most prevalent. The few women mentioned included Harriet Tubman, Rosa Parks, and Eleanor Roosevelt (Hahn, 1999).

Interestingly, ninth graders born in the United States were more supportive of women's rights than those born out of the country, and White students were more supportive than Black students (Baldi et al., 2001). Furthermore, students with more books in the home (a proxy for socioeconomic status) were more supportive of women's rights than those with fewer.

Other Nations, Other Governments

One way in which young people can be exposed to diversity is through the study of other countries and governments. U.S. students have traditionally scored low in terms of knowledge of and interest in international affairs. In the first IEA study conducted in 1971 (Torney et al., 1975), students in only one other country, Ireland, scored below U.S. students on items tapping international knowledge. Subsequent national studies have suggested that students' knowledge of and interest in other countries is weak (Lutkus, Weiss, Campbell, Mazzeo, & Lazer, 1999; Niemi & Junn, 1998). In the recent CivEd study, U.S. students reported only a moderate amount of exposure to international politics. For example:

- Only 49% of students said they had studied other countries' governments in the past year;
- Only 43% of students report they have studied international organizations;
- Students are much more likely to report talking about U.S. government affairs as opposed to international politics;
- When students do engage in discussions about international politics, it is most likely with their teachers (52%) as opposed to their parents (43%) or friends (18%);

- Only 53% of U.S. students report that they "sometimes" or "often" read articles in the newspaper about what is happening in other countries, as compared to 62% who say they read about national news; and
- Students born in the United States were significantly less likely to read international news than those born outside the U.S.; there were no differences in reading national news. (Baldi et al., 2001)

Somewhat paradoxically, three-fourths of all students "agreed" or "strongly agreed" that they had learned in school to be concerned about events in other countries. What this suggests, however, is that U.S. students learn about other countries in the context of problems or issues, rather than from a more holistic or historical context. Further, they may be developing an affective sympathy, rather than becoming knowledgeable about others with whom they share an interdependent global society and environment.

Analyses of the civics and U.S. history textbooks in phase 1 of the CivEd study indicated that the countries and/or governments mentioned are either strong allies (e.g., Britain, Israel) or foes (e.g., Cuba, Iran) of the United States (Avery & Simmons, 2000/2001). "Enemies" of the United States are usually mentioned in the context of armed conflicts or for the purpose of contrasting a political or economic system with that of the United States. Few, if any, references are made to countries on the continents of Africa, Australia, or South America. All the texts mention the United Nations, but while the structure and organization of the UN may be described in some detail, the issues that come before the international body are rarely mentioned.

How does students' limited exposure to the world outside the United States impact their understanding of the world? We cannot know for sure, but it is doubtful that the current course of study helps students to appreciate the complexity of international issues, to understand other governments' perspectives on foreign affairs, or to develop a sense of a global "common good."

Diversity of Ideas

Tolerance for the diversity of ideas is at the heart of a democracy. It is through the expression and exchange of ideas that democracy sustains itself. To the degree that one group dominates and silences others, democracy is weakened. U.S. students, similar to adults, express strong belief in the right to free expression. Ninety percent of the 14-year-olds in the CivEd study say that it is "somewhat good" or "very good" for democracy when "everyone has the right to express their opinions freely." The percentage drops to 78%, however, when students are asked whether the right to protest laws believed to be unjust is good for democracy. Numerous other studies indicate that support for free expression decreases even further when young people (and adults) are asked about the rights of specific groups, particularly those groups with whom people strongly disagree (Avery, Bird, Johnstone, Sullivan, & Thalhammer, 1992; Conover & Searing, 2000; Hahn, 1998; Sullivan, Pierson, & Marcus, 1982). In other words, Americans tend to offer strong support for freedom of expression in the abstract, but the support is fragile because it quickly erodes when students are asked about groups that are particularly offensive to them.

Classroom Climate and Discussion

Equally important as students' exposure to diversity in terms of content is their experience with the exchange of diverse ideas in the classroom. Bickmore (1993) offers a very useful differentiation between conflictual content and conflictual pedagogy. Conflictual content is curricular material that presents multiple perspectives on a political or social issue. Conflictual pedagogy is an instructional approach that supports and encourages student expression of ideas. A teacher may choose conflictual content but not support students' exploration of ideas and opinions. For example, a teacher could require students to study *Roe v. Wade,* the 1972 U.S. Supreme Court decision supporting a woman's right to choose abortion, but review the case with students by limiting the "discussion" to factual questions, such as "When was this case decided? How many justices dissented?" Conversely, a teacher may encourage students to express their opinions in class but not present them with significant and enduring social science issues. In these classes, students may feel free to talk about whether Senior Day should be held at the local entertainment park or picnic grounds, but they do not engage in discussions about significant social and political issues over which citizens disagree. Students in these classes are frequently invited to share their opinions, but the focus is on trivial issues and students' opinions are rarely challenged.

One of the more interesting findings of the 1971 IEA study (Torney et al., 1975) was that students' perceptions that they were free to express their opinions in class was positively related to students' support for democratic values (e.g., tolerance, the right to vote, the right to be represented, respect for others). Subsequent studies support this finding (Ehman, 1980; Hahn, 1998). What explains the relationship between a positive classroom climate and support for democratic values? Political theorists suggest that the act of participating in discussions of political and social issues contributes to the development of students' "social capital" (Conover & Searing, 2000). Participation in regular class discussions helps students develop skills in analyzing issues, formulating and defending positions, and listening to others. These skills are an important resource when students enter the more formal political sphere.

In a well-structured class discussion, students also often come to appreciate the complexity of public issues. They are less likely to categorize issues as "good" or "bad," "pro" or "con." They understand that there are vast gray areas associated with most significant issues. All of these are important skills for active, participatory citizenship. It is likely that the more one has developed these skills ("social capital"), the more likely one is to use them as an adult citizen.

Items designed to measure classroom climate were included in the CivEd study. The majority of U.S. students perceive an open classroom climate for discussion. For example, students report that:

- they are encouraged to make up their own minds about issues (85%);
- they are free to express their opinions (78%);
- they free to disagree with teachers about social and political issues (73%);
- their teachers encourage them to discuss political and social issues about which people have different opinions (69%);
- teachers respect their opinions (79%);
- teachers present several sides of an issue (79%) (Baldi et al., 2001, p. 34; see also Hahn, 1998).

In comparison to students from other countries, U.S. students scored above the international mean on the measure of classroom climate. Although these results are positive, other findings suggest a more complex picture.

First is the concern that although students are encouraged to express their views and they feel free to express them, this could be with respect to trivial or noncontentious matters. Almost a third of students reported that teachers did not encourage them to discuss political or social issues about which people have different opinions. In a pluralistic democracy, it is important that citizens be able to discuss such issues across their differences. Second, the CivEd study found students from lower socioeconomic backgrounds, those least likely to accumulate social capital outside of school, report a less open classroom climate than do their peers (Baldi et al., 2001). Other studies suggest that discussions of political issues, while not a frequent occurrence in any school, are more likely to occur in suburban and rural communities and least likely to occur in urban and immigrant communities (Conover & Searing, 2000).

In the focus groups we noted several indications that students in urban schools, particularly those with largely African American student populations, were less likely to experience discussions of issues in an open classroom climate than students in suburban schools (Hahn, 1999). Concern for order and basic skill development seem to work against schools fostering democratic discourse. For example, middle school teachers in several different schools in one urban district said that it was difficult to teach about democracy and speaking one's opinion when the atmosphere of the school worked against that. They said that although they encouraged their students to speak out, many of their colleagues told students to be quiet, listen, and take notes or work on assignments at their seats. Furthermore, the students had to be quiet in the halls and the lunchroom, where a "quiet lunch" policy was enforced. Other teachers also said that it was a challenge trying to teach about democracy and encouraging students to express their opinions when school policies aimed at "keeping kids silent and powerless." A teacher in another part of the country also expressed concern, saying that when she had taught in an urban school, "What the administrators in our building were most concerned about was order, and the last thing they wanted was for kids to speak out on issues."

It is not only a concern for order that appears to be working against the creation of a democratic climate in schools and classrooms. Many well-intentioned teachers feel they must spend every available minute helping their urban students acquire the basic facts. One high school teacher explained why he and his colleagues in an urban area serving African American students did not engage students in a variety of activities, including discussions:

> We do the traditional things—lectures and have students answer questions in the text. . . . We've got to do whatever we can to get the students to read the textbook, and answering questions is one way to guarantee that we can have a conversation about what they've read. The students are not reading it at home, so we end up having to do it in the classroom, which none of us likes. Number one, we'd rather be doing other things and number two, our students are falling behind. If somebody else's students are reading at home and then doing stuff in the classroom, they're getting more than ours are. But we've got to play with the cards that we're dealt.

And so the cycle perpetuates itself. Those students who come to school with less social capital are also those least likely to acquire it in school and hence are least prepared to exercise the rights and responsibilities of citizenship.

CONCLUSION

In conclusion, the IEA CivEd study provides a beginning from which to increase our understanding of young people's experiences with and orientations toward diversity. Three themes are apparent, and related to each, there are remaining challenges.

First, national contexts matter. Students learn about diversity in schools and families that are embedded in wider national cultures. Earlier studies revealed clear country differences in students' willingness to extend rights to diverse groups (Hahn, 1998). That was similarly found in the CivEd study. Students in countries with high unemployment rates and low gross national products reported more negative attitudes toward others (on the immigrants' rights and women's rights scales) than did students in countries that were more economically secure and had long democratic traditions (Torney-Purta et al., 2001).

Readers might be tempted to feel that in the United States, which is comparatively well off economically and which has a long democratic tradition, students are sufficiently supportive of rights for all. Indeed, U.S. ninth graders were among students from only four countries who scored above the international mean in support for rights for both women and immigrants (the other countries were Norway, Sweden, and Cyprus).

Second, this study also suggests that there are numerous reasons for educators and concerned citizens not to be complacent. There is still much work to be done. Textbooks still give insufficient attention to women, Hispanics, and Asians—and we fear the situation may get worse as new state curriculum standards tie textbook publishers to traditional narrative histories. If the experiences of our focus group participants are typical, classroom instruction also seems to give scant attention to women, Hispanics, and Asians. Most importantly, not all students within the country hold equally positive attitudes toward rights for immigrants and women.

On the one hand, it may seem logical that females are more supportive of women's rights than are men and that immigrants are more supportive of immigrants' rights than are those born in the United States. In a pluralistic democracy, however, it is important that everyone be concerned about rights for the "other" as well as for themselves. We need to learn more about why some male students, African American students, and students born outside the United States, are not fully supportive of women's rights. Similarly, more needs to be learned about why some students born in the United States, White students, and male students are less than fully supportive of immigrants' rights.

Third, schools do matter. Perhaps one reason that there was a generally positive attitude toward rights for immigrants is that in the United States students do hear positive messages about being "a nation of immigrants." That is not true for other countries that participated in the IEA study. Moreover, students in our focus groups told us that they learn much about democracy and diversity through their experiences in extracurricular activities with peers who are racially and culturally diverse. Students spoke positively about the diversity they experienced in sports, band, and various clubs. However, numerous students do not now have such experiences. Ironically, busing to promote integration, along with constraints on school budgets, may have reduced opportunities that some students have to participate in extracurricular activities.

Fourth, because schools matter, we are concerned about the insufficient attention given to international topics in U.S. classrooms. Students are not learning as much as they might about other countries, international organizations, and global issues. The fact that 75% of students reported that in their social studies classes they discuss current events (Baldi et al., 2001) suggests one way to address this problem. Too often such discussions are brief reviews of who has done what in national and local events, rather than deeper explorations into international events and issues. That needs to be changed. Furthermore, considerably more students said they watch news broadcasts on television than read newspapers; yet today network news programs give little attention to international news. Teachers and parents need to encourage students to seek out and pay attention to international news. Such encouragement can have positive results. For example, in one study, students in different schools reported that although they had not previously been interested in the news, when teachers asked them to keep up and then talked to them about issues in the news, they became interested (Hahn, 1998). Moreover, the Internet now provides an opportunity for students to follow events as they are reported from news sources in other nations. In the process, young people can gain insights into multiple perspectives and may gain a greater appreciation of diverse views internationally.

Fifth, classrooms need to become microcosms of societies in which citizens with diverse views, as well as cultures, wrestle with the difficult issues that face society. We are concerned about the number of students who say that in their classes they do not investigate social and political issues about which people have different views. Those are precisely the issues that citizens of the future will need to resolve. By the time students are in the ninth grade, they should be investigating and discussing problematic issues. Discussions of controversial issues are not easy and they are not something that comes naturally. They take practice—on the part of teachers and students. In the focus groups, some teachers said they did not teach more about diversity because they were not comfortable handling the controversial nature of the related issues. Clearly, if we are to help prepare youth for their roles as citizens in a multicultural society in a world of diverse peoples, teachers must be confident in their abilities to help students investigate controversial issues. Pre-service teacher education and professional development programs alike need to give greater attention to teaching how to lead discussions of controversial issues in supportive classroom environments.

Engaging in deliberation across differences is at the heart of democratic living. It needs to be practiced in the classroom as well as in local communities and among nation-states. Such deliberation needs to be combined with an appreciation of minority rights and the common good. In a multicultural, pluralistic society, the extent of democratic practices and the quality of democratic discourse hinge on citizens' orientations toward diversity. When minority rights are respected, when thoughtful deliberations around public issues purposefully include diverse perspectives, and when self-interest is tempered by a concern for the common good, democracy thrives.

We began this chapter by asking, "What is the status of young people's orientations toward diversity today?" In the results of the most recent international study, we find cause for hope and optimism but also for concern and action. Like democracy itself, students' attitudes toward diversity require constant vigilance.

NOTE

1. Student report of the number of books in the home was used as the indicator of socioeconomic status. This is, of course, only an indirect measure, but it is one that is commonly used in studies such as this one when more direct measures are impractical.

Chapter 12

Conditions in the Organizational Environment That Support Positive Intergroup Relations

Kenneth Cushner

In schools, perhaps more than in any other social setting, opportunities exist to have close and regular interactions with a wide variety of people. It is thus critical that educators take the opportunity to become proactive in improving intergroup relations. However, just because teachers, administrators, and other authorities may sanction such efforts, changing schools and institutions to make them more supportive of positive intergroup relations, attentive to issues of diversity, and inclusive of all people in society is no easy task. Although theory and current ideology encourage certain changes in the educational context (Glazer, 1997) and a continually expanding knowledge base exists to bring about such changes, there is less evidence that teachers and administrators actually apply much of what is known or that their efforts have the intended impact. Facilitating intergroup relations in schools is dependent not only on the knowledge and desires of educators but also on the organizational climate that is maintained in the school district and in the schools.

The field of organizational behavior offers insights into the mechanisms that facilitate change. An organization is an integrated system of interdependent structures and functions made up of groups of people who must work together, while knowing what the others in the system are doing (Berrien, 1976). Organizational behavior is a field that can link the work of social scientists and educators as they seek to bridge the gap between academic inquiry and the everyday challenges of improving intergroup relations in the schools.

The path to support such efforts, while paved with good intentions, is obstructed by numerous roadblocks, detours, and areas that are still under construction. We are only now beginning to understand the organizational processes involved in affecting such changes. The chapters in this volume have identified a wide range of successful programs designed to improve intergroup relations, but unless the schools' organizational structures are supportive of such efforts, the effects of these programs are likely to be reduced. This chapter will explore the structural features of institutions, primarily K–12 schools, that promote positive intergroup relations. It begins by reviewing Allport's contact hypothesis, looks at problems that hinder institutional change, and discusses factors that can support positive intergroup relations in the school environment.

THE CONTACT HYPOTHESIS REVISITED

Most of the chapters in this volume refer to Gordon Allport's foundational work, *The Nature of Prejudice*, published in 1954. While this work was originally developed to address prejudice in settings outside of schools, it provided both the groundwork for much of what happened in the early efforts at school desegregation and a viable framework for efforts to improve intergroup relations in schools. The elements that Allport first identified as being critical to improving intergroup relations remain as solid today as they were when they were originally proposed. It is clear that merely putting students from differing backgrounds together in the same environment does not guarantee positive relations among them. Relations between students from different racial, ethnic, religious, and cultural groups are most likely to improve when Allport's conditions are met: (1) Students are on an equal status with one another in the contact situation, implying that they have equal access to the rewards available in the school; (2) students interact with one another on a repeated basis while in pursuit of some common goals; (3) students have the opportunity to get to know one another as individuals in a rather intimate manner, thus interacting with a wide range of people and disproving the prevailing stereotypes of the group; and (4) their interactions are sanctioned by administrators and others in authority.

Applying the contact hypothesis directly to school settings has been problematic for a variety of reasons. For example, many schools are relatively monocultural, thus providing little opportunity for intergroup contact to occur. In many schools, patterns of racial and ethnic segregation remain, often because of segregated housing patterns in the communities in which they are located; residential segregation thus reduces the possibility of intergroup contact in schools (Bagley, Mizuno, & Collins, 1992; Feld & Carter, 1998). If contact is to lead to intergroup understanding, then segregation constitutes a major obstacle that must be addressed. Even when cultural, ethnic, racial, and socioeconomic diversity is present in a school, other factors often militate against regular, meaningful intergroup interaction. One potential problem is evident in what has been called the "power-threat" or group-threat hypothesis (Blumer, 1958; Vogt, 1997), which suggests that when a minority group increases in size, the dominant group is likely to feel increasingly threatened and act in a hostile manner. Blumer argued that racial prejudice is not a result of personality traits, but rather a product of situational variables such as group ratios that, in turn, affect psychological processes.

Hallinan (1982) tested this hypothesis in the school context by studying friendship choices of children in 20 elementary schools in northern California over the period of a schoolyear. Surprisingly, fewer instances of cross-racial friendships were found in classes where the racial balance was equal. Hallinan (1982) explained this as being a consequence of the fact that racially balanced classrooms contained sufficient numbers of Black and White students that they could segregate themselves into subgroups. There was a greater tendency to make cross-racial friendships, for both Black and White students, when the students were in majority-White classrooms. This was thought to occur because majority-White classrooms reflected the racial ratios in the world from which students came.

Another problem involved in applying the contact hypothesis in schools centers on Allport's criterion of equal-status contact (Vogt, 1997). Although equal-status contact provides much of the foundational structure that underlies many group activities in the classroom, including cooperative learning strategies, it may be undermined by inequalities that exist among groups outside the school. Students do not leave their social status at home when they come to school. Unless efforts are made to counteract these inequalities, contact in the schools may lead to increased stereotyping (Cohen, 1984; Henderson-King & Nisbett, 1996). Note, however, that Cohen (Chapter 3, this volume) cites strong evidence that specially trained teachers can counter such effects.

Generalizing changed attitudes beyond the immediate context where an intervention occurs also presents a problem when applying the equal-status concept. That is, while intergroup relations may appear to improve between individuals who come into contact in the school setting, such attitude change may not transfer to other contexts. Also, equal status between two specific groups in school may not generalize to other out-groups or to situations in which status is not equal, as in many community contexts.

FACTORS THAT HINDER CHANGE AT THE INDIVIDUAL LEVEL

In his early work, Lewin (1951) proposed a model of change suggesting that the status quo is maintained when opposing forces—that is, those supportive of change and those resistant to change—are relatively equal in strength. He argued that the most effective way to institute change is to reduce the resistance rather than add to the forces favoring change. Resistance to change, and resistance to efforts designed to improve intergroup relations in particular, exists at both the individual and organizational level (Cushner, McClelland, & Safford, 2000; Greenman & Kimmel, 1995). It is important that we consider both individual and institutional characteristics when considering factors that facilitate or hinder change efforts. The greatest opportunities for real change arise when the individuals and the organization work in concert.

At the individual level, one of the factors that can hinder changes that might lead to improvements in intergroup relations is the relative lack of diversity among the teachers themselves. Teachers, by and large, are a relatively homogeneous group of individuals (Cushner et al., 2000; Zimpher, 1989). Roughly 88% of teachers are European American. Most teachers have limited experience living and working with people from other cultural backgrounds; and teachers are considerably older, on average, than the general working population (Hussar, 1999). Close to 70% of teacher education students spend all or most of their free time with people of their own background. Fewer than 10% of teachers are fluent in a second language, with three-fifths being fully monolingual. Of course, teachers are well ahead of the general population of the United States in these respects, where monolingualism is the rule, except among recent immigrants. And there is ample evidence that teachers and schools compensate in many important ways for shortcomings in social contacts with other children (Alexander, Entwisle, & Olson, 2001). Still, the majority of teachers live within 100 miles of where they were born and wish to teach in communities and schools similar to those in which they were raised (Cushner et al., 2000). This is one of the reasons that schools most in need of good teachers tend to be staffed by teachers with fewer qualifications and less experience (Lankford, Loeb, & Wyckoff, 2002). These characteristics of schools and teaching may often lead them to be less responsive to change and to diversity than would be ideal for fostering improved intergroup relations in schools. While schools and teachers are surely less diverse and progressive than what most authors of this book would consider ideal (Cummings, Dyas, Maddux, & Kochman, 2001), they tend to be more receptive to efforts to improve intergroup relations than is the general population. One way to increase educators' receptivity to improving intergroup relations is change at the organizational level.

FACTORS THAT INFLUENCE CHANGE AT
THE ORGANIZATIONAL LEVEL

Initially, the picture for institutions could seem less encouraging than that for individuals. Institutions tend to adhere to tradition and maintain the status quo. Sociologists have long argued that this institutional "conservatism" may be especially characteristic of educational institutions (Brint, Contreras, & Matthews, 2001). For example, one study undertaken by the National Council for the Accreditation of Teacher Education (NCATE) suggested that although a growing number of educational institutions professed to address issues of cultural diversity, very few actually did so (Gollnick, 1992). However, this finding was one of the factors that lead NCATE to place increased emphasis in support of diversity as one of its central criteria for accrediting programs of teacher education.

Recent support for the theory of institutional conservatism of schools comes from a study by Brint and colleagues (2001), who analyzed the socialization messages conveyed in schools. The study examined 64 different classrooms for the expression of 16 different values that were categorized into four areas: work-related performance (orderliness, promptness); interaction between self and others (respect for others, self-control); "traditional virtues" (honesty, fairness, reliability); and "modern values" (appreciation of cultural diversity, individual uniqueness). The results of the study indicated that the majority (84%) of socialization messages address the foundations of work performance and effort (in 40% of the classrooms surveyed these were the only messages). The least frequent messages delivered to students were those related to "modern values," with multicultural integration evident only in a relatively few surface-level classroom projects per year. The authors state, "New ideas and values have a chance to become popular only if they fit, or at least do not significantly threaten, the organizational priorities of schools" (p. 171).

Many critics have contended that schools and classrooms are not particularly democratic institutions and that they must be restructured if they are to adequately serve all students (Engel, 1988; Ladson-Billing, 1992; McLaren, 1989). Banks (2002) argues that school restructuring must occur because the dominant approaches, techniques, and practices do not, and probably never will, succeed with large numbers of students of color.

Resistance to organizational change may have historical roots that are often related to the failure of past change efforts (Morey, 1997). Because most changes involve some sense of loss, anxiety, or conflict, resistance can also arise due to the anticipation of the turbulence, chaos, and stress that change will cause. If the uncertainty and disruption occasioned by the threat of change are ignored, resistance can become even more deeply entrenched, often driving conflict underground to such an extent that it may be difficult to overcome (Bolman & Deal, 1991).

The effective management of change must take into consideration the nature of the educational institution. There is evidence to suggest that those institutions that tend to be internally focused are less likely to espouse change. Conversely, those institutions that are externally oriented—that is, those with greater links to the community—are generally better able to respond to social and political factors and thus more responsive to change efforts (J. W. Schofield, 1991). Fullan (1993) has suggested that if change is not perceived to be part of the organizational culture, efforts to bring it about are likely to fail. He argues that "you cannot have an educational environment in which change is continuously expected alongside a conservative system and expect anything but constant aggravation" (p. 3).

Myers, Caruso, and Birk (1999), when they studied organizational change efforts related to improving intergroup relations and intercultural understanding, found that teachers expressed a range of concerns and issues. Teachers in this study reported that it took a significant amount of time and money to initiate change and that most schools are currently struggling to meet basic expenses. There was also a perceived lack of ownership of the problem of change; no one seemed willing to take responsibility for addressing it. They said that there was often a failure to endorse diversity, equity, and justice as institutional objectives from the top down—in other words, Allport's critical criterion of administrative support was absent. The teachers felt that an appreciation and understanding of the time and effort required to change students were lacking. They also complained of insufficient collaboration with families and guardians. One reason for this lack of collaboration is that low-income working parents are much less likely to have jobs that allow them the scheduling flexibility conducive to meeting with teachers and participating in school programs (Heyman & Earle, 2000). This often leads to poor connections with minority communities and a lack of understanding of their unique needs. In addition, there is often a lack of minority faculty and staff involved from the very beginning. Frequently, there is also a shortage of follow-up and support services once a program or experience has been provided. These findings suggest that a wide range of organizational barriers to change must be overcome if intergroup relations are to be improved.

It is not simply resistance within educational institutions that creates difficulties in improving intergroup relations in the schools. Community level factors also play a role. Blau, Lamb, Sterns, and Pellerin (2001) looked at the relationship between equal-status contact in neighborhoods and subsequent achievement in school. They found that all students, regardless of race, achieved at lower levels in their social studies courses when they lived in homogeneous communities in which race and socioeconomic status were closely related. That is, neighborhoods that were one-dimensional with respect to race and class did not provide a favorable background for the challenges of learning about social studies and key social science concepts such as social differentiation.

Another organizational problem is that many integrated schools resegregate themselves through the practice of ability tracking. Grouping students by academic ability continues to be practiced in many schools, especially high schools, and may result in the unintended segregation of students by ethnicity or race (Stephan, 1999). Tracking often relegates a disproportionate number of low-income students and students of color to lower-track classes, which has the result of limiting equal-status intergroup interaction. Segregation can also occur for other reasons. In some instances, students segregate themselves into like groups on the playground, in the lunchroom, or as a result of participation in extracurricular activities. For whatever reason it occurs, within-school resegregation limits intergroup interactions.

In brief, schools are faced with a number of organizational barriers to changes that could, if lowered, improve intergroup relations. Among the barriers that must be addressed are classroom environments that are not conducive to egalitarian intergroup relations, a lack of communication with ethnic and racial groups in the community, the internal conservative focus of many institutions, a lack of money and leadership, segregation in the communities from which students are drawn, and resegregation through tracking in the schools.

CREATING AN ENVIRONMENT THAT SUPPORTS POSITIVE INTERGROUP RELATIONS

The public seems to be as concerned with the school's responsibility in solving social problems as it is in dealing with more traditional educational issues (Brint et al., 2001). Attitudes and behaviors toward others—be they racially, culturally, or ethnically different—develop over a lifetime. However, as the chapters in this book attest, they can be changed by well-developed educational efforts. Changing structures in the school can also set the stage for promoting equal and high-quality educational experiences for all students that can go far in improving intergroup relations. Some caution must be exercised in implementing changes because relations among groups can be negatively affected by structural changes that exacerbate or re-create problems of social inequality (Nieto, 1992). Intergroup contact may, if Allport's criteria are not met, exacerbate problems among groups.

It is not possible to prepare a single plan of action that will work for all schools, which is why the programs described in this book stress the need to build context-specific plans of action. The nature of change itself is such that it is impossible to predict the obstacles and opportunities that will present themselves once the process has begun (Baker, 2001; Fullan, 1993). This makes effective planning more of a process than an event. Scholars have begun to reconceptualize their understanding of change from being a rational, linear process to one that is more nonlinear and dynamic. In addition, the complexities of relationships of individuals and communities viewed within the culture of the organization must be understood and dealt with if change is to be effective (Beer, Eisenstat, & Spector, 1990; Lincoln, 1985). Identifying and addressing the obstacles and constraints to change is a critical first step to designing and implementing a successful change effort that is congruent with the organization's prevailing culture.

Little evidence exists to document that enduring institutional change occurs as a result of short-term programs, individual-level staff development, or ready-made curriculum packages or applications of a new technology that can easily be adapted or integrated into existing school structures (Cuban, 1984). Rather, institutional change is more likely to be evident when individuals within the organization are supported by institutional structures that enable the desired changes to take place. This is why the programs described in earlier chapters of this volume place so much emphasis on building communities to ensure that programs fit in the school's organizational environment. Change comes about by a focused and balanced interaction among individuals, communities, and institutions.

Change efforts have proven successful at creating environments that support positive intercultural relations. The factors associated with successful organizational change discussed below include leadership, policy statements, staff development, development of role models, creation of a diverse faculty and staff, school–community relations, creation of a sense of community in the schools, pedagogy and curriculum transformation, and evaluation.

Leadership

Effective leadership is central to change in institutions; without it, most change efforts fail. Educational leaders who have a vision, who are transformative in orientation, and who are comfortable with ambiguity and openness are the most successful in creating true reform. Such leaders identify themselves as agents of change, empower others to assume leadership roles, foster learning, and assist others in understanding the core values driving the change effort (Fullan, 1993; Morey, 1997). When restructuring occurs, the total system is recognized as the problem and thus must be the target of reform. Piecemeal changes are typically insufficient as a reform strategy

(Darling-Hammond, 1997). For change to occur, an awareness of the need, and a willingness to address it, must be apparent. With regard to intergroup relations, such awareness can be furthered by a strong leader who promotes institutional communications and actions that are designed to foster increased understanding of issues related to diversity and their relationships to the educational mission of the schools.

Stringfield, Datnow, Ross, and Snively (1998) studied restructuring in multicultural environments in 13 schools that had implemented an internationally recognized change program. Their investigation showed that, 2 to 4 years later, these schools were "all over the map." That is, some appeared to have full implementation, a committed staff, and successful intergroup relations. Some showed half the teachers implementing most of the components. And still others demonstrated little impact from the program. In those schools where implementation was less than desired, teachers reported not fully understanding the model, feeling it was inconsistent with what they believed was best for children, having insufficient time allotted, and experiencing too many conflicting demands. Although some of these teachers were enthusiastic about the program, many felt that they lacked the necessary skills to implement the change. In addition, many teachers either felt powerless (i.e., they felt the change was imposed upon them and that they didn't have a choice in the change effort) or believed that the administrators were not fully invested in the process. In the programs that were working well, the situation was quite different. The desired skills and knowledge were integrated across the disciplines, especially in bilingual settings, and staff were sensitive to local culture and community needs. Successful change efforts in these studies were found to have a strong leader, usually the principal, who had a vision of what the institution was trying to achieve. These principals worked well with all staff members and built on their strengths. They also ensured that the goals of the school incorporated all the students.

Policy Statements

Policies that clearly communicate support for positive relationships among groups are an essential feature of change efforts. It is important that schools have a written policy, mission, or vision statement that frames the institution's goals and directions as they relate to diversity and intergroup relations. Ideally, these statements would reflect a commitment from the top level of the system that communicates a board of education's dedication to fostering diversity and creating equal opportunity. Such statements legitimize the issue of intergroup relations, facilitate the establishment of programs and practices, and convey a message to all stakeholders that the issue is a priority.

A good example of such a statement was created in 1996 by the Indianapolis public schools. Their policy statement included three major objectives supportive of multicultural education. The first objective was to promote and foster intergroup understanding, awareness, and appreciation by students and staff of the diverse ethnic, racial, cultural, and linguistic groups represented in the school district, the United States, and the world. The second objective was to help children develop more positive attitudes toward cultural diversity, especially in the early grades, by dispelling misconceptions, stereotypes, and negative beliefs about themselves and others. The third objective was to identify the impact of racism and other barriers to acceptance of differences (Banks, 2002).

Once a policy is in place, an action plan can be developed that brings the school's goals to life (Sue, 1999). Good plans outline specific time frames for the implementation of diversity goals, differentiate short-term from long-term goals, identify an individual or department to be responsible, and include periodic assessments to determine how well the plan is progressing as time unfolds. Good plans also lay the foundation for continuing professional development plans for teachers and staff.

School policies should be implemented that make it very clear to all that prejudice and discrimination will be actively discouraged. Students should know that overt acts of intergroup aggression and intentional hate speech will not be tolerated. In addition, reward structures, such as incentives for nondiscriminatory behavior, can be established that will have a positive impact on intergroup relations (Stephan, 1999). Although it is a policy more difficult to put into action than to plan, students can be rewarded for behaving in ways that support positive intergroup relations, as numerous studies have demonstrated. For instance, Hauserman, Walen, and Behling (1973) report on a study in which students were rewarded for sitting next to students of another race during lunchtime. Providing such rewards resulted in increased cross-racial interaction during, and after, the lunch period. The goal of these policies is to undermine hostility and discriminatory behavior and in its place promote civility, respect, and tolerance between groups.

Disciplinary policies, too, should be analyzed, as the manner in which discipline is administered sometimes functions to exclude minority-group students from a meaningful educational experience. Insensitivity to cultural, linguistic, and social differences may interact with racism, discrimination, and low expectations of student achievement to produce an environment where minority-group students are at a disadvantage. Successful schools involve students in determining disciplinary policies. They also analyze the rates of detention, suspension, and assignment to "special" classes or alternative programs to ensure that they are fair to all various groups.

Staff Development

Teachers are sometimes poorly equipped with the knowledge and skills that are necessary to improve intergroup relations. They may need more training and continuing education if they are to be successful in this regard (Stephan, 1999). Effective preparation, as described in Chapters 2 through 10 in this volume, goes beyond simply knowing about the cultures of the students in their schools and includes training in techniques used to improve intergroup relations. Sleeter (1992) points out the importance of changing teachers as individuals through staff development, while simultaneously focusing on organization-level change. She studied a 2-year staff intergroup relations development project that involved 30 teachers from two contiguous school districts. After 2 years, minimal impact was observed in the classroom; the greatest change was that more classes incorporated cooperative learning on a regular basis. The teachers reported the following reasons for the limited classroom impact: lack of time, large class sizes, excessive curriculum requirements, the structure of the programs, the disjuncture between school and community, and a poorly supported administrative and bureaucratic structure. Sleeter concludes that efforts must focus as much on changing the school structure and processes as on educating individuals or adding an array of special programs or activities.

Teachers, unfortunately, often lack the power to make many of the changes that are needed or expected of them. As Banks (2002) explains:

> It is unreasonable to expect disempowered and victimized teachers to empower and motivate disaffected youths of color. Consequently, major goals of school restructuring must be to give teachers respect, to provide them the ability and authority to make decisions that matter, and to hold them accountable as professionals for the decisions they make. School reform will succeed only if we treat teachers in ways that we have long admonished them to treat their students. (p. 42)

Development of Role Models

The organizational culture of the school should reflect the kinds of intergroup relations that are desired among all groups in the school. Since so much of human behavior is acquired through observation, it is imperative that students be exposed to a range of role models who display the types of desirable interactions sought between the various racial, ethnic, and cultural groups in the school (Bandura, 1986). The most effective role models tend to be those who are respected by the observers (because of their high status, perceived competence, and power), to whom the observers are attracted, and who seem to find the behaviors rewarding themselves. School adminis-trators, teachers, counselors, and support staff who behave in warm, respect-ful, and egalitarian ways toward one another become important role models for students as they work to improve their own intergroup relations skills and behaviors (Sue, 1999).

Creation of a Diverse Faculty and Staff

The racial, ethnic, and gender composition of the administration, teach-ers, and support staff should reflect those of the students and the commu-nity (J. W. Schofield, 1995). Schools should develop and implement a strong policy for the recruitment, hiring and promotion of people from diverse backgrounds. Institutions that are serious about increasing their diversity can employ a number of creative strategies. Schools that maintain balanced fac-ulty and staff could be rewarded by their districts with additional resources that otherwise might not be available to them. School districts can actively recruit applicants from underrepresented groups at professional conferences or universities that train teachers or by advertising in publications that mi-nority candidates are most likely to read. They may also develop "grow your own" programs designed to identify talented students from within the dis-trict who can be supported through their college years and invited back to teach. Increasingly, local businesses and universities are teaming up with schools to provide the support, development, and encouragement that are necessary to recruit a diverse teaching staff.

The retention of minority-group faculty members, once they have been attracted to an institution, is also important. Institutions that have been suc-cessful with retention efforts have employed a wide range of strategies. Mentoring programs for minority-group faculty members are often success-ful at ensuring that newcomers feel welcome in the institution and that they clearly understand what is expected of them to succeed (Boice & Turner, 1989). Likewise, opportunities for minority teachers to meet together to share concerns and perceptions and to promote networking have proven benefi-cial (Wadsworth, 1999).

School–Community Relations

Another important aspect involved in favorable intergroup relations is the relationship between the schools and the community. It can be valuable to develop a dialogue between the community and its schools so that both sides can enter into an ongoing negotiation concerning the purposes of the schools and the community's expectations. For instance, a frequent complaint of many immigrant families is that the school does not value respect for age or authority, or that children appear to waste time in school without significant teacher-directed instruction. These complaints suggest that distinctly different values exist in different segments of the community. Their voices need to be heard and heeded by teachers and administrators. If both sides think about approaching such problems from the point of view of the other, modifications in their expectations are possible. Both sides can develop a bicultural or multicultural orientation that will facilitate the development of new approaches to their joint concerns. Culturally appropriate means to introduce the schools to the community are critical. Gaining the participation of members of the minority community may require different strategies than gaining participation from members of the majority group. Finally, it must be remembered that a single, united "community" hardly ever exists. Rather, citizens are often bitterly divided about school issues, with alienated parents who feel schools are hostile to their values just as likely, if not more likely, to be middle-class European Americans as members of ethnic-minority groups (Sikkink, 1999). Fissures within communities make it more difficult to build a sense of common purpose between the school and the citizens whose children attend it.

Creation of a Sense of Community in the Schools

Schools that accept and integrate various cultures, languages, abilities, and experiences, and work at the community level to improve intergroup relations, help their students learn to negotiate life in a society characterized by multiple layers of identity and affiliation. The students themselves can contribute to this effort by working to create a sense of community within the school environment. Intercultural pairings of younger and older students within a school and between schools can help individuals reach out and participate in the lives of those around them who may be different from themselves. Successful "reading buddy" programs that bring early readers and older students together over a continuous period of time can help to develop bonds that lead students to look out for one another. These programs can be structured to cross ethnic, racial, and gender lines. Efforts should be made to include individuals from different groups in all the activities of the school. Providing recognition and encouragement for a wide range of contributions to the school community can enable diverse individuals to find their niches. The goal is to develop a sense of belonging that facilitates personal identity development and that reduces anxiety and ambiguity.

Simply altering the physical surroundings to make the school look less "institutional" in ways that reflect the various groups that are present can have a significant impact on school climate. Hallway walls may include photographs of children, of families, and of the local community. Inclusive schools integrate the ideas, perspectives, and contributions of all and come to look like a place where real people live and work together—people who can be identified, recognized, and admired for being who they are. Such efforts go far in helping children to see the ethnic, racial, or cultural makeup of their schools as making a positive contribution to the school community.

In addition, a sense of community can be developed within the ranks of teachers and administrators as well as between students and teachers. In successful schools, teachers share ideas, materials, and feedback, and they perceive themselves as helpers to their colleagues. Persuasive evidence suggests that this kind of collective responsibility for one's colleagues and commitment to students' learning is more likely to develop in smaller schools (Lee & Loeb, 2000). This conclusion has stimulated the adoption—in many urban areas supported by the Gates Foundation—of the schools-within-schools reform. This attempts to approximate the advantages of small schools, such as an accepting environment, without incurring the expense of relocating students to new buildings. For some children, life at home and in the neighborhood is chaotic and hazardous, a circumstance that creates a relatively high degree of anxiety, ambiguity, and uncertainty. In order for children to feel safe and secure, and thus open to developing positive intergroup relations, the school should become a safe haven by striving to be an orderly, predictable, accepting environment.

Pedagogy and Curriculum Transformation

Improving intergroup relations requires teachers and schools to look at curriculum and instruction issues. Teachers should determine what knowledge, skills, and attitudes already exist among their students as a prelude to focusing on those that must be developed. They should strive to teach multiple perspectives by emphasizing many different groups, not just the experiences of one group. In a pluralistic nation such as the United States, more than one kind of cultural content is valid and worth knowing. Beyond providing an expanded knowledge base, presenting multiple perspectives helps to reduce the tendency people have to form and use racial, ethnic, cultural, and religious stereotypes.

Efforts to address issues of diversity should not be restricted to the social studies, language arts, or performing arts. Attention to diversity in all areas, including mathematics, the sciences, and physical education, can be beneficial. If the curriculum is to help students make broad connections, it must not focus solely on the cognitive domain but must address affective and behavioral development as well. Especially in the areas of culture learning and development of students' skills in relating to people from different groups, active participation should be stressed. In efforts to bring people from different backgrounds into closer contact and thus to improve intergroup understanding, teachers should include local populations whenever it is appropriate. Individuals from the community who are able to share their lives and their special knowledge and talents can broaden the offerings of the school and promote intergroup relations.

Creating successful interventions to improve intergroup relations is a complicated process that is influenced by a number of factors, including the teachers' racial attitudes and skills, the length of the intervention, content coverage, and classroom atmosphere, as well as the ethnic and racial composition of the school and community. It has been known for quite some time that a wide range of curriculum intervention strategies using multiethnic materials can have a positive impact on racial attitudes when compared to the more traditional standard materials (Banks, 2002). Until relatively recently, however, little attention was given to the more subtle or hidden messages conveyed by school curricula and classroom materials. Ignoring differences in gender, ethnicity, and disability, among many other sources of diversity, was not thought to be harmful. However, excluding such factors undermines the legitimacy of the groups that have been marginalized and leads majority-group members to develop an unrealistic perception of the complexity of the world around them. (See the textbook analysis in Chapter 11, this volume.)

In order to develop positive self-identities for all children, to build a sense of inclusion, and to work to bridge intergroup differences, the manner in which educational materials are presented to children should reflect the diversity of groups found in the society at large. An increasing number of students will feel empowered and included in the educational endeavor when teachers and other school personnel accommodate and adapt learning activities to the needs and abilities of these students. In particular, attention should be paid to differences in learning styles. For example, cooperative learning has been shown to increase the achievement of minority-group students as well as to improve intergroup relations (see Chapter 4, this volume).

Evaluation

Continuous assessment affords institutions an opportunity to determine how effective their diversity efforts have been. Effective institutions examine such things as student perceptions of the classroom and school experiences (through small focus group discussions), faculty perceptions and experiences of diversity-related issues (through exit interviews when faculty or staff leave), the degree to which teachers integrate issues related to diversity in their teaching, and the overall sensitivity to cultural diversity on the part of faculty and staff.

Assessment is also used in determining student achievement. Methods of student assessment that consider the complex interrelationships of race, class, ethnicity, religion, gender, and disability are crucial to maintaining perceptions of fairness in schools. Studies of test validity have indicated that considerable bias (e.g., cultural, gender, linguistic, experiential) may exist in standardized tests. This is, of course, an enormously controversial and technical topic. But the evidence is strong enough about the effects of stereotyping on test results (Stangor, Carr, & Kiang, 1998) and about the effects of status processes on measures of mental ability (Houser, Thye, & Markovsky, 1998) that responsible educators will use standardized tests with extreme caution and will not simply assume that such tests are culturally neutral. Based on such testing, students can be excluded from the variety of curricular and instructional choices available in their schools. For example, students with inferior skills in the majority language who perform poorly on language tests given early in their educational careers may have their subsequent educational experiences unfairly restricted. Thus, schools must be sensitive to how such tests are employed if they are to avoid the unfair treatment of groups that might be disadvantaged by them.

If tracking based on ability testing is a problem, de-tracking is the first, but not the only, step needed to alleviate the situation. One problem is that teachers can inadvertently reverse the effects of de-tracking. In some cases, due to large class sizes and the difficulty of dealing with heterogeneity in the classroom, teachers may do their own ability grouping, thus reestablishing a form of tracking. Professional development and learning from schools that have been successful at dismantling tracking can help individual teachers better understand the process and their role. As tracking also occurs in extracurricular activities, ways must be found to appeal to, and include, a wider range of students in these activities.

CONCLUSION

Schools provide an incredibly rich context in which to focus efforts to improve intergroup relations. The task is complicated by the intricate social nature of organizations and the roles that individuals play within them. Understanding the dynamics of change, within individuals as well as within organizations, and how these relate to community structures and cultures can provide valuable insights into how to fashion a more effective environment for improving intergroup relations. Understanding the origins of the barriers reformers face provides us clues about how to get around them. Pinpointing barriers, even seemingly intractable ones, is to suggest, if only indirectly, paths to improvement in school environments that can make them more welcoming to the efforts of intergroup relations programs.

Chapter 13

The Evaluation of Multicultural Education Programs: Techniques and a Meta-Analysis

Cookie White Stephan
Lausanne Renfro
Walter G. Stephan

For the last 25 years, school-based anti-smoking programs have been very popular. For example, two tobacco companies have funded a school-based tobacco prevention program for 250,000 teenagers in 18 states (Kaufman, 2000). Program directors, school officials, and students have received the program enthusiastically and given it high praise. In the state of Washington, an even more extensive 50-hour program was implemented, based on the "best practices" guidelines from the Centers for Disease Control and Prevention and the National Cancer Institute in addition to the material used in the tobacco-company-funded program. This program included a puppet play for third graders on the dangers of secondhand smoke, role playing for middle school students on how to turn down offers of tobacco, and high school student reenactments of testimony from tobacco-liability trials showing the industry's attempts to conceal the consequences of smoking. However, a 15-year study of 8,400 students followed from third grade until after high school recently concluded that the Washington program was ineffective. Students exposed to the anti-smoking program were just as likely to smoke as students who did not receive the training. Given the popularity and the strong belief in the efficacy of these anti-smoking programs, without evaluation even more money might have been spent on completely ineffective programs.

Education Programs for Improving Intergroup Relations. ISBN 0-8077-4459-X (paper). Prior to photocopying items for classroom use, please contact the Copyright Clearance Center, Customer Service, 222 Rosewood Drive, Danvers, MA, 01923, USA, telephone (978) 750-8400.

Less than 2 months after the anti-smoking data were released, the DARE (Drug Abuse Resistance Education) advisory board announced it would revamp its program in response to repeated reports, most recently from the Surgeon General and the National Academy of Sciences, showing that children who participate in the program in elementary school are just as likely to use drugs later in life as children who do not participate (Kalb, 2001; Zernike, 2001). Begun in 1983, the $126 million program was taught in 75% of elementary schools nationwide. Its "just say no" message delivered by police officers was long suspected of being ineffective, but the DARE board resisted accepting evaluation results, in part because of the avid testimonials of participants and DARE officials and trainers. But as one writer put it, "while DARE may feel good, it doesn't do good" (Kalb, 2001, p. 56). Unfortunately, the DARE program was not halted immediately. While a new DARE was being tested, many students continued to participate in the original ineffective program!

Therein lies the message of this chapter. A program that "looks good" may be ineffective, as may one that follows the best professional advice available. Worse yet, a program may have negative effects. Caring multicultural education program designers with materials they think are having positive effects may be increasing racism and prejudice among program participants, even when the participants say they like the program and the participants believe its effects are positive. Participants', program designers', and implementers' beliefs about effectiveness may be dead wrong. Simply put, all programs need to be evaluated. Then the results of the evaluation need to be acted on.

Programs designed to improve intergroup relations should be evaluated to establish what their effects are and to understand why they occur; then this information should be used to improve them. Evaluations make it possible to pinpoint the elements of a program that are most effective as well as determine which aspects of the program need to be changed. In addition, information on the effectiveness of programs can be used to seek funding, justify expenditures, and disseminate the program more widely. Furthermore, understanding why different techniques work can enable practitioners to design better techniques in the future. Without systematic evaluations, it is impossible to make informed decisions about such matters.

The purpose of this chapter is to present information on the evaluation of multicultural education programs and the usefulness of such evaluations. First, it provides a "primer" on evaluating multicultural education programs by discussing various types of data and designs. Then it shows what can be learned from multicultural education program evaluations by summarizing the published evaluations of these programs in a meta-analysis.

Little has been published about the effects of most multicultural education programs. For this reason, even a complete and precise description of multicultural education programs (such as those in the above chapters) makes a valuable contribution to the literature for practitioners who are selecting a program. A published evaluation of the program outcomes is even more useful.

EVALUATING MULTICULTURAL EDUCATION PROGRAMS

Evaluating the effects of multicultural education programs can be both easy and inexpensive. Evaluation research data consist of observations made about the program. The data can answer such questions as "What occurred during the programs?" "Why did these effects occur?" and "Did the program achieve its goals?" The first step in any evaluation must be the careful consideration of the intended effects of the program. Clarifying the specific goals of the program and how they can be measured is often a useful exercise in itself because it leads practitioners to carefully assess whether or not the techniques they are planning to use can achieve their goals.

The two basic types of evaluation research data are quantitative and qualitative. Quantitative data are numerical, while quantitative techniques rely on measurement instruments such as questionnaires and systematic observation. When using quantitative techniques, the type and magnitude of effects produced by the programs are measured. These data are then subjected to statistical analysis. In the best quantitative evaluations, the variables thought to produce these effects are also assessed in such a way that the link between cause and effect becomes clear. If a program with the goal of stereotype reduction does reduce stereotyping in students exposed to it, but stereotypes are not reduced in similar students not attending the program, the researchers can infer that the program was responsible for the reduction in stereotyping.

Qualitative approaches to evaluation consist of observations that are nonnumerical; they often include descriptions of the program and the participants' responses to the program using language and images. Each type of technique has benefits and liabilities. Quantitative techniques are better than qualitative techniques at establishing the actual effects of the program and providing more precise information regarding the exact processes that may be responsible for these effects. Qualitative techniques are better at producing in-depth information and information about subtle nuances of attitudes and behaviors. We begin our discussion with quantitative techniques.

Quantitative Techniques

We will discuss three quantitative designs, going from most to least preferred: the pre-test/post-test with control group design, the post-test only with control group design, and the pre-test/post-test with no control group design.

The Pre-Test/Post-Test with Control Group Design. In this design, both the treatment group and the control group (a comparable group of individuals who are not participants in the multicultural education program) are tested before and after the treatment group participates in the multicultural education program. If the results show changes in intergroup relations attitudes, feelings, or behaviors of the treatment group, whereas no changes occur in the control group, these data strongly suggest that the program is responsible for these changes.

In the ideal situation, the participants are randomly assigned to the treatment and control groups, thus ensuring that they are equivalent. In practical terms, random assignment is often not possible, in which case the two groups should be as comparable as possible. A particularly good control group consists of people who will participate in the program but have not yet done so (e.g., Dunnette & Motowildo, 1982). For example, if many people sign up for a program, but some have to wait to participate until there is space for them, the waiting group would be an ideal control group. Other control groups that can provide useful comparisons are students in the same grade who will not participate in the program and college students with the same major as those in the treatment group. The most important dimensions of equivalence are racial/ethnic composition, sex, age, grade in school, and experience with the relevant out-groups (the target groups for the training). When random assignment is impossible, the pre-test/post-test with control group design allows the evaluator to establish whether or not the treatment group and the control group are equivalent on relevant multicultural education measures before the program begins. Thus, any relevant characteristics should be measured in the treatment and control group at the beginning of the program so that the researcher will know how they might differ. Pre-test equivalence increases the chances that any observed differences between these two groups at the post-test are due to the program.

This design eliminates most of the alternative explanations for the differences between the treatment and control groups. One disadvantage of this design is that it requires more testing than the other designs and thus is more labor intensive. In addition, pre-testing presents a liability: It alerts the participants to the measures of interest and the types of changes anticipated. If the time interval between pre- and post-test is relatively short, participants may remember their responses on the pre-test. Those motivated to help the trainers may report positive changes only because they think the presenters want them to provide these types of responses.

Research indicates that receiving training can have positive effects on people simply because it makes them feel appreciated. To counteract such effects, the control group could receive some type of training program other than multicultural education training (e.g., computer skills training) so that both groups would receive some type of special treatment.

One example of a pre-test/post-test design with a matched control group is provided by an analysis of the effects of a program to reduce racial prejudice by strengthening individual rather than racial attributions for behavior (Aboud & Fenwick, 1999). Four groups of mixed-race fifth graders participated in the study. Students in the treatment group used a textbook including 11 activities, each taking one or two classes. The activities included group discussion, dyadic problem solving, and individual work. The theme of all the activities was that the internal qualities of individuals are more important than the external features of race. Students in the control group followed a standard curriculum on personal and social development. Both groups of students were tested before the beginning of the training and 2 months after the program ended on measures of attention to individual differences and racism. Students in the treatment group increased significantly in their use of individual attributions, whereas students in the control group showed no attributional changes. Highly prejudiced students in the treatment group had significantly decreased racism scores, in contrast to highly prejudiced students in the control group, whose scores did not change. Low-prejudice students in both groups remained low in race prejudice at the post-test. The presence of the control group allowed the researchers to make the inference that the changes in the treatment group were due to the course curriculum.

If a program is multifaceted, the pre-test/post-test with control group approach usually will not provide information on the specific aspects of the program that created the obtained effects. This problem can be remedied in this and all other quantitative approaches by adding questions about variables that might be responsible for (mediate) the effects of the programs. A wide variety of psychological processes may be responsible for the success of multicultural education programs, such as increasing empathy (Stephan & Finlay, 2000), providing more knowledge about the out-group (Stephan & Stephan, 1984), decreasing anxiety about interacting with the out-group (Stephan & Stephan, 1985), reducing stereotyping (Rothbart & John, 1985), increasing perceptions of in-group–out-group similarities (Byrne, 1971), creating superordinate groups (Gaertner, Mann, Murrell, & Dovidio, 1989), emphasizing multiple identities (Brewer, 2000), reinforcing and modeling positive behaviors (Bandura, 1986), and correcting misattributions (Pettigrew, 1979). By measuring the mediating variables appropriate to the program, it is possible to perform statistical analyses that provide indications of the degree to which these psychological processes have created the observed changes in values, attitudes, and behaviors. (For more information on mediating variables, see Chapter 14, this volume.)

For example, if a particular program is designed to change attitudes toward a specific out-group by increasing empathy toward its members, at the pre-test both attitudes and level of empathy toward this group could be measured. At the post-test, they could be measured again. If a positive correlation exists between changes in empathy and changes in attitudes, it is likely that the changes in empathy brought about by the program are responsible for the changes in attitudes. Although this conclusion is only suggestive, since it is based on correlational evidence and correlation does not prove causation, additional statistical tests (structural equation analyses) can be performed that help determine whether the mediators could have been responsible for the outcomes.

An example of an evaluation that examined the mediators of intergroup bias is provided by Wittig and Molina (2000). These authors explored the effect of a multicultural education program in which college students led discussions in middle school and high school classrooms that included the history of various groups, cultural awareness, anti-prejudice, and respect for others. As well as exploring the effect of a multicultural education program on bias, Wittig and Molina (2000) also examined the role of two mediators of intergroup bias. One of these mediators was a combined measure of out-group orientation (interest in people from different groups) and ethnic identity (pride in one's own group). They found that pre-program measures of school interracial climate (see the chapter by Cushner in this volume) significantly influenced out-group orientation and ethnic identity and that out-group orientation and ethnic identity mediated the effect of the program on post-test measures of affective bias against out-group members.

The Post-Test only with Control Group Design. In this design, no pre-testing takes place. The responses of the treatment group are compared to those of a control group only on a post-test. If the control group is comparable to the treatment group in all respects except for not receiving the treatment, comparing the treatment and control groups provides information on the effectiveness of the program. However, if the treatment and the control groups are not completely comparable, any differences between the two groups at the post-test may be due to preexisting differences between the groups. The solution to this potential flaw is random assignment to conditions. If the sample is large enough, random assignment almost guarantees the pre-test equivalence of the two groups.

An example of a post-test–only design with a control group is provided by Henington (1981), who assessed the effect of a 21-hour multicultural and anti-sexism course on the racial and gender knowledge of pre-service secondary student teachers. Knowledge was also assessed in a control group of similar students receiving different training. The results showed a significant difference between the treatment and control groups on racial and gender knowledge immediately after training, and this difference was retained 26 days after instruction.

Henington (1981) attempted to establish equivalence between treatment and control groups by randomly assigning teachers to conditions. She also examined 12 demographic factors, none of which varied between the two groups. When using the post-test only with control group design, collecting appropriate demographic data is a good way of lowering suspicions regarding the possible lack of equivalence of the treatment and control groups.

The Pre-Test/Post-Test without Control Group Design. This design consists of a pre-test and post-test of the treatment group. There is no control group. The participants are simply asked the same questions at the pre-test and at the post-test. For example, attitudes toward specific groups, knowledge, or skill levels might be measured before and after the multicultural education program to determine the difference between them at the two points in time. The pre-test/post-test design should be used to assess the effects of programs only if no control group is available.

This design can provide information about whether or not the program had the desired effects, but it is subject to several limitations. It cannot furnish definitive knowledge about the effects of the program because no control group exists. It is possible that the observed changes would have occurred even without the program (e.g., as children mature during the schoolyear), or they might be due to external events that have nothing to do with the program (e.g., other programs in the school may have had a positive impact on intergroup relations). In addition, if some participants have dropped out between the pre-test and the post-test, the meaning of any differences obtained is questionable, because the group composition has changed. It is possible, for example, that dropouts are due to the fact that only the most interested or most receptive individuals remained through the entire training and that the bored or hostile participants dropped out. If so, the difference between the pre-test and post-test would overstate the effectiveness of the training. Similar to the pre–post with control group design, the pre-test may alert participants to the desired effects of the program, and participants may give the trainers the answers they want to hear.

Grant and Grant (1985) provide an example of a study employing a pre-test/post-test design. They studied the effects of a 2-week in-service multicultural education program on teachers and principals from school districts across the country. The participants were tested before and after the training on measures of racism, sexism, classism, ableism, and ageism. The data show that scores on all these measures decreased (showed less prejudice) after the training. Although the training appeared to be effective, two design problems exist. It is possible that the observed changes would have occurred even without the program (e.g., other events occurring in society, such as a well-publicized hate crime, could have created the changes). In addition, the desired outcome of the training was obvious; teachers may have given the responses desired by the trainers, rather than their true feelings.

Thus, a variety of quantitative techniques exist. None of them are perfect, but all can add important numerical data about programs. Qualitative techniques are discussed next. In some situations, quantitative techniques cannot be applied. For example, some types of observations are very difficult to quantify (e.g., How do the participants' journal entries about race change over time?). In other situations, the evaluators may be uncertain of what to measure (e.g., trainers may know one aspect of the program is not working well, but they do not know why). In still other circumstances, in-depth or subtle information about attitudes and behavior may be particularly useful. For instance, the researchers may be interested in the unique self-insights acquired by participants in the program. In addition, detailed program descriptions provide useful information to all practitioners and researchers. In such circumstances, evaluators turn to qualitative data to supplement or replace quantitative data.

Qualitative Techniques

We present two types of qualitative techniques, post-program surveys and observation.

Post-Program Survey. Post-program surveys, one of the simplest types of evaluations of multicultural education programs, consist of asking participants to evaluate the program after completion. Often participants are asked "What aspects of the program were most effective?" and "What aspects of the program were least effective?" Another commonly asked question is "What did you learn from this program?" Participants can also be asked to discuss the impact of specific facets of the program. It is often useful to ask "What aspects of the program should be changed?" To be effective, the questions should be short, clear, and precise. In general, the questions should be asked anonymously so participants will feel comfortable providing negative as well as positive feedback. Indicating the purpose of the questions (e.g., to improve the program) may encourage honest and open responses to the questions. Because these types of evaluations are so simple and inexpensive, they should be conducted routinely for all multicultural education programs.

Although responses to these types of questions provide valuable information about the participants' perspectives on the program, self-reports are limited by the insight of the participants and their willingness to report their feelings accurately. In particular, participants may be reluctant to report on the portions of the program that they did not like for fear of hurting the trainers' feelings or of being identified.

More important, these types of evaluations cannot be taken as valid evidence of the actual effects of the program. Many types of training lead participants to feel good about themselves and the other people in the training. These participants honestly think that the program has had beneficial effects, and they will report that the program had these positive effects. Such comments, however, do not necessarily mean that individuals have changed their attitudes and behaviors in lasting ways.

Adlerfer (1992) examined the effects of a 3-day diversity training program at a large corporation by asking the participants about their reactions to the program. Although most of them agreed that the program had helped race relations in the corporation, more Blacks than Whites thought the program was useful. Nearly 20% of the White males actually thought the program hurt race relations in the corporation. Although these data do not provide evidence that the program actually hurt race relations, they do suggest that the program needed modification to be more effective for all participants.

Observation. Observation consists of asking the presenters, the participants, and others who are affiliated with the program to describe and analyze their observations of the program. This approach can yield insights into the strengths and weaknesses of the program. The observations of those who are most intimately involved in it are likely to be rich and detailed. But presenters and participants can also be biased by their hopes and expectations. They may be too close to the programs and too vested in the outcomes to be objective in their observations. Observations can also be made by "neutral" observers who may be less influenced by their preconceptions and less subject to bias. Their neutrality and background may enable them to see aspects of the program that the presenters and participants do not, but they are unlikely to be as knowledgeable about the program as the presenters are, and they may miss some program nuances and subtleties.

Fine's (1993a, 1995) observations of the Facing History and Ourselves program provide an elaborate example of the technique of observation. Facing History and Ourselves is a multidisciplinary moral education program that employs a one-semester history course about Nazi Germany before and during World War II to help adolescents reflect critically on contemporary moral issues. (For more information on Facing History and Ourselves, see Chapter 6, this volume.) The curriculum focuses on the Nazi rise to power and the

Holocaust, and takes students back and forth between this historical case study and reflection on the causes and consequences of present-day prejudice, intolerance, violence, and racism. Fine (1991/1992, 1993a, 1995) has observed the entire curriculum and qualitatively documented the students' increased abilities to reflect critically on their own beliefs and behaviors and their responsibilities toward one another as a result of the program. She used students' class discussions, writings, and behaviors in and outside of class to document changes.

In summary, all multicultural education programs need evaluation. You have now seen some of the ways in which they can be conducted and the advantages of evaluation. The better the design, the richer the inferences that can be drawn from the data. However, even the simplest evaluations can provide useful information regarding the effects of the program. Next we turn to an analysis of the published quantitative evaluations of multicultural education programs to determine the overall effectiveness of these programs.

THE EFFECTIVENESS OF MULTICULTURAL EDUCATION PROGRAMS

Some evaluations of multicultural education programs have been published, but with the exception of cooperative learning groups, the literature is sparse. Again with the exception of cooperative learning groups (see Chapter 4, this volume), we found no inclusive review articles on the overall effectiveness of programs in general and only a few on a single technique or context (but see Aboud & Fenwick [1999] on school-based interventions and Bigler [1999] on multicultural curricula). Since considerable time, money, and energy are invested in these programs, and particularly with the ever-present possibility of interventions doing harm rather than good, a thorough evaluation of multicultural education programs other than cooperative learning appears to be needed.

Accordingly, we conducted a meta-analysis of the published articles evaluating multicultural education programs that presented quantitative findings. Meta-analysis is a methodology that allows researchers to combine data from a variety of quantitative studies to evaluate the overall outcomes of the various research studies. This technique enables individual studies to be quantified in the same way through the use of a standardized index of change attributable to the intergroup training, called an effect size. Individual effect sizes are combined and weighted by sample size to produce a single weighted effect size that provides the overall size and direction of the outcome on a given measure from all the studies examined. We used meta-analysis to produce overall effect sizes for attitude and behavior measures to determine whether these programs improved intergroup relations and, if so, what features of the programs were most effective.

Using as keywords *prejudice, racism, intergroup relations,* and *multicultural education,* we searched the following databases from their beginning to the present: PsychLit, PsycFirst, PsycINFO, Article First, ERIC, Education Abstracts, and the Social Science Citation Index. In addition, we contacted researchers to locate books, articles, and chapters in press; found review articles and chapters for additional relevant materials; and examined the references of all the academic materials we had. Evaluations of multicultural education programs began to be published in the 1940s. Programs to improve relations among groups that did not include racial and ethnic groups (e.g., sex discrimination programs) were so few in number that they were eliminated from the analyses. Evaluations of intercultural training (e.g., training individuals to work in Turkey) were also excluded because both the training goals and the targets of change differed from those of the remaining studies.

We located 58 articles containing quantitative data. Of these, we excluded 9 studies reporting interventions lasting less than 3 hours under the assumption that such short programs were unlikely to have lasting effects on intergroup attitudes or behaviors. Of the 49 quantitative articles that reported training longer than 3 hours, 6 were excluded because the dependent variables did not measure intergroup relations attitudes or behaviors, another 6 because the reported data were too incomplete to be included in analyses, and 2 due to problems of design or analysis. We were thus able to include 35 articles in the meta-analysis. (They are indicated in the References by an asterisk.)

These 35 articles are quite diverse. The participants' ages ranged from kindergarten through adulthood. The treatment programs took place all across the United States, as well as in several other countries, and ranged from 4 to 80 hours in length. The participants and the target groups included Whites and all types of ethnic minorities. The programs contained one or more of the following treatments: lectures, readings, library research, films/videos, discussions involving all the participants, small-group discussions, experiential exercises (e.g., simulations, role playing), contact with target-group members, and one-on-one dialogues. Most programs took place in educational institutions, but they also were conducted in work and recreational (e.g., summer camp) settings.

Our four dependent measures consisted of attitude change, behavior change, delayed attitude change (post-measures assessed from 8 to 64 weeks after the intervention), and delayed behavior change. Examples of the measures included stereotypes, racial awareness, social distance, racial preference, perceived group differences, liking for members of an outgroup, the importance of diversity, knowledge of stereotype effects, out-group attributes, discouraging racist comments, encouraging open discussion of cultural differences, and demonstrations of multicultural skills. The dependent measures are diverse because the goals of the programs varied and the measures were designed to assess the specific effects the intervention was intended to produce. All relevant dependent measures from these interventions were included in the meta-analyses, yielding 35 attitude measures, 11 behavior measures, 6 delayed-attitude measures, and 3 delayed-behavior measures.

Effect size was calculated with Cohen's d. Positive effects signify a positive change in intergroup attitudes or behaviors. Z statistics (standard normal deviate) were calculated on the weighted effect sizes to determine their level of statistical significance. In pre–post studies with a control group, the effect sizes were calculated from the difference between pre–post difference scores for both groups. In post-test studies without a control group, effect size was calculated from the pre–post difference score for the treatment group. If the means were missing, the effect sizes were calculated from the F, t, chi-square, or r statistics. The standard deviation was calculated from the pooled standard deviations of the conditions included (Rosenthal, 1994; Shadish & Haddock, 1994; Wolf, 1986).

Before examining the results of the meta-analysis, we should include one note on validity. Since authors are more likely to submit—and journals are more likely to publish—evaluations with positive and significant findings (Bradley & Gupta, 1997; Kramer, Gardner, Brooks, & Yesavage, 1998; Rosenthal, 1979), it is likely that these 35 studies are not representative of the entire pool of evaluations conducted since the 1940s. It is almost certain that evaluations showing no or negative differences were conducted but did not see print. Thus, the results reported here undoubtedly overstate the positive nature of the findings evaluating multicultural education programs.

Table 13.1 displays the effect sizes, standard deviations, confidence intervals (CIs), and Z statistics for the four dependent measures. The immediate attitude and behavior measures showed small but significant positive mean changes. Thus, unlike the anti-smoking and anti-drug programs mentioned at the beginning of the chapter, multicultural education programs have been successful in changing attitudes and behaviors. The magnitude of the effect suggests that, although the programs overall had a positive effect, they are not as successful as they might be. It is possible that the relatively small effect sizes for the immediate post-measures are attenuated by the fact that programs may have been evaluated after their initial implementations and the programs may become more effective as they evolve. The effect sizes were also doubtless lessened by the fact that in some programs trainers were not systematically prepared or experienced; also, some measures of success were not as specific or tailored to the training as they could have been.

Table 13.1. Effect Sizes by Dependent Measures

Dependent Measure	Number of Studies	Weighted effect size (Cohen's *d*)	Standard deviation	95% Confidence Interval	*Z* test for statistical significance
Attitude change	35	.25	.03	.19/.30	8.72*
Behavior change	11	.38	.05	.27/.49	6.97*
Delayed attitude change	6	.80	.11	.57/1.02	7.05*
Delayed behavior change	3	.86	.17	.52/1.20	4.99*

Note: * = $p < .05$.

Obviously, good techniques—carefully selected and pre-tested training components, experienced and well-trained implementers, thoughtfully chosen and appropriate measures of success—are likely to yield more positive outcomes.

Although calculated from a small number of studies and thus having less generalizability, the delayed-attitude and -behavior effect sizes were more than twice as large. These data are important despite their flaws, for they indicate that attitude and behavior changes can be sustained over time.

In an effort to determine which factors were most successful in producing positive intergroup relations changes, we dichotomized these multicultural education programs on the basis of whether or not they included the following components: lectures, assigned readings, videos, group discussions involving all the participants, small-group discussions, one-on-one interactions, and contact with (nonparticipant) target group members. We then conducted statistical tests (one-way analyses of variance or ANOVAs) to determine if programs had more positive attitude or behavior outcomes with the inclusion of these program components.

No single program component significantly contributed to immediate positive attitudes. Surprisingly, programs containing discussions that included all the participants had less positive attitude change than programs that did not (see Table 13.2 for immediate-attitude and -behavior measures). Only one program component, contact with target-group members, produced significant positive behavior changes; interventions including contact showed more positive behavior change than those without such contact. Another unexpected finding was that programs including assigned readings had less positive behavior change than programs that did not.

We also examined the effects of the individual interventions on the delayed-attitude and -behavior measures. We found a single, unanticipated

Table 13.2. Significant One-Way ANOVAs for Presence/Absence of Program Content for Immediate-Attitude and -Behavior Measures

	Means					
	Attitudes			Behaviors		
Program feature	Present	Absent	F	Present	Absent	F
All participant discussions	.34	.91	6.65*			
Readings				.18	.84	8.38*
Nonparticipant contact				.95	.27	10.12*

Note: * = $p < .05$.

finding: Interventions including small-group discussions produced marginally less positive change on delayed-attitude measures than interventions without such discussions (present = .47, absent = 1.43, $F = 5.00$, $p < .10$).

Combining interventions (i.e., any experiential intervention, any academic component, any group work, experiential plus academic, experiential plus groups, academic plus groups) and examining the effects of these combined interventions versus those that contained none of the components produced no significant differences in any of the four attitude and behavior measures (calculations not shown).

We then combined the four dependent measures and examined the effect of the interventions on this dependent variable. A single marginally significant result was found: Interventions including some type of experiential exercise led to somewhat greater positive change than those that did not include such exercises (experiential component present = 1.14, absent = .43, $F = 3.29$, $p < .10$).

In addition, we examined the effects of the number of hours of intervention, geographic location of the intervention, and age and ethnicity of participants. None were significantly associated with degree of attitude or behavior change. The quality of the design of the evaluation was also unrelated to degree of attitude or behavior change.

In evaluating the results of the meta-analysis, we can conclude that multicultural education programs generally have significantly positive effects on attitudes and behaviors, but we have little information as to the sources of this success. The only clear statement we can make is that these results confirm the contact hypothesis: Programs including contact with nonparticipant target persons resulted in more positive behavior change than those that did not include this type of contact. Research on the contact hypothesis indicates that some of the necessary conditions for contact to improve multicultural education are equal-status interactions, the pursuit of common goals, support by authority figures, and a perception of common interests and humanity (Allport, 1954; Pettigrew, 1971, 1998; Stephan, 1987; Stephan & Stephan, 1996; Williams, 1947).

Weak evidence suggests that programs containing experiential interventions are more successful than those that do not. These data are consistent with the findings from intercultural communication training showing the effectiveness of experiential over less-involving techniques (Goldstein & Smith, 1999; Gudykunst, Hammer, & Wiseman, 1977; Landis, Brislin, & Hulgus, 1985). The uninvolving nature of completing assigned readings may help explain the finding that programs with readings produce less behavior change than those that do not include readings. Some data from the meta-analysis also suggest that discussions, whether small-group discussions or those that include all participants, may inhibit attitude and behavior change.

It thus appears that successful attitude and behavior changes are dependent not on specific interventions in multicultural education programs but on the manner in which the program contents are conveyed. With the exception of contact, it seems that all other content can either facilitate or inhibit positive changes—depending on the way in which it is delivered. Clearly, trainers must be ever-vigilant regarding the way in which program components are presented. It is easy, for example, to imagine a discussion that promotes negative attitudes toward multicultural education through the expression of prejudice by participants or the unintentional confirmation of stereotypes—or one that has no effect because it is uninvolving. One can also imagine a discussion that has positive effects because it engages participants, provides knowledge, creates empathy, and reduces stereotyping.

Little information on program content was presented in the manuscripts we reviewed, so we were able to code information only in gross categories (e.g., role playing). With more information regarding the way the techniques were employed (e.g., What was the content of the role playing? Was a script provided? How were role players prepared? How long did the role plays last? Were all participants involved? Did role players get feedback?), better measures of training processes could have been created. It is possible that more training detail would have provided clearer information regarding successful and unsuccessful training components and processes. A more precise examination of the techniques will not be possible until researchers present more information regarding the details of their training. We urge authors to provide this detailed qualitative type of information. Ideally, a combination of both quantitative and qualitative data would be used to assess any multicultural education program.

The fact that few clear content suggestions can be made at present further underscores the importance of evaluations of multicultural education programs. A magic list of successful program components does not now and may never exist. It is likely that different types of programs can have positive, negative, or no effects, depending on the way in which they are implemented. It is imperative that program designers and implementers ascertain which outcomes their program produces.

Clearly, more information on the outcomes of multicultural education programs is needed. Every evaluation should provide detailed information on the programs and the outcomes of the programs. In addition, research that attempts to identify mediators of the training effects, and to assess the extent to which the proposed mediators accounted for the programs' effects, is almost unknown in the literature and is greatly needed. Until researchers are certain they understand why their programs produced the outcomes that were found, they will know less than they should know to make their programs maximally effective. Finally, extremely few comparative studies exist. Information regarding the outcomes of two or more programs in the same population is invaluable to researchers and trainers in selecting ideal training programs.

We have presented strong evidence that multicultural education programs work. We need more detailed evaluations, however, to determine why and how they work so we may reach our ultimate goal—to make them even more effective.

SUMMARY

We argued for the importance of evaluating multicultural education programs and suggested a number of analytic strategies. In addition, we conducted a meta-analysis of the available quantitative data on the outcomes of multicultural education programs and found that these programs typically have positive effects on intergroup attitudes and behaviors. However, we found few predictors of program success, other than contact with the target group. Much more research is needed on the outcomes of various types of programs. In particular, the literature lacks studies showing the mechanisms by which effects occur and studies comparing different types of multicultural education training techniques. It also lacks detailed information on the content of successful multicultural education training programs.

Chapter 14

From Intervention to Outcome: Processes in the Reduction of Bias

John F. Dovidio
Samuel L. Gaertner
Tracie L. Stewart
Victoria M. Esses
Marleen ten Vergert
Gordon Hodson

Intergroup relations programs, many of which have been illustrated in detail in this volume, share the overall common objective of reducing intergroup bias. Bias, however, is a multifaceted phenomenon, involving beliefs, emotions, and behavioral orientations. Moreover, intergroup relations programs differ substantially in the nature and emphases of the interventions they involve, also as amply demonstrated in the present volume. Thus, although it is important to ask *whether* a particular program is effective in reducing bias (see Chapter 13, this volume), it is also critical, both theoretically and practically, to consider *how* different types of interventions may reduce different types of bias. Theoretically, understanding how interventions can reduce bias helps to illuminate the underlying psychological processes responsible for the origins and maintenance of orientations that produce intergroup discord and conflict. Pragmatically, a comprehensive appreciation of the intervening mechanisms can help practitioners tailor their emphasis on different aspects of training to address most effectively the nature of the problems or issues that need to be addressed.

In this chapter, we explore the ways in which different types of antibias interventions can reduce bias. We summarize this process in Figure 14.1,

Education Programs for Improving Intergroup Relations. ISBN 0-8077-4459-X (paper). Prior to photocopying items for classroom use, please contact the Copyright Clearance Center, Customer Service, 222 Rosewood Drive, Danvers, MA, 01923, USA, telephone (978) 750-8400.

which illustrates the organization of this chapter. As Figure 14.1 depicts, although specific types of intergroup relations strategies, such as multicultural education and intergroup dialogues, differ considerably in their approaches and techniques, there may also be important similarities in their components and content. Essentially, these different programs and interventions may operate through one of two processes, or both. One process involves change and enlightenment in the program participant, for example, by increasing understanding of and sensitivity to the plight of others or to one's own role and responsibilities in creating social change. The second process, which is supported by the significant evidence that has accumulated over the past 50 years on the contact hypothesis (Allport, 1954; Pettigrew & Tropp, 2000), involves the beneficial outcomes of structured interactions between majority- and minority-group members.

Enlightenment and contact, in turn, can stimulate a number of more basic, underlying processes that have been identified as important *mediators* of reductions in bias. Mediators are the psychological mechanisms through which outside forces produce change. In the context of this chapter, they are the internal processes that translate external influences and interventions into reductions of prejudice, stereotyping, and discrimination. We have classified these mediators as primarily cognitive, involving the ways people think about others, and primarily emotional, relating to the ways that people feel about others. Finally, on the far right of Figure 14.1, we note that bias, the target of change, is a multifaceted phenomenon, involving prejudice, stereotypes, negative affect, and discrimination.

We use Figure 14.1 as an organizing theme for this chapter. However, we move through this figure from right to left, beginning with a consideration of the nature of bias and recognition of its different aspects. We start here because we believe that understanding the nature of bias is an essential first step in taking action to combat it. Next, we identify a range of processes, based on extensive psychological research, that are candidates for mediation. After that, we introduce the basic distinction between enlightenment and interaction approaches. We then review the ways in which different types of interventions and programs can relate both to the mediating mechanisms and to different types of reductions in bias. Finally, we consider the implications of this analysis for practice and for program evaluation.

THE NATURE OF BIAS

Intergroup bias comes in many forms. It is reflected in attitudes toward another group, in beliefs about another group, in emotional reactions, and in behavioral orientations or actual behavior toward members

Figure 14.1. From intervention to outcome: The intervening role of content and mediating processes on the reduction of bias

Program/ Training/ Intervention	Approach/ Component	Mediating Mechanism Process	Target of Change (Bias)
Multicultural Education	*Enlightenment* Knowledge Meta-Information Models Perspectives	*Cognitive* Social Categorization Social Knowledge Standards	Prejudice
Intergroup Dialogues			Stereotypes
Cooperative Learning	*Contact* Interaction Cooperation Equal Status Supportive Norms Personalization	*Emotional* Empathy Self-Directed Emotion	Negative Affect
Moral & Values Education			Discrimination

of another group or toward the group as a whole. These types of bias reflect four main components of bias that have been studied extensively in psychological research: prejudice, stereotypes, negative affect, and discrimination. We also note that bias can be expressed unconsciously as well as intentionally (Blair, 2001; Devine, 1989). In this section we will first briefly describe the basic types of bias and the levels at which they manifest themselves. We will then review evidence of the interrelationships among the different facets of bias.

Types of Bias

Prejudice has been commonly defined as a negative attitude, but theorists have disagreed about whether a negative attitude must have other distinguishing characteristics to be classified as a prejudice. On the one hand, researchers have argued that a defining feature of prejudice is that the negative attitude must be unfounded or unjustified. Allport (1954) defined prejudice as "an antipathy based on faulty and inflexible generalization. It may be felt or expressed. It may be directed toward a group as a whole, or toward an individual because he is a member of that group" (p. 9). On the other hand, other definitions, reflecting our own perspective, focus on the importance of group membership as a determinant of orientation toward an individual. Jones (1997), for example, used the term *prejudice* to refer to "a positive or negative attitude, judgment, or feeling about a person that is generalized from attitudes or beliefs about the group to which the person belongs" (p. 10).

Prejudice is also generally conceptualized, like other attitudes, as having a cognitive component (e.g., beliefs about a target group), an affective component (e.g., dislike), and a conative component (e.g., a behavioral predisposition to avoid the target group [Esses, Haddock, & Zanna, 1993; Zanna & Rempel, 1988]). The cognitive component involves specific thoughts or beliefs about the attitude object; the affective component involves feelings and emotions associated with the attitude object; and the behavioral component reflects associations with the person's past or intended action toward the attitude object. However, as Eagly and Chaiken (1998) note: "Even though attitudes may be expressed through cognitive, affective, and behavioral responses and formed through responding of each of these types, attitudes do not necessarily have all three aspects, either at the point of their formation or at the point of attitudinal responding. Attitudes can be formed primarily or exclusively on the basis of any one of the three types of processes" (p. 272). Prejudice is typically measured using standardized scales reflecting people's degree of endorsement of a range of statements about attributes of the group, feelings about the group, and support for policies that affect the group (see Dovidio, Brigham, Johnson, & Gaertner, 1996).

Whereas prejudice is an attitude toward a social group, a *stereotype* represents a constellation of beliefs about the members of a particular social category. As with definitions of *prejudice*, conceptualizations of stereotypes range from those that characterize stereotyping as general processes, which may often be functional, to those that consider inaccuracy as a defining feature of stereotypes. In fact, stereotypes were initially considered to have a functional component. Lippmann (1922), who has been recognized for coining the term *stereotype*, described a stereotype as a "picture inside [one's] head" that helped to manage the complexity of one's environment by simplifying the social world. Within the cognitive orientation that has dominated research on stereotyping over the past three decades, theorists have also stressed the role of stereotypes in helping people process and comprehend complex information about people and groups while deemphasizing value judgments about using them. For example, Hamilton and Trolier (1986) defined *stereotypes* simply as "cognitive categories that are used by the social perceiver in processing information about people" (p. 128). From this perspective, stereotypes are not *necessarily* distorted or erroneous.

Nevertheless, even recognizing the possible functions of stereotyping and the predisposition of people to reduce uncertainty and cognitive demand by classifying people as well as objects based on perceived similarity and group membership (Fiske & Taylor, 1991), most contemporary definitions of *stereotypes* explicitly address their faulty nature. Stereotypes have been defined as overgeneralizations resulting from irrational processes (e.g., Allport, 1954) and as beliefs characterized by inordinate rigidity and resistance to change (e.g., Adorno, Frenkel-Brunswik, Levinson, & Sanford, 1950). More recently, Ryan, Judd, and Park (1996) have identified another dimension of possible stereotype inaccuracy, "dispersion inaccuracy." Specifically, a trait attribution (e.g., that members of a group are athletic) could be accurate in its estimate of the average level of a characteristic within a group, but it may still be an inaccurate overgeneralization in that it underestimates the range or variability of that trait within the group. That is, people may overattribute the extent to which different members of a group share the same trait. Stereotypes thus involve the out-group homogeneity effect (Mullen & Hu, 1989), the phenomenon in which people overestimate the extent to which members of other groups are alike (e.g., the belief that all members of a group are athletic). Stereotypes are typically measured by asking respondents to provide descriptions of members of a group or by rating the extent to which specific traits (e.g., athleticism) are associated with the group.

Whereas stereotypes represent a predominantly cognitive response to members of other groups, *affective reactions* are primarily emotional in content. Bias has often been considered in terms of strong negative affect (Mackie, Devos, & Smith, 2001). For example, the scapegoat theory of prejudice

(Dollard, Doob, Miller, Mowrer & Sears, 1939) defines *prejudice* as a form of displaced hostility. However, negative intergroup affect does not necessarily have to involve hostility toward members of another group to be problematic. Emotions such as discomfort and anxiety are typically dominant features of intergroup contact and interaction that can interfere with effective communication and lead to negative intergroup perceptions (e.g., Hyers & Swim, 1998; Stephan & Stephan, 1985). In addition, intergroup bias can take the form of less-positive feelings toward members of other groups than toward one's own group (e.g., in terms of less admiration and respect) rather than more negative feelings toward members of the out-group (Brewer, 1979; Pettigrew & Meertens, 1995; Smith & Ho, 2002).

In most research involving affect and intergroup bias, emotions are measured by simply asking participants to indicate—for example, on a 7-point scale from "not at all" to "very much"—the extent in which they experienced a range of emotions. Attempting to examine more automatic and spontaneous expressions of affect, researchers have studied facial expressions and used advanced techniques to measure facial muscle activity, heart rate, and other physiological responses (e.g., Vanman, Paul, Ito, & Miller, 1997).

In the context of intergroup relations, *discrimination* has a pejorative meaning. It implies more than simply distinguishing among social objects; it also implies inappropriate treatment of individuals due to their group membership—a selectively unjustified negative behavior toward members of the target group. According to Allport (1954), discrimination involves denying "individuals or groups of people equality of treatment which they may wish" (p. 51). Jones (1972) defined *discrimination* as "those actions designed to maintain own-group characteristics and favored position at the expense of the comparison group" (p. 4).

Although discrimination in judicial terms implies an act of conscious and intentional behavior, psychological studies have demonstrated that bias can often expressed in subtle ways without a person's awareness. Racial discrimination has been measured in terms of failure to help, self-disclosure, seating distances, and nonverbal behaviors (Dovidio & Gaertner, 1998; Gaertner & Dovidio, 1986).

Relations Among Prejudice, Stereotypes, Negative Affect, and Discrimination

Traditional views of prejudice, stereotypes, negative affect, and discrimination suggest, at least at first glance, that these are likely closely clustered facets of intergroup bias. To the extent that stereotypes represent the cognitive component of prejudice, stereotyping would be expected to be positively related to prejudice. In addition, because attitudes have an emotional component, affective reactions and prejudice would also be expected to be strongly positively related. Given the long-term focus on attitudes in psychology, because of their presumed ability to predict behavior, prejudice, as a negative attitude, would be expected to predict discrimination directly.

Furthermore, some scholars have proposed that stereotypes can be a consequence, as well as a cause, of discrimination. Allport (1954), for instance, described stereotypes as "primarily rationalizers" of discrimination. He added, "While it does no harm (and may do some good) to combat them in schools and colleges, and to reduce them in mass media of communication, it must not be thought that this attack alone will eradicate the roots of prejudice" (p. 204). More recently, Jost and Banaji (1994) similarly concluded that "individuals generate beliefs about themselves and stereotypes about social groups in such a way that existing situations are justified" (p. 3). For example, people may make dispositional attributions, such as "lazy," to members of a group to provide a causal explanation for the group's disadvantaged economic status.

Despite ample and seemingly obvious reasons why prejudice, stereotypes, negative affect, and discrimination would be expected to be strongly associated, the empirical evidence indicates that their relations are actually quite modest. Dovidio and colleagues (1996) conducted a quantitative, meta-analytic review of the literature on racial prejudice, stereotyping, and discrimination. They found that the average correlation between prejudice and discrimination was only moderate ($r = .32$). The correlations between prejudice and stereotyping ($r = .25$) and between stereotyping and discrimination ($r = .16$) were even weaker. Similarly, in other research, Whites' negative affect is a significant but moderate predictor of bias toward a range of groups (Dovidio, Esses, Beach, & Gaertner, 2002; Stangor, Sullivan, & Ford, 1991).

Overall, this pattern of consistently significant interrelations among prejudice, stereotypes, negative affect, and discrimination theoretically suggests that these phenomena reflect some underlying theme of bias. However, the modest magnitude of their relations further indicates that, in many ways, these phenomena also reflect unique aspects of bias. Thus, from a practitioner's perspective, prejudice, stereotyping, negative affect, and discriminatory behavior may all be considered separate, legitimate targets of interventions. In the next section, we examine different processes that can mediate the relationship between these interventions and reductions in attitudinal, cognitive, affective, and behavioral biases.

MEDIATING PROCESSES

Mediating mechanisms may be viewed as the most proximate processes responsible for reductions in bias. Although the distinction is not always fully clear-cut and mutually exclusive, the processes that can mediate the reduction of bias can be classified as primarily cognitive or primarily affective. Cognitive processes involve the ways people think about and categorize others, whereas affective processes relate to emotional factors that lead to reductions in bias.

Cognitive Processes

Interventions that operate through cognitive processes can influence the ways that people conceive of others (for example, in terms of group membership or as individuals), what they know about others and how they construe their relations with others, and how they assess what are appropriate or inappropriate standards of behavior.

Social Categorization. One of the most basic processes in social cognition, the ways in which people think about others, involves social categorization. Because of the complexity of one's environment and the demands on one's cognitive resources, people operate as "cognitive misers" (Fiske & Taylor, 1991) and rely on heuristics (i.e., mental shortcuts) in making many everyday decisions. One such process involves social categorization, the classification of people into groups based on similarity or perceived group membership.

Social categorization is particularly important when the categorization of others is in terms of membership in one's own group (the in-group) or in a different group (the out-group). Upon social categorization, people favor in-group members in terms of evaluations, attributions, material resources, helping, and social support (see Gaertner & Dovidio, 2000). This type of social categorization also profoundly influences the ways in which people think of others. For instance, people are more generous and forgiving in their explanations for the behaviors of in-group relative to out-group members. Positive behaviors and successful outcomes are more likely to be attributed to internal, stable characteristics (the personality) of in-group than out-group members, whereas negative outcomes are more likely to be ascribed to the personalities of out-group members than of in-group members (Hewstone, 1990; Pettigrew, 1979).

The process of social categorization, however, is not completely unalterable. Categorization of a person into the in-group or the out-group is dependent on the criteria used to distinguish the groups. For instance, African Americans can be seen as an out-group by White Americans when race is salient but as a member of the in-group in situations in which nationality is more salient. Besides flexibility in defining categories, people may also see others as unique individuals and in personalized ways, given appropriate interest and motivation. By modifying a perceiver's goals, motives, perceptions of past experiences, expectations, and factors within the social context more broadly, there is opportunity to alter the level of category inclusiveness that will be primary or most influential in a given situation. This malleability of the level at which others are perceived and categorized is important because of its implications for altering the way people think about members of in-groups and out-groups and consequently about the nature of intergroup relations.

Because categorization is a basic process that is fundamental to intergroup bias, researchers have targeted this process as a starting point to begin to improve intergroup relations. From the social categorization perspective, the issue to be addressed is how situations can be structured to alter inclusive–exclusive collective representations of others. Recent work (Gaertner & Dovidio, 2000) identifies two ways in which original members of two different groups can be re-represented—conceived as separate individuals or reconceptualized as a member of one's own group. These representations map directly onto two processes that can reduce intergroup bias, decategorization and recategorization.

Decategorization refers to influencing whether people identify themselves on the continuum proposed by Tajfel and Turner (1979; see also Brewer, 1988; Brewer & Miller, 1984; Fiske, Lin, & Neuberg, 1999) primarily as group members or as distinct individuals. With decategorization, group boundaries are degraded, inducing members of different groups to conceive of themselves and others as separate individuals and encouraging more personalized interactions.

Recategorization, in contrast, is not designed to reduce or eliminate categorization but rather to structure a definition of group categorization at a higher level of category inclusiveness in ways that reduce intergroup bias and conflict (Allport, 1954; see also Gaertner & Dovidio, 2000). As proposed by the common in-group identity model (Gaertner & Dovidio, 2000), recategorization induces members of different groups to conceive of themselves as a single, more inclusive superordinate group rather than as two completely separate groups. Recategorization extends the benefits of pro–in-group bias to former out-group members who are now recategorized as part of the in-group, thus leading to more positive attitudes toward them. That is, the processes that lead to favoritism toward in-group members would now be directed toward former out-group members as they become redefined from exclusive to inclusive categories.

Social Knowledge. Increasing what people know about others can reduce bias in at least four ways. First, with more information about others, people will be more likely to see others in individuated and personalized ways. As we noted in the previous section, this type of decategorization reduces bias. Second, greater knowledge of others may reduce uncertainty about how to interact with them, which reduces the likelihood of avoidance of members of other groups and reduces discomfort in interactions that do occur (Crosby, Bromley, & Saxe, 1980; Gaertner & Dovidio, 1986). Third, enhanced intercultural understanding, in terms of better historical background or increased cultural sensitivity, can reduce bias by increasing recognition of injustice. As Stephan and Finlay (1999) explained, "learning about suffering and discrimination while empathizing with the victims may lead people to . . . come to believe that the victims do not deserve the mistreatment. . . . If the victims do not deserve this unjust treatment, it may no longer be tenable to hold such negative attitudes toward them" (p. 735).

A fourth way in which increased social knowledge can reduce intergroup bias is by changing the way that people view the functional relations between groups and their members. On the basis of their work on their classic Robbers Cave study, Sherif, Harvey, White, Hood, and Sherif (1961) proposed that competition between groups produces prejudice and discrimination, whereas intergroup interdependence and cooperative interaction result in successful outcomes that reduce intergroup bias. More recently, realistic group conflict theory (Campbell, 1965; see also Bobo, 1988), the instrumental model of group conflict (Esses, Dovidio, Jackson, & Armstrong, 2001), and social dominance theory (Sidanius & Pratto, 1999) have also emphasized the importance of how people view the competitive or cooperative nature of intergroup relations as a critical mediator of intergroup relations. Thus, appropriately structured information that leads people to see the relations between their group and another group as cooperative and interdependent rather than as competitive and adversarial can substantially reduce intergroup biases (Esses et al., 2001).

Standards of Behavior. Information can also lead people to reevaluate or change their personal standards of behavior in ways that reduce biases. This information can influence people's perceptions of what they believe to be appropriate and just, and how they construe social norms and the standards expected by others. The study of the influence of norms on prejudice and expressions of bias has a long-standing tradition in social psychology (see Duckitt, 1992). This research frequently makes a distinction between personal norms and standards on the one hand, and social norms and standards on the other (Allport, 1954; Devine, 1989).

Information or interventions that make people's own egalitarian standards more salient reduce the likelihood that people will exhibit biases toward others. Macrae, Bodenhausen, and Milne (1998) found that increasing people's self-focus, which presumably heightens their attention to personal standards, resulted in less stereotypical descriptions of others. Consistent with the argument that the nature of personal standards is a key factor, this reduction in stereotyping occurred only among participants whose personal standards dictated an avoidance of using stereotypes in thinking about or acting toward others.

Information that influences perceptions of the standards of others, and thus social norms, also systematically affects the expression of stereotypes. For example, with respect to race, Wittenbrink and Henly (1996) provided White college students with information that suggested that other Whites generally were relatively low or high in their racial biases. As the researchers hypothesized, when participants were led to believe that other Whites were less biased, White students themselves displayed lower levels of self-reported prejudice and, in a simulated juror task, evaluated a Black defendant more positively, were less confident of the defendant's guilt, and advocated shorter prison sentences (see also Stangor, Sechrist, & Jost, 2001).

Taken together, then, there is consistent evidence of the impact of cognitive factors that influence how people categorize others, how they perceive their relation to others, and how they define appropriate standards of conduct on the expression of prejudice, stereotypes, negative feelings, and discrimination. In the next section, we review evidence on the role of affect in the reduction of bias.

Emotional Influences

Because negative emotions are an important facet of bias, affective processes are also implicated as critical mediators of reductions in bias. These processes may either involve the development of more positive emotional bonds with others—for example, through empathy—or focus on the arousal of negative emotions directed toward the self. Negative self-affect, if appropriately channeled, can motivate a person to change his or her attitudes and behavior. As we observed earlier, cognitive and affective processes are not necessarily independent. For instance, information that makes people aware that they are not meeting personal or social standards can also produce negative emotions that contribute, in their own right, to the reduction of bias. In this section, we consider how these factors reduce bias.

Affective Connections to Others. Interventions aimed at enhancing empathy toward members of another group appear particularly promising in reducing intergroup biases. For example, a study by Batson and colleagues (1997) demonstrated the effect of empathy on attitudes toward stigmatized groups. Participants who were instructed to focus on the feelings of the person (a high-empathy condition) rather than on the facts of the person's problem (low-empathy condition) while listening to an interview with a member of a stigmatized group subsequently exhibited more positive attitudes toward the other person's group (people suffering from AIDS or homeless people). Finlay and Stephan (2000) reported similar improvements in Whites' attitudes toward Blacks after participants read a set of short essays ostensibly written by Black college students describing their personal experiences with discrimination (e.g., being falsely accused of wrongdoing, being denied check-writing privileges). The empathy procedures instructed participants to either imagine how the writer of the essay would feel, or how they themselves would feel, in that situation. Finlay and Stephan (2000) found that both empathy conditions eliminated differences in the evaluations of Blacks and Whites found in a control condition.

There are at least two ways in which empathy can have its effect. Empathy can reduce bias by leading people to feel more positively about others or by motivating them to behave in a more supportive way toward others. With respect to changing the way people feel about others, Batson and colleagues (1997) found that asking participants to imagine how the other person was feeling, compared to attending primarily to the information presented, increased liking for a specific member of another group, which generalized to more positive attitudes toward the group as a whole. In terms of arousing motivations to behave in a more supportive way toward others, Batson (1991) has also shown that empathy can stimulate a particular emotional experience, empathic concern (e.g., compassion, sympathy), that produces an altruistic motivation to improve the welfare of the other person. To the extent that prejudice is commonly seen as threatening the welfare of the other person, one manifestation of this altruistic response may be increasing one's motivation to respond without prejudice to that person's group.

Other types of interventions involve having people focus on their own emotions rather than the emotions of others. Some of these techniques are aimed at reducing negative emotions and, when possible, creating new, positive affective connections. Other techniques are designed to influence particular self-directed negative emotions, such as guilt, that arouse motivations to change one's attitudes in ways that will improve intergroup relations.

Reducing Negative Feelings. The aversive racism framework (Dovidio & Gaertner, 1998; Gaertner & Dovidio, 1986) proposes that most Whites' attitudes toward Blacks are primarily characterized by feelings of anxiety and discomfort that lead to avoidance, rather than by hatred and antipathy that produce open hostility toward Blacks. Stephan and Stephan (1985) also proposed that intergroup anxiety is a dominant factor in intergroup responses and bias (see also Hyers & Swim, 1998; Islam & Hewstone, 1993). In addition, building on the work on contemporary forms of racism in the United States, Pettigrew and Meertens (1995) hypothesized that, compared to traditionally blatant forms, contemporary forms of intergroup bias may reflect differential positive affective reactions, rather than overt negative reactions to outgroups. These approaches thus suggest that reducing intergroup fear and anxiety and substituting more positive emotions is a critical factor for facilitating more favorable responses of Whites toward Blacks.

Supportive of this reasoning, Esses and Dovidio (2002) asked participants to focus on their feelings or on their thoughts while they viewed a videotape depicting various everyday forms of discrimination against Blacks or a control videotape. Participants who focused on their feelings while watching the Black discrimination video were substantially less likely to report fear and more likely to report respect among their feelings toward Blacks than participants in the other conditions. Furthermore, in part because of this reduction of negative affect and the development of respect, these participants were also more willing to engage in interactions and intergroup contact with Blacks.

Arousing Self-Directed Negative Emotion. Recent survey and experimental research indicates that most people in North America strongly support principles of equality and fairness (see Dovidio & Gaertner, 1998). Because of this commitment to equality, people typically experience distress at obvious evidence of their bias toward other groups. Thus, engaging people to discover inconsistencies among their self-images, values, and behaviors may arouse cognitive dissonance—an unpleasant state that is experienced when people become aware of inconsistencies in how they think, feel, and act toward others (Leippe & Eisenstadt, 1994)—or other negative emotional states (Devine & Monteith, 1993; Rokeach, 1973) that can produce more favorable attitudes toward members of stereotyped groups in general and Blacks in particular.

Devine and Monteith (1993; see also Monteith, 1993), for example, have found that people who hold egalitarian standards experience emotions such as guilt or compunction as a consequence of deviating from these standards, and, as a result, they show increased motivation to respond in nonprejudiced ways or in ways that reaffirm their nonprejudiced self-images (see also Dutton & Lake, 1973). Similarly, viewing unfair discriminatory acts against others while empathizing with them may arouse feelings associated with moral indignation for violations of egalitarian values (see also Stephan & Finlay, 1999). These perceptions of injustice and wrongdoing may, in turn, produce an increased commitment to personal efforts to respond in nonprejudiced ways.

Cognitive and Affective Mediators and the Reduction of Bias

In this section, we have reviewed a range of cognitive and emotional processes that can be engaged to reduce intergroup biases. However, as we highlighted earlier, bias is a multifaceted concept that involves prejudice, stereotypes, negative affect, and discrimination. In addition, as we have explained, cognitive and emotional responses are not necessarily independent. Making people aware that they are behaving in ways that deviate from their personal standards may not only heighten the salience of these standards (a cognitive effect) but also generate feelings of guilt and compunction (emotional reactions) that contribute to self-regulatory processes that will bring one's actions in line with one's standards (Devine, Plant, & Buswell, 2000). Furthermore, each of the types of bias we identified has both cognitive and emotional aspects. Prejudice, as an attitude, has both a belief and an affective component (Esses et al., 1993; Zanna & Rempel, 1988). In addition, although stereotypes are primarily cognitive structures, they involve emotional associations as well (Dovidio et al., 1996). How affective responses are labeled or interpreted by those who experience them, a cognitive activity, critically influences the nature of the emotional experience (Schachter & Singer, 1962). Also, some behaviors, such as willingness to engage in intergroup contact, may have a strong affective basis, whereas other actions, such as support for public policies, may have a stronger cognitive basis (Dovidio et al., 2002). Thus, each of these mediators can have quite diffuse effects on reductions in a range of different facets of bias.

Nevertheless, in terms of applications, practitioners might consider placing their emphasis on particular mediating mechanisms in light of the types of bias that they are most interested in targeting. In previous work (Dovidio et al., 1996, 2002), we have suggested that the effectiveness of a particular mechanism for reducing bias may be a function of the extent to which the mechanism and the outcome correspond in their balance of affective and cognitive influences. For instance, we (Dovidio et al., 2002; Esses & Dovidio, 2002) have found that interventions that emphasize emotional processes (i.e., focusing on one's feelings) are more effective in reducing bias in behaviors that have a relatively strong affective component (willingness to engage in intergroup contact) than behaviors that have a stronger cognitive component (support for public policies benefiting minorities). Conversely, we observed that interventions that emphasize cognitions more than emotions (i.e., focusing on one's thoughts) had a somewhat stronger impact on support for public policies than on willingness to engage in intergroup contact. Thus, by understanding the range of processes that can mediate reductions of different types of biases, practitioners can be more effective in their interventions. In the next two sections we examine more closely the nature of these interventions.

CONTENT AND COMPONENTS OF INTERVENTIONS

As illustrated in Figure 14.1, different types of intergroup relations and training programs may be classified broadly according to the extent to which they focus on personal enlightenment or involve direct or symbolic intergroup contact.

Enlightenment

Enlightenment approaches, broadly defined, involve expanding the knowledge that people have of other groups or altering people's perspective of their relations with others. These approaches can reduce bias mainly through cognitive but also through affective mechanisms. For example, multicultural education programs that provide information about other cultures and their traditions can allow people to see members of another group in a more individuated and personalized fashion, while at the same time reducing the anxiety and fear that come from ignorance. Information about history and historical injustices may allow people to develop more inclusive representations (e.g., as Americans) or arouse feelings of collective guilt or moral indignation that can motivate more positive orientations and reductions in bias toward other groups (Swim & Miller, 1999).

These types of approaches, which focus directly on changes in the knowledge and sensitivity of participants, also convey important messages indirectly. This "meta-information" involves important messages, communicated implicitly, that go beyond the specific training and leads people to reflect more broadly on their orientation toward members of other groups relative to members of their own group. The emphases of these approaches on the positive aspects of other cultures provide models of acceptance and understanding for participants. These models make salient and reinforce social norms of equality and nonprejudice. In addition, for children, who may be limited in their opportunity for moral development and for abstract reasoning, modeling can be even more effective at reducing bias and creating more positive orientations toward others than direct instruction or "moral exhortation" (Grusec, 1982; see also Schroeder, Penner, Dovidio, & Piliavin, 1995). Modeling can teach children, in a concrete way, how they should behave toward others, and it can reinforce the positive beliefs and motivations that they may already be in the process of forming.

In developing awareness and understanding, these types of approaches also encourage participants to be more flexible in the perspectives that they adopt toward members of other groups. Perspective taking is an important factor in creating emotional empathy, which we have seen is an important emotional mediator of reductions in bias. In addition, Galinsky and Moskowitz (2000) have proposed that taking the perspective of another person produces more individuated perceptions and, as a consequence, may reduce the use of stereotypes. They found that White participants who were instructed to take the perspective of a Black person in writing an essay about "a day in the life" of the person exhibited less bias on an implicit measure of stereotypes than White participants who wrote the essay without receiving these instructions. Because automatic stereotypes are believed to shape perceptions, memory, and judgment at the earliest stages of information processing, influencing these stereotypes can have a positive effect on the expression of explicit stereotypes as well as attitudes (Galinsky & Moskowitz, 2000).

Intergroup Contact

Programs and interventions, particularly those that have a significant intergroup experiential component, can exert their impact through processes more directly associated with intergroup contact. For the past 50 years the contact hypothesis (Allport, 1954; Pettigrew, 1998; Pettigrew & Tropp, 2000) has represented a promising and popular strategy for reducing intergroup bias and conflict. This hypothesis proposes that simple contact between groups is not automatically sufficient to improve intergroup relations. Rather, for contact between groups to reduce bias successfully, certain prerequisite features must be present. These characteristics of contact include equal status between the groups; cooperative (rather than competitive) intergroup interaction; opportunities for personal acquaintance between the members, especially with those whose personal characteristics do not support stereotypic expectations; and supportive norms by authorities within and outside of the contact situation (Cook, 1985; Pettigrew, 1998; Wright, Aron, McLaughlin-Volpe, & Ropp, 1997). Many of these factors relate directly to the types of organizational environmental factors, described in Chapter 12 of this volume, that support positive intergroup relations. Research in laboratory and field settings generally supports the efficacy of the list of prerequisite conditions for achieving improved intergroup relations (see Pettigrew & Tropp, 2000).

Structurally, however, the contact hypothesis has represented a list of loosely connected and diverse conditions, rather than a unifying conceptual framework that explains *how* these prerequisite features achieve their effects. Recent approaches have extended research on the contact hypothesis by attempting to understand the potential common processes and mechanisms that these diverse factors engage to reduce bias. With respect to potential mediators, appropriately structured intergroup contact can reduce bias by changing the nature of interdependence between members of different groups from perceived competition to cooperation and by creating greater opportunity for equal-status contact between members of different groups (Cook, 1985; Stephan, 1987; see also Chapter 3, this volume). Cooperative learning (Slavin, 1985; see also Chapter 4, this volume), Jigsaw classroom interventions (Aronson & Patnoe, 1997), and more comprehensive approaches in schools (e.g., Peacekeepers [Johnson & Johnson, 2000]), are all programs designed to increase interdependence between members of different groups and to establish a cooperative community.

Furthermore, these programs may also reduce bias by altering members' perceptions of group boundaries and memberships. On the one hand, intergroup cooperative interaction can create more inclusive categories, transforming members' representations of the memberships from "us" versus "them" to a more inclusive "we" (see Gaertner & Dovidio, 2000). On the other hand, personalized interactions with a variety of out-group members can undermine the value and meaningfulness of the social category stereotype as a source of information about members of that group.

Several alternative explanations for the positive effects of intergroup contact have been proposed (see Brewer & Miller, 1984; Miller & Davidson-Podgorny, 1987; Worchel, 1986). For example, cooperation may induce greater intergroup acceptance as people attempt to reduce the cognitive dissonance they experience as a result of the inconsistency between their current positive interaction and their previous negative attitude toward a member of another group (Miller & Brewer, 1986). It is also possible that the rewarding consequences of achieving success through cooperative efforts can reduce intergroup anxiety (Stephan & Stephan, 1985) or become directly associated with members of other groups (Lott & Lott, 1965), thereby increasing attraction (Gaertner et al., 1999). Pettigrew and Tropp (2000) have found that, across the range of studies in the literature, a substantial amount of the effect of contact on the reduction of bias is mediated by improvements in affect.

As with our attempts to classify cognitive and affective mediators, we acknowledge that our delineation of approaches as emphasizing enlightenment or intergroup contact may be overly broad and imprecise. Nevertheless, we offer this taxonomy as a device for examining how different types of programs and training that are dramatically different on the surface may have important functional similarities. In the next section, we review the range of different types of programs that have been used to combat bias and promote diversity in the context of the overall framework that we outlined in Figure 14.1.

TYPES OF TRAINING AND PROGRAMS

In their recent book, *Improving Intergroup Relations*, Stephan and Stephan (2001) describe a number of different types of training and education approaches and experiences that have been systematically adopted to reduce bias. These approaches include multicultural education, intergroup dialogues, cooperative learning, and moral and values education. We will not describe these programs in great depth. Stephan and Stephan provide cogent descriptions in their book. In addition, several different examples of these approaches are illustrated in detail in the chapters of the present volume. Our purpose is to sketch out the defining features of each and show how they may map onto the processes we depict in Figure 14.1 and have described in the present chapter.

Multicultural Education

As Stephan and Stephan (2001) observed, "Multicultural education programs vary enormously. . . . Some programs rely on the use of textbooks and formal instructional materials, whereas others incorporate an array of more involving materials and procedures, including movies, videos, field trips, class visits by members of the groups being studied, group exercises, simulation games, and role-playing" (p. 51). Chapters 2, 5, and 7 of this volume describe examples of these approaches in more detail. What these approaches all share is a strong emphasis on conveying information about others and, directly or indirectly, what appropriate social and personal standards of acceptance and inclusiveness are. Consequently, multicultural programs generally focus strongly on enlightenment.

Given the emphasis on gaining new knowledge and awareness, the impact of multicultural education on the reduction of bias is therefore more likely to occur through cognitive than through affective mechanisms. For instance, as Stephan and Stephan (2001) observed, multicultural programs reinforce values of justice, equality, and acceptance implicitly or explicitly by presenting information about various groups in a positive and respectful manner. Also, these programs, by providing information about the diversity and variability within other groups, can facilitate more individuated impressions of members of other groups (i.e., decategorization) or, by emphasizing common group membership (e.g., nationalism or common humanity), they can promote more superordinate, inclusive representations of members of these groups (i.e., recategorization).

To the extent that multicultural education programs also involve direct experience with members of other groups, they can have a secondary impact through structured intergroup contact and can activate emotional mediating mechanisms. Exercises that involve role playing and encourage different perspective taking can produce emotions such as empathic concern that lead to more positive orientations toward members of the other groups, or they can produce personal reactions such as moral indignation or guilt that can motivate actions that lead to reductions in bias.

Intergroup Dialogues

Intergroup dialogues also occur in a variety of ways. However, they typically share the goal of allowing members of different groups to address areas of contention through active discussion and recognition of different perspectives and worldviews (Dubois & Hutson, 1997). In one form of intergroup dialogue in educational settings (see Chapter 8, this volume), groups first learn about the norms and guidelines for the dialogues and then address issues of collective identity. After that, the participants consider specific issues of contention, often in the context of broader issues of social justice (compare Chapter 9, this volume). Finally, participants are encouraged to build alliances across former group boundaries.

In terms of our framework, because of the strong emphasis on intergroup interaction, dialogues of this type would be expected to have their primary effect through processes associated with intergroup contact. These dialogues are structured in a way that reflect the conditions of positive intergroup contact (equal status and personalized interaction with supportive norms and interdependence). Through discussion, people may also gain an important understanding of the perspectives of other groups, which can facilitate empathy, and valuable information about their cultural and history, which can enhance positive feelings toward these groups. These effects, however, are likely to be secondary to the contact effects. Thus, the mediating mechanisms that are most likely to be invoked are those that are most strongly associated with the contact hypothesis, such as changes in social categorization and in the perceptions of functional relations between the groups.

Cooperative Learning

Cooperative learning approaches can take a variety of forms (see, for example, Chapters 3 and 4, this volume). In some cases, the primary objective of these techniques is to foster effective classroom learning (Slavin, 1985). In other cases, like the Jigsaw classroom technique (Aronson & Patnoe, 1997), improving intergroup relations is the primary, explicit goal. The fundamental aspects that define cooperative learning, cooperative interdependence with supportive norms, and personalized interaction place their emphasis directly on the processes affiliated with the contact hypothesis.

During these cooperative interactions, participants are likely to recategorize people who were formerly viewed in terms of their different racial- or ethnic-group membership as members of a new common in-group (e.g., as members of the same team [Gaertner & Dovidio, 2000]). Thus, the processes of in-group favoritism that originally contributed to bias will become redirected to improve attitudes and orientations toward those now considered part of the in-group. Biases based on racial and ethnic categorization will thus be reduced. In addition, through equal-status, cooperative interactions people will gain insights that dilute and undermine stereotypic conceptions of others and accumulate experiences that reduce intergroup anxiety and produce more positive emotional responses (e.g., happiness with mutual success). Through these processes, bias may be substantially reduced without participants dramatically increasing their factual knowledge of another group's culture or history.

Moral and Values Education

Moral and values education programs have been developed not to involve anti-bias education or intergroup relations training but rather to foster the moral development of children, adolescents, and young adults. These programs typically occur in schools, including within college curricula (see Chapter 9, this volume). Stephan and Stephan (2001) identify a number of different dimensions of moral and values education programs, but they primarily distinguish them on the basis of whether the major goal is to change individuals or the community as a whole and whether specific values are directly taught. For instance, a program such as Facing History and Ourselves (see Chapter 6, this volume), which is a moral education program that teaches about Nazi Germany before and during World War II and encourages students to reflect on the implications for current moral issues, does not attempt to change an entire community, nor does it directly advocate specific values. A program such as Just Communities, which is based on Kohlberg's work on moral development (Kohlberg, 1984), is designed to help develop a more moral community, but not by advocating specific values. In contrast, character education programs (e.g., Lickona, 1991) focus on individual rather than community development and directly teach values such as respect and responsibility. Civics education (see Chapter 11, this volume) emphasizes the civic responsibilities of the individual members of society.

Stephan and Stephan (2001) propose that these programs generally operate through enhancing enlightenment, although some may work through the processes associated with intergroup contact as well. These programs emphasize cognitive factors dealing with standards of behavior and make consideration of the values of social justice, fairness, and equality central to the experience. To the extent that these programs develop and strengthen values that are inconsistent with bias, they are also likely to invoke cognitive and emotional mediating mechanisms in situations in which individuals become aware that they are not meeting their own personal standards. As a consequence, people will engage in self-regulatory processes that can lead to more positive intergroup orientations.

Stephan and Stephan (2001) also explain how some moral and values education programs can improve intergroup relations through processes associated with social contact. They state, "The creation of moral communities could be successful in intergroup settings in part because they replicate the conditions under which face-to-face contact has been shown to reduce prejudice: The contact involves equal status and is cooperative and personal" (p. 230).

In general, although there is not a clear one-to-one correspondence between particular programs and the types of intervening mechanisms that they are likely to activate in the process of reducing bias, we have attempted to provide some structure to understanding how apparently diverse programs, strategies, and interventions function to reduce bias. We conclude the chapter by presenting the implications of this type of analysis for implementing anti-bias programs and for evaluating them.

Implications for Program Design and Evaluation

The success of intergroup relations programs depends on several factors. Many of these elements are concrete and relate to the quality of the program, the skill of the trainers or facilitators, the receptivity of the audience, and the presence of possible precipitating events (such as a racial incident) that motivated the organization to seek outside consultation. In addition to these contextual features, we suggest, at a conceptual level, that the effectiveness of programs may be related to how well they address the specific outcomes that are desired and how much they invoke the specific mechanisms that will most effectively accomplish the objectives. Although there is no clear roadmap to success, we note that it is important to consider whether the primary goal is to change attitudes, stereotypes, feelings, or behavior—or some combination of these aspects of bias—at the explicit or implicit levels of expression. Then, after assessing the extent to which problems may be conscious and deliberate, and thus rooted in cognitive control, or more spontaneous and emotional, and thus related to affective mechanisms, practitioners may be able to determine what types of programs or kinds of interventions within a given program may be most appropriate to introduce. This approach suggests that it is not sufficient to have a "good" program; it is equally important to have an "appropriate" program—one that is well suited to the problems to be addressed or objectives to be achieved.

Understanding the range of mechanisms that can mediate the impact of specific interventions on reducing bias not only has theoretical benefits in terms of developing a more comprehensive model of the processes involved in bias and bias reduction; it also has practical benefits. To the extent that different types of interventions (e.g., aspects of multicultural education and intergroup dialogues) activate similar mediating processes, a practitioner can choose, from a large repertoire of tools, the most effective and appropriate intervention for a given context and audience. Moreover, to the extent that the current nature of intergroup relations might preclude the use of some paths (for example, it might be difficult to create empathy when conflict is intense), practitioners can rely on other interventions that will place more emphasis on techniques (e.g., intergroup dialogues) and mechanisms (e.g., creating cooperative interdependence) that will be more efficient and effective in that situation. Examining mediators in program evaluation studies can also provide valuable information about why a program might have been ineffective at improving intergroup relations. If the intervention did not influence the mediating mechanisms as expected, then one would not expect to achieve the program's desired objectives fully. Thus, appreciating the role of mediating mechanisms can help illuminate why programs fail as well as why programs succeed.

The framework we present in Figure 14.1 also has implications for how programs can be evaluated. Many forms of evaluation basically relate the presence or absence of an intervention (e.g., a treatment versus a control group) to differences in specific measures of bias. In its simplest form, an evaluation would examine whether a particular type of training produces a difference on one measure of bias, such as prejudice. Our analysis encourages evaluators to consider multiple measures of bias that represent at least the four facets that we have identified (prejudice, stereotypes, negative affect, and discrimination). In addition, it suggests that evaluators might also include measures of the hypothesized intervening processes (e.g., amount of knowledge gained, degree of personalized interaction, attempts to adopt others' perspectives, experience of positive feelings toward others or negative feelings toward oneself for violating personal standards).

The inclusion of these additional measures not only can offer valuable conceptual insights into the processes involved but also can have tangible benefits in the evaluation of a program. If an evaluator finds that a particular program successfully reduces bias, these additional measures can help to clarify what aspects of the program are most important in achieving this outcome. In the event that an evaluator cannot demonstrate that a program directly reduces bias, examination of these additional measures may help identify indirect effects. For example, although a program may not lead to an overall decrease in prejudice, it may enhance the extent to which people engage in perspective taking, which is one step on the road to reducing prejudice. In addition, within the sample of participants in a program, those who engage in more perspective taking may demonstrate greater reductions in prejudice. Results such as these can then aid practitioners in fine-tuning their interventions in ways that can enhance their impact on specific mediating processes and improve overall program effectiveness.

In conclusion, we acknowledge that bias is deeply rooted in history, economics, culture, institutional practices, and the ways people think about others. As a consequence, efforts to reduce bias must be carefully planned and skillfully executed to have any desirable effects. Within these efforts, science and practice play important roles that can support and reinforce each other. Through experience, practitioners can develop tools that are increasingly effective at reducing bias. Informed by this effectiveness, researchers can investigate how and why these tools work as they do. In addition, research under highly controlled conditions can shed light on the basic causes of bias, on the types of underlying processes that can most effectively eliminate this bias, and on the conditions under which different processes operate best. Once these processes have been identified and tested, they can be incorporated directly into interventions to address bias in more complex and intense naturalistic circumstances. Thus, we see practice and theory as complementary enterprises. If appreciated and managed appropriately, this partnership can contribute more important and lasting benefits to society than either approach could achieve alone.

Chapter 15

Conclusion: Understanding Intergroup Relations Programs

Walter G. Stephan

One cannot read the preceding chapters without coming away with a sense of excitement about the field of intergroup relations. Certainly the problems these programs address are daunting ones, and the implementation of these programs is difficult and demanding. However, if they achieve their goals, they promise to transform our society from the bottom up. The ultimate value of employing an educational approach to address intergroup relations is that we are able to deal with problems before they emerge by shaping the hearts and minds of children as they grow to adulthood. The programs reviewed in this book do exactly that. From preschool through college, they aim to break down the barriers among groups that have had such devastating effects on our country and on other countries around the world. We are now in a position to confront the age-old problems of prejudice, stereotyping, discrimination, and oppression that have plagued humankind since the first groups of peoples came into contact with one another. The programs reviewed in this book are in their initial stages of development, but they have already shown themselves to be effective and they hold the promise of becoming even more effective in the future.

The number and variety of these programs are astonishing. Despite this variety, there is a common underlying vision that animates these programs. In this vision of a future world, group differences are prized, not disparaged; people from different groups treat each other with respect, not disdain; social justice is a lived reality, not just an ideal; and coexistence means more than merely tolerating the presence of other groups. This positive vision of the future has evolved spontaneously in communities across the country and in other countries as well. Nearly all the programs reported in this book, as well as most other intergroup relations programs, were developed to meet perceived local needs. The people who developed them were often unaware that similar programs existed elsewhere or were being developed in other communities. They simply recognized the same domain of problems and held a similar vision for the future.

The intergroup relations programs covered in this book differ in so many ways that it is tempting to think of each of them as being unique and, in a sense, each is. But underlying the variability among these programs are sets of dimensions that can be used to classify them and to understand their differences and similarities. In this concluding chapter, I will provide a framework for understanding intergroup relations programs. This framework will follow the creation of intergroup relations programs from conception to an analysis of their effects. I will start by simply describing the different types of programs that exist and the dimensions along which they differ. Then I will analyze the goals of these programs and the techniques they employ to achieve these goals. The following section will explore the psychological processes underlying the success of these techniques. After this, I will examine some issues associated with the implementation of these programs. Next, the outcomes of these programs will be explored. In the final section, I will discuss techniques of evaluating the effectiveness of intergroup relations programs and the process of making adjustments to such programs in light of these assessments. In all of these sections, my primary focus will be on material presented in this volume, but I will also draw on other types of intergroup relations programs.

TYPES OF INTERGROUP RELATIONS PROGRAMS

Broadly conceived, intergroup relations programs are designed to address the racial, ethnic, cultural, religious, and other central group differences that exist in a specific society. In educational settings, these programs provide knowledge about different groups and skills for interacting with their members. They generally aim to change biased attitudes, feelings, and behaviors. The most ambitious of these programs attempt to change not only individuals but also the institutions in which they are being implemented.

As we have seen in the preceding chapters, intergroup relations programs take many forms, including those specifically labeled as such but also programs labeled as multicultural education, anti-bias education, diversity education, moral education, cooperative learning, dialogue groups, and coexistence education. Other related programs include intercultural training and conflict resolution training. The principal ways in which these programs differ can be conceptualized along two dimensions: direct versus indirect and didactic versus interactive (Stephan & Stephan, 2001).

Some programs aimed at improving relations among groups take a direct approach to this task. These programs are designed teach students about the nature of the different groups that coexist in a given society by providing students with information about the similarities and differences among the groups. They generally focus on the history of these groups and their practices, norms, and values. Often they explicitly address the existence of conflict among these groups, both in the past and in the present. Most of the programs that were originally labeled as multicultural education take this direct approach, but it is also true to some extent of programs such as anti-bias education and dialogue groups.

Other programs take an indirect approach to improving intergroup relations. In these programs, little or no mention is made of different racial, ethnic, religious, or other groups. Some of these indirect programs rely for their success on contact between members of different groups under very specific conditions that can lead to improved relations among group members—as is the case with cooperative learning groups. In other programs, the goal is to change or develop certain underlying values or principles that are incompatible with prejudice, stereotyping, and discrimination. This approach is characteristic of moral education programs and programs that teach conflict resolution skills.

All intergroup relations programs emphasize didactic and interactive approaches to teaching, but in varying degrees. Some are heavily oriented toward relatively traditional teaching styles involving explicit instruction and rely on readings, lectures, and discussions led by teachers or group leaders. Courses involving textbooks on multicultural education typify this approach. Other programs employ more interactive approaches to learning, such as dialogues, role playing, simulation games, and interactive group exercises. Cooperative learning and dialogue groups are good examples of programs that take an interactive approach. In practice, most intergroup relations programs employ both of these approaches to teaching and learning, but most tend to focus more on one approach than the other.

In addition to these two central dimensions on which intergroup relations programs differ, there are a host of other dimensions than can be used to understand the ways in which they vary. Some programs are aimed at helping participants understand just one other group, but most are aimed at creating an understanding of some set of outgroups. Racial, ethnic, religious, and cultural groups are the most commonly covered, but additional groups may include gender, sexual preference, and disability status, among others. Programs vary in the degree to which they emphasize group differences or the common humanity underlying these group differences. Some are oriented primarily toward creating changes within individuals, whereas others are more oriented toward social action and changing institutions.

GOALS

Although intergroup relations programs share certain underlying goals, the degree to which the specific goals of individual programs vary is remarkable. Traditional multicultural education programs that are taught in a course format and take a direct approach to improving intergroup relations. They have as their goals preparing students to function in a multicultural society, acknowledging the contributions of all groups to society, promoting justice and equality of opportunity, and strengthening group identities (Banks, 1997). The program that most closely resembles multicultural education among those covered in this book is Hands Across the Campus (Chapter 7). The goals of this program are to foster an appreciation of America's multicultural heritage, improve communication across group boundaries, and reinforce democratic ideals and social justice. Anti-bias education (Chapter 2) is also similar in many respects to multicultural education programs, although it tends to be more oriented toward younger children than are most multicultural education programs. It aims to create an empathic understanding of diverse groups, foster critical thinking about bias, teach children how to confront bias, and nurture self-identity.

A third program that shares the direct approach taken by multicultural education is the World of Difference program, which was created to combat prejudice, promote democratic ideals, and strengthen pluralism (Chapter 5). This program is designed to foster intergroup understanding and raise awareness about the harm inflicted by prejudice and discrimination. It also aims to provide participants with skills to challenge prejudice and discrimination and equip them to function effectively in a diverse society. Critical thinking and personal responsibility in these domains are also stressed.

In a related vein, dialogue groups proclaim their goals to be understanding the worldview of other groups, creating an awareness of the ways social institutions shape relations between groups, and promoting social action (Chapter 8). Positive in-group identities are also promoted in dialogue groups. In addition, dialogue participants are expected to learn about group differences and similarities.

The Brandeis Initiative in Intercommunal Coexistence also takes a direct approach to intergroup relations, using the arts and humanities to enhance coexistence on campus and internationally (Chapter 10). For this program, coexistence means greater intergroup understanding, empathy, and cooperation. This initiative focuses on the ethical dimensions of coexistence practice (e.g., respecting different cultures' values without falling into the trap of relativism) by addressing moral challenges and tensions. Through such techniques as research projects, courses, conversation groups, campus activities, and international outreach, the Initiative explores interethnic, interreligious, and interracial tensions and possibilities. Different activities have different goals. For example, the goals of the conversation groups are to deepen an understanding of majority/minority issues and relate respectfully across group differences.

The programs that take an indirect approach to improving intergroup relations have somewhat different goals. Among the goals of cooperative learning groups are to promote cooperative, individualized contact with out-group members; create egalitarian treatment of out-group members, and increase empathy for out-group members (Chapters 3 and 4). In complex instruction, the goal is to alter the expectations of students with respect to low-status peers (Chapter 3). Multiple cooperative tasks requiring a variety of abilities are used to change expectations. Changes in expectations are designed to lead to more equal-status interaction in the classroom.

Moral education programs are oriented toward increasing levels of moral reasoning, improving critical thinking and reflection, and teaching students to learn to act in accordance with principles of justice and caring. The moral education courses at SUNY at Albany are designed to prepare students to deal with moral issues in the public life of a pluralistic society (Chapter 9). These programs attempt to teach students to resolve intergroup relations issues in a just and fair manner. Students are expected to learn to make collective decisions in accordance with principles of social morality.

The Facing History and Ourselves program strives to teach an appreciation of human rights as well as prevent violence, racism, prejudice, stereotyping, and anti-Semitism through a confrontation with the events of the Holocaust (Chapter 6). It attempts to foster critical thinking and interpersonal understanding. It emphasizes taking multiple perspectives and developing psychosocial competencies by establishing a climate of trust in which the personal views of students can be challenged. It also stresses individual and group identity.

Although the goals of these programs do not appear to be incompatible, they are often quite different. There seem to be several key dimensions along which they differ. One dimension is the relative emphasis they place on creating understanding and knowledge versus changing behavior. Many of these programs aim to increase understanding of other groups in society and provide knowledge of basic concepts such as prejudice, stereotyping, and discrimination that are relevant to intergroup relations. Other programs are oriented more toward skill acquisition and behavior change. They wish to help people change their own behaviors and become more adept at intervening when they see instances of prejudice and discrimination. Still other programs are more concerned with social action or creating social change in the larger society. A few programs try to accomplish all of these goals.

A second dimension on which intergroup relations programs differ is the degree to which they emphasize issues of morality. A number programs have an explicit focus on morality and ethics. These programs usually emphasize issues of justice, fairness, equality, and perspective taking. In contrast, many other programs are more pragmatic in orientation, emphasizing the costs of discrimination and prejudice and the suffering they cause.

In some programs, issues of individual and group identity are explicitly addressed, but in others these issues are hardly mentioned and instead the common humanity shared by all groups may be stressed. Cooperation between groups is either an explicit goal or is actually practiced in some programs, but in many programs these issues are not explicitly addressed. Nearly all the programs strive to change individuals, but some also go further and attempt to change the institutional contexts in which they are conducted.

Obviously, no program can accomplish all the potential goals of education in intergroup relations, so strategic decisions must be made concerning what goals to pursue and what techniques to use in accomplishing them. Some of the potential techniques are addressed in the next section.

TECHNIQUES

Given the multiplicity of programs and the differences in their goals, it should come as no surprise that the techniques they employ are similarly varied. These techniques range from traditional to highly innovative. Among the more traditional approaches are those typically employed in didactic styles of teaching, including lectures, readings, class discussions, invited speakers, videos, and films. Even didactically oriented programs often use small-group discussions and other interactive exercises such as role playing and simulation games. Common supplementary techniques include keeping journals, analyzing case histories, field trips, and celebratory events. The more innovative techniques include skills training (for instance, in conflict resolution techniques), the integration of the arts into coexistence programs, attempts to encourage social activism and coalition building, dialogues that focus directly on issues of conflict, and changing institutional policies and procedures to be more sensitive to diversity-related issues.

The principal dimension on which these techniques differ is the degree to which they are active versus passive in terms of the role of the students in the learning process (Stephan & Stephan, 2001). The experientially oriented techniques such as role playing and simulation games are good examples of active techniques, while reading and listening to lectures are more passive techniques. Both types of technique can be effective, and most programs employ a mixture of both. Active approaches are probably more effective in conveying skills, whereas passive techniques are probably more effective in conveying information.

To understand why these techniques work, it is necessary to examine the mediating mechanisms. That is, it is necessary to examine the psychological processes that are activated by these techniques and are responsible for bringing about the effects they have on intergroup relations.

MEDIATING PROCESSES

Intergroup relations programs draw on a host of psychological processes to bring about changes in intergroup relations. Some of these processes were covered in Chapter 14. These include the beneficial effects of intergroup contact under the conditions established by the contact hypothesis (cooperative, equal status, personalized, and supported by authority figures), decategorization, recategorization (creating superordinate groups), increasing social knowledge, changing standards of behavior, empathy, reducing intergroup anxiety, and invoking guilt or compunction.

In addition to those processes, there are a variety of other psychological processes that promote change (Stephan & Stephan, 2001). Some techniques counteract negative stereotypes with information on counterstereotypical behavior. Implicitly if not explicitly, most programs provide information that breaks down monolithic conceptions of out-groups, which leads to more differentiated perceptions of these groups and thereby reduces stereotypes. In some programs, information is provided that counteracts misattributions for the behavior of out-group members. Other programs (e.g., dialogue groups) draw on the powerful process of personal self-disclosure to bring people closer together. Most programs spend some time emphasizing the underlying similarity of all groups—the common humanity shared by all people. Many programs acknowledge the fact that intergroup conflict is often founded in group differences, and they attempt to teach respect for, and acceptance of, group differences. Programs oriented toward institutional change establish new norms to govern intergroup relations. In these programs, administrators and teachers are often asked to model the types of behavior expected of students.

The dimensions on which these psychological process differ include the degree to which they elicit cognitive, affective, and behavioral responses and the extent to which they rely on conscious processes or processes that are outside of awareness. Providing information about out-groups that increases understanding and reduces stereotyping calls predominantly on cognitive processes, as do techniques that create superordinate groups and lead to greater differentiation of out-groups. Techniques that lead to awareness of uncomfortable discrepancies between cognitions and behavior, create guilt, or reduce anxiety about interacting with out-group members all involve affect. Processes that bring about change through modeling or reinforcement or that use self-criticism to induce change are aimed primarily at behavior change, although cognition and affect also play a role.

Many of these psychological processes operate outside of the awareness of the students involved. This is true of the processes involved in cooperative learning programs, in which students change their attitudes and learn to empathize with out-group members as a natural by-product of engaging in structured interactions with students who are different from themselves. Learning to like out-group members in the process of engaging in mutual self-disclosures, as occurs in dialogue groups, also brings about change without conscious awareness. In contrast, processes such a learning to suppress stereotypes require conscious effort and motivation. Likewise, learning conflict resolution skills requires a conscious learning process; so, too, does learning to correct misattributions. There are circumstances under which it may be desirable to employ processes that do not entail conscious awareness to be effective. This may occur in communities that are polarized by intergroup conflict. In such situations, dealing with intergroup issues indirectly may be viable because resistance to more direct programs of change is likely. Under ordinary circumstances, it is probably desirable to employ a range of techniques that call on cognitive, affective, and behavioral process that are both conscious and nonconscious.

In creating intergroup relations programs, practitioners should integrate the goals of the program with the techniques and processes most likely to achieve them. Many programs currently in existence, including those covered in this book, implicitly match goals, techniques, and processes, but few programs do so explicitly. It is now growing increasingly possible to create programs with a full awareness of the particular techniques and processes that will achieve specific goals. For instance, complex instruction, which relies on cooperative interdependence supplemented by treatments to offset status inequalities, has been found to increase egalitarian behavior (Chapter 3). Similarly, the Facing History and Ourselves program, which increases moral reasoning through an analysis and discussion of the implications of the Holocaust, leads to reductions in prejudice and fighting behavior (Chapter 6). Programs that employ role playing create empathy for outgroups, which has been shown to reduce prejudice.

Once program materials have been developed and choices about techniques have been made, the program must be implemented, which raises a whole new set of issues.

PROGRAM IMPLEMENTATION

The programs presented in this book are intended for a wide range of audiences, although they are all conducted in educational settings. Clearly, the manner in which these programs are implemented and the choice of materials and techniques must take into account the emotional, cognitive, and social maturity of the students. These programs must also take into account the specific groups that are present in the educational context, the prior relations among these groups in the community, the current issues of contention among the groups, and any status or power differences between the groups—both in the educational setting itself and in the community.

It may also be valuable to take into consideration the preferred learning styles of the students who are participating in the program, along with other factors such as the strength of their identification with their in-groups, their attitudes and beliefs about out-groups (especially their levels of ethnocentrism), and the degree to which they are alienated from society.

The settings in which these programs are conducted are of great importance. It matters greatly whether the schools are integrated or segregated by race, ethnicity, religion, or social class. For instance, techniques that are based on intergroup contact cannot be employed in segregated schools. School size and classroom size are also relevant. Interactive exercises are more difficult to use as classroom size increases. The racial, ethnic, and gender composition of the administration and teaching staff will have an impact on the effectiveness of the program and the manner in which it is implemented. A monocultural staff can hardly model positive intergroup relations among themselves. The types of classes (social studies, history, languages) in which intergroup relations programs are introduced obviously affect what materials and techniques can be used.

Textbooks and other curriculum materials that can be employed in intergroup relations programs are widely available, and many school districts use these materials in their classrooms. At the university level, fewer resources exist, and many multicultural courses are one-of-a-kind—developed by the professors who present them.

One of the central features that differentiates the implementation of intergroup relations programs is that some of these programs are conducted by outside teams of experts, whereas others are developed and conducted by teachers themselves. One advantage of locally created programs is that they are likely to be specifically tailored to the needs and circumstances of the local community. When school districts bring in outside agencies, these agencies usually provide teacher training, assistance in implementing the program, follow-up support, and in some cases evaluations of the effectiveness of the programs. All these components can help to create successful programs, and some of them are likely to be absent in programs that are created locally.

Although pre-service teachers commonly take courses that prepare them to teach students from diverse backgrounds, most teachers are still not trained to teach multicultural education courses or to incorporate this approach into the courses they teach. For this reason, additional teacher training is necessary (Chapter 12). Many of these programs, particularly those involving cooperative learning, require the teachers to play new roles, and this, too, necessitates training. Implementing intergroup relations programs, especially initially, can be difficult, and having skilled professionals available to provide back-up support can make the difference between success and failure. Because these programs are demanding, often deal with sensitive issues, and create some level of conflict, they may not be sustained without follow-up support and ongoing teacher training.

All intergroup relations programs should be evaluated to determine their effectiveness and the need for modifications. Programs created by outside agencies are often in the best position to be evaluated because agency staff know what the intended effects of the program are and they may have developed measures to assess them. Unfortunately, all too often even these programs go unevaluated. School districts that create their own programs should also evaluate them, but they seem even less likely to do so.

Intergroup relations programs sometimes meet with resistance that can affect how they are implemented or even whether they are implemented at all. These types of programs are sometimes viewed as unnecessary or even counterproductive. Critics of intergroup relations programs believe that they undermine traditional approaches to education and detract from the learning of basic skills (see Banks, 1993; Sleeter, 1995). Such critics worry that these programs do not promote a national identity and that they may hinder assimilation. They are also concerned that teaching students about racism, sexism, and ethnocentrism may make relations between groups worse. In contrast, the proponents of intergroup relations programs believe they promote social cohesion by fostering respect and acceptance among different groups (Banks, 1993). They think that members of all groups should have the option of maintaining a strong identity with their ethnic, cultural, and religious groups of origin. In addition, proponents also argue that multicultural education promotes the underlying principles of participatory democracy, rather than creating divisiveness, by fostering egalitarian relations among groups. The proponents also think that multicultural education furthers the learning of basic skills (Banks, 1993).

To dispel these criticisms and counteract resistance, it is important to seek community involvement in the selection, design, and implementation of intergroup relations programs. As the programs covered in this book make clear, there is an enormous range of intergroup relations programs and only the most direct ones are even potentially subject to these criticisms. By including community leaders, parents, and other stakeholders in the planning and implementation process, it may be possible to overcome the reservations of critics or to select programs that are not subject to their concerns.

After any of these programs have been implemented, the next question that arises concerns the effects of the program.

EFFECTS

The range of documented effects of intergroup relations programs is remarkably broad. These effects can be categorized into three basic types: cognitive, affective, and behavioral (Stephan & Stephan, 2001; Chapter 13, this volume). Among the cognitive effects that have been documented in outcome studies are positive changes in ethnocentrism, stereotypes, and perceptions of out-group differentiation, as well as less-biased attributions for out-group behavior. Intergroup relations programs have also been found to lead to greater acceptance of, tolerance of, respect for, and trust of out-groups. Knowledge and understanding of out-groups increase, as does awareness of institutional discrimination. Some programs have noted improvements in analytical, critical, and reflective thought.

Intergroup relations programs also have an impact on affect and feelings. They have been found to reduce prejudice, hostility, anxiety, stress, and negative affect. On the positive side, they increase empathy, caring, and positive affect. Strengthened identification with the ingroup (with no increase in negative attitudes toward out-groups) can also occur.

Some of the most impressive outcomes can be found in the behavioral domain. Intergroup relations programs can increase intergroup relations skills, improve intergroup communication, reduce intergroup conflict, and increase intergroup friendships and willingness to interact with out-group members. In addition, they can lead to more egalitarian treatment of out-group members and a greater emphasis on fair treatment of out-group members. In some cases, these programs lead to greater social activism and an increased concern for social justice. An enhanced ability to interact with out-groups in a cooperative and interdependent manner has also been observed. Also, participants learn to treat others as individuals, not as group members.

As diverse as these documented outcomes of intergroup relations are, there are many more that merit investigation. Particularly interesting are the long-term effects of these programs on such outcomes as participation in democracy, selection of integrated colleges, choice of jobs in integrated settings, choice of integrated neighborhoods, involvement in civic or recreational activities across group boundaries, and adult friendship choices.

The reason that these effects are known is because of the research that has been conducted on the effects of these programs. Unfortunately, not nearly enough evaluations of these programs have been done and there is much that remains to be learned.

EVALUATION

The pathway to program improvement is program evaluation. Evaluations provide essential information on the effects of intergroup relations programs and the processes by which these effects were brought about. In a number of cases, intergroup relations programs have been found to be less effective than had been anticipated. In general, the research on intergroup relations programs indicates that multicultural education and related programs have beneficial effects on intergroup relations, but on average these effects are not very large (Chapter 13). When the results of large numbers of intergroup relations programs are examined together, they reveal that these programs are more effective with some groups than with others, they affect some of the desired outcomes but not others, and they often have immediate beneficial effects—but these effects sometimes are lost as time goes by. The value of evaluation efforts is that, when done effectively, they can pinpoint the aspects of a program that need improvement. As such evidence accumulates, the circumstances under which different programs and techniques are most effective become clear, and we gain a better understanding of why these techniques are effective. The future development and growth of intergroup relations programs in educational settings depend on the development and elaboration of this knowledge. The only way to create it is to conduct evaluations of all types and publish them.

CONCLUSIONS

The intergroup relations programs covered in this book were created by thoughtful and dedicated professionals with years of experience teaching and training students. They were guided by a sense of what techniques they had found to be effective and the goals they wished to accomplish.

The evidence indicates that these efforts were largely successful, but the evidence also suggests that in nearly all cases these programs were not as effective as they could have been. Practitioners are now able to make choices about intergroup relations programs based on research on the effectiveness of existing programs and techniques. Program design should start with a comprehensive understanding of the particular context in which the program will be introduced. Based on this initial assessment and consultations with the various stakeholders in the process—including school boards, school administrators, teachers, students, staff, parents, and members of the community—specific goals for the program should be formulated. Once these goals have been identified, techniques that are known to be effective in achieving these goals can be selected and modified for this context. At the same time, it is possible to select the psychological processes most likely to be operative in these techniques and to design the techniques to optimize the effectiveness of these processes. Programs are most likely to be effective if they attempt to bring about changes both among students and at the institutional level.

Before any program is implemented, empirical data should be collected on the state of intergroup relations in this context and valid pre-measures should be collected on those variables that the program is expected to influence. One option is to initially conduct the program with only about half of the available students in order to create a control group of students who have not yet received the program. After the program has been conducted, the same measures should be collected again and the results should be used to evaluate the effectiveness of the program, along with other assessment tools that are more qualitative in nature, such as the reactions of teachers and program administrators. The results of these evaluations should then be used to refine and strengthen the program so that it can achieve its goals more effectively in the future. It is important that follow-up support and guidance be provided in order to maintain the program. The results of programs of demonstrated effectiveness should be widely disseminated to aid other practitioners in increasing the impact of their programs.

Education in intergroup relations should be a lifelong process. Currently, most programs are conducted in a piecemeal fashion, and students are fortunate if they are able to participate in any type of intergroup relations program at any time in their entire educational careers. In an ideal world, students would be provided with education in intergroup relations throughout their education. These programs should be attuned to students' emotional, social, and intellectual skills as they evolve over time. They should be sensitive to the local context and current needs, but they should also take into consideration the fact that the students will eventually become engaged in the larger society and the wider world. Thus, they should be prepared to deal with diversity beyond that which exists in their local communities. And, of course, intergroup relations issues will continue to arise during adulthood on the job and in the community, as well as nationally and internationally. For this reason, education in intergroup relations should not be limited to educational settings but should also involve diversity training in organizational settings, community dialogues, and other related programs for adults.

If we are going to live together productively in a multicultural world, we will have to be constantly vigilant about the potentially destructive effects of its intergroup differences. But we should not lose sight of the fact that these same differences are a source of strength, creativity, increased performance, and joy.

References

Note: * denotes studies included in Chapter 13's meta-analysis

Aboud, F. E. (1997). Interest in ethnic information: A cross-cultural developmental study. *Journal of Behavioral Science, 9,* 134–146.

*Aboud, F. E., & Fenwick, V. (1999). Exploring and evaluating school-based interventions to reduce prejudice. *Journal of Social Issues, 55,* 767–786.

Abu-Nimer, M. (1999). *Dialogue, conflict resolution, and change: Arab–Jewish encounters in Israel.* Blue Mountain Lake, NY: State University of New York Press.

Adlerfer, C. P. (1992). Changing race relations embedded in organizations: Report on a long-term project with the XYZ corporation. In S. E. Jackson et al. (Eds.), *Diversity in the workforce* (pp. 138–166). New York: Guilford.

Adoff, A. (1973). *Black is brown is tan.* New York: HarperCollins.

Adorno, T. W., Frenkel-Brunswik, E., Levinson, D. J., & Sanford, R. N. (1950). *The authoritarian personality.* New York: Harper.

Alexander, K. L., Entwisle, D. R., & Olson, L. S. (2001). Schools, achievement and inequality: A seasonal perspective. *Educational Evaluation and Policy Analysis, 23,* 171–191.

Allport, G. W. (1954). *The nature of prejudice.* Reading, MA: Addison-Wesley.

Alperin, D. J. (1990). Social diversity and the necessity of alliances: A developing feminist perspective. In L. Albrecht & R. M. Brewer (Eds.), *Bridges of power: Women's multicultural alliances* (pp. 23–33). Santa Cruz, CA: New Society Publishers.

Alvarado, C., Derman-Sparks, L., et al. (1999). *In our own way: How antibias work shapes our lives.* St. Paul, MN: Redleaf.

Arendt, H. (1977). *The life of the mind: Thinking.* New York: Harcourt.

Aronson, E. (1978). *The Jigsaw classroom.* Beverly Hills, CA: Sage

Aronson, E., & Patnoe, S. (1997). *The Jigsaw classroom.* New York: Longman.

Astin, A. (1996). "Involvement in Learning" revisited: Lessons we have learned. *Journal of College Student Personnel, 37,* 123–134.

*Avery, P. G., Bird, K., Johnstone, S., Sullivan, J. L., & Thalhammer, K. (1992). Exploring political tolerance with adolescents. *Theory and Research in Social Education, 20,* 386–420.

Avery, P. G., & Simmons, A. M. (Fall/Winter 2000/2001). Civic life as conveyed in U.S. civics and history textbooks. *International Journal of Social Education, 15(2),* 105–130.

Ayers, W. (1993). *To teach: The journey of a teacher.* New York: Teachers College Press.

Bagley, C., Mizuno, Y., & Collins, G. (1992). Schools and opportunities for multicultural contact. In C. Grant (Ed.), *Research and multicultural education: From the margins to the mainstream* (pp. 203–217). London: Falmer.

Baker, P. J. (2001). Fullan's compelling vision of educational change. *Planning and Changing, 32*, 128–143.

Baldi, S., Perie, M., Skidmore, D., Greenberg, E., & Hahn, C. (2001). *What democracy means to ninth-graders: U.S. results from the International IEA Civic Education Study* (NCES 2001–096). U. S. Department of Education, National Center for Education Statistics. Washington, DC: U.S. Government Printing Office.

Bandura, A. (1986). *Social foundations of thought and action: A social cognitive theory.* Englewood Cliffs, NJ: Prentice-Hall.

Banks, J. A. (1988). *Multiethnic education: Theory and practice.* Boston: Allyn & Bacon.

Banks, J. A. (1993). Multicultural education and its critics: Britain and the United States. *The New Era, 65*, 58–64.

Banks, J. A. (1997). *Educating citizens in a multicultural society.* New York: Teachers College Press.

Banks, J. A. (2002). *An introduction to multicultural education* (3rd ed.). Boston: Allyn & Bacon.

Barber, B. (1984). *Strong democracy: Participatory politics for a new age.* Berkeley: University of California Press.

Barber, B. (1993, November). America skips school. *Harper's*, pp. 39–46.

Bardige, B. (1981). Facing History and Ourselves: Tracing development through an analysis of students' journals. *Moral Education Forum, 4*, 42–48.

Bardige, B. (1983). *Reflective thinking and prosocial awareness.* Unpublished doctoral dissertation,: Harvard Graduate School of Education, Cambridge, MA.

Bardige, B. (1988). Things so finely human: Moral sensibilities at risk in adolescence. In C. Gilligan, J. V. Ward, J. M. Taylor, & B. Bardige (Eds.), *Mapping the moral domain: A contribution of women's thinking to psychological theory and education* (pp. 87–110). Cambridge, MA: Harvard University Press.

Barth, R. S. (2001). *Learning by heart.* San Francisco: Jossey-Bass.

Batson, C. D. (1990). How social an animal? The human capacity for caring. *American Psychologist, 45*, 336–346.

Batson, C. D. (1991). *The altruism question: Toward a social-psychological answer.* Hillsdale, NJ: Erlbaum.

Batson, C. D., Polycarpou, M. P., Harmon-Jones, E., Imhoff, H. J., Mitchener, E. C., Bednar, L. L., Klein, T. R., & Highberger, L. (1997). Empathy and attitudes: Can feeling for a member of a stigmatized group improve feelings toward the group? *Journal of Personality and Social Psychology, 72*, 105–118.

Beer, M., Eisenstat, R., & Spector, B. (1990). Why change programs don't produce change. *Harvard Business Review, 68*, 158–166.

Berger, J. B., Cohen, B. P., & Zelditch, M., Jr. (1966). Status characteristics and expectation states. In J. Berger & M. Zelditch, Jr. (Eds.), *Sociological theories in progress* (Vol. 1; pp. 9–46). Boston: Houghton Mifflin.

Berger, J. B., Cohen, B. P., & Zelditch, M., Jr. (1972). Status characteristics and social interaction. *American Sociological Review, 37*, 241–255.

Berger, J. B., Rosenholtz, S. J., & Zelditch, M., Jr. (1980). Status organizing processes. *Annual Review of Sociology, 6*, 479–508.

Berkowitz, M. W. (1985). The role of discussion in moral education. In M. W. Berkowitz & F. Oser (Eds.), *Moral education: Theory and application* (pp. 197–218). Hillsdale, NJ: Erlbaum.

Berkowitz, M. W. (1988). Try and catch the wind: Dialogue, dialectics and development in Kohlberg's life and legacy. *Journal of Counseling and Values, 32,* 179–186.

Berkowitz, M. W., & Gibbs, J. C. (1983). Measuring the developmental features of moral discussion. *Merrill-Palmer Quarterly, 29,* 399–410.

Berman, S. (nd). *Comparison of dialogue and debate.* Unpublished manuscript. (Available from Educators for Social Responsibility, 19 Garden St, Cambridge, MA 02138).

Berrien, F. K. (1976). A general systems approach to organizations. In M. D. Dunnette (Ed.), *Handbook of industrial and organizational psychology.* Chicago: Rand McNally & Company.

*Best, D. L., Smith, S. C., Graves, D. J., & Williams, J. E. (1975). The modification of racial bias in preschool children. *Journal of Experimental Child Psychology, 20,* 193–205.

Bickmore, K. (1993). Learning inclusion/inclusion in learning: Citizenship education for a pluralistic society. *Theory and Research in Social Education, 21,* 341–384.

Biggs, D. A., Colesante, R. J., & Smith, J. (2000). Two tracks to citizenship in the United States. In M. Leicester, C. Modgil, & S. Mogdil (Eds.), *Education, culture and values: Vol. I. Systems of education: Theories, policies and implicit values* (pp. 144–151). New York: Falmer.

Bigler, R. S. (1999). The use of multicultural curricula and materials to counter racism in children. *Journal of Social Issues, 55,* 687–706.

Bisson, J. (1997). *Celebrate! An antibias guide to enjoying holidays in early childhood programs.* St. Paul, MN: Redleaf.

Blair, I. V. (2001). Implicit stereotypes and prejudice. In G. B. Moskowitz (Ed.), *Cognitive social psychology: The Princeton Symposium on the Legacy and Future of Social Cognition* (pp. 359–374). Mahwah, NJ: Erlbaum.

Blaney, N. T., Stephan, C., Rosenfield, D., Aronson, E., & Silkes, J. (1977). Interdependence in the classroom: A field study. *Journal of Educational Psychology, 69,* 121–128.

Blatt, M. (1969). *The effects of classroom discussion programs upon children's level of moral development.* Unpublished doctoral dissertation, University of Chicago.

Blatt, M., & Kohlberg, L. (1975). The effects of classroom moral discussion upon children's moral judgment. *Journal of Moral Education, 4,* 129–161.

Blau, J., Lamb, U., Stearns, E., & Pellerin, C. (2001). Cosmopolitan environments and adolescents' gains in social studies. *Sociology of Education, 74,* 121–138.

Bluestein, J. (2001). *Creating emotionally safe schools: A guide for educators and parents.* Deerfield Beach, FL: Health Communications.

Blumer, H. (1958). Race prejudice as a sense of group position. *Pacific Sociological Review, 1,* 3–7.

Blyth, D. A., Saito, R., & Berkas, T. (1997). A quantitative study of the impact of service-learning programs. In A. S. Waterman (Ed.), *Service-learning: Applications from the research* (pp. 39–56). Mahwah, NJ: Erlbaum.

Bobo, L. (1988). Group conflict, prejudice, and the paradox of contemporary racial attitudes. In P. A. Katz & D. A. Taylor (Eds.), *Eliminating racism: Profiles in controversy* (pp. 85–114). New York: Plenum.

Bohm, D. (1996). *On dialogue*. London: Routledge.

Boice, R., & Turner, J. (1989). The FIPSE-CSULB mentoring project for new faculty. *To Improve the Academy, 8,* 117–139.

Bolman, L. G., & Deal, T. E. (1991). *Reframing organizations: Artistry, choice and leadership*. San Francisco: Jossey-Bass.

Bradley, M. T., & Gupta, R. D. (1997). Estimating the effect of the file drawer problem in meta-analysis. *Perceptual and Motor Skills, 85,* 719–722.

Brawarsky, S. (1996). *Improving intergroup relations among youth*. New York: Carnegie Corporation of New York.

Bredekamp, S., & Rosegrant, T. (Eds.). (1992). *Reaching potentials: Appropriate curriculum and assessment for young children*. Washington, DC: National Association for the Education of Young Children.

Brewer, M. B. (1979). Ingroup bias in the minimal intergroup situation: A cognitive motivational analysis. *Psychological Bulletin, 86,* 307–324.

Brewer, M. B. (1988). A dual process model of impression formation. In T. S. Srull & R. S. Wyer (Eds.), *Advances in social cognition: Vol. I. A dual process model of impression formation* (pp. 1–36). Hillsdale, NJ: Erlbaum.

Brewer, M. B. (2000). Reducing prejudice through cross-categorization: Effects of multiple social identities. In S. Oskamp (Ed.), *Reducing prejudice and discrimination* (pp. 211–238). Mahwah, NJ: Erlbaum.

Brewer, M. B., & Miller, N. (1984). Beyond the contact hypothesis: Theoretical perspectives on desegregation. In N. Miller & M. B. Brewer (Eds.), *Groups in contact: The psychology of desegregation* (pp. 281–302). Orlando, FL: Academic Press.

Brint, S., Contreras, M. F., & Matthews, M. T. (2001). Socialization messages in primary schools: An organizational analysis. *Sociology of Education, 74,* 157–180.

*Brooks, G. S., & Kahn, S. E. (1990). Evaluation of a course in gender and cultural issues. *Cultural Education and Supervision, 30,* 66–76.

*Brown, S. P., Parham, T. A., & Yonker, R. (1996). Influence of cross-cultural training course on racial identity attitudes of White women and men: Preliminary perspectives. *Journal of Counseling & Development, 74,* 510–516.

Brown, B. (2001). *Combining discrimination: Persona dolls in action*. Stoke on Trent, UK: Trentham.

Bruner, J. S. (1986). *Actual minds, possible worlds*. Cambridge, MA: Harvard University Press.

Bryant, B. (1982). An index of empathy for children and adolescents. *Child Development, 53,* 413–425.

Burton, R.V. (1963). The generality of honesty reconsidered. *Psychological Review, 35,* 481–499.

Burton, R. V., & Kunce, L. (1995). Behavioral models of moral development: A brief history and integration. In W. M. Kurtines & J. L. Gewirtz (Eds.), *Moral education: An introduction* (pp. 141–171). Boston: Allyn & Bacon.

*Byington, K., Fischer, J., Walker, L., & Freedman, E. (1997). Evaluating the effectiveness of a multicultural counseling ethics and assessment training. *Journal of Applied Rehabiliation Counseling, 28,* 234–248.

Byrne, D. (1971). *The attraction paradigm*. New York: Academic Press.

Byrnes, D. A. (1988). Children and prejudice. *Social Education, 52,* 267–271.

*Byrnes, D. H., & Kiger, G. (1990). The effect of a prejudice reduction simulation on attitude change. *Journal of Applied Social Psychology, 20,* 341–356.

Campbell, D.T. (1965). Ethnocentric and other altruistic motives. In D. Levine (Ed.), *Nebraska symposium on motivation* (Vol. 13; pp. 283–311). Lincoln: University of Nebraska Press.

*Carrell, L. J. (1997). Diversity in the communication curriculum: Impact on student empathy. *Communication Education, 46,* 234–244.

Chang, H., Muckrlory, A., & Pulido-Tobiassen, D. (1996). *Looking in, looking out: Redefining child care and early education in a diverse society.* Oakland, CA: California Tomorrow.

Chesler, M. (2001). Extending intergroup dialogue: From talk to action. In D. Schoem & S. Hurtado (Eds.), *Intergroup dialogue: Deliberative democracy in school, college, community, and workplace* (pp. 294–305). Ann Arbor: University of Michigan Press.

Clark, K. (1955). *Prejudice and the young child.* Boston: Beacon.

Clinton, W. (1997). Remarks by the president in meeting with the Advisory Board to the President on Race. June 13, 1997, http://www.whitehouse.gov/Initiatives/19970616–14199.html.

Cohen, E. G. (1982). Expectation states and interracial interaction in school settings. *Annual Review of Sociology, 8,* 209–235.

Cohen, E. G. (1984). The desegregated school: Problems in status power and interethnic climate. In N. Miller & M. B. Brewer (Eds.), *Groups in contact: The psychology of desegregation* (pp. 77–96). New York: Academic Press.

Cohen, E. G. (1992). *Restructuring the classroom: Conditions for productive small groups.* Madison: Wisconsin Center for Educational Research.

Cohen, E. G. (1994a). *Designing groupwork: Strategies for heterogeneous classrooms* (rev. ed.). New York: Teachers College Press.

Cohen, E. G. (1994b). *Status treatments for the classroom.* [Video]. New York: Teachers College Press.

Cohen, E. G. (1997).Understanding status problems: Sources and consequences. In E. G. Cohen & R. A. Lotan (Eds.), *Working for equity in heterogeneous classrooms: Sociological theory in practice* (pp. 61–76). New York: Teachers College Press.

Cohen, E. G., Bianchini, J. A., Cossey, R., Holthuis, N. C., Morphew, C. C., & Whitcomb, J. A. (1997). What did students learn? In E. G. Cohen & R. A. Lotan (Eds.), *Working for equity in heterogeneous classrooms: Sociological theory in practice* (pp. 137–165). New York: Teachers College Press.

Cohen, E. G., Lockheed, M., & Lohman, M. (1976). The Center for Interracial Cooperation: A field experiment. *Sociology of Education, 49,* 47–58.

Cohen, E. G., & Lotan, R. A. (1995). Producing equal status interaction in the heterogeneous classroom. *American Educational Research Journal, 32,* 99–120.

Cohen, E. G., & Lotan, R. A. (1997a). Raising expectations for competence: The effectiveness of status interventions. In E. G. Cohen & R. A. Lotan (Eds.), *Working for equity in heterogeneous classrooms: Sociological theory in practice* (pp. 77–91). New York: Teachers College Press.

Cohen, E. G., & Lotan, R. A. (Eds.). (1997b). *Working for equity in heterogeneous classrooms: Sociological theory in practice.* New York: Teachers College Press.

Cohen, E. G., Lotan, R., & Catanzarite, L. (1988). Can expectations for competence be treated in the classroom? In M. Webster, Jr., & M. Foschi (Eds.), *Status generalization: New theory and research* (pp. 27–54). Stanford, CA: Stanford University Press.

Cohen, E. G., Lotan, R. A., & Holthuis, N. C. (1997). Organizing the classroom for learning. In E. G. Cohen & R. A. Lotan (Eds.), *Working for equity in heterogeneous classrooms: Sociological theory in practice* (pp. 31–43). New York: Teachers College Press.

Cohen, E. G., Lotan, R. A., & Leechor, C. (1989). Can classrooms learn? *Sociology of Education, 62*, 75–94.

Cohen, E. G., & Roper, S. (1972). Modification of interracial interaction disability: An application of status characteristic theory. *American Sociological Review, 37*, 648–655.

*Colca, C., Lowen, D., Colca, L., & Lord, S. A. (1982). Combating racism in the schools. *Social Work in Education, 5*, 5–15.

Colesante, R. J., & Biggs, D. A. (1999). Teaching about tolerance with stories and arguments. *Journal of Moral Education, 28*, 185–199.

Conover, P. J., & Searing, D. D. (2000). A political socialization perspective. In L. M. McDonnell, P. M. Timpane, & R. Benjamin (Eds.), *Rediscovering the democratic purposes of education* (pp. 91–124). Lawrence: University Press of Kansas.

Cook, S. W. (1978). Interpersonal and attitudinal outcomes of cooperative interracial groups. *Journal of Research and Development in Education, 12*, 7–113.

Cook, S. W. (1985). Experimenting on social issues: The case of school desegregation. *American Psychologist, 40*, 452–460.

Cooper, L., Johnson, D.W., Johnson., R., & Wilderson, F. (1980). Effects of cooperative, competitive, and individualistic experiences on interpersonal attraction among heterogeneous peers. *Journal of Social Psychology, 111*, 243–252.

Cooper, R., & Slavin, R. E. (2001). Cooperative learning programs and multicultural education: Improving intergroup relations. In F. Salili & R. Hoosain, *Research on Multicultural Education and International Perspectives* (pp. 15–33). Greenwich, CT: Information Age.

Cotton, K. (1992). *Developing empathy in children and youth* (Close-Up No. 13). Portland, OR: Northwest Regional Educational Laboratory.

Covey, S. (1990). *The seven habits of highly effective people.* New York: Simon & Schuster.

Creaser, B., & Dau, E. (1996). *The anti-bias approach in early childhood.* Australia: HarperCollins.

Cronin, S., Derman-Sparks, L., Henry, S., Olatunji, S., & York, S. (1998). *Future vision, present work: Learning from the culturally relevant anti-bias leadership project.* St. Paul, MN: Redleaf.

Crosby, F., Bromley, S., & Saxe, L. (1980). Recent unobtrusive studies of Black and White discrimination and prejudice: A literature review. *Psychological Bulletin, 87*, 546–563.

Cross, W. E. (1987). A two-factor theory of Black identity: Implications for the study of identity development in minority children. In J. Phinney & M. J. Rotheram (Eds.), *Children's ethnic socialization* (pp. 117–133). Beverly Hills, CA: Sage.

Cross, W. E. (1991). *Shades of black.* Philadelphia, PA: Temple University Press.

Cuban, L. (1984). *How they taught.* New York: Longman.

Cummings, R., Dyas, L., Maddux, C., & Kochman, A. (2001). Principled moral reasoning and the behavior of preservice teacher education students. *American Educational Research Journal, 38,* 143–158.

Cushner, K., McClelland, A., & Safford, P. (2000). *Human diversity in education: An integrative approach* (3rd ed.). New York: McGraw-Hill.

*D'Andrea, M., Daniels, J., & Heck, R. (1991). Evaluating the impact of multicultural counseling training. *Journal of Counseling and Development, 70,* 143–150.

Darder, A. (1991). *Culture and power in the classroom.* New York: Bergin & Garvey.

Darling-Hammond, L. (1995). Inequality and access to knowledge. In J. A. Banks & C. A. McGee Banks (Eds.), *Handbook of research on multicultural education* (pp. 465–483). New York: Macmillan.

Darling-Hammond, L. (1997). *The right to learn: A blueprint for creating schools that work.* San Francisco: Jossey-Bass.

Darling-Hammond, L., & McLaughlin, M. W. (1995). *Practices and policies to support teacher development in an era of reform.* New York: National Center for Restructuring Education, Schools, and Teaching.

Day, J. M. (1991). Role-taking revisited: Narrative and cognitive-developmental interpretations of moral growth. *Journal of Moral Education, 20,* 305–315.

DeAvila, E. A., & Duncan, S. (1982). *Finding out/Descubrimiento.* San Rafael, CA: Linguametrics Group.

Deering, P. D. (1989, October). *An ethnographic approach for examining participants' construction of a cooperative learning class culture.* Paper presented at the annual meeting of the American Anthropological Association, Washington, DC. (Eric Document Reproduction Service, ED 319 083).

Delpit, L. (1996). *Other people's children: Cultural conflict in the classroom.* New York: New Press.

Dennis, R. (1981). Socialization and racism: The White experience. In B. Bowser & R. Hunt (Eds.), *Impacts of racism on White Americans* (pp.71–85). Beverly Hills, CA: Sage.

Derman-Sparks, L., & ABC Task Force. (1989). *Anti-bias curriculum: Tools for empowering young children.* Washington, DC: National Association for the Education of Young Children.

Derman-Sparks, L., & Ramsey, P. (2000). *A framework for culturally relevant, multicultural, and antibias education in the 21st century.* In J. L. Roopnarine & J. E. Johnson (Eds.), *Approaches to early childhood education* (pp. 379–404). Columbus, OH: Merrill/Prentice Hall.

Derman-Sparks, L., Higa, C., & Sparks, B. (1980). Children, race, and racism: How race awareness develops. *Bulletin, 11,* 3–9.

Deutsch, M. (1992). *The effects of training in cooperative learning and conflict resolution in an alternative high school.* New York: Teachers College Press.

Devine, P. G. (1989). Stereotypes and prejudice: The automatic and controlled components. *Journal of Personality and Social Psychology, 56,* 5–18.

Devine, P. G., & Monteith, M. J. (1993). The role of discrepancy-associated affect in prejudice reduction. In D. M. Mackie & D. L. Hamilton (Eds.), *Affect, cognition, and stereotyping: Interactive processes in intergroup perception* (pp. 317–344). Orlando, FL: Academic Press.

Devine, P. G., Plant, E. A., & Buswell, B. N. (2000). Breaking the prejudice habit:

Progress and obstacles. In S. Oskamp (Ed.), *Reducing prejudice and discrimination* (pp. 185–208). Hillsdale, NJ: Erlbaum.

DeVries, D. L., Edwards, K. J., & Slavin, R. E. (1978). Biracial learning teams and race relations in the classroom: Four field experiments on Teams-Games-Tournament. *Journal of Educational Psychology, 70*, 356–362.

Dewey, J. (1963). *Experience and education.* New York: Collier. (Original work published 1938)

Dewey, J. (1966). *Democracy and education.* New York: Macmillan. (Original work published 1916)

Dollard, J., Doob, L. W., Miller, N., Mowrer, O. H., & Sears, R. R. (1939). *Frustration and aggression.* New Haven, CT: Yale University Press.

Dovidio, J. F., Brigham, J. C., Johnson, B. T., & Gaertner, S. L. (1996). Stereotyping, prejudice and discrimination: Another look. In C. N. Macrae, C. Stangor, & M. Hewstone (Eds.), *Stereotypes and stereotyping* (pp. 276–319). New York: Guilford.

Dovidio, J. F., Esses, V. M., Beach, K. R., & Gaertner, S. L. (2002). The role of affect in determining intergroup behavior: The case of willingness to engage in intergroup contact. In D. M. Mackie & E. R. Smith (Eds.), *From prejudice to intergroup emotions: Differentiated reactions to social groups* (pp. 153–171). New York: Psychology Press.

Dovidio, J. F., & Gaertner, S. L. (1998). On the nature of contemporary prejudice: The causes, consequences, and challenges of aversive racism. In J. Eberhardt & S. T. Fiske (Eds.), *Confronting racism: The problem and the response* (pp. 3–32). Newbury Park, CA: Sage.

Dubois, P. M., & Hutson, J. J. (1997). *Intergroup dialogues across America.* Hadley, MA: Common Wealth Printing.

Duckitt, J. (1992). Psychology and prejudice: A historical analysis and integrative framework. *American Psychologist, 47*, 1182–1193.

Dunnette, M. D., & Motowildo, S. J. (1982). Estimating benefits and costs of antisexist training programs in organizations. In H. J. Bernardin (Ed.), *Women in the workplace* (pp. 156–182). New York: Praeger.

Durkheim, E. (1973). *Moral education: A study in the theory and application of the sociology of education.* New York: Free Press.

Dutton, D. G., & Lake, R. A. (1973). Threat of own prejudice and reverse discrimination in interracial situations. *Journal of Personality and Social Psychology, 28*, 94–100.

Eagly, A. H., & Chaiken, S. (1998). Attitude structure and function. In D. T. Gilbert, S. T. Fiske, & G. Lindzey (Eds.), *The handbook of social psychology* (4th ed.; Vol. 1; pp. 269–322). New York: McGraw-Hill.

Ehman, L. H. (1980). Change in high school students' political attitudes as a function of social studies classroom climate. *American Educational Research Journal, 17*, 253–265.

Ellis, N., & Lotan, R. A. (1997). Teachers as learners: Feedback, conceptual understanding, and implementation. In E. G. Cohen & R. A. Lotan (Eds.), *Working for equity in heterogeneous classrooms: Sociological theory in practice* (pp. 209–222). New York: Teachers College Press.

Ender, S. C., Saunders-McCaffrey, S., and Miller, T. K. (1979). Students helping students: A training manual for peer helpers on college campuses. Athens, GA: Student Development Associates.

Engel, S. (1988). Conformity or independent thought: Why teach the social studies in a democracy? *Democratic Schools, 3,* 12–13.

Esses, V. M., & Dovidio, J. F. (2002). The role of emotions in determining willingness to engage in intergroup contact. *Personality and Social Psychology Bulletin, 28*(9), 1202–1214.

Esses, V. M., Dovidio, J. F., Jackson, L. M., & Armstrong, T. L. (2001). The immigration dilemma: The role of perceived group competition, ethnic prejudice, and national identity. *Journal of Social Issues, 57,* 389–412.

Esses, V. M., Haddock, G., & Zanna, M. P. (1993). Values, stereotypes, and emotions as determinants of intergroup attitudes. In D. M. Mackie & D. L. Hamilton (Eds.), *Affect, cognition, and stereotyping: Interactive processes in group perception* (pp. 137–166). New York: Academic Press.

Facing History and Ourselves (FHAO). (1999). *The Facing History Alumni Project: 25th Anniversary Follow-up Interviews with Students, Teachers, and Parents.* Brookline, MA: FHAO.

Facing History and Ourselves (FHAO). (1994). *A discussion with Elie Wiesel.* Brookline, MA: FHAO

Facing History and Ourselves (FHAO). (1996). *Annual report.* Brookline, MA: FHAO

Fantuzzo, J. W., Polite, K., & Grayson, N. (1990). An evaluation of reciprocal peer tutoring across elementary school settings. *Journal of School Psychology, 28,* 309–323.

Fantuzzo, J. W., Riggio, R. E., Connelly, S., & Dimeff, L. A. (1989). Effects of reciprocal peer tutoring on academic achievement and psychological adjustment: A component analysis. *Journal of Educational Psychology, 81,* 173–177.

Faust, D., & Arbuthnot, J. (1978). Relationship between moral and Piagetian reasoning and the effectiveness of moral education. *Developmental Psychology, 14,* 435–346.

Fein, H. (1979). *Accounting for genocide.* New York: Free Press.

Feld, S. L., & Carter, W. C. (1998). When desegregation *reduces* interracial contact: A class size paradox for weak ties. *American Journal of Sociology, 103,* 1165–1186.

Fine, M. (1991/1992). Facing history and ourselves: Portrait of a classroom. *Educational Leadership, 49,* 44–49.

Fine, M. (1993a). Collaborative innovations: Documentation of the Facing History and Ourselves program at an Essential School. *Teachers College Record, 94,* 771–789.

Fine, M. (1993b). You can't just say that the only ones who can speak are those who agree with your position: Political discourse in the classroom. *Harvard Educational Review, 63,* 412–433

Fine, M. (1995). *Habits of mind: Struggling over values in America's classrooms.* San Francisco: Jossey-Bass.

Finlay, K., & Stephan, W. G. (2000). Reducing prejudice: The effects of empathy on intergroup attitudes. *Journal of Applied Social Psychology, 30,* 1720–1737.

Finn, J. D. (1989). Withdrawing from school. *Review of Educational Research, 59,* 117–142.

Fishbein, M., & Ajzen, I. (1975). *Belief, attitude, intention, and behavior: An introduction to theory and research.* Reading, MA: Addison-Wesley.

Fiske, S. T., Lin, M., & Neuberg, S. L. (1999). The continuum model: Ten years later. In S. Chaiken & Y. Trope (Eds.), *Dual process theories in social psychology* (pp. 231–254). New York: Guilford.

Fiske, S. T., & Taylor, S. E. (1991). *Social cognition.* New York: McGraw-Hill.

Fox, D. J., & Jordan, V. B. (1973). Racial preference and identification of Black, American Chinese, and White children. *Genetic Psychology Monographs, 88,* 229–286.

Fredrickson, G. (1999). Models of American ethnic relations: A historical perspective. In D. Prentice & D. Miller (Eds.), *Cultural divides: Understanding and overcoming group conflict* (pp. 23–34). New York: Russell Sage Foundation.

Freire, P. (1970). *Pedagogy of the oppressed.* New York: Continuum International Publishing Group.

Freire, P. (1998). *Teachers as cultural workers: Letters to those who dare teach.* Boulder, CO: Westview.

Fullan, M. (1990). Staff development, innovation, and institutional development. In J. Bruce (Ed.), *Changing School Culture through Staff Development* (pp. 244–262) (ASCD Yearbook). Alexandria, VA: Association for Supervision and Curriculum Development

Fullan, M. (1991). Overcoming barriers to educational change. In *Changing schools, insights.* Washington, DC: U.S. Department of Education, Office of Policy and Planning.

Fullan, M. (1993). *Change forces: Probing the depths of educational reform.* New York: Falmer.

Gaertner, S. L., & Dovidio, J. F. (1986). The aversive form of racism. In J. F. Dovidio & S. L. Gaertner (Eds.), *Prejudice, discrimination, and racism* (pp. 61–89). Orlando, FL: Academic Press.

Gaertner, S. L., & Dovidio, J. F. (2000). *Reducing intergroup bias: The common ingroup identity model.* Philadelphia: Psychology Press.

Gaertner, S. L., Dovidio, J. F., Rust, M. C., Nier, J., Banker, B., Ward, C. M., Mottola, G. R., & Houlette, M. (1999). Reducing intergroup bias: Elements of intergroup cooperation. *Journal of Personality and Social Psychology, 76,* 388–402.

Gaertner, S. L., Mann, J., Murrell, A., & Dovidio, J. F. (1989). Reducing intergroup bias: The benefits of recategorization. *Journal of Personality and Social Psychology, 57,* 239–249.

Galinsky, A. D., & Moskowitz, G. B. (2000). Perspective-taking: Decreasing stereotype expression, stereotype accessibility, and in-group favoritism. *Journal of Personality and Social Psychology, 78,* 708–724.

Gallos, J. V., & Ramsey, J. (1997). *Teaching diversity: Listening to the soul, speaking from the heart.* San Francisco: Jossey-Bass.

Galston, W. (1989). Civic education in the liberal state. In N. L. Rosenblum (Ed.), *Liberalism and the moral life.* Cambridge, MA: Harvard University Press.

Garcia, E. E., & Hurtado, A. (1995). Becoming American: A review of current research on the development of racial and ethnic identity in children. In W. Hawley & A. Jackson (Eds.), *Toward a common destiny: Improving race and ethnic relations in America.* San Francisco: Jossey-Bass.

Garcia, J., Powell, R., & Sanchez, T. (1990, April). *Multicultural textbooks: How to use them more effectively in the classroom.* Paper presented at the annual meeting of the American Educational Research Association, Boston. (ERIC Document Reproduction Service No. ED 320 262)

Garcia Coll, C. T., & Vasquez Garcia, H. A. (1995). Developmental processes and their influence on interethnic and interracial relations. In W. Hawley & A. Jackson (Eds.), *Toward a common destiny: Improving race and ethnic relations in America*. San Francisco: Jossey-Bass.

Gardner, H. (1983). *Frames of mind: The theory of multiple intelligences*. New York: Basic Books.

Garet, M., Porter, A., Desimone, L., Birman, B., & Youn, K. (2001). What makes professional development effective? Results from a national sample of teachers. *American Educational Research Journal, 38*, 915–945.

Gilligan, C. (1982). *In a different voice: Psychological theory and women's development*. Cambridge, MA: Harvard University Press.

Gilligan, C. (1998). Remembering Larry. *Journal of Moral Education, 27*, 125–140.

*Gimmestad, B. J., & De Chiara, E. (1982). Dramatic plays: A vehicle for prejudice reduction in the elementary school. *Journal of Educational Research, 76*, 45–49.

Ginott, H. (1975). *Teacher and child: A book for parents and teachers*. New York: Scribner.

Giroux, H. (1983). Critical theory and rationality in citizenship education. In H. Giroux & D. Purpel (Eds.), *The hidden curriculum and moral education* (pp. 321–360). Berkeley: McCutchan.

Giroux, H. (1992). *Border crossing: Cultural workers and the politics of education*. New York: Routledge.

Glazer, M. (1997). *We are all multiculturalists now*. Cambridge, MA: Harvard University Press.

Goldstein, D. L., & Smith, D. H. (1999). The analysis of the effects of experiential training on sojourners' cross-cultural adaptability. *International Journal of Intercultural Relations, 23*, 157–173.

Goleman, D. (1998). *Working with emotional intelligence*. New York: Bantam Books.

Gollnick, D. (1992). Multicultural education: Policies and practices in teacher education. In C. A. Grant (Ed.), *Research and multicultural education* (pp. 218–239). London: Falmer.

Gonzales, A. (1979, April). *Classroom cooperation and ethnic balance*. Paper presented at the annual convention of the American Psychological Association, New York.

Gonzales, A. (1981). *An approach to independent-cooperative bilingual education and measures related to social motives*. Unpublished manuscript, California State University, Fresno.

Goodman, D., & Shapiro, S. (1997). Sexism curriculum design. In M. Adams, L. A. Bell, & P. Griffin (Eds.), *Teaching for diversity and social justice: A sourcebook* (pp. 110–140). New York: Routledge.

Goodman, M. E. (1952). *Race awareness in young children*. New York: Collier.

*Grant, C. A., & Grant, G. A. (1985). Staff development and education that is multicultural. *British Journal of In-Service Education, 12*, 6–18.

Graves, N., & Graves, T. (1991). Candida Graves: Complex teamwork in action. *Cooperative Learning, 12*, 12–16.

Green, J. A., & Gerard, H. (1974). School desegregation and ethic attitudes. In F. Franklin & J. Sherwood (Eds), *Integrating the organization*. New York: Free Press.

Greenman, N. P., & Kimmel, E. B. (1995). The road to multicultural education: Potholes of resistance. *Journal of Teacher Education, 46,* 360–368.

Grusec, J. E. (1981). Socialization processes and the development of altruism. In J. P. Rushton & R. M. Sorrentino (Eds.), *Altruism and helping behavior: Social, personality, and developmental perspectives* (pp. 65–90). Hillsdale, NJ: Erlbaum.

Grusec, J. E. (1982). The socialization of altruism. In N. Eisenberg (Ed.), *The development of prosocial behavior* (pp. 139–166). New York: Academic Press.

Gudykunst, W. B., Hammer, M. R., & Wiseman, R. I. (1977). An analysis of an integrated approach to cross-cultural training. *International Journal of Intercultural Relations, 1,* 99–110.

Gurin, P. (1999). Selections from "The Compelling Need for Diversity in Higher Education," expert reports in defense of the University of Michigan: Expert report of Patricia Gurin. *Equity and Excellence in Education, 32,* 37–62.

Gurin, P., Dey, E. L., Hurtado, S., & Gurin, G. (2002). Diversity and higher education: Theory and impact on educational outcomes. *Harvard Educational Review, 72,* 330–366.

Guttman, A. (2000). Why should schools care about civic education? In L. M. McDonnell, P. M. Timpane, & R. Benjamin (Eds.), *Rediscovering the democratic purposes of education* (pp. 73–90). Lawrence: University Press of Kansas.

Habermas, J. (1990). *Moral consciousness and communicative action* (C. Lenhardt & S. W. Nicholsen, Trans.). Cambridge, MA: MIT Press. (Original work published 1983)

Hahn, C. (1996). Gender and political learning. *Theory and Research in Social Education, 24,* 8–35.

Hahn, C. (1998). *Becoming political: Comparative perspectives on citizenship education.* Albany: State University of New York Press.

Hahn, C. (1999). Challenges to civic education in the United States. In J. Torney-Purta, J. Schwille, & J. Amadeo (Eds.), *Civic education across countries: Twenty-four national case studies from the IEA Civic Education Project* (pp. 583–607). Amsterdam: IEA.

Hallinan, M. T. (1982). Classroom racial composition and children's friendships. *Social Forces, 61,* 56–72

Hamilton, D. L., & Trolier, T. K. (1986). Stereotypes and stereotyping: An overview of the cognitive approach. In J. F. Dovidio & S. L. Gaertner (Eds.), *Prejudice, discrimination, and racism* (pp. 127–163). Orlando, FL: Academic Press.

*Hanover, J. M. B., & Cellar, D. F. (1998). Environmental factors and the effectiveness of workforce diversity training. *Human Resource Development Quaterly, 9,* 105–124.

Hartshorne, H., & May, M. (1928–1930). *Studies in the nature of character* (Vols 1, 2, 3). New York: Macmillan.

Hauserman, N., Walen, S. R., & Behling, M. (1973). Reinforced racial integration in the first grade: A study of generalization. *Journal of Applied Behavioral Analysis, 6,* 193–200.

Heath, S. B. (1995). Race, ethnicity and the defiance of categories. In W. Hawley & A. Jackson (Eds.), *Toward a common destiny: Improving race and ethnic relations in America* (pp. 39–70). San Francisco: Jossey-Bass.

Henderson-King, E., & Nisbett, R. E. (1996). Anti-Black prejudice as a function of exposure to the negative behavior of a single Black person. *Journal of Personality and Social Psychology, 71,* 654–664.

*Henington, M. (1981). Effect of intensive multicultural non-sexist instruction on secondary student teachers. *Educational Research Quarterly, 6,* 65–75.

*Hertz-Lazarowitz, R., Kuppermintz, H., & Lang, J. (1998). Arab-Jewish coexistence: Beit Hagafen coexistence programs. In E. Weiner (Ed.), *The handbook of interethnic coexistence* (pp. 565–584). New York: Continuum.

Hewstone, M. (1990). The "ultimate attribution error"? A review of the literature on intergroup attributions. *European Journal of Social Psychology, 20,* 311–335.

Hewstone, M., & Brown, R. (1986). *Contact and conflict in intergroup encounters.* Oxford: Blackwell.

Heyman, J. S., & Earle, A. (2000). Low-income parents: How do working conditions affect their opportunity to help school-age children at risk? *American Educational Research Journal, 37,* 833–848.

Hofheimer Bettmann, E., Green, M. B., & Dovidio, J. F. (1993). *Who says you can't mandate change in attitudes?* Unpublished manuscript.

*Hohn, R. L. (1973). Perceptual training and its effect on racial preferences of kindergarten children. *Psychological Reports, 32,* 435–441.

hooks, b. (1995). *Killing rage: Ending racism.* New York: Holt.

Horton, M., & Freire, P. (1990). *We make the road by walking: Conversations in education and social change.* Philadelphia: Temple University Press.

Houser, J., Thye, S., & Markovsky, B. (1998). Status processes and mental ability test scores. *American Journal of Sociology, 104,* 195–228.

Howard, G. (1999). *We can't teach what we don't know: White teachers, multiracial schools.* New York: Teachers College Press.

Hussar, W. (1999). *Predicting the need for newly hired teachers in the United States.* Washington, DC: National Center for Education Statistics.

Hyers, L. L., & Swim, J. K. (1998). A comparison of the experiences of dominant and minority group members during an intergroup encounter. *Group Processes and Intergroup Relations, 1,* 143–163.

Hyman, H. H., & Wright, C. R. (1979). *Education's lasting influence on values.* Chicago: University of Chicago Press.

Islam, M. R., & Hewstone, M. (1993). Dimensions of contact as predictors of intergroup anxiety, perceived outgroup variability and outgroup attitude: An integrative model. *Personality and Social Psychology Bulletin, 19,* 700–710.

Jackson, P. W., Boostrom, R. E., & Hansen, D.T. (1993). *The moral life of schools.* San Francisco: Jossey-Bass.

Jaffee, S., & Hyde, J. S. (2000). Gender differences in moral orientation: A meta-analysis. *Psychological Bulletin, 126,* 703–726.

James, R. B. (1981). Why civic virtue and self-interest should provide the moral core of citizenship education. In T. C. Hunt & M. M. Maxson (Eds.), *Religion and morality in public schooling* (pp. 147–164). Washington DC: University Press of America.

Johnson, D., Johnson, T., & Holubec, E. (1993). *Circles of learning: Cooperation in the classroom* (4th ed.). Edina, MN: Interaction Books.

Johnson, D.W., & Johnson, R. T. (1981). Effects of cooperative and individualistic learning experience on interethnic interaction. *Journal of Educational Psychology*, *73*, 444–449.

Johnson, D.W., & Johnson, R.T. (1987). *Learning together and alone: Cooperative, competitive, and individualist learning* (2nd ed.). Englewood Cliffs, NJ: Prentice-Hall.

Johnson, D. W., & Johnson, R. T. (2000). The three Cs of reducing prejudice and discrimination. In S. Oskamp (Ed.), *Reducing prejudice and discrimination* (pp. 239–268). Hillsdale, NJ: Erlbaum.

Jones, J. M. (1972). *Prejudice and racism*. Reading, MA: Addison-Wesley.

Jones, J. M. (1997). *Prejudice and racism* (2nd ed.). New York: McGraw-Hill.

Jost, J. T., & Banaji, M. R. (1994). The role of stereotyping in system-justification and the production of false consciousness. *British Journal of Social Psychology*, *33*, 1–27.

Kagan, S., Zahn, G. L., Widaman, K. F., Schwarzwald, J., & Tyrell, G. (1985). Classroom structural bias: Impact of cooperative and competitive classroom structures on cooperative and competitive individuals and groups. In R. E. Slavin, S. Sharan, S. Kagan, R. Hertz-Lararowitz, C. Webb, & R. Schmuck (Eds.), *Learning to cooperate, cooperating to learn* (pp. 277–312). New York: Plenum.

Kalb, C. (2001, February 26). DARE checks into rehab: A new stragegy for the popular anti-drug program. *Time*, p. 56.

*Kamfer, L., & Kenter, D. J. L. (1994). First evaluation of a stereotype reduction workshop. *South African Journal of Psychology*, *24*, 13–20.

*Katz, J. H., & Ivey, A. (1977). White awareness: The frontier of racism awareness training. *Personnel and Guidance Journal*, *55*, 485–489.

Katz, P. A. (1976). The acquisition of racial attitudes in children. In P.A. Katz (Ed.), *Towards the elimination of racism* (pp. 125–154). New York: Pergamon.

Katz, P. A. (1982). Development of children's racial awareness and intergroup attitudes. In L. G. Katz (Ed.), *Current topics in early childhood education* (pp. 17–54). Norwood, NJ: Pergamon.

Kaufman, M. (2000, December 20). Anti-smoking units failed to stop teens. *Washington Post*, p. A3.

*Kehoe, J. W., & Rogers, W. T. (1978). The effects of principle testing discussions on student attitudes toward selected groups subjected to discrimination. *Canadian Journal of Education*, *3*, 73–80.

Kissinger, K. (1997). *All the colors we are*. St. Paul, MN: Redleaf.

Kohlberg, L. (1967). Moral and religious education, and the public schools: A developmental view. In T. Sizer (Ed.), *Religion and public education*. Boston: Houghton Mifflin.

Kohlberg, L. (1969). Stage and sequence: The cognitive developmental approach to socialization. In D. Goslin (Ed.), *Handbook of socialization, theory and research*. New York: Academic Press.

Kohlberg, L. (1970). The moral atmosphere of the school. In N. Overley (Ed.), *The unstudied curriculum*. Washington, DC: Association for Supervision and Curriculum Development.

Kohlberg, L. (1976). This special section in perspective. *Social Education*, 213–215.

Kohlberg, L. (1984). *Essays on moral development: Vol. 2. The psychology of moral development*. San Francisco: Harper & Row.

Kohlberg, L. (1985). A just community approach to moral education in theory and practice. In M. Berkowitz & F. Ozer (Eds.), *Moral education: Theory and practice.* Hillsdale, NJ: Erlbaum.

Kohlberg, L., Levine, C., & Hewer, A. (1983). *Moral stages: A current formulation and response to critics.* Basel, Switzerland: Karger.

*Kowalski, K. (1998). The impact of vicarious exposure to diversity on preschoolers' emerging ethnic/racial attitudes. *Early Child Development and Care, 146,* 41–51.

Kramer, H. C., Gardner, C. B., Brooks, J. O., III, & Yesavage, J. A. (1998). Advantages of excluding underpowered studies in meta-analysis: Inclusionist versus exclusionists viewpoints. *Psychological Methods, 3,* 23–31.

Kressel, N. J. (2002). *Mass hate. The global rise of genocide and terror.* New York: Westview.

Ladson-Billings, G. (1992). Culturally relevant teaching: The key to making multicultural education work. In C. Grant (Ed.), *Research and multicultural education: From the margins to the mainstream* (pp. 106–121). London: Falmer.

Ladson-Billings, G. (1997). *Dreamkeepers: Successful teachers of African-American children.* San Francisco: Jossey-Bass.

Ladson-Billings, G. (2001). *Crossing over to Canaan: The journey of a new teacher.* New York: Wiley.

Landis, D., Brislin, R. W., & Hulgus, J. F. (1985). Attributional training versus contact in acculturative learning: A laboratory study. *Journal of Applied Social Psychology, 15,* 466–482.

Lankford, H., Loeb, S., & Wyckoff, J. (2002). Teacher sorting and the plight of urban schools. *Educational Evaluation and Policy Analysis, 24,* 37–62.

Lantieri, L. (1998). *Waging peace in our schools.* Boston: Beacon.

Leahy, R. L. (1983). The development of the conception of social class. In R. Leahy (Ed.), *The child's construction of inequality* (pp. 79–107). New York: Academic Press.

Lederach, J. P. (1997). *Building peace: Sustainable reconciliation in divided societies.* Washington, DC: U.S. Institute of Peace.

Lee, C. (1997, June). *Cooperative learning in the thinking classroom: Research and theoretical perspectives.* Paper presented at the International Conference on Thinking, Singapore. (Eric Document Reproduction Services No. ED 408 570)

Lee, V., & Loeb, S. (2000). School size in Chicago elementary schools: Effects on teachers' attitudes and students' achievement. *American Educational Research Journal, 37,* 3–31.

*Lefley, H. P. (1985). Impact of cross-cultural training on Black and White mental health professionals. *International Journal of Intercultural Relations, 9,* 305–318.

Leippe, M. R., & Eisenstadt, D. (1994). Generalization of dissonance reduction: Decreasing prejudice through induced compliance. *Journal of Personality and Social Psychology, 67,* 395–413.

Leming, J. S. (1993). In search of effective character education. *Educational Leadership, 51,* 63–71.

Leming, J. S. (1997). Whither goes character education? Objectives, pedagogy, and research in education programs. *Journal of Education, 179,* 11–34.

*Lessing, E. E., & Clark, C. C. (1976). An attempt to reduce ethnic prejudice and assess its correlates in a junior high school sample. *Educational Research Quarterly, 1,* 3–16.

Lewin, K. (1951). *Field theory in social science.* New York: Harper & Row.

Lickona, T. (1991). *Educating for character.* New York: Bantam.

Lieberman, M. (1991). Program Evaluation, "A Summary of Responses of Teachers and Students to Surveys and Tests Administered during Spring and Summer, 1990" and "Summary of Summer Institute Participants' Responses to a Follow-up Survey, 1991." Wellesley, MA: Responsive Methodology (unpublished).

Lieberman, M. (1993). Project Submissions to U.S. Department of Education Joint Dissemination Review Panel in 1980 (285:80–33),1985 (451:80–33R), and submission to U.S. Department of Education Program Effectiveness Panel.

Lieberman, M. (1995). *Results of the Facing History and Ourselves teacher survey.* Wellesley, MA: Responsive Methodology (unpublished).

Lieberman, M. (1999). *Facing History and Ourselves educator survey report, Cleveland Ohio area.* Unpublished manuscript. Albuquerque, NM: Responsive Methodology.

Lieberman, M. (2000). *Facing History Tennessee teacher survey: An analysis of responses.* Unpublished manuscript. Albuquerque, NM: Responsive Methodology.

Lightfoot, S. L. (1983). *The good high school: Portraits of character and culture.* New York: Basic Books.

Lim, S., Biggs, D. A., & Colesante, R. J. (1998, March). *The influence of justice and care moral orientations in teaching about controversial moral issues.* Paper presented at the meeting of the Association of Moral Education, Hanover, NH.

Lincoln, Y. S. (1985). *Organizational theory and inquiry.* London: Sage.

Lind, G. (2000). The importance of role-taking opportunities for self-sustaining moral development. *Journal of Research in Education, 10,* 9–15.

Lippmann, W. (1922). *Public opinion.* New York: Harcourt-Brace.

*Litcher, J. H., & Johnson, D. W. (1969). Changes in attitudes toward Negroes of White elementary school students after use of multicultural readers. *Journal of Educational Psychology, 60,* 148–152.

Lloyd, P., & Cohen, E. G. (1999). Peer status in the middle school: A natural treatment for unequal participation. *Social Psychology of Education, 4,* 1–24.

*Lopez, G., Gurin, P., & Nagda, B. R. (1998). Education and understanding structural causes of group inequalities. *Political Psychology, 19,* 305–329.

Lopez-Reyna, N.A (1997). The relation of interactions and story quality among Mexican American and Anglo American students with learning disabilities. *Exceptionality, 7,* 245–261.

Lotan, R. A. (1997). Principles of a principled curriculum. In E. G. Cohen & R. Lotan (Eds.), *Working for equity in heterogeneous classrooms: Sociological theory in practice* (pp. 105–116). New York: Teachers College Press.

Lotan, R. A., Cohen, E. G., & Morphew, C. C. (1997). Principals, colleagues, and staff developers: The case for organizational support. In E. G. Cohen & R. A. Lotan (Eds.), *Working for equity in heterogeneous classrooms: Sociological theory in practice* (pp. 223–239). New York: Teachers College Press.

Lott, A. J., & Lott, B. E. (1965). Group cohesiveness as interpersonal attraction: A review of relationships with antecedent and consequent variables. *Psychological Bulletin, 64,* 259–309.

Lutkus, A. D., Weiss, A. R., Campbell, J. R., Mazzeo, J., & Lazer, S. (1999). *The NAEP civics report card for the nation*. Washington, DC: National Center for Education Statistics.

Mackie, D. M., Devos, T., & Smith, E. R. (2001). Intergroup emotions: Explaining offensive action tendencies in an intergroup context. *Journal of Personality and Social Psychology, 79*, 602–616.

Macrae, C. N., Bodenhausen, G. V., & Milne, A. B. (1998). Saying no to unwanted thoughts: Self-focus and the regulation of mental life. *Journal of Personality and Social Psychology, 74*, 578–589.

Maeroff, G. I. (1999). *Altered destinies: Making life better for school children in need*. New York: St. Martin's Griffin.

Maller, J. B. (1934). General and specific factors in character. *Journal of Social Psychology, 5*, 97–102.

Mariaskin, L., & Sofo, R. (1992). Culturally diverse communities. *Kappa Delta Pi Record*.

Marsh, M. M. (1992). Implementing anti-bias curriculum in the kindergarten classroom. In S. Kessler & B. Swadner (Eds.), *Reconceptualizing the early childhood curriculum: Beginning the dialogue* (pp. 267–282). New York: Teachers College Press.

McClellan, B. E. (1999). *Moral education in America*. New York: Teachers College Press.

McConahay, J. B. (1986). Modern racism, ambivalence, and the Modern Racism Scale. In J. F. Dovidio & S. L. Gaertner (Eds.), *Prejudice, discrimination, and racism* (pp. 91–125). Orlando, FL: Academic Press.

McLaren, P. (1989). *Life in schools*. New York: Longman.

McLaughlin, M. W. (1978). Implementation as mutual adaptation: Change in classroom organization. In D. Mann (Ed.), *Making change happen*. New York: Teachers College Press.

McLaughlin, T. H. (1992). Citizenship, diversity, and education. *Journal of Moral Education, 21*, 235–250.

McLoyd, V. (1990). Minority children: Introduction to the special issue. *Child Development, 61*, 263–266.

Mezirow, J. (2000). Learning to think like an adult: Core concepts of transformation theory. In J. Mezirow (Ed.), *Learning as transformation: Critical perspectives on a theory in progress* (pp. 3–33). San Francisco: Jossey-Bass.

Miller, K. A., Kohn, M. L., & Schooler, C. (1986). Educational self-direction and personality. *American Sociological Review, 51*, 372–390.

Miller, N., & Brewer, M. B. (1986). Categorization effects on ingroup and outgroup perception. In J. F. Dovidio & S. L. Gaertner (Eds.), *Prejudice, discrimination, and racism* (pp. 209–230). Orlando, FL: Academic Press.

Miller, N., & Davidson-Podgorny, G. (1987). Theoretical models of intergroup relations and the use of cooperative teams as an intervention for desegregated settings. In C. Hendrick (Ed.), *Review of personality and social psychology: Vol. 9. Group processes and intergroup relations* (pp. 41–67). Beverly Hills, CA: Sage.

Monteith, M. J. (1993). Self-regulation of prejudiced responses: Implications for progress in prejudice-reduction efforts. *Journal of Personality and Social Psychology, 65*, 469–485.

Monteith, M., & Voils, C. (1998). Proneness to prejudiced responses. *Journal of Personality and Social Psychology, 75*, 901–916.

Morey, A. I. (1997). Organizational change and implementation strategies for multicultural infusion. In A. Morey & M. Kitano (Eds.), *Multicultural course transformation in higher education: A broader truth* (pp. 279–296). Boston: Allyn & Bacon.

Mosher, R., & Sprinthall, N. (1970). Psychological education in secondary schools: A program to promote individual and human development. *American Psychologist, 25*, 911–924.

Mullen, B., & Hu, L. T. (1989). Perception of ingroup and outgroup variability: A meta-analytic integration. *Basic and Applied Social Psychology, 10*, 233–252.

Myers, K. A., Caruso, R., & Birk, N. A. (1999). The diversity continuum: Enhancing student interest and access, creating a staying environment, and preparing students for transition. In J. Q. Adams & J. R. Welsch (Eds.), *Cultural diversity: Curriculum, classroom and climate* (pp. 429–442). Macomb, IL: Illinois Staff and Curriculum Developers Association.

Myers, P., & Zúñiga, X. (1993). Concentric circles exercise. In D. Schoem, L. Frankel, X. Zúñiga, & E. Lewis (Eds.), *Multicultural teaching in the university* (pp. 318–319). Westport, CT: Praeger.

Nagda, B. A. (2001). *Creating spaces of hope and possibility: A curriculum guide for intergroup dialogues.* Seattle, WA: IDEA Training & Resource Institute.

Nagda, B. A., & Moise-Swanson, D. (2001, March). *Intergroup dialogues: An empowerment approach to educating students for social justice work.* Paper presented at the annual program meeting for the Council on Social Work Education, Dallas, TX.

Nagda, B. A., Kim, C. W., & Truelove, Y. (2004). Learning about difference, learning with others, learning to transgress. *Journal of Social Issues, 60*(1), 195–214.

Nagda, B. A., Spearmon, M., Holley, L. C., Harding, S., Balassone, M. L., Moise-Swanson, D., & de Mello, S. (1999). Intergroup dialogues: An innovative approach to teaching about diversity and justice in social work programs. *Journal of Social Work Education, 35*, 433–449.

Nagda, B. A., & Zúñiga, X. (2003). Fostering meaningful racial engagement through intergroup dialogues. *Group Processes and Intergroup Relations, 6*, 111–128.

National Association for the Education of Young Children (NAEYC). (1989). *Antibias curriculum: Tools for empowering young children.* Washington, DC: NAEYC.

National Conference for Community and Justice (NCCJ). (2000a). *NCCJ unveils first comprehensive nationwide survey on interracial and intergroup relations since 1993: Daily experiences of discrimination continue at alarming rates* (press release). Washington, DC: Author.

National Conference for Community and Justice (NCCJ). (2000). *Taking America's pulse II.* Washington, DC: Author.

*Neville, H., & Furlong, M. (1994). The impact of participation in a cultural awareness program on the racial attitudes and social behaviors of first-year college students. *Journal of College Student Development, 35*, 371–377.

*Neville, H. A., Heppner, M. J., Louie, C. E., Thompson, C. E., Brocks, L., & Baker, C. E. (1996). The impact of multicultural training on White racial identity attitudes and therapy competencies. *Professional Psychology: Research and Practice, 27*, 83–89.

Nie, N. H., Junn, J., & Stehlik-Barry, K. (1996). *Education and democratic citizenship in America.* Chicago: University of Chicago Press.

Niemi, R., & Junn, J. (1998). *Civic education: What makes students learn.* New Haven, CT: Yale University Press.

Nieto, S. (1992). *Affirming diversity: The sociopolitical context of multicultural education.* New York: Longman.

Noddings, N. (1994). Conversation as moral education. *Journal of Moral Education, 23,* 107–118.

Oishi, S. (1983). *Effects of team assisted individualization in mathematics on cross-race interactions of elementary school children.* Unpublished doctoral dissertation, University of Maryland, College Park, MD.

Oishi, S., Slavin, R. E., & Madden, N.A. (1983, April). *Effects of student teams and individualized instruction on cross-race and cross-sex friendships.* Paper presented at the annual meeting of the American Educational Research Association, Montreal, Canada.

Orfield, G. (1975). How to make desegregation work: The adaptation of schools to their newly-integrated student bodies. *Law and Contemporary Problems, 39,* 314–340.

*Ottavi, T. M., Pope-Davis, D., & Dings, J. (1994). The relationship between White racial identity attitudes and self-reported multicultural counseling competencies. *Journal of Counseling Psychology, 41,* 149–154.

Pascarella, E., Edison, M., Hagedorn, L., Nora, A., & Terenzini, P. (1996). Influences on students' openness to diversity. *Journal of Higher Education, 67,* 174–195.

Pascarella, E. T., & Terenzini, P.T. (1991). *How college affects students.* San Francisco: Jossey-Bass.

Pelo, A., & Davidson, F. (2000). *That's not fair! A teacher's guide to activism with young children.* St. Paul: MN: Redleaf.

Pettigrew, T. F. (1971). *Racially separate or together?* New York: McGraw-Hill.

Pettigrew, T. F. (1979). The ultimate attribution error: Extending Allport's cognitive analysis of prejudice. *Personality and Social Psychology Bulletin, 5,* 461–476.

Pettigrew, T.F. (1986). The intergroup contact hypothesis reconsidered. In M. Hewstone & R. Brown (Eds.), *Contact and conflict in intergroup encounters* (pp. 169–195). Oxford: Basil Blackwell.

Pettigrew, T. F. (1998). Prejudice and discrimination on the college campus. In J. L. Eberhardt & S. T. Fiske (Eds.), *Confronting racism: The problem and the response* (pp. 263–279). Thousand Oaks, CA: Sage.

Pettigrew, T. F., & Meertens, R. W. (1995). Subtle and blatant prejudice in Western Europe. *European Journal of Social Psychology, 25,* 57–76.

Pettigrew, T. F., & Tropp, L. R. (2000). Does intergroup contact reduce prejudice? Recent meta-analytic findings. In S. Oskamp (Ed.), *Reducing prejudice and discrimination* (pp. 93–114). Mahwah, NJ: Erlbaum.

Phinney, J. S. (1989). Stages of ethnic identity development in minority group adolescents. *Journal of Early Adolescence, 9,* 34–49.

Phinney, J. S. (1992). The Multigroup Ethnic Identity Measure: A new scale for use with diverse groups. *Journal of Adolescent Research, 7,* 156–176.

Piaget, J. (1970). *Structuralism.* New York: Basic Books.

Piaget, J. (1983). Piaget's theory. In P. H. Mussen (Ed.), *Handbook of child psychology* (pp. 103–128). New York: Wiley.

Pierce, C. (1980). Social trace contaminants: Subtle indicators of racism. In S. Withey,

R. Abeles, & L. Erlbaum (Eds.), *Television and social behavior: Beyond violence and children* (pp. 249–257). Hillsdale, NJ: Erlbaum.

Pope, D. C. (2001). *Doing school.* New Haven, CT: Yale University Press.

Power, C. (1985). Democratic moral education in the large public high school. In M. Berkowitz & F. Ozer (Eds.), *Moral education: Theory and practice* (pp. 219–238). Hillsdale, NJ: Erlbaum.

Power, C., Higgins, A., & Kohlberg, L. (1989). *Lawrence Kohlberg's approach to moral education.* New York: Columbia University Press.

Pratte, R. (1988). *The civic imperative: Examining the need for civic education.* New York: Teachers College Press.

Quintanilla, M. (1995, November 17). The great divide. *The Los Angeles Times,* pp. E1, E7.

Ramsey, P. G. (1998). *Teaching and learning in a diverse world: Multicultural education for young children* (2nd ed.). New York: Teachers College Press.

Ramsey, P. G., William, L. R., with Void, E. B. (in press). *Multicultural education: A source book* (2nd Ed.). New York: Garland.

Rest, J. (1979). *Development in judging moral issues.* Minneapolis: University of Minnesota Press.

Rest, J. R. (1983). Morality. In J. H. Flavell & E. Markham (Eds.), *Handbook of child psychology* (Vol. 3; 4th ed.). New York: Wiley.

Rokeach, M. (1973). *The nature of human values.* New York: Free Press.

Romo, H. D., & Falbo, T. (1996). *Latino high school graduation: Defying the odds.* Austin: University of Texas Press.

Rosenberg, M. (1965). *Society and the adolescent's self image.* Princeton, NJ: Princeton University Press.

Rosenholtz, S. J., & Rosenholtz, S. H. (1981). Classroom organization and the perception of ability. *Sociology of Education, 54,* 132–140.

Rosenthal, R. (1979). The file drawer problem and tolerance for null effects. *Psychological Bulletin, 86,* 638–641.

Rosenthal, R. (1994). Parametric measures of effect size. In H. Cooper & L. Hedges (Eds.), *The handbook of research synthesis* (pp. 231–244). New York: Russell Sage Foundation.

Rothbart, M., & John, O. P. (1985). Social categorization and behavioral episodes: A cognitive analysis and the effects of intergroup contact. *Journal of Social Issues, 41,* 81–104.

Rowe, I., & Marcia, J. (1980). Ego identity status, formal operations, and moral development. *Journal of Youth and Adolescence, 9,* 87–99.

Rushton, J. P. (1981). The altruistic personality. In J. P. Rushton & R. M. Sorrentino (Eds.), *Altruism and helping behavior* (pp. 251–266). Hillsdale, NJ: Erlbaum.

Ryan, C. S., Judd, C. M., & Park, B. (1996). Assessing stereotype accuracy: Implications for understanding the stereotyping process. In C. N. Macrae, C. Stangor, & M. Hewstone (Eds.), *Stereotypes and stereotyping* (pp. 121–157). New York: Guilford.

Schachter, S., & Singer, J. E. (1962). Cognitive, social, and physiological determinants of emotional state. *Psychological Review, 69,* 379–399.

Schlaefli, A., Rest, J., & Thoma, S. (1985). Does moral education improve moral judgment? A meta-analysis of intervention studies using the DIT. *Review of Educational Research, 55,* 319–352.

Schoem, D., & Hurtado, S. (Eds.). (2001). *Intergroup dialogue: Deliberative democracy in school, college, community and workplace.* Ann Arbor: University of Michigan Press.

Schofield, A. (1991). *Improving the effectiveness of the management of innovation and change in higher education.* Paris: International Institute for Educational Planning.

Schofield, J. W. (1991). School desegregation and intergroup relations: A review of the literature. In G. Grant (Ed.), *Review of Research in Education, 17,* 335–409. Washington, DC: American Educational Research Association.

Schofield, J. W. (1995). Improving intergroup relations among students. In J. Banks & C. Banks (Eds.), *Handbook of research on multicultural education* (pp. 635–645). New York, NY: MacMillan.

Schofield, J. W. (1995a). Promoting positive intergroup relations: A review of the literature. *Reviews in Education, 17,* 335–409.

Schofield, J. W. (1995b). Promoting positive intergroup relations in school settings. In W. Hawley & A. Jackson (Eds.), *Toward a common destiny: Improving race and ethnic relations in America.* San Francisco: Jossey-Bass.

Schroeder, D. A., Penner, L. A., Dovidio, J. F., & Piliavin, J. A. (1995). *Psychology of helping and altruism.* New York: McGraw-Hill.

Schultz, L., Barr, D., & Selman, R. (2001). The value of a developmental approach to evaluating character development programs: An outcome study of "Facing History and Ourselves." *Journal of Moral Education, 30,* 3–27.

Schultz, L., & Selman, R. (1998). *Toward the construction of two developmental social competence measures: The GSID Relationship Questionnaires.* Unpublished manuscript, Harvard University.

Selman, R. (1980). *The growth of interpersonal understanding.* New York: Academic Press.

Selman, R., & Schultz, L. (1990). *Making a friend in youth: Developmental theory and pair therapy.* Chicago: University of Chicago Press.

Selman, R., Watts, C., & Schultz, L. (1997). *Fostering friendship: Pair therapy for treatment and prevention.* Hawthorne, NY: Aldine de Gruyter.

Shadish, W. R., & Haddock, C. K. (1994). Combining estimates of effect size. In H. Cooper & L. Hedges (Eds.), *The handbook of research synthesis* (pp. 261–281). New York: Russell Sage Foundation.

Sharan, S., Hertz-Lazarowitz, R., Bejarano, Y., Raviv, S., & Sharan, Y. (1984). *Cooperative learning in the classroom: Research in desegregated schools.* Hillsdale, NJ: Erlbaum.

Sharan, Y., & Sharan, S. (1992). *Expanding cooperative learning through group investigation.* New York: Teachers College Press.

Shavit, Y., & Blossfeld, H. (1993). *Persistent inequality: Changing educational attainment in thirteen countries.* San Francisco: Westview.

Sherif, M. (1966). *Group conflict and cooperation.* London: Routledge & Kegan Paul.

Sherif, M., Harvey, O. J., White, B. J., Hood, W. R., & Sherif, C. W. (1961). *Intergroup conflict and cooperation. The Robbers Cave experiment.* Norman: University of Oklahoma Book Exchange.

Shulman, J., Lotan, R. A., & Whitcomb, J.A. (1998). *Groupwork in diverse classrooms: A casebook for educators.* New York: Teachers College Press.

Sidanius, J., & Pratto, F. (1999). *Social dominance: An intergroup theory of social hierarchy and oppression.* New York: Cambridge University Press.

Sikkink, D. (1999). The social sources of alienation from public schools. *Social Forces, 78,* 51–86.

Sizer, T., & Sizer, N. F. (1999). *The students are watching: Schools and the moral contract.* Boston: Beacon.

Slavin, R. E. (1977). How student learning teams can integrate the desegregated classroom. *Integrated Education, 15,* 5–58.

Slavin, R. E. (1979). Effects of biracial leaning teams on cross-racial friendships. *Journal of Educational Psychology, 71,* 381–387.

Slavin, R. E. (1983). *Cooperative learning.* New York: Longman.

Slavin, R. E. (1985). Cooperative learning: Applying contact theory to desegregated schools. *Journal of Social Issues, 41,* 45–62.

Slavin, R. E. (1986). *Using student team learning* (3rd ed.). Baltimore: Center for Research on Elementary and Middle Schools, Johns Hopkins University.

Slavin, R. E. (1990). *Cooperative learning: Theory, research, and practice.* Englewood Cliffs, NJ: Prentice-Hall.

Slavin, R. E. (1991). Synthesis of research on cooperative learning. *Educational Leadership, 48,* 71–82.

Slavin, R. E. (1992). When and why does cooperative learning increase achievement? Theoretical and empirical perspectives. In R. Hertz-Lazarowitz & N. Miller (Eds.), *Interaction in cooperative groups* (pp. 145–173). New York: Cambridge University Press.

Slavin, R. E. (1995a). Cooperative learning and intergroup relations. In J. Banks & C. Banks (Eds.), *Handbook of research on multicultural education.* New York: Macmillian.

Slavin, R. E. (1995b). *Cooperative learning: Theory, research, and practice* (2nd ed.). Boston: Allyn & Bacon.

Slavin, R. E. (1995c). Enhancing intergroup relations in schools: Cooperative learning and other strategies. In W. D. Hawley & A. Jackson (Eds.), *Toward a common destiny: Improving race and ethnic relations in America* (pp. 291–312). San Francisco: Jossey-Bass.

Slavin, R. E., Leavy, M., & Madden, N. A. (1984). Combining cooperative learning and individualized instruction: Effects on students mathematics achievement, attitudes, and behaviors. *Elementary School Journal, 84,* 409–422.

Slavin, R. E., & Madden, N. A. (1979). School practices that improve race relations. *American Educational Research Journal, 16,* 169–180.

Slavin, R. E., & Oickle, E. (1981). Effects of cooperative learning teams on student achievement and race relations: Treatment by race interactions. *Sociology of Education, 54,* 174–180.

Sleeter, C. (1992). Restructuring schools for multicultural education. *Journal of Teacher Education, 43,* 141–148.

Sleeter, C. E. (1995). An analysis of critiques of multicultural education. In J. A. Banks & C. A. McGee Banks (Eds.), *Handbook of research on multicultural education* (pp. 81–93). Boston: Allyn & Bacon

Smith, E. R., & Ho, C. (2002). Prejudice as intergroup emotion: Integrating relative deprivation and social comparison explanations of prejudice. In I. Walker &

H. J. Smith (Eds.), *Relative deprivation: Specification, development, and integration* (pp. 332–348). New York: Cambridge University Press.

Smith, T.W. (1990). *Ethnic images* (General Social Survey Topical Report No. 19). Chicago: National Opinion Research Center, University of Chicago.

*Sodowsky, G., Kus-Jackson, P., Richardson, M., & Corey, A. (1998). Correlates of self-reported multicultural competencies: Counselor multicultural social desirability, race, social inadequacy, locus of control, racial ideology, and multicultural training. *Journal of Counseling Psychology, 45*, 256–264.

Stahl, R., & VanSickle, R. (1992). *Cooperative learning in the social studies classroom: An invitation to social study.* Washington, DC: National Council for the Social Studies.

Stallings, J., & Stipek, D. (1986). Research on early childhood and elementary school teaching programs. In M. Wittrock (Ed.), *Handbook of research on teaching and learning.* Thousand Oaks, CA: Sage.

Stangor, C., Carr, C., & & Kiang, L. (1998). Activating stereotypes undermines task performance. *Journal of Personality and Social Psychology, 75*, 1191–1197.

Stangor, C., Sechrist, G., & Jost, J. (2001). Social influence and intergroup beliefs: The role of perceived social consensus. In J. P. Forgas & K. D. Williams (Eds.), *Social influence: Direct and indirect processes. The Sydney symposium of social psychology* (pp. 235–252). Philadelphia: Psychology Press/Taylor & Francis.

Stangor, C., Sullivan, L. A., & Ford, T. E. (1991). Affective and cognitive determinants of prejudice. *Social Cognition, 9*, 359–380.

Staub, E. (1979). *Positive social behavior and morality: Vol. 2: Socialization and development.* New York: Academic Press.

Staub, E. (1981). Promoting positive behavior in schools, in other educational settings and in the home. In J. P. Rushton & R. M. Sorrentino (Eds.), *Altruism and helping behavior* (pp. 109–133). Hillsdale, NJ: Erlbaum.

Stephan, W. G. (1978). School desegregation: An evaluation of the predictions made in *Brown v. Board of Education. Psychological Bulletin, 85*, 217–238.

Stephan, W. G. (1987). The contact hypothesis in multicultural education. In C. Hendrick (Ed.), *Group processes and multicultural education* (pp. 13–40). Beverly Hills: Sage.

Stephan, W. G. (1999). *Reducing prejudice and stereotyping in schools.* New York: Teachers College Press.

Stephan, W. G., & Brigham, J. C. (1985). Intergroup contact: Introduction. *Journal of Social Issues, 41*, 1–8.

Stephan, W. G., & Finlay, K. A. (2000). The role of empathy in improving multicultural education. *Journal of Social Issues, 55*(4), 729–744.

Stephan, W. G., & Stephan, C. W. (1984). The role of ignorance in multicultural education. In N. Miller & M. B. Brewer (Eds.), *Groups in contact: The psychology of desegregation* (pp. 229–257). New York: Academic Press.

Stephan, W. G., & Stephan, C. W. (1985). Intergroup anxiety. *Journal of Social Issues, 41*, 157–175.

Stephan, W. G., & Stephan, C. W. (1996). *Intergroup relations.* Boulder, CO: Westview.

Stephan, W. G., & Stephan, C. W. (2001). *Improving intergroup relations.* Thousand Oaks, CA: Sage.

Sternberg, R. J. (1985). *Beyond IQ: A triarchic theory of human intelligence*. Cambridge, UK: Cambridge University Press.

Stevens, R. J., Madden, N. A., Slavin, R. E., & Farnish, A. (1987). Cooperative integrated reading and composition: Two field experiments. *Reading Research Quarterly, 22,* 433–454.

Stringfield, S., Datnow, A., Ross, S. M., & Snively, F. (1998). Scaling up school restructuring in multicultural multilingual contexts: Early observations from Sunland Country. *Education and Urban Society, 30,* 326–357.

Strom, M. S. (1980). Facing History and Ourselves: Holocaust and human behavior. In R. Mosher (Ed.), *Moral education: A first generation of research and development*. New York: Praeger.

Sue, D. (1999). Creating conditions for a constructive dialogue on "race": Taking individual and institutional responsibility. In J. Adams & J. Welsch (Eds.), *Cultural diversity: Curriculum, classroom and climate* (pp. 15–20). Illinois Staff and Curriculum Developers Association.

Sullivan, H. S. (1953). *The interpersonal theory of psychiatry*. New York: Norton.

Sullivan, J. L., Piereson, J., & Marcus, G. (1982). *Political tolerance and American democracy*. Chicago: University of Chicago Press.

Swim, J. K., & Miller, D. L. (1999). White guilt: Its antecedents and consequences for attitudes toward affirmative action. *Personality and Social Psychology Bulletin, 25,* 500–514.

Tajfel, H., & Turner, J. C. (1979). An integrative theory of intergroup conflict. In W. G. Austin & S. Worchel (Eds.), *The social psychology of intergroup relations* (pp. 33–48). Monterey, CA: Brooks/Cole.

*Tansik, D. A., & Driskill, J. (1977). Temporal persistence of attitudes induced through required training. *Group and Organization Studies, 2,* 310–323.

Tatum, B. D. (1997). *"Why are all the Black kids sitting together in the cafeteria?" and other conversations about race*. New York: Basic Books.

Torney, J. V., Oppenheim, A. N., & Farnen, R. F. (1975). *Civic education in ten countries: An empirical study*. New York: Wiley.

Torney-Purta, J., Schwille, J., & Amadeo, J. (1999). *Civic education across countries: Twenty-four national case studies form the IEA Civic Education Project*. Amsterdam: International Association for the Evaluation of Educational Achievement.

Trager, H., & Radke-Yarrow, M. (1952). *They learn what they live*. New York: Harper & Brothers.

Ury, W. V. (1999). *Getting to peace*. New York: Viking.

U.S. Department of Education, National Center for Education Statistics. (2000). *The condition of education 2000*. Washington, DC: U.S. Government Printing Office.

Van Ausdale, D., & Feagin, J. R. (2001). *The first R: How children learn race and racism*. New York: Rowman & Littlefield.

Van Keulen, A. (2000). *Ik ben ik en jij bent jij: Methodiek en praktijkboek voor de Kinderopvang over opvoeden zonder vooroordelen*. Nederlands: Instituut voor Zorg en Welzijn/ NIZW.

Vanman, E. J., Paul, B. Y., Ito, T. A., & Miller, N. (1997). The modern face of prejudice and structural features that moderate the effect of cooperation on affect. *Journal of Personality and Social Psychology, 73,* 941–959.

*Van Soest, D. (1996). Impact of social work education on student attitudes and behavior concerning oppression. *Journal of Social Work Education, 32,* 191–202.

*Verma, G. K., & Bagley, C. (1973). Changing racial attitudes in adolescents. *International Journal of Psychology, 8,* 55–58.

Vitz, P. C. (1990). The use of stories in moral development: New psychological reasons for an old educational method. *American Psychologist, 45,* 709–720.

Vogt, W. P. (1997). *Tolerance and education: Learning to live with diversity and difference.* Thousand Oaks, CA: Sage.

Vogt, W. P. (2002, April). *Isn't this program too complex to evaluate? A case study of an evaluation of a multi-method, multi-level, multi-university teacher education grant.* Paper presented at the annual meeting of the American Educational Research Association, New Orleans.

Wadsworth, E. C. (1999). Faculty development programs in support of multicultural education. In J. Adams & J. Welsch (Eds.), *Cultural diversity: Curriculum, classroom and climate* (pp. 457–462). Macomb, IL: Illinois Staff and Curriculum Developers Association.

Walker, H. (October 17, 2000). *Responding to diversity, rethinking curriculum, reinventing the future: Evaluation of the National Community College Early Childhood Education & Leadership Institute.* New York: Consortium of Early Childhood Foundations (unpublished).

Walker, L. J. (1980). Cognitive and perspective-taking prerequisites for moral development. *Child Development, 51,* 131–139.

Walker, L. J. (1983). Sources of cognitive conflict for stage transition in moral development. *Developmental Psychology, 19,* 103–110.

*Wang, V. O. (1998). Curriculum evaluation and assessment of multicultural genetic counseling. *Journal of Genetic Counseling, 7,* 87–111.

Wark, G. R., & Krebs, D. L. (1996). Gender and dilemma differences in real-life moral judgment. *Developmental Psychology, 32,* 220–230.

Weinstein, J. (1997). Facing History and Ourselves. *High School Magazine,* p. 5.

Wentzel, K. R. (1991). Social competence at school: Relationships between social responsibility and academic achievement. *Review of Educational Research, 61,* 1–24.

*Werner, M. J., & Wright, F. E. (1973). Effects of undergoing arbitrary discrimination upon subsequent attitudes toward a minority group. *Journal of Applied Social Psychology, 3,* 94–102.

Whitney, T. (1999). *Kids like us: Using persona dolls in the classroom.* St. Paul, MN: Redleaf.

Wiegel, R. H., Wiser, P. L., & Cook, S. W. (1975). Impact of cooperative learning experiences on cross-ethnic relations and attitudes. *Journal of Social Issues, 31,* 219–245.

Wijeyisinghe, C., Griffin, P., & Love, B. (1997). Racism curriculum design. In M. Adams, L. A. Bell, & P. Griffin (Eds.), *Teaching for diversity and social justice* (pp. 82–109). New York: Routledge.

Williams, R. M., Jr. (1947). *The reduction of intergroup tensions*. New York: Social Science Research Council.

Wittenbrink, B., & Henly, J. (1996). Creating social reality: Informational social influence and the content of stereotypic beliefs. *Personality and Social Psychology Bulletin, 22*, 598–610.

*Wittig, M., & Molina, L. (2000). Moderators and mediators of prejudice reduction in intergroup relations. In S. Oskamp (Ed.), *Reducing prejudice and discrimination* (pp. 295–318). Mahwah, NJ: Erlbaum.

Wolf, F. M. (1986). *Meta-analysis: Quantitative methods for research synthesis*. Newbury Park, CA: Sage.

Wolpert, E. (1999). *Start seeing diversity: A basic guide to an anti-bias classroom* [Video and Guide]. St. Paul, MN: Redleaf.

Worchel, S. (1986). The role of cooperation in reducing intergroup conflict. In S. Worchel & W. Austin (Eds.), *The psychology of intergroup relations* (pp. 288–304). Chicago: Nelson-Hall.

Wright, S. C., Aron, A., McLaughlin-Volpe, T., & Ropp, S. A. (1997). The extended contact effect: Knowledge of cross-group friendships and prejudice. *Journal of Personality and Social Psychology, 73*, 73–90.

Wynne, E. (1985/1986). The great tradition in education: Transmitting moral values. *Educational Leadership, 43*, 4–8.

*Yawkey, T. D. (1973). Attitudes toward Black Americans held by rural and urban White early childhood subjects based upon multi-ethnic social studies materials. *Journal of Negro Education, 42*, 164–169.

Yeakley, A. M. (1998). *The nature of prejudice change: Positive and negative change processes arising from intergroup contact experiences*. Unpublished doctoral dissertation, University of Michigan, Ann Arbor.

York, S. (1998). *As big as life: The everyday inclusion curriculum* (Vols. 1, 2). St.Paul, MN: Redleaf.

Zanna, M. P., & Rempel, J. K. (1988). Attitudes: A new look at an old concept. In D. Bar-Tal & A. W. Kruglanski (Eds.), *The social psychology of knowledge* (pp. 315–334). Cambridge, UK: Cambridge University Press.

Zernike, K. (2001, February 15). Antidrug program says it will adopt a new strategy. *The New York Times*.

Ziegler, S. (1981). The effective of cooperative learning teams for increasing cross-ethic friendship: Additional evidence. *Human Organization, 40*, 24–268.

Zimpher, N. L. (1989). The RATE project: A profile of teacher education students. *Journal of Teacher Education, 40*, 27–30.

Zúñiga, X., & Nagda, B. A. (1993). Dialogue groups: An innovative approach to multicultural learning. In D. Schoem, L. Frankel, X. Zúñiga, & E. Lewis (Eds.), *Multicultural teaching in the university* (pp. 233–248). Westport, CT: Praeger.

Zúñiga, X., Nagda, B. A., & Sevig, T. D. (2002). Intergroup dialogues: An educational model for cultivating engagement across differences. *Equity and Excellence in Education, 35*, 7–17.

About the Editors and the Contributors

Patricia G. Avery is a Professor in the Department of Curriculum and Instruction at the University of Minnesota, where she teaches research methods and secondary social studies methods courses to postbaccalaureate and graduate students. She received her Ph.D. from Emory University in Atlanta, Georgia in 1987. Her research focuses on civic education, political socialization, and political tolerance. Her work has been published in journals such as *American Educational Research Journal, Social Education, Theory into Practice*, and *Theory and Research in Social Education*. From 1995–2001, she served as a member of the Expert Panel on Civic Education for the International Association for the Evaluation of Educational Achievement (IEA).

Dennis J. Barr is currently a Program Evaluator for Facing History and Ourselves (FHAO), a national nonprofit teacher professional development organization, and Lecturer of Education at the Harvard Graduate School of Education, where he teaches a course on theory, research, and practice in moral education. Dr. Barr completed a doctorate in Human Development and Psychology at the Harvard Graduate School of Education and has conducted a number of research studies and published articles focusing on psychosocial development in early adolescence and the prevention of adolescent risk-taking behavior. He was the Principal Investigator of the study, "Intergroup Relations Among Youth: A Study of the Impact and Processes of Facing History and Ourselves," funded by the Carnegie Corporation of New York. In addition, Dr. Barr is a licensed psychologist and served as a clinical supervisor at the Judge Baker Children's Center. He currently lives in the Boston area with his wife and two daughters.

Ellen Hofheimer Bettmann is the national director of Training and Resources for the Anti-Defamation League. She is one of the creators of A WORLD OF DIFFERENCE®, ADL's international anti-bias education program, and has designed and presented programs around the world. A graduate of Connecticut College, Ms. Bettmann is the author of numerous training manuals and articles, and is the co-author of the book *Hate Hurts* (2000). She serves on several national advisory boards, including Family Diversity Projects and Women's Educational Media, and is the recipient of many awards, including the Martin Luther King, Jr. Award from Boston College.

Donald A. Biggs is a Professor of Educational Psychology and Director of Urban Education programs at the University at Albany. Prior to his work at Albany, Dr. Biggs served on the faculty of the University of Minnesota and served as the Director of Student Life Studies and Planning. He received his Ed.D. in Educational Psychology from UCLA. He is the editor of the *Journal of Research in Education* and serves on the editorial board of the *Journal of Educational Psychology*. His research interests include moral development, citizenship and urban education. He is the author of several books including *Foundations of Ethical Counseling* and *The Dictionary of Counseling*.

Cynthia Cohen is the Director of Coexistence Research and International Collaborations in the Slifka Program in Intercommunal Coexistence at Brandeis University. She writes on the ethical and aesthetic dimensions of coexistence and reconciliation, including "Working with Integrity: A Guide-book for Peacebuilders Asking Ethical Questions" (available on-line) and "Engaging with the Arts to Promote Coexistence" in Imagine Coexistence (Jossey-Bass, 2003). Dr. Cohen holds degrees from Wesleyan University, the Massachusetts Institute of Technology, and the University of New Hampshire. She works as a facilitator, teacher, trainer, and researcher in the Middle East, Sri Lanka, the United States, and other conflict regions.

Elizabeth G. Cohen is Professor Emerita of the School of Education and Department of Sociology at Stanford. She founded and directed the Program for Complex Instruction, a model of instruction that permits teaching at a very high conceptual level to classrooms with a diverse population and a wide range of academic achievement. Her publications include *Designing Groupwork, Strategies for Heterogeneous Classrooms*; *Working for Equity in Heterogeneous Classrooms: Sociological Theory in Practice*, co-edited with Rachel Lotan; and *Teaching Cooperative Learning: The Challenge for Teacher Education*, co-edited with Brody and Sapon-Shevin. Currently she is writing a book on educational policy, *And Never Mind the Children*.

Robert J. Colesante is an Associate Professor of Education at Siena College in Loudonville, New York. He received his Ph.D. from the University at Albany in the Department of Educational Psychology and Statistics. His research interests include moral development, urban youth development, and the use of narratives in teaching. Recent articles appear in the *School*

Community Journal and the *Journal of Moral Education*. He has co-directed an Urban Youth Leadership Institute that is designed as an opportunity for talented urban youth to learn about citizenship by exercising the skills of good citizens.

Robert Cooper is Assistant Professor of Education at the Graduate School of Education and Information Studies at the University of California, Los Angeles. He received his B.A. from Pomona College and his Ph.D. from UCLA. Dr. Cooper conducts research on the implementation and scale up of school reform models. His research focuses on the politics and policies of school reform, particularly as they relate to issues of race and equity for at-risk students. Specializing in the use of a mixed-methods approach, he has published and presented numerous papers on the varying aspects of school reform and school change, including recent articles in *Urban Education*, *Journal of Negro Education*, *Education and Urban Society*, and *Journal of Education for Students Placed at Risk*.

Kenneth Cushner is Associate Dean and Professor of Education at Kent State University, Kent, Ohio. A former East-West Center Scholar, he is a frequent contributor to the professional development of educators through writing, workshop presentations, and travel program development. Dr. Cushner is author of several books and articles in the field of intercultural education and training, including: *Human Diversity in Education: An Integrative Approach*, 4th edition (2003) and *Intercultural Interactions: A Practical Guide*, 2nd edition (1996). He has developed and led intercultural programs on all seven continents, and is actively involved in university partnerships in Turkey, the Bahamas, and Kenya.

Louise Derman-Sparks is a long-time human development faculty member at Pacific Oaks College. She has authored and co-authored several books, including: *Anti-Bias Curriculum: Tools for Empowering Young Children*; *Teaching/Learning Anti-Racism: A Developmental Approach*; *In Our Own Way: How Anti-Bias Work Shapes Our Lives and Future Vision*; and *Current Work: Lessons from the Culturally Relevant Anti-Bias Education Leadership Project*. She is currently writing a book with Dr. Patricia Ramsey about doing anti-bias/multicultural education with White children and families. Ms. Derman-Sparks speaks, conducts workshops, and consults widely throughout the United States and internationally. She served on the Governing Board of the National Association for the Education of Young Children from 1998–2001 and currently serves on the National Advisory Board of Crossroads Ministry: An Interfaith and Community Based Anti-Racism Training Organization.

Amelia Seraphia Derr, M.S.W., is the Director of Education at the Hate Free Zone Campaign of Washington, an immigrant rights organization. She received her Master of Social Work degree from the University of Washington where she specialized in multi-ethnic social work practice and international social work. She has taught courses on intergroup dialogue, assisted in curriculum development, and conducted research on student learning in intergroup dialogues. Her long-term professional interests include working on issues of international trafficking of women and children as well as using intergroup dialogues internationally.

John F. Dovidio is Charles A. Dana Professor of Psychology at Colgate University, where he serves as Provost and Dean of the Faculty. He is currently Editor of the *Journal of Personality and Social Psychology—Interpersonal Relations and Group Processes*. He has been Editor of *Personality and Social Psychology Bulletin* and Associate Editor of *Group Processes and Intergroup Relations*. His research interests are in stereotyping, prejudice, and discrimination; social power and nonverbal communication; and altruism and helping.

Victoria M. Esses is Professor of Psychology at the University of Western Ontario. She has served as Associate Editor of *Personality and Social Psychology Bulletin, Group Processes and Intergroup Relations*, and *Canadian Journal of Behavioural Science*, and on the editorial board of *Journal of Personality and Social Psychology*. Dr. Esses' research interests include intergroup relations, prejudice, and discrimination, with a particular focus on issues relating to immigrants and immigration.

Lindsay J. Friedman is the Director of ADL's A WORLD OF DIFFERENCE® Institute, which delivers anti-bias training and diversity education programs throughout the United States and abroad. Ms. Friedman provides oversight to the League's anti-bias education efforts, including staff training and support, program and resource development and evaluation, and coordination for special education initiatives and partnerships. Ms. Friedman has worked in the anti-bias education field for over 13 years, with the ADL and Facing History and Ourselves. Ms. Friedman holds a Bachelor of Arts in History from Northwestern University and Masters Degree in Education from the University of Vermont.

Samuel L. Gaertner is Professor of Psychology at the University of Delaware. He received his Ph.D. from the City University of New York, Graduate Center in 1970. He shared the Gordon Allport Intergroup Relations Prize awarded by the Society for the Psychological Study of Social Issues in 1985 with John Dovidio for their work on aversive racism and also in 1998 for their work on the Common Ingroup Identity Model. Dr. Gaertner serves on the editorial boards of *The Journal of Personality and Social Psychology*, *Personality and Social Psychology Bulletin*, and *Group Processes and Intergroup Relations*.

Carole L. Hahn is Professor in the Division of Educational Studies at Emory University. She is the National Research Coordinator for the United States and Chair of the U.S. Steering Committee for the Civic Education Study (CivEd) conducted by the International Association for the Evaluation of Educational Achievement (IEA).

Gordon Hodson completed his Ph.D. at the University of Western Ontario, and is a Lecturer (Assistant Professor) at the University of Wales, Swansea. His research interests involve stereotyping, prejudice, and discrimination, with a focus on individual differences, social identity, and perceived threat.

Sharon Hicks-Bartlett received her Ph.D. from the University of Chicago in Sociology in 1994. She holds a M.A. degree in sociology; a M.A. in gerontology; and a B.A. degree in American History. In 1996 she held two postdoctoral fellowships from the University of Michigan (Ann Arbor). For 7 years she operated Hands Across the Campus™, an American Jewish Committee program on prejudice reduction and conflict resolution in schools. She now presides over Terrapin Training Strategies, Inc., a diversity training and cross-cultural communication group that assists institutions and organizations to best meet the challenges of living in an increasingly global world. She is completing two books, one on diversity in school settings, and one on work and family life in a small town.

Biren (Ratnesh) A. Nagda, Ph.D., M.S.W., is Associate Professor and Director of the Intergroup Dialogue, Education and Action (IDEA) Training & Resource Institute at the University of Washington School of Social Work. His teaching and research interests focus on cultural diversity and social justice, intergroup dialogue, and multicultural- and empowerment-oriented social work practice with individuals, groups, and organizations. In 2001, he received the University of Washington Distinguished Teaching Award. He has published extensively on intergroup dialogues in educational and community settings. He recently completed a 2-year community-based research project looking at best practices in community-wide dialogues on race and racism.

Lausanne Renfro is a doctoral candidate in social psychology at New Mexico State University. She received her B.A. in psychology from St.

Edward's University in Austin, Texas and her M.A. in experimental psychology from New Mexico State University. Her research interests include intergroup relations, discrimination, prejudice, stereotypes, realistic and symbolic threats, group and individual threats, group-individual interactions, and prejudice reduction.

Robert E. Slavin is currently Co-Director of the Center for Research on the Education of Students Placed at Risk at Johns Hopkins University and Chairman of the Success for All Foundation. He received his B. A. in Psychology from Reed College in 1972, and his Ph.D. in Social Relations in 1975 from Johns Hopkins University. Dr. Slavin has authored or co-authored more than 200 articles and 18 books, including *Educational Psychology: Theory into Practice* (1986, 1988, 1991, 1994, 1997, and 2000); *Effective Programs for Students at Risk* (1989); *Cooperative Learning: Theory, Research, and Practice* (1990, 1995); *Preventing Early School Failure* (1994); *Every Child, Every School: Success for All* (1996); *Show Me the Evidence: Proven and Promising Programs for America's Schools* (1998); and *Effective Programs for Latino Students* (2000). He received the American Educational Research Association's Raymond B. Cattell Early Career Award for Programmatic Research in 1986, the Palmer O. Johnson award for the best article in an AERA journal in 1988, the Charles A. Dana award in 1994, the James Bryant Conant Award from the Education Commission of the States in 1998, the Outstanding Leadership in Education Award from the Horace Mann League in 1999, and the Distinguished Services Award from the Council of Chief State School Officers in 2000.

Cookie White Stephan is Emerita Professor of Sociology at New Mexico State University. She received her Ph.D. in psychology from the University of Minnesota in 1971. Stephan's major research focus is on intergroup relations, specifically the antecedents of prejudice and ethnic identity. With Walter G. Stephan, she is the author of *Intergroup Relations* (1996) and *Improving Intergroup Relations* (2001).

Walter G. Stephan received his Ph.D. in psychology from the University of Minnesota in 1971. He has taught at the University of Texas at Austin and at New Mexico State University, where he currently holds the rank of Emeritus Professor. He has published articles on attribution processes, cognition and affect, intergroup relations, and intercultural relations. He co-authored (with Cookie Stephan) *Intergroup Relations* (1996) and *Improving Intergroup Relations* (2001). He has also published *Reducing Prejudice and Stereotyping in the Schools* (1998), and is co-authored (with W. Paul Vogt) *Multicultural Education Programs: Research and Theory* (2004).

Margot Stern Strom has spent more than 30 years as an educator, author, and lecturer. Since 1979, she has been executive director and president of the Facing History and Ourselves National Foundation. Since 1994, Strom has also served as senior officer for the Harvard/Facing History and Ourselves Project and co-chair of the project's Advisory Committee. She is the recipient of numerous civic and education awards, including the 1997 Charles A. Dana Foundation Award for Pioneering Achievement in Education. She has been featured in many national and local media and has co-authored several articles and books on moral education and citizenship education. Strom received a B.A. in liberal arts and sciences from the University of Illinois, an M.A. in history from Memphis State University, and a C.A.S. in human development from Harvard Graduate School of Education. She has been awarded an L.L.D. Honorary Degree from Hebrew College, and Doctor of Humane Letters Honorary Degrees from Lesley College and Northeastern University.

Tracie L. Stewart received her Ph.D. from Purdue University and is Assistant Professor of Psychology at Georgia State University. Her research in the area of intergroup relations focuses on automatic and controlled stereotype processes, individual differences in stereotyping and prejudice, and prejudice reduction. She recently conducted a program evaluation of a well-known diversity training exercise (in press) and has designed classroom activities to facilitate discussion of bias-related issues (e.g., "The Small Talk Activity," 2001). From 1997–2000, she was a board member for the Poughkeepsie Institute, a nonprofit organization dedicated to research in the public interest.

Terry Tollefson has been the Director of Administration for Policy, Planning, and Evaluation at Facing History and Ourselves since 1990. During that time he has co-authored publications on the impact of the Facing History program. He serves as Project Administrator of the Harvard/Facing History Project—a research partnership designed to bring together scholars and practitioners around issues such as the origins of violence and hatred, and opportunities for promoting courage and compassion through education. Dr. Tollefson has been a teacher and administrator in public and private schools both in the United States and abroad. He was a founding director of Intercollege, a private, accredited college that introduced liberal arts education to the country of Cyprus. Dr. Tollefson's research at the Harvard Graduate School of Education focused on education and cultural differences. In addition to completing a doctorate in Teaching, Curriculum, and Learning Environments at Harvard, Dr. Tollefson holds Master's degrees in Teaching, Educational Administration, and Philosophy.

Marleen ten Vergert graduated in Family Studies as well as Social Psychology from the University of Nijmegen, the Netherlands. In 2001, she was employed by Colgate University as a research coordinator and assisted Professor John F. Dovidio in his research on stereotyping and prejudice. She has worked as a behavioral expert with the police force in the Netherlands and is currently working for SISA, a governmental agency for youth policy in the city of Rotterdam.

W. Paul Vogt is Professor of Research and Evaluation in the College of Education at Illinois State University. He specializes in the evaluation of educational programs and is particularly interested in integrating multiple methods in program evaluation. His books include: *Tolerance and Education* (1997); *Dictionary of Statistics and Methodology, 2nd edition* (1998); and *Quantitative Research Methods for Educators* (2004).

Index

SUBJECTS